PSYCHOLOGY LIBRARY EDITIONS:
PSYCHOLOGY OF READING

Volume 2

SPEECH AND READING

SPEECH AND READING

A Comparative Approach

Edited by
BEATRICE DE GELDER AND JOSÉ MORAIS

Routledge
Taylor & Francis Group
LONDON AND NEW YORK

First published in 1995 by Erlbaum (UK) Taylor & Francis

This edition first published in 2018
by Routledge
4 Park Square, Milton Park, Abingdon, Oxon OX14 4RN
605 Third Avenue, New York, NY 10017

Routledge is an imprint of the Taylor & Francis Group, an informa business

British Library Cataloguing in Publication Data
A catalogue record for this book is available from the British Library

ISBN: 978-1-138-08065-2 (Set)
ISBN: 978-0-203-70345-8 (Set) (ebk)
ISBN: 978-1-138-08440-7 (Volume 2) (hbk)
ISBN: 978-1-315-11181-0 (Volume 2) (ebk)

Publisher's Note
The publisher has gone to great lengths to ensure the quality of this reprint but points out that some imperfections in the original copies may be apparent.

Disclaimer
The publisher has made every effort to trace copyright holders and would welcome correspondence from those they have been unable to trace.

Speech and Reading
A Comparative Approach

Edited by

Beatrice de Gelder
Tilburg University, The Netherlands

José Morais
Université Libre de Bruxelles, Belgium

Erlbaum (UK) Taylor & Francis

Erlbaum (UK) Taylor & Francis, Publishers
27 Church Road
Hove
East Sussex BN3 2FA
UK

British Library Cataloguing in Publication Data
A catalogue reord for this book is available from the British Library

ISBN 0-86377-355-9 (Hbk)

Indices by Christine Boylan
Typeset by Litho Link Ltd., Welshpool, Powys, Wales
Printed and bound in the United Kingdom by Redwood Books, Trowbridge, Wiltshire

Contents

List of Contributors

Paul Bertelson
Université Libre de Bruxelles, Laboratoire de Psychologie Expérimentale, 117, Av. Ad Buyl, 1050 Bruxelles, Belgium.

Peter Bryant
Department of Experimental Psychology, University of Oxford, South Park Road, Oxford OX1 3UD, UK.

Vivian Burden
Department of Psychology, Goldsmiths' College, University of London, London SE14 6NW, UK.

Ruth Campbell
Goldsmiths' College, Lewisham Way, London SE14 6NW, UK.

Alfonso Caramazza
Cognitive Neuropsychology Laboratory, The Johns Hopkins University, Baltimore, MD 21218, USA.

Thomas H. Carr
Department of Psychology, Michigan State University, East Lansing, MI 48824-1117, USA.

Robert C. Crowder
Department of Psychology, Yale University, New Haven, CT 06520, USA.

Anne Cutler
MRC Applied Psychology Unit, 15 Chaucer Road, Cambridge CB2 2EFR, UK.

Beatrice de Gelder
Department of Psychology, Tilburg University, P.O. Box 90153, 5000 LE Tilburg, The Netherlands.

Elizabeth Whitney Goodell
Haskins Laboratories, 270 Crown Street, New Haven, CT 06511–6695, USA.

J.M. Gurd
Department of Experimental Psychology, University of Oxford, South Park Road, Oxford OX1 3UD, UK.

Daisy L. Hung
Graduate Institute of Psychology, National Chung-Cheng University, 160 San-Hsing, Min-Hsiung, Chia-Yi, 621, Taiwan.

Pratibha Karanth
All India Institute of Speech and Hearing, Manasagangothri, Mysore 570 006, India.

Régine Kolinksy
Université Libre de Bruxelles, Laboratoire de Psychologie Expérimentale, 117, Av. Ad Buyl, 1050 Bruxelles, Belgium.

Asha Kudva
All India Institure of Speech and Hearing, Manasa Gangothri, Mysore – 570 006, India.

Sam-Po Law
City Polytechnic of Hong Kong, Department of Chinese, Translation and Linguistics, Tat Chee Avenue, Kowloon, Hong Kong.

Wei Ling Lee
Graduate Institute of Psychology, National Chung-Cheng University, 160 Dan-Hsing, Min-Hsiung, Chia-Yi, 621, Taiwan.

Alvin M. Liberman
Haskins Laboratories, 270 Crown Street, New Haven, CT 06511-6695, USA.

Zhong Hui Lin
Graduate Institute of Psychology, National Chung-Cheng University, 160 Dan-Hsing, Min-Hsiung, Chia-Yi, 621, Taiwan.

Georgije Lukatela
Elektrotehn. Fakultet, Bul. Revolvcije 73, Beograd, Serbia.

John C. Marshall
The Radcliff Infirmary, Woodstock Road, Oxford, 0X2 6HE, UK.

James M. McQueen
MRC Applied Psychology Unit, 15 Chaucer Road, Cambridge, CB2 2EF, UK.

José Morais
Laboratoire de Psychologie Experimentale, Université Libre de Bruxelles, 117, Av. Ad Buyl, 1050 Bruxelles, Belgium.

Karalyn Patterson
MRC Applied Psychology Unit, 15 Chaucer Road, Cambridge, CB2 2EF, UK.

Michael I. Posner
Institute of Cognitive and Decision Sciences, University of Oregon, Straub Hall, Eugene, OR 97403, USA.

Sumiko Sasanuma
Department of Communication Research, Tokyo Metropolitan Institute of Gerontology, 35–2 Sakeicho, Itabashu, Tokyo 173, Japan.

Michael Studdert-Kennedy
Haskins Laboratories, 270 Crown Street, New Haven, CT 06511-6695, USA.

Aimeé Suprenant
Department of Psychology, Yale University, New Haven, CT 06520, USA.

Michael T. Turvey
Haskins Laboratories, 270 Crown Street, New Haven, CT 06511–6695, USA.

Ovid T. Tzeng
Graduate Institute of Psychology, National Chung-Cheng University, 160 San-Hsing, Min-Hsiung, Chia-Yi, 621, Taiwan.

Aparna Vijayan
All India Institute of Speech and Hearing, Manasa Gangothri, Mysore – 570 006, India.

Jean Vroomen
Department of Psychology, Tilburg University, P.O. Box 90153, 5000 LE Tilburg, The Netherlands.

To the memory of Isabelle Y. Liberman

Preface

The impetus for the present collection of papers came from a desire to tie closer links between the work on phonological processes implicated in reading—whether by beginning or by skilled readers—and that of speech processing. Most of the papers appearing in this volume were first presented at a meeting bringing together researchers in the domain of speech processing with students of reading and reading acquisition. The meeting took place at the Rockefeller Study Centre in Bellagio, Italy. We are pleased to express our gratitude to the Rockefeller Foundation for making possible the organisation of the conference and providing us with the most congenial aesthetic and social surroundings. Additional support for the organisation of the conference as well as for the preparation of the manuscript was received from the Belgian National Fund for Scientific Research (FNRS), the Loterie Nationale (Conventions 2.4562.86 and 8.4505.92), as well as from the Belgian Ministère de l'Education de la Communauté Française ("Action de Recherche concertée: language processing in different modalities. Comparative approaches". Convention no. 91–96/148). Ms. S. Struyken from Tilburg University provided valuable assistance with the organisation of the conference.

We thank Paul Bertelson for having been a source of encouragement throughout the whole project.

The first plans for the Bellagio conference were made by a trio which comprised, beside the two present editors, the late Isabelle Y. Liberman. Isabelle's work was central to the main theme of the meeting and is universally recognised for its essential role in the emergence of modern approaches to the analysis of reading acquisition processes. She participated in the early preparations for the meeting with her usual enthusiasm. It is thus only fitting that the present volume is dedicated to the memory of that great lady of science who, to many of the contributors, was also a dear and sadly missed friend.

Beatrice de Gelder and José Morais

Introduction
Speech and Reading: One Side to Two Coins

Beatrice de Gelder
Tilburg University, The Netherlands

José Morais
Université Libre de Bruxelles, Belgium

Speaking and understanding speech stand out as natural linguistic activities, whereas reading qualifies commonly as a highly artificial skill. Speech and reading have been studied by different groups of researchers with different explanatory agendas, for different purposes and with very different methods. As a consequence, it is so far mostly the differences between speech and reading that have captured attention. However, as they are both linguistic activities what could be more natural than to expect them to be closely linked and to assume they are two expressions of the human competence for language that have a common core? This book continues the tradition inaugurated nearly 25 years ago with the volume edited by Kavanagh and Mattingly (1972) *Language by ear and by eye*. The notion that reading acquisition has close links with speech processing competence has gained momentum during the last two decades of research when in a different area of research it became increasingly clear that there was a specific biological basis for language and a dedicated information-processing infrastructure.

The present volume is built around the search for links between speech, reading and reading acquisition. The common theme is that the most promising approach to understanding the acquisition of reading skill is to see it as building upon speech skills. On such an approach the problem of understanding reading acquisition squarely belongs to the domain of investigations of the biology of language, and specifically that of phonological processes. This vantage point allows one to outline new perspectives and brings into focus little explored domains of research with the hope of showing results to be relevant for the biology of reading. The most obvious implication of this perspective is that the study of spoken language processing might contribute to our understanding of the process of reading acquisition.

In their classic paper "Perception of the speech code", Liberman, Cooper, Shankweiler, and Studdert-Kennedy (1967) noted that although written language is parasitic on speech, reading and writing do not follow necessarily from the maturation of the speech machinery. The perception and production of speech develop naturally and below the level of consciousness as part of a biological specialisation that is universal. Reading and writing, in contrast, do not ordinarily develop without direct instruction and also have been rare among the peoples of the world. The difficulty of literacy acquisition is further compounded in the alphabetic writing system which, it is assumed, requires of the learner an awareness of the internal phonological structure of words, an awareness found to be lacking in both preliterate children and illiterate adults. This perspective has been elaborated in a series of well-known papers (see Bertelson & de Gelder, 1989; 1991; Gleitman & Rozin, 1977; Liberman, 1971; 1983; Morais, Alegria, & Content, 1987; Rozin & Gleitman, 1977) and has dominated the research on reading acquisition for the last 15 years. It is clearly the case that conscious phonological representations remain a topic of central interest. But more recently the importance of phonological representations has come to the foreground in models of reading that have an indirect or phonology-based route.

The subtitle of this volume indicates the focus and the direction of inquiry common to a majority of the articles. The notion of a comparative approach is to be understood in a number of interlocking ways. By adequate use of the comparative method it should be possible to identify the components of reading acquisition and track down the specific problems encountered in each domain. A number of domains can be distinguished.

A first issue concerns the distinction between specific effects of literacy training and the general cognitive influence of schooling. Literacy training is usually provided in school, together with training in other activities, some of which also imply the development of analytic skills. The specific effects of literacy training, as far as the first stages of literacy acquisition are concerned, may be assessed by comparing illiterate adults and ex-illiterates, i.e. people who are learning, or have learned, to read and write as adults in special classes. On the other hand, possible effects of literacy acquisition on the development of other skills, such as those involved in visual analysis and in memory encoding and retrieval, are worth investigating.

Next, various metaphonological abilities need to be distinguished. It has recently become clear that the set of abilities called metaphonological is highly heterogeneous, not only because they concern different aspects or units of the phonology of language, but also—and above all—because they involve different kinds of mental operations. An intriguing question, for instance, is how some people manage to detect rhyme in word sets, apparently without being able to analyse their internal phonological structure. In this context the evidence from the illiterates is highly relevant. Adults who are illiterates for socio-economic or cultural reasons rather than as a consequence of failure to benefit from instruction offer a unique opportunity to disentangle the effects of literacy itself from those of cognitive maturation. Likewise, evidence from nonalphabetic literates promises an essential contribution to our understanding of the relation between speech and reading. The study of nonalphabetic literates (for instance readers of Japanese or Chinese writing systems exclusively) is necessary to determine the extent to which phonemic awareness, as a special form of phonological awareness, depends on learning an alphabet.

None of the above reduces in any way the need to study the populations traditionally studied: pre-school children, developmental and acquired dyslexics. The study of pre-school children provided useful information both about the precursors of metaphonological skills and about the relationships between the emergence of these skills and a still developing primary phonological awareness. Complementary evidence is supplied by the study of developmental dyslexics. Detailed assessment of failures both in metaphonological operations (knowledge of these operations, attained degree in automaticity, etc.) and in reading and writing performance should contribute to the understanding of the role of conscious processes in literacy acquisition as well as be useful for prevention and remediation. Different types of acquired dyslexia and dysgraphia are an important source of information about the normal processes underlying word recognition and spelling. The study of such patients may also provide suggestions as to the role that metaphonological abilities play in the skilled reader and writer, as well as to the modularity of these abilities.

This comparative approach has two additional dimensions. One concerns the relevance of questions on the representation of speech for understanding reading and reading acquisition. The latter provides a new system of language processes and representations, which, although being derived from the primary, biologically determined system for spoken language, may in turn affect it. It is of great importance for the study of the architecture of language to specify which levels, in the perception of speech, are affected by the development of a reading skill and which are not. The second dimension concerns evidence from sensory-deprived subjects. Both deaf and blind people have acquired alternative means and procedures for dealing with spoken and written language. The development of these procedures may require special forms of linguistic awareness. The differential development of phonological awareness in deaf and blind subjects can help to define crucial components of the literacy acquisition process.

The volume is organised in four sections. The organisation of the sections respects a so far accepted division of labour as well as a logical order of topics, starting with studies of speech representation and continuing with reading acquisition. It proceeds by contrasting adult studies with developmental research, by looking at alphabetic vs. nonalphabetic reading and by examining language skills in the case of normal auditory input vs. less usual or exceptional nonauditory input such as lip-reading in deaf subjects or tactile reading in blind subjects. Common themes run across all these subdivisions, and these as much as the cross-modal comparisons represent the major impetus for putting these various domains of research together and expecting some degree of cross-fertilisation. In what follows we first point to common issues and then give an overview of the major dimensions of the present comparative approach.

SPEECH PROCESSING, ITS SPECIFICITY AND ITS RELATION TO READING

The chapters in Part I of this volume deal with speech processing and this may appear surprising. When the issue of reading is considered on its own, like in familiar dual-route models of reading, speech processing receives very little attention indeed. A basic assumption of the classic dual-route model is that meaning can be obtained by accessing the phonological input lexicon on the basis of an assembled phonological representation. Other models draw attention to a phonology-mediated reading route. Theories of reading that stress the involvement of phonological processes thus add independent support to the central point made by Liberman about reading acquisition building on spoken language representations. Most importantly, they draw attention to the relevance of the study of spoken word representation for understanding reading and reading acquisition. Indeed, the whole point about the indirect route is that the link must be made between the written representation and the phonological representation of the word. Therefore, the student of reading and *a fortiori* the student of reading acquisition cannot ignore the research aimed at understanding speech processing. At least three sub-domains in the area of speech processing are likely to be relevant for investigating the final details of the phonological representations contacted in the reading process. The most obvious area is that of the nature of speech representations in on-line processing. The study of short-term memory is also important because of the observations of phonological memory impairments in poor readers. The third and equally critical issue concerns the development of speech representations. These three aspects are addressed in the chapters following Liberman's general statement of the speech and reading relation.

A forceful statement of the logic underlying the present collection is found in the chapter by Alvin Liberman. He emphasises the notion that speech is natural and orthographies are artifacts. At the same time he claims that our understanding of reading and reading acquisition must be built on our understanding of speech. He argues against a traditional approach of reading that ignores the importance of the readers' spoken language competence and emphasises instead the visual aspects of the reading process. This focus on spoken language competence orients the study of reading acquisition and its impairments towards the domain of phonological and metaphonological processes and away from peripheral visual explanations of reading difficulties. The picture that seems to emerge clearly from current research on reading acquisition is that phonological processes are the critical component in successful reading acquisition.

Anne Cutler and James McQueen defend a specific position in the debate regarding ongoing speech segmentation. A central problem confronting the student of speech processing is one that has no equivalent in reading because in the latter, but not in the former, word boundaries are marked unambiguously. Is the segmentation issue addressed in the course of the word recognition process or, alternatively, is it more plausible to have two separate processes or stages, one pre-lexical and another lexical? In the former case, the representational format of the spoken words is one that allows the speaker to segment words in the speech stream in the course of word identification itself. The phonological form may thus contain multiple components, some of which are important vehicles in the print-to-sound mapping, for example, segmental format of the phonological representations, while others are not, for example, metrical or prosodic aspects. Cutler and McQueen argue for the existence of a segmentation strategy based on the assumption that strong syllables signal word beginnings. This procedure operates at a pre-lexical level. The phoneme monitoring task as well as phonetic categorisation have been extensively used to investigate the issue of speech representation. Even independently of the issue of a pre-lexical segmentation stage, data obtained with phoneme monitoring have been taken as evidence for the phonemic structure of implicit speech representations. Cutler and McQueen present evidence obtained with these tasks that supports the notion of a lexicon-independent segmentation procedure. Besides this major claim, the approach defended in the chapter stresses the linguistic specificity of segmentation procedures. The authors argue that the pre-lexical segmentation strategy they propose is specifically suited to the phonological properties of English but not, for example, to those of French. That position is an important one in the debate on phonological representations. Intuitively, one might expect that in languages where segmentation strategies build on a clearly syllabically segmented speech stream a syllabic procedure would be the platform from where reading acquisition takes off. Against this background of language-specific phonological procedures, there is room for different patterns of written to spoken language conversion procedures in different languages. Later chapters introduce a second dimension of complexity in the speech-to-reading issue, one following from cross-linguistic differences in written representation. Needless to say, a realistic picture of reading must acknowledge contrasting phonologies as well as contrasting orthographies.

Phonological processes in short-term memory are the second area where concerns of the students of speech processing overlap with those of the student of reading and reading acquisition. The research of Crowder and collaborators fits in with the notion that there is a subsystem of short-term memory that is specifically devoted to phonological processes. In a series of interesting experiments Robert Crowder and Aimee Surprenant show that recency and suffix effects, which in the 1960s and 1970s were typically taken as the signature of auditory processes, in fact result from the involvement of the speech processor in short-term memory. Examining short-term retention for different kinds of auditory materials like speech, music or animal sounds, and considering general properties of auditorily presented information like discriminability and familiarity, they arrive at the conclusion that the critical dimension of processing is whether subjects perceive the input as speech.

So far, issues of phonological representation, contrasting phonologies and contrasting orthographies were mentioned as they arise in the context of understanding normal adult listening and reading. In the final chapter of Part I the authors tackle what is the third area of speech processing investigations relevant for speech and reading, i.e. the development of speech representations. Michael Studdert-Kennedy and Elizabeth Whitney Goodell suggest that phonemes emerge at an unconscious level from units of articulatory action, called gestures, which are progressively organised within the word. They report evidence from a child about two years of age who produces deviant forms, which can be readily accounted for according to this conceptual framework, but not using a featural description. The emergence of phonemes is seen as a biologically based process where the developmental process of selecting a representational format is driven by imperatives of economical storage and rapidity of access.

The chapters in Part I all support the importance of studies of speech processing for understanding reading but they also present new challenges to the received view in these matters. The most straightforward statement of the relation between spoken and written language pictures the issue as one of mapping graphemic units onto the units of spoken word perception. It was at some time tacitly accepted that the latter were phonemes and that the critical intellectual contribution required from the apprentice reader consisted of accessing the corresponding implicit spoken representations. The study of reading acquisition problems as well as, more recently, the evidence from illiterates and from nonalphabetic readers have challenged this view. Evidence of the latter type showed that explicit alphabetic training is still needed. On the other hand, reading disorders such as developmental phonological dyslexia showed that access remained elusive notwithstanding intensive phonics tuition.

LANGUAGE AND READING IN DIFFERENT MODALITIES

The study of speech processing in input modalities other than audition presents opportunities for addressing in a novel way some of the issues so far mentioned. Cross-modal research of linguistic processes should offer a privileged avenue for disentangling abstract linguistic and modality specific aspects of language processing. Two different routes are open for such cross-modal studies. One is to look for commonalities across different input modalities, whether in normal adult processing, in development, or in impairment. The other is to examine systematically processing in populations in which one of the input modes for language is absent, or impaired for peripheral reasons. Besides understanding the nature of the impairment and how it explains the difficulties, we might gain from these studies a better understanding of the normal phonological skills, their subcomponents and their interaction in the building of the speech-to-reading interface.

Comparisons between input modalities have so far been largely limited to the cases of listening to speech and of visual reading. As a consequence it is often difficult to know which of several coexistent modality characteristics are responsible for observed intermodal differences in performance. Paul Bertelson argues that consideration of other, generally neglected, input modes is necessary for a full use of the comparative approach. He draws supporting examples from the work of his group on braille reading by the blind. One study shows that so-called garden-path effects occur in the reading of braille just as in that of printed prose, but that they affect different parameters of exploratory behaviour. In another study it was shown that the manifestations of sequential use of input information for word recognition demonstrated in previous work with spoken words can be replicated for braille words and also for printed words presented letter-by-letter. Those findings suggest that sequential processing is not contingent on a particular input mode, but rather on the temporal distribution of the input.

Ruth Campbell and Vivian Burden re-examine and challenge the old view that deaf children are poor at tasks requiring phonological skills thought to be associated with sensitivity to sound regularities and sound similarities between words. Deaf youngsters generally become poor readers. For a long time it was considered evident that, being deaf, they lacked phonological representations of speech and thus could not resort to them to transcode written language into meaning. The study of Campbell and Burden emphasises that the phonological decoding skills of the deaf are in most respects normal. Why this picture of poor reading in the presence of normal phonological skills? The authors suggest that as a consequence of absent spoken input the interactions between the separate components of the phonological system do not become properly established. As poor reading is thus not explained by the absence of separate decoding skills, but also manifests itself in reduced skills to take advantage of the context, one might ask to what extent training the existing decoding abilities will improve reading.

Poor reading ability is often associated with deficits in short-term phonological codes. So far these studies have been limited to speech input in the auditory modality. As we noted, the chapter by Crowder and Surprenant underscored the existence of a specifically phonological storage in short-term memory. This is a finding that combines well with the evidence from impaired short-term memory performance for spoken input in young poor readers. Based on these two lines of evidence one might predict that poor short-term memory for linguistic material would also be shown when poor readers had to recall memory items present in the lip-read modality. Beatrice de Gelder and Jean Vroomen present a systematic study of serial recall performance in young as well as in adult poor readers and find very symmetrical performance in the two modalities. On the basis of recency as well as suffix effects, they conclude that, compared to normal controls, performance is normal except for an overall reduced span. The overall reduction is the same in the two modalities and this for young as well as for adult readers. The picture of a specifically phonological memory disorder is thus complemented by evidence from an unusual speech input modality.

READING IN DIFFERENT ORTHOGRAPHIES

One may address the evidence from studies of reading, reading acquisition, and reading impairments in nonalphabetic orthographies from different perspectives. At the very least, the existence of nonalphabetic orthographies raises the issue of the generality of the findings on reading ability in alphabetic orthographies. In this sense evidence from nonalphabetic readers should be welcome because of its potential disentangling general and orthography-specific aspects of reading. In the context of this volume, such evidence allows us also to tackle another issue, that of the degree of intimacy between speaking and reading skills and the question of whether some orthographies do make spoken language more visible than others (DeFrancis, 1989).

A phrase which has been repeatedly called into service to characterise the job of the apprentice reader is that of the critical moment of "discovering the alphabetic principle". In the perspective of researchers of the 1970s such as, for example, Gleitman and Rozin (1977), this formulation reflected the view that the alphabetic system maps onto an existing level of spoken language representation. Discovery of the alphabetic principle was viewed as a matter of access to speech representations. Reading acquisition difficulties were blamed on children's problems with grasping the alphabetic principle, but no more detailed proposals were made. Evidence concerning the difference between good and poor readers in conscious manipulations of subsyllabic units fitted well with this conception and its emphasis on access to unconscious speech representations.

In the 1970s nonalphabetic orthographies served already as a reference point. It was assumed that Chinese orthography was logographic instead of phonology-based. Anecdotal evidence about the absence of reading difficulties in cultures where logographic writing systems like Japanese or Chinese were in use seem to support this picture. In the past decade the notion of Chinese as an exclusively logogaphic writing system has been attacked by students of Chinese writing who called attention to the importance of the phonetic components of Chinese characters (DeFrancis, 1989) and by psychologists inquiring into Chinese reading behaviour. Foremost among them, Ovid Tzeng and his collaborators have advanced evidence for the importance of sound-based processing of characters, thereby criticising the misleading opposition between purely phonographic and purely logographic writing systems. Their chapter in this volume offers a new and fascinating insight into the role of the phonetic information contained in the characters for children's reading development. They examine the role played by the phonetic radical in a task requiring the beginning and advanced readers to read pseudocharacters. The leading notion is that once children have mastered a sizable set of Chinese characters they will read pseudocharacters by adopting a naming strategy based on their knowledge of sound/orthography regularities derived from the known words.

The evidence advanced by the study of Chinese pseudocharacters lends support to the notion of a biological basis of reading skills because it shows that phonological representations are also important for reading in nonalphabetic orthography. This is just the phonology-based view of reading that Lukatela, Turvey, and collaborators have been arguing for since a decade and it represents a challenge to the dominant position of a direct visual route for reading. On the latter view phonological information is only available after lexical access and can have no influence on written word recognition. On this picture speech processing skills are not called upon in fluent reading. Evidence from Serbo-Croatian as well as from English shows the existence of a phonological ambiguity effect for nonwords as well as for words. In their chapter Georgije Lukatela and Michael Turvey return to this issue and argue, as they did in earlier articles, in favour of an important role of prelexical phonology in word recognition. Their contribution presents a comprehensive review of the arguments and the data supporting this role and a comparison of results obtained with Serbo-Croatian with results obtained in English. To integrate these results in a general perspective they argue for a difference between languages in the distinctiveness of the phonemic level and, correspondingly, to a differential contribution of that level to prelexical processes. In Serbo-Croatian as contrasted with English, the phonemic level comes much more to the foreground because there are fewer phoneme/grapheme pairs and these have stronger connections than is the case in English. In the latter case only weak phonological priming effects are found, but they still testify to the role of a prelexical phonological level.

The research presented by Sam-Po Law and Alfonso Caramazza addresses the same issue as Tzeng et al. but now in the context of a neuropsychological approach. They describe the basic features of the Chinese writing system and present data from six Cantonese aphasics. These patients produced responses that phonologically resembled the target, as do patients who write alphabetically. Errors involving either the signific or the phonetic component of a character are analysed and two main suggestions arise. First, the components are apparently treated as wholes at some level of processing; and second, information about the position and the identity of the component can be disrupted selectively. These neuropsychological findings thus point in the same direction as the findings from the developmental study by Tzeng et al.

The chapter by Sumiko Sasanuma and Karalyn Patterson takes as its point of departure the apparent inconsistency observed in some patients who show nonsemantic reading while at the same time making regularisation errors on exception words. The aim of the chapter is to see to what extent the comparison of these cases with data from Japanese patients also displaying nonsemantic reading can throw light on this specific phenomenon and thereby on the ways in which orthography constrains word reading. The critical contribution here concerns kanji word reading performance in the Japanese subjects as the correct reading of the kanji characters making up a multi-character word is fixed by the whole intra-word context. In this sense kanji word reading can be assimilated to exception word reading in alphabetic orthographies. The authors discuss the similarities between the patient populations across the linguistic differences. Yet they also point to relevant differences in the reading impairments for the English vs. the Japanese subjects. They suggest that one major difference between reading in these two languages might be related to the fact that the English orthography, even in the case of fully irregular spellings, is still based on a fine-grained network of graphemes that scaffolds impaired performance.

READING, THE IMPACT OF ITS ACQUISITION ON LANGUAGE PROCESSES AND READING DISORDERS

While the above picture is relevant for the study of reading per se, it also touches directly on long-standing issues in reading acquisition. As will be seen in Part IV, students of reading acquisition and of its problems are very much confronted with the issue of phonological awareness as this remains the single best indicator of reading progress in young children. Yet it is still very much an open question whether single phoneme manipulation skill is the critical component of phonological awareness. This issue is touched on in the chapters by Bryant, by Morais and Kolinsky, and by Karanth et al., as well as in the chapters by de Gelder and Vroomen and by Campbell and Burden dealing with language in other modalities.

In the past, the role of phonological awareness in learning to read has been stressed quite often, whereas the role of other language capacities such as grammatical awareness received much less attention. Peter Bryant recalls his position on how metaphonological awareness precedes and facilitates learning to read and goes on to present evidence in favour of the notion that awareness of grammatical properties may also play a causal role in reading development. He discusses which aspects of the reading progress these sensitivities may act on. Grammatical awareness may help children to take advantage of the context to read words they cannot read in isolation. But then, the effect of grammatical awareness might be on language comprehension in general rather on reading itself.

The study of the language skills of patients with brain lesions has become a major source of information about the possibility that separate subsystems are involved in the cognitive processing of language. A new promising tool is provided by the techniques of brain imagery. Thomas Carr and Michael Posner review the most important findings obtained with the subtractive method on PET images with regard to written word cognition. They report evidence in favour of a specific subsystem concerned with the orthographic encoding of letter sequences and localised in the left-medial prestriate visual cortex of literate adults. The authors argue that the data present a good illustration of the functional reorganisation of the brain driven by the experience of learning to read and write.

Illiterate adults have provided clear evidence of the close relationship between some forms of phonological awareness, particularly awareness of phonemes, and learning to read and write in an alphabetic system. There are, on the other hand, only few data concerning grammatical awareness in illiterates. Prathibha Karanth, Asha Kudva and Vaparna Vijayan present here a study of a large range of grammatical knowledge to ascertain which aspects of it illiterate adults are aware of. The results suggest that many aspects of grammatical awareness are influenced by the experience of written language. A comparison between school-going and nonschool-going children provided converging evidence. Interestingly, lack of syntactic awareness seems to affect comprehension in listening as well as in reading. The authors admit that these efforts would be larger in Kannada, a highly inflected agglutinative language, than in languages, like English, that depend more on free morphemes and on word order.

José Morais and Régine Kolinsky address the issue of the consequences of phonemic awareness. After having recalled that in their view phonemic awareness is critical for reading ability, they address the two sides of this coin. Phonemic awareness is a crucial factor of successful alphabetic literacy acquisition as is illustrated clearly by studies showing the effects of phonemic training on reading acquisition. Moreover, the bulk of available evidence converges on the importance of combining explicitly taught grapheme–phoneme correspondences with phonemic awareness in bringing about successful reading acquisition. As a corollary to this view, the authors review evidence in favour of effects of phonemic awareness on speech recognition and suggest possible loci for this influence in the speech-processing system.

As far as the general theme of lexical activation is concerned, the study of the difficulties of lexical search may fruitfully complement that of difficulties in word access. Indeed, lexical access triggered by speech or print as well as lexical search initiated deliberately by the subject occur during comprehension of both spoken and written language. In reading as well as in conversation and listening to discourse, words consistent with the context are called to mind more or less intentionally. Jennifer Gurd and John Marshall report a study of word-finding difficulties in patients with Parkinson's disease. They argue for the existence of a double dissociation between two types of internal retrieval from a single lexical semantic store, namely a routinised vs. a nonroutinised retrieval.

One general comment is in order. Very likely, reading acquisition is an interactive process involving a succession of quantal steps, some in the sphere of phonological ability and some in other domains of the skill. A full understanding of the process of reading acquisition requires identification of those steps. Moreover, among the many studies that have attempted to analyse the mental representations and processes required for learning to read, the majority have taken as subject the younger reader in a normal school environment. This volume defends an approach that goes beyond that bias and integrates relevant expertise in spoken and written language developed in closely related research domains.

As is to be expected, such a comparative venture is based on the existence of common themes, but also introduces new areas of possible disagreement as well as potentially misleading areas of agreement. Aside from the common themes we have reviewed, some contentious issues emerge from the new materials presented in the volume. One such major issue concerns not so much disagreement as uncertainty. What is the format of phonological representations? Is it affected by cross-linguistic differences as well as by cross-orthographic ones? Is there a developmental course for the phonological formats as Studdert-Kennedy and Goodell claim? Is this developmental course partly driven by orthographic experience as Morais and Kolinsky argue? Or should more emphasis be put on the role of early phonological awareness and its role in early reading acquisition?

At the same time, some convergences may be misleading. Is reading in nonalphabetic orthographies based on phonological processes and representations just as much and in the same way as it is in alphabetic orthographies? The traditional dual-route model may not give one the appropriate handle on that issue. Reading, for example, Chinese cannot depend on phonological representation assembly in the same way it does in alphabetic reading. Evidence on phonological representation in Chinese and in Serbo-Croatian may not involve the same level of fine-grained phonological representations even if phonological effects in written language tasks point in the same direction. Thus learning to read in alphabetic writing systems may capitalise more directly on the kinds of representations that arise in the course of phonological development as outlined by Studdert-Kennedy and Goodell and assumed by Liberman. Finally, it is worth noting that the controversy on the relation between phonological awareness and reading acquisition now seems to expand into the area of syntactic development. For example, whereas Bryant highlights the causal role of these capacities, Karanth et al, present evidence of limited syntactic knowledge in illiterates.

REFERENCES

Bertelson, P., & de Gelder, B. (1989). Learning about reading from illiterates. In A.M. Galaburda (Ed.), *From neurons to reading* (pp. 1–23). Cambridge, MA: MIT Press.

Bertelson, P., & de Gelder, B. (1991). The emergence of phonological awareness: Comparative approaches. In I.G. Mattingly & M. Studdert-Kennedy (Eds.), *Modularity and the motor theory of speech perception* (pp. 393–412). Hillsdale, NJ: Lawrence Erlbaum Associates Inc.

DeFrancis, J. (1989). *Visible speech: The diverse oneness of writing systems.* Honolulu: University of Hawaii Press.

Gleitman, L.R., & Rozin, P. (1977). The structure and acquisition of reading I: Relations between orthographies and the structure of language. In A.S. Reber & D.L. Scarborough (Eds.), *Toward a psychology of reading* (pp. 1–53). Hillsdale, NJ: Lawrence Erlbaum Associates Inc.

Kavanagh, J.F., & Mattingly, I.G. (1972). *Language by ear and by eye.* Cambridge, MA: MIT Press.

Liberman, A.M., Cooper, F.S., Shankweiler, D., & Studdert-Kennedy, M. (1967). Perception of the speech code. *Psychological Review, 24,* 431–461.

Liberman, I.Y. (1971). Basic research in speech and lateralization of language: Some implications for reading disabilities. *Bulletin of the Orton Society, 21,* 7–87.

Liberman, I.Y. (1983). A language-oriented view of reading and its disabilities. In H. Myklebust (Ed.), *Progress in learning disabilities* (Vol. 5, pp. 81–101). New York: Grune & Stratton.

Morais, J., Alegria, J., & Content, A. (1987). The relationships between segmental analysis and alphabetic literacy: An interactive view. *Cahiers de Psychologie Cognitive, 7,* 415–438.

Rozin, P., & Gleitman, L.R. (1977). The structure and acquisition of reading II: The reading process and the acquisition of the alphabetic principle. In A.S. Reber & D.L. Scarborough (Eds.), *Toward a psychology of reading* (pp. 55–141). Hillsdale, NJ: Lawrence Erlbaum Associates Inc.

I
SPEECH PROCESSING, ITS SPECIFICITY AND ITS RELATION TO READING

1 The Relation of Speech to Reading and Writing

Alvin M. Liberman
Haskins Laboratories, New Haven, CT, USA

Theories of reading–writing and theories of speech typically have in common that neither takes proper account of an obvious fact about language that must, in any reckoning, be critically relevant to both: There is a vast difference in naturalness (hence ease of use) between its spoken and written forms. In my view, a theory of reading should begin with this fact, but only after a theory of speech has explained it.

My aim, then, is to say how well the difference in naturalness is illuminated by each of two theories of speech—one conventional, the other less so—and then, in that light, to weigh the contribution that each of these can make to an understanding of reading and writing and the difficulties that attend them. More broadly, I aim to promote the notion that a theory of speech and a theory of reading–writing are inseparable, and that the validity of the one is measured, in no small part, by its fit to the other.

WHAT DOES IT MEAN TO SAY THAT SPEECH IS MORE NATURAL?

The difference in naturalness between the spoken and written forms of language is patent, so I run the risk of being tedious if I elaborate it here. Still, it is important for the argument I mean to make that we have explicitly in mind how variously the difference manifests itself. Let me, therefore, count the ways.

1. Speech is universal. Every community of human beings has a fully developed spoken language. Reading and writing, on the other hand, are relatively rare. Many, perhaps most, languages do not even have a written form,

and when, as in modern times, a writing system is derived—usually by missionaries—it does not readily come into common use.

2. Speech is older in the history of our species. Indeed, it is presumably as old as mankind, having emerged as perhaps the most important of our species-typical characteristics. Writing systems, on the other hand, are developments of the last few thousand years.

3. Speech comes earlier in the history of the individual; reading–writing come later, if at all.

4. Speech must, of course, be learned, but it need not be taught. For learning to speak, the necessary and sufficient conditions are but two: membership of the human race and exposure to a mother tongue. Indeed, given that these two conditions are met, there is scarcely any way that the development of speech can be prevented. Thus, learning to speak is a precognitive process, much like learning to perceive visual depth and distance or the location of sound. In contrast, reading and writing need to be taught, although, given the right ability, motivation, and opportunity, some will infer the relation of script to language and thus teach themselves. But however learned, reading–writing is an intellectual achievement in a way that learning to speak is not.

5. There are brain mechanisms that evolved with language and that are, accordingly, largely dedicated to its processes. Reading–writing presumably engage at least some of these mechanisms, but they must also exploit others that evolved to serve nonlinguistic functions. There is no specialisation for reading–writing as such.

6. Spoken language has the critically important property of "openness": unlike nonhuman systems of communication, speech is capable of expressing and conveying an indefinitely numerous variety of messages. A script can share this property, but only to the extent that it somehow transcribes its spoken-language base. Having no independent existence, a proper (open) script is narrowly constrained by the nature of its spoken-language roots and by the mental resources on which they draw. Still, within these constraints, scripts are more variable than speech.

One dimension of variation is the level at which the message is represented, although the range of that variation is, in fact, much narrower than the variety of possible written forms would suggest. Thus, as DeFrancis (1989) convincingly argues, any script that communicates meanings or ideas directly, as in ideograms, for example, is doomed to arrive at a dead end. Ideographic scripts cannot be open – that is, they cannot generate novel messages—and the number of messages they can convey is never more than the inventory of one-to-one associations between (holistically different) signals and distinctly different meanings that human beings can master. Indeed, it is a distinguishing characteristic of language, and a necessary condition of its openness, that it communicates meanings indirectly, via specifically linguistic structures and processes, including, nontrivially, those of the phonological component. Not surprisingly, scripts must follow suit; in the matter of language, as with so many other natural processes, it is hard to improve on nature.

Constraints of a different kind apply at the lower levels. Thus, the acoustic signal, as represented visually by a spectrogram, for example, cannot serve as a basis for a script; although spectrograms can be puzzled out by experts, they, along with other visual representations, cannot be read fluently. The reason is not primarily that the relevant parts of the signal are insufficiently visible; it is, rather, that, owing to the nature of speech, and especially to the coarticulation that is central to it, the relation between acoustic signal and message is complex in ways that defeat whatever cognitive processes the "reader" brings to bear. Narrow phonetic transcriptions are easier to read, but there is still more context-, rate-, and speaker-conditioned variation than the eye is comfortable with. In any case, no extant script offers language at a narrow phonetic level. To be useable, scripts must, apparently, be pitched at the more abstract phonological and morphonological levels. That being so, and given that reading–writing require conscious awareness of the units represented by the script, we can infer that people can become conscious of phonemes and morphoponemes. We can also infer about these units that, standing above so much of the acoustic and phonetic variability, they correspond approximately to the invariant forms in which words are presumably stored in the speaker's lexicon. A script that captures this invariance certainly has advantages. At all events, some scripts (e.g. Finnish, Serbo-Croatian) do approximate to purely phonological renditions of the language, while others depart from a phonological base in the direction of morphology. Thus, English script is rather highly morphophonological, Chinese even more so. But, as DeFrancis (1989; see also Wang, 1981) makes abundantly clear, all these scripts, including even the Chinese, are significantly phonological, and, in his view, they would fail if they were not; the variation is simply in the degree to which some of the morphology is also represented.

Scripts also vary somewhat, as speech does not, in the size of the linguistic segments they take as their elements, but here, too, the choice is quite constrained. Surely, it would not be correct to make a unit of the script equal to the phoneme and a half, a third of a syllable, or some arbitrary stretch—say 100 milliseconds—of the speech stream. Still, scripts can and do take as their irreducible units either phonemes or syllables, so in this respect, too, they are more diverse than speech.

7. All of the foregoing differences are, of course, merely reflections of one underlying circumstance—namely, that speech is a product of biological evolution, whereas writing systems are artifacts. Indeed, an alphabet—the writing system that is of most immediate concern to us—is a triumph of applied biology,

part discovery, part invention. The discovery—surely one of the most momentous of all time—was that words do not differ from each other holistically, but rather by the particular arrangement of a small inventory of the meaningless units they comprise. The invention was simply the notion that if each of these units were to be represented by a distinctive optical shape, then everyone could read and write, provided they knew the language and were conscious of the internal phonological structure of its words.

HOW IS THE DIFFERENCE IN NATURALNESS TO BE UNDERSTOOD?

Having seen in how far speech is more natural than reading–writing, we should look first for a simple explanation, one that is to be seen among the surface appearances of the two processes. But when we search there, we are led to conclude, in defiance of the most obvious facts, that the advantage must lie with reading–writing, not with speech. Thus, it is the eye, not the ear, that is the better receptor; the hand, not the tongue, that is the more versatile effector; the print, not the sound, that offers the better signal-to-noise ratio; and the discrete alphabetic characters, not the nearly continuous and elaborately context-conditioned acoustic signal, that offers the more straightforward relation to the language. To resolve this seeming paradox and to find the enlightenment we seek, we shall have, therefore, to look more deeply into the biology of speech. To that end, I turn to two views of speech to see what each has to offer.

The Conventional View of Speech as a Basis for Understanding the Difference in Naturalness.

The first assumption of the conventional view is so much taken for granted that it is rarely made explicit. It is, very simply, that the phonetic elements are defined as sounds. This is not merely to say the obvious, which is that speech is conveyed by an acoustic medium, but rather to suppose, in a phrase made famous by Marshall McLuhan, that the medium *is* the message.

The second assumption, which concerns the production of these sounds, is also usually unspoken, not just because it is taken for granted, although surely it is, but also because it is apparently not thought by conventional theorists to be even relevant. But, whatever the reason, one finds among the conventional claims none that implies the existence of a phonetic mode of action—that is, a mode adapted to phonetic purposes and no other. One therefore infers that the conventional view must hold (by default, as it were) that no such mode exists. Put affirmatively, the conventional assumption is that speech is produced by motor processes and movements that are independent of language.

The third assumption concerns the perception of speech sounds, and, unlike the first two, is made explicitly and at great length (Cole & Scott, 1974; Crowder

& Morton, 1969; Diehl & Kluender, 1989; Fujisaki & Kawashima, 1970; Kuhl, 1981; Kuhl & Miller, 1975; Miller, 1977; Oden & Massaro, 1978; Stevens, 1975). In its simplest form, it is that perception of speech is not different from perception of other sounds; all are governed by the same general processes of the auditory system. Thus, language simply accepts representations made available to it by perceptual processes that are generally auditory, not specifically linguistic. So, just as language presumably recruits ordinary motor processes for its own purposes, so, too, does it recruit the ordinary processes of auditory perception; at the level of perception, as well as action, there is, in the conventional view, no specialisation for language.

The fourth assumption is required by the second and third. For if the acts and percepts of speech are not, by their nature, specifically phonetic, they must necessarily be made so, and that can be done only by a process of cognitive translation. Presumably, that is why conventional theorists say about speech perception that after the listener has apprehended the auditory representation they must elevate it to linguistic status by attaching a phonetic label (Crowder & Morton, 1969; Fujisaki & Kawashima, 1970; Pisoni, 1973), fitting it to a phonetic prototype (Oden & Massaro, 1978), or associating it with some other linguistically significant entity, such as a "distinctive feature" (Stevens, 1975).

I note, parenthetically, that this conventional way of thinking about speech is heir to two related traditions in the psychology of perception. One, which traces its origins to Aristotle's enumeration of the five senses, requires of a perceptual model that it have an end organ specifically devoted to its interests. Thus, ears yield an auditory mode; eyes, a visual mode; the nose, an olfactory mode; and so on. Lacking an end organ of its very own, speech cannot, therefore, be a mode. In that case, phonetic percepts cannot be the immediate objects of perception; they can only be perceived secondarily, as the result of a cognitive association between a primary auditory representation appropriate to the acoustic stimulus that excites the ear (and hence the auditory mode) and, on the other hand, some cognitive form of a linguistic unit. Such an assumption is, of course, perfectly consistent with another tradition in psychology, one that goes back at least to the beginning of the 18th century, where it is claimed in Berkeley's *New theory of vision* (1709) that depth (which cannot be projected directly onto a two-dimensional retina) is perceived by associating sensations of muscular strain (caused by the convergence of the eyes as they fixate objects at various distances) with the experience of distance. In the conventional view of speech, as in Berkeley's assumption about visual depth, apprehending the event or property is a matter of perceiving one thing and calling it something else.

Some of my colleagues and I have long argued that the conventional assumptions fail to account for the important facts about speech. Here, however, my concern is only with the extent to which they enlighten us about the relation of spoken language to its written derivative. That the conventional view enlightens us not at all becomes apparent when one sees that, in contradiction of all the differences enumerated earlier, it leads to the conclusion that speech and reading–writing must be equally natural. To see how comfortably the conventional view sits with an (erroneous) assumption that speech and reading–writing are psychologically equivalent, one need only reconsider the four assumptions of that view, substituting, where appropriate, "optical" for "acoustic" or "visual" for "auditory".

One sees then that, just as the phonetic elements of speech are, by the first of the conventional assumptions, defined as sounds, the elements of a writing system can only be defined as optical shapes. As for the second assumption—namely that speech production is managed by motor processes of the most general sort—we must suppose that this is exactly true for writing; by no stretch of the imagination can it be supposed that the writer's movements are the output of an action mode that is specifically linguistic. The third assumption of the conventional view of speech also finds its parallel in reading–writing, for, surely, the percepts evoked by the optical characters are ordinarily visual in the same way that the percepts evoked by the sounds of speech are supposed to be ordinarily auditory. Thus, at the level of action and perception, there is in reading–writing, as there is assumed to be in speech, no specifically linguistic mode. For speech, that is only an assumption—and, as I think, a very wrong one—but for reading–writing it is an incontrovertible fact; the acts and percepts of reading–writing did not evolve as part of the specialisation for language, hence they cannot belong to a natural linguistic mode.

The consequence of all this is that the fourth of the conventional assumptions about speech is, in fact, necessary for reading–writing and applies perfectly to it: Like the ordinary, nonlinguistic auditory and motor representations seen in the conventional view of speech, the correspondingly ordinary visual and motor representations of reading–writing must somehow be made relevant to language, and that can only be done by a cognitive process; the reader–writer simply has to learn that certain shapes refer to units of the language and that others do not.

It is this last assumption that most clearly reveals the flaw that makes the conventional view useless as a basis for understanding the most important difference between speech and reading–writing—namely, that the evolution of the one is biological, the other cultural. To appreciate the nature of this shortcoming, we must first consider how either mode of language transmission meets a requirement that is imposed on every communication system, whatever its nature and the course of its development. This requirement, which is commonly ignored in arguments about the nature of speech, is that the parties to the message exchange must be bound by a common understanding about which signals, or which aspects of which signals, have communicative significance; only then can communication succeed. Mattingly and I have called this the requirement for "parity" (Liberman & Mattingly, 1985; Liberman & Mattingly, 1989; Mattingly & Liberman, 1988). One asks, then, what is entailed by parity as the system develops in the species and as it is realised in the normal communicative act.

In the development of writing systems, the answer is simple and beyond dispute: Parity was established by agreement. Thus, all who use an alphabet are parties to a compact that prescribes just which optical shapes are to be taken as symbols for which phonological units, the association of the one with the other having been determined arbitrarily. Indeed, this is what it means to say that writing systems are artifacts, and that the child's learning the linguistic significance of the characters of the script is a cognitive activity.

Unfortunately for the validity of the conventional assumptions, they require that the same applies to the development of parity in speech. For if the acts and percepts of speech are, as the conventional assumption would have it, ordinarily motor and ordinarily auditory, one must ask how, why, when, and by whom they were invested with linguistic significance. Where is it written that the gesture and percept we know as [b] should count for language, but that a clapping of the hands should not? Is there somewhere a commandment that says, Thou shalt not commit [b] except when it is thy clear intention to communicate? Or are we to assume, just as absurdly, that [b] was incorporated into the language by agreement? It is hard to see how the conventional view of speech can be made to provide a basis for understanding the all-important difference in evolutionary status between speech and reading–writing.

The problem is the worse confounded when we take account of both sides of the normal communicative act. For in the conventional view the speaker deals in representations of a generally motor sort and the listener in representations of a generally auditory sort. What is it, then, that these two representations have in common, except that neither has anything to do with language? Therefore, one must suppose for speech, as for writing and reading, that there is something like a phonetic idea—a cognitive representation of some kind—to connect these representations to each other and to language, and so to make communication possible.

Thus it is that at every biological or psychological turn the conventional view of speech makes reading and writing the equivalents of speech perception and production. As these processes are plainly not equivalent, the conventional view of speech can hardly be the starting point for an account of reading and writing.

The Unconventional View of Speech as a Basis for Understanding the Difference in Naturalness.

The first assumption of the unconventional view is that the units of speech are defined as gestures, not as the sounds that those gestures produce. (For recent accounts of the unconventional view, see: Liberman & Mattingly, 1985; Liberman & Mattingly, 1989; Mattingly & Liberman, 1988; Mattingly & Liberman, 1990.) The rationale for this assumption is to be understood by taking account of the function of the phonological component of the grammar and of the requirements it imposes. As for the function of phonology, it is, of course, to form words by combining and permuting a few dozen meaningless segments, and so to make possible a lexicon tens of thousands of times larger than could ever have been achieved if, as in all natural but nonhuman communication systems, each "word" were conveyed by a signal that was holistically different from all others. But phonology can serve this critically important function only if its elements are commutable; and if they are to be commutable, they must be discrete and invariant.

A related requirement concerns rate, for if all utterances are to be formed by variously stringing together an exiguous set of signal elements, then, inevitably, the strings must run to great lengths. It is essential, therefore, if these strings are to be organised into words and sentences, that they be produced and perceived at reasonable speed. But if the auditory percepts of the conventional view are to be discrete and invariant, the sounds and gestures must be discrete and invariant, too. Such sounds and gestures are possible, of course, but only at the expense of rate. Thus one could not, in the conventional view, say "bag", but only [bə] [a] [gə], and to say [bə] [a] [gə] is not to speak but to spell. Of course, if speech were like that, then everyone who could speak or perceive a word would know exactly how to write and read it, provided only that they had managed the trivial task of memorising the letter-to-sound correspondences. The problem is that there would be no language worth writing or reading.

There seems, indeed, no way to solve the rate problem and still somehow preserve the acoustic-auditory strategy of the conventional view. It would not have helped, for example, if mankind had evolved not with a vocal tract but with acoustic devices adapted to producing a rapid sequence of sounds—a drumfire or tattoo—for that strategy would have defeated the ear. The point is that speech proceeds at rates that transmit up to 15 or even 20 phonemes per second, but if each phoneme were represented by a discrete sound, then rates that high would seriously strain and sometimes overreach the ability of the ear to resolve the individual sounds and to divine their order.

According to the unconventional view, in the evolution of speech the problem was solved by avoiding the acoustic-auditory strategy that would have caused it. The alternative was to define the phonetic elements as gestures, as the first assumption of the unconventional view proposes. Thus, [b] is a closing at the lips, [h] an opening at the glottis, [p] a combination of lip closing and glottis opening, and so forth. In fact, the gestures are far more complex than this, for a gesture usually comprises movements of several articulators, and these movements are exquisitely context-conditioned. Given such complications, one must wait for others to discover how best to characterise these gestures and how to derive the articulatory movements from them. However, one can be reasonably sure that the unconventional view leads the theoretical enterprise in the right direction, for it permits co-articulation. That is, it permits the speaker to overlap gestures that are produced by different organs—for example, the lips and the tongue in [ba]—and to merge gestures that are produced by different parts of the same organ—for example, the tip and body of the tongue, as in [da]—and so to achieve the high rates that are common.

But the gestures that are co-articulated, and the means for controlling them, were not lying conveniently to hand, just waiting to be appropriated by language, which brings us to the second assumption of the unconventional view: The gestures of speech and their controls are specifically phonetic, having been adapted for language and for nothing else. As for the gestures themselves, they are distinct as a class from those movements of the same organs that are used for such nonlinguistic purposes as swallowing, moving food around in the mouth, licking the lips, and so on. Presumably, they were selected in the evolution of speech in large part because of the ease with which they lent themselves to being co-articulated. But the control and co-ordination of these gestures is also specific to speech. Co-articulation is constrained by the special demands of phonological communication. Thus, co-articulation must produce enough overlap and merging to permit the high rates of phonetic segment production that do, in fact, occur, while yet preserving the details of phonetic structure.

The third assumption of the unconventional view is that, just as there is a specialisation for the production of phonetic structures, so, too, is there a specialisation for their perception. Indeed, the two are but complementary aspects of the same specialisation, one for deriving the articulatory movements from the (abstract) specification of the gestures, the other for processing the acoustic signals so as to recover the co-articulated gestures that are its distal cause. The rationale for this assumption about perception arises out of the consequences of the fact that co-articulation folds information about several gestures into a single piece of sound, thereby conveying the information in parallel. This is of critical importance for language because it relaxes by a large factor the constraint on rate of phonetic-segment perception that is set by the temporal resolving power of the ear. But this gain has a price, for co-articulation produces a complex and singularly linguistic relation between acoustic signal and the phonetic message it conveys. As is well known, the signal for each particular phonetic element is vastly different in different contexts, and there is no direct correspondence in segmentation between signal and phonetic structure. It is to manage this language-specific relation between signal and appropriate percept that the specialisation for speech perception is adapted. Support for the hypothesis that there is such a specialised speech mode of perception is to be found elsewhere. (See the references given at the beginning of this section.) What is important for our present purposes is only that, according to this hypothesis, the percepts evoked by the sounds of speech are immediately and specifically phonetic. There is no need, as there is in the conventional view, for a cognitive translation from an initial auditory representation, simply because there is no initial auditory representation.

Now one can see plainly the difference between speech and reading–writing. In reading, to take the one case, the primary perceptual representations are, as we have seen, inherently visual, not linguistic. Thus, these representations are, at best, arbitrary symbols for the natural units of language, hence unsuited to any natural language process until and unless they have been translated into linguistic form. On the other hand, the representations that are evoked by the sounds of speech are immediately linguistic in kind, having been made so by the automatic processes of the phonetic module. Accordingly, they are, by their very nature, perfectly suited for the further automatic and natural processing that the larger specialisation for language provides.

As for parity and its development in evolution and in the child, it is, in the unconventional view, intrinsic to the system. For what evolved, in this view, was a specifically phonetic process, together with representations that were thus categorically set apart from all others and reserved for language. The unconventional view also allows us to see, as the link between sender and receiver, the specifically phonetic gestures that serve as the common coin for the conduct of their linguistic business. There is no need to establish parity by means of (innate) phonetic ideas—e.g. labels, prototypes, distinctive features—to which the several nonlinguistic representations must be cognitively associated.

HOW CAN READING–WRITING BE MADE TO EXPLOIT THE MORE NATURAL PROCESSES OF SPEECH?

The conventional view of speech provides no basis for asking this question, as there exists, in this view, no difference in naturalness. It is perhaps for this reason that the (probably) most widely held theory of reading in the United States explicitly takes as its premise that reading and writing are, or at least can be, as natural and easy as speech (Goodman & Goodman, 1979). According to this theory, called "whole language", reading and writing prove to be difficult only because teachers burden children with what the theorists call "bite-size abstract chunks of language such as words, syllables, and phonemes" (Goodman, 1986). If teachers were to teach children to read and write the way they were (presumably) taught to speak, then there would be no problem. Other theorists simply ignore the primacy of speech as they describe a reading process in which purely visual representations are sufficient to take the reader from print to meaning, thus implying a "visual" language that is somehow parallel to a language best described as "auditory" (see, for example, Massaro & Schmuller, 1975; Smith, 1971).

In the unconventional view, however, language is neither auditory nor visual. If it seems to be auditory, that is only because the appropriate stimulus is commonly acoustic (*pace* Aristotle). But optical stimuli will, under some conditions, evoke equally convincing phonetic percepts, provided (and this is a critical proviso) they specify the same articulatory movements (hence, phonetic gestures) that the sounds of speech evoke. This so-called "McGurk effect" works powerfully when the stimuli are the natural movements of the articulatory apparatus, but not when they are the arbitrary letters of the alphabet. Thus, language is a mode, largely independent of end organs, that comprises structures and processes specifically adapted to language, hence easy to use for linguistic purposes. Therefore, the seemingly sensible strategy for the reader is to enter that mode, for once there, everything else that needs to be done by way of linguistic processing is done for him or her automatically by virtue of his or her natural language capacity. As for where the reader should enter the language mode, one supposes that earlier the better, and that the phonological component of the mode is early enough. Certainly, making contact with the phonology has several important advantages: It makes available to the reader a generative scheme that comprehends all the words of the language, those that died yesterday, those that live today, and those that will be born tomorrow; it also establishes clear and stable representations in a semantic world full of vague and labile meanings; and, not least, it provides the natural grist for the syntactic mill—that is, the phonological representations that are used by the working memory as it organises words into sentences.

The thoroughly visual way to read, described earlier, is the obvious alternative, doing everything that natural language does without ever touching its structures and processes. But surely that must be a hard way to read, if, indeed, it is even possible, because it requires the reader to invent new and cognitively taxing processes just in order to deal with representations that are not specialised for language and for which he or she has no natural ability.

WHAT OBSTACLE BLOCKS THE NATURAL PATH?

As we have seen, the conventional view allows two equivalent representations of language—one auditory, the other visual—hence two equally natural paths that language processes might follow. In that case, such obstacles as there might be could be no greater for the visual mode; indeed, accepting the considerations I mentioned earlier, we should have to suppose that visual representations would offer the easier route.

The unconventional view, on the other hand, permits one to see just what it is that the would-be reader and writer (but not the speaker–listener) must learn, and why the learning might be at least a little difficult. The point is that, given the specialisation for speech, anyone who wants to speak a word is not required to know how it is spelled; indeed, they do not even have to know that it has a spelling. They have only to think of the word; the speech specialisation spells it for them, automatically selecting and co-ordinating the appropriate gestures. In an analogous way, the listener need not consciously parse the sound so as to identify its constituent phonological elements. Again, he or she relies on the phonetic specialisation to do all the hard work; he or she has only to listen. Because the speech specialisation is a module, its processes are automatic and insulated from consciousness. There are, therefore, no cognitively formed associations that would make one aware of the units being associated. Of course, the phonological representations, as distinguished from the processes, are not so insulated; they are available to consciousness—indeed, if they were not, alphabetic scripts would not work—but there is nothing in the ordinary use of language that requires the speaker–listener to give them attention. The consequence is that experience with speech is normally not sufficient to make one consciously aware of the phonological structure of its words, yet it is exactly this awareness that is required of all who would enjoy the advantages of an alphabetic scheme for reading and writing.

Developing an awareness of phonological structure, and hence an understanding of the alphabetic principle, is made the more difficult by the co-articulation that is central to the function of the phonetic specialisation. Although such co-articulation has the crucial advantage of allowing speech production and perception to proceed at reasonable rates, it has the disadvantage from the would-be reader–writer's point of view that it destroys any simple correspondence between the acoustic segments and the phonological segments they convey. Thus, in a word like "bag", co-articulation folds three phonological segments into one seamless stretch of sound in which information about the several phonological segments is thoroughly overlapped. Accordingly, it avails the reader little to be able to identify the letters, or even to know their sounds. What the reader must know, if the script is to make sense, is that a word like "bag" has three pieces of phonology even though it has only one piece of sound. There is now much evidence (1) that pre-literate and illiterate people (adults and children) lack such phonological awareness; (2) that the amount of awareness they do have predicts their success in learning to read; and (3) that teaching phonological awareness makes success in reading more likely. (For a summary, see, for example, Liberman & Liberman, 1990.)

WHY SHOULD THE OBSTACLE LOOM ESPECIALLY LARGE FOR SOME?

Taking the conventional view of speech seriously makes it difficult to avoid the assumption that the problem of the dyslexic must be in the visual system. It is, therefore, not in the least surprising to find that by far the largest group of theories about dyslexia does, in fact, place the problem there. Thus, some believe that the trouble with dyslexics is that they cannot control their eye movements (Pavlides, 1985), or that they have problems with vergence (Stein, Riddell & Fowler, 1988), or that they see letters upside down or reversed left to right (Orton, 1937), or that their peripheral vision is better than it should be (Geiger & Lettvin, 1989), and so on.

The unconventional view of speech directs one's attention not to the visual system and the various problems that might afflict it, but rather to the specialisation for language and the reasons why the alphabetic principle is not self-evident. As we have seen, this view suggests that phonological awareness, which is necessary for application of the alphabetic principle, does not come automatically with mastery of the language. As for dyslexics—that is, those who find it particularly hard to achieve that awareness—the unconventional view of speech suggests that the problem might well arise out of a malfunction of the phonological specialisation, a malfunction sufficient to cause the phonological representations to be less robust than normal. Such representations would presumably be just that much harder to become aware of. Although it is difficult to test that hypothesis directly, it is possible to look for support in the other consequences that a weak phonological faculty should have. Thus, one would expect the dyslexics would show such other symptoms as greater-than-normal difficulty in holding and manipulating verbal (but not nonverbal) materials in working memory, in naming objects (that is, in finding the proper phonological representation), in perceiving speech (but not nonspeech) in noise, and in managing difficult articulations. There is some evidence that dyslexics do show such symptoms. (For a summary, see Liberman, Shankweiler, & Liberman, 1985.)

WHAT ARE THE IMPLICATIONS FOR A THEORY OF SPEECH?

Those who investigate the perception and production of speech have been little concerned to explain how these processes differ so fundamentally in naturalness from those of reading and writing. Perhaps this is because the difference is so obvious as to be taken for granted and so to escape scientific examination. Or perhaps the speech researchers believe that explaining the difference is the business of those who study reading and writing. In any case, neglect of the difference might be justifiable if it were possible for a theory of speech to have no relevant implications. But a theory of speech does inevitably have such implications, and, as has been shown, the implications of the conventional theory run counter to the obvious facts. My concern in this chapter has been to show that, as a consequence, the conventional theory is of little help to those who would understand reading and writing. Now I would suggest that, for exactly the same reason, the theory offers little help to those who would understand speech, for if the theory fails to offer a reasonable account of a most fundamental fact about language, then we should conclude that there is something profoundly wrong with it.

The unconventional theory of speech described in this chapter was developed to account for speech, not for the difference between its processes and those of reading and writing. That it nevertheless shows promise of also serving the latter purpose may well be taken as one more reason for believing it.

ACKNOWLEDGEMENT

This work was supported by NIH grant HD–01994 to Haskins Laboratories.

REFERENCES

Berkeley, G. (1709). *An essay towards a new theory of vision*. Dublin: Printed by Aaron Rhames for Jeremy Pepyal.

Cole, R.A., & Scott, B. (1974). Toward a theory of speech perception. *Psychological Review, 81*, 348–374.

Crowder, R.G. & Morton, J. (1969). Pre-categorical acoustic storage (PAS). *Perception and Psychophysics, 5*, 365–373.

DeFrancis, J. (1989). *Visible speech: The diverse oneness of writing systems*. Honolulu: University of Hawaii Press.

Diehl, R., & Kluender, K. (1989). On the objects of speech perception. *Ecological Psychology*, 1, 121–144.

Fujisaki, M., & Kawashima, T. (1970). Some experiments on speech perception and a model for the perceptual mechanism. *Annual Report of the Engineering Research Institute* (Faculty of Engineering, University of Tokyo), *29*, 207–214.

Geiger, G., & Lettvin, J.Y. (1988). Dyslexia and reading as examples of alternative visual strategies. In C. von Euler, I. Lundberg, & G. Lennerstrand (Eds.), *Wenner-Gren Symposium Series, 54, Brain and Reading*. London: Macmillan Press.

Goodman, K.S. (1976). Reading: A psycholinguistic guessing game. In H. Singer & R.B. Ruddell (Eds.), *Theoretical models and processes of reading*. Newark, DE: International Reading Association.

Goodman, K.S. (1986). *What's whole in whole language: A parent-teacher guide*. Portsmouth, NH: Heinemann.

Goodman, K.S., & Goodman, Y.M. (1979). Learning to read is natural. In L.B. Resnick & P.A. Weaver (Eds.), *Theory and practice of early reading*, Vol. 1. Hillsdale, NJ: Lawrence Erlbaum Associates Inc.

Kuhl, P.K. (1981). Discrimination of speech by nonhuman animals: Basic auditory sensitivities conducive to the perception of speech-sound categories. *Journal of the Acoustic Society of America, 70*, 340–349.

Kuhl, P.K., & Miller, J.D. (1975). Speech perception by the chinchilla: Voiced-voiceless distinction in alveolar plosive consonants. *Science, 190*, 69.

Liberman, A.M., & Mattingly, I.G. (1985). The motor theory of speech perception revised. *Cognition, 21*, 1–36.

Liberman, A.M., & Mattingly, I.G. (1989). A specialization for speech perception. *Science, 243*, 489–494.

Liberman, I.Y., & Liberman, A.M. (1990). Whole language vs. code emphasis: Underlying assumptions and their implications for reading instruction. *Annals of Dyslexia, 40*, 51–76.

Liberman, I.Y., Shankweiler, D., & Liberman, A.M. (1989). The alphabetic principle and learning to read. In D. Shankweiler & I.Y. Liberman (Eds.), *Phonology and reading disability: Solving the reading puzzle*. Research Monograph Series. Ann Arbor: Michigan University Press.

Mattingly, I.G., & Liberman, A.M. (1988). Specialized perceiving systems for speech and other biologically significant sounds. In G.M. Edelman, W.E. Gall, & W.M. Cowan (Eds.), *Functions of the auditory system* (pp. 775–793). New York: Wiley.

Mattingly, I.G. & Liberman, A.M. (1990). Speech and other auditory modules. In G.M. Edelman, W.E. Gall, & W.M. Cowan (Eds.), *Signal and sense: Local and global order in perceptual maps*. New York: Wiley.

Miller, J.D. (1977). Perception of speech sounds in animals: Evidence for speech processing by mammalian auditory mechanisms. In T.H. Bullock (Ed.), *Recognition of complex acoustic signals* (Life Sciences Research Report 5). Berlin: Dahlem Konferenzen.

Oden, G.C. & Massaro, D.W. (1978). Integration of featural information in speech perception. *Psychological Review, 85*, 172–191.

Orton, S.J. (1937). *Reading, writing and speech problems in children.* New York: W.W. Norton & Co.

Pavlides, G.T. (1985). Eye movement differences between dyslexics, normal, and retarded readers while sequentially fixating digits. *American Journal of Opto and Physiological Optics, 62*, 820–832.

Pisoni, D.B. (1973). Auditory and phonetic memory codes in the discrimination of consonants and vowels. *Perception and Psychophysics, 13*, 253–260.

Smith, F. (1971). *Understanding reading.* New York: Holt, Rinehart, & Winston.

Stein, J., Riddell, P., & Fowler, S. (1988). Disordered right hemisphere function in developmental dyslexia. In C. von Euler, I. Lundberg, & G. Lennerstrand (Eds.), *Brain and reading.* London: The Macmillan Press Ltd.

Stevens, K.N. (1975). The potential role of property detectors in the perception of consonants. In G. Fant & M.A. Tatham (Eds.), *Auditory analysis and perception of speech.* New York: Academic Press.

Wang, W.S-Y. (1981). Language structure and optimal orthography. In O.J.L. Tzeng & H. Singer (Eds.), *Perception of print: Reading research in experimental psychology.* Hillsdale, NJ: Lawrence Erlbaum Associates Inc.

2 The Recognition of Lexical Units in Speech

Anne Cutler and James M. McQueen
MRC Applied Psychology Unit, Cambridge, UK

In order to understand language, a listener or reader must be able to recognise discrete lexical units. The range of possible utterances (or texts) that we may be confronted with is infinite, so it is impossible to store them in memory. Instead, we must store smaller units, usually words. Incoming spoken or written language must therefore be mapped onto these stored units, held in a mental lexicon.

The recognition of these lexical entries depends upon identification of where each corresponding unit in the input begins and ends—that is, on the recognition of word *boundaries*. The written forms of many languages facilitate the segmentation of visual language into discrete lexical units by providing an explicit boundary marker: the white spaces between words. There is, however, no equivalent to these white spaces in spoken language. The spectrogram shown in Fig. 2.1 illustrates this point. In the absence of a phonetic transcription, it is difficult to identify either how many words there are, or where they might begin. The continuous nature of speech prevents any objective marking of the onsets and offsets of each phoneme. Co-articulation operates both word-internally and across word boundaries. As the beginnings of phonemes cannot be reliably identified, it is impossible to mark word onsets. A trained spectrogram reader is likely to hypothesise phoneme candidates and then word candidates for the utterance in Fig. 2.1 without marking the precise location of any segment or word boundaries.

In the absence of reliable word boundary markers in speech, how might the *lexical segmentation problem* be solved? We suggest that listeners develop specific strategies to deal with this problem. These strategies tend to exploit the

Both authors are now at the Max Planck Institute for Psycholinguistics, Nijmegen, The Netherlands.

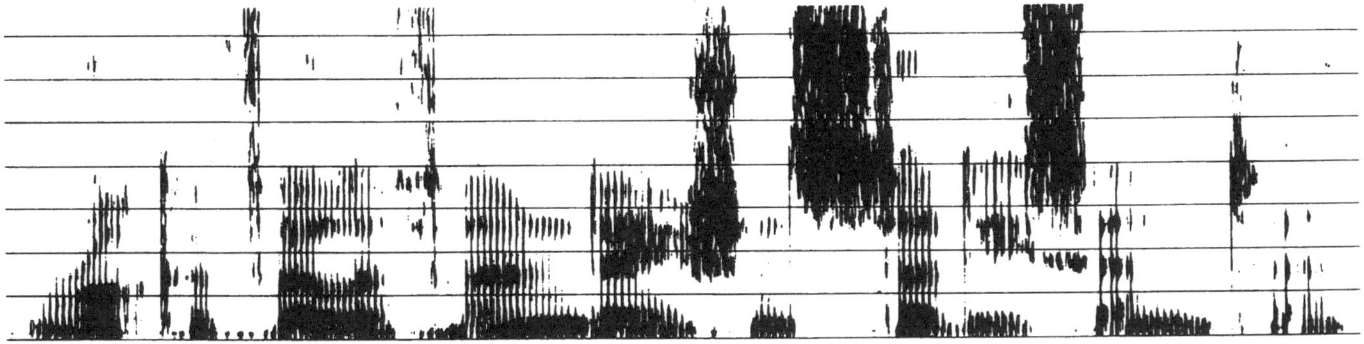

FIG.2.1 A spectrogram of a short phrase, spoken by a native speaker of British English. The phrase is "Rockefeller Foundation Study Centre."

structural regularities of the listener's language, and are therefore likely to be language-specific. In this chapter, we outline a segmentation strategy for English, based on the prosodic structure of the language. Note that prosodic information is not given to the reader of English. The failure of alphabetic scripts to code prosody may be one reason why these scripts have adopted the explicit boundary marker of white space between words.

THE METRICAL SEGMENTATION STRATEGY

The strategy that English listeners apparently use to solve the lexical segmentation problem in speech recognition exploits the rhythmic structure of the English language. English is a stress language, and its rhythm is stress-based. Languages with stress rhythm have, in effect, two distinct syllable types: strong and weak. Strong syllables contain full vowels: weak syllables contain reduced vowels (in English, often schwa). Words like "a-buse", "sa-loon", and "pro-ject" start with a weak syllable followed by a strong one. This distinction is insensitive to lexical stress: For a syllable to be strong it need only contain a full vowel; it does not matter whether this syllable carries the primary stress of a word, or only a secondary stress (e.g. "projectile" contains three syllables; the first is weak, the second is strong with primary stress, the final syllable is also strong with secondary stress).

The "metrical segmentation strategy" exploits stress rhythm in the following way: English listeners assume that every strong syllable is the onset of a new content word. Evidence in support of this claim has come from an analysis of misperceptions of speech (Cutler & Butterfield, 1992), from an examination of the prosodic structure of the English lexicon (Cutler & Carter, 1987), and from laboratory word-recognition tasks (Cutler & Norris, 1988). Here we will focus on the data from misperception, and on the statistical analyses of the vocabulary. First, we will discuss how speech appears to be misperceived exactly as the operation of the metrical segmentation strategy would predict. Secondly, we will show how a strategy of segmenting speech at the onsets of strong syllables is likely to be successful most of the time, because it accurately exploits the structure of the English vocabulary.

The misperceptions of speech that are of relevance to lexical segmentation are those which involve word boundaries. These *juncture misperceptions* are of two kinds. Word boundaries can be erroneously inserted or erroneously deleted. These errors can occur in two places: before strong syllables and before weak syllables. The metrical segmentation strategy predicts that two types of juncture misperception should be relatively common: erroneous insertions before strong syllables (postulating a word boundary before a strong syllable) and erroneous deletions before weak syllables (failing to detect a word boundary before a weak syllable). The strategy also predicts that the other two types of error should be rare. Listeners should tend not to insert word boundaries before weak syllables, nor should they tend to delete boundaries before strong syllables.

Cutler and Butterfield (1992) examined these predictions in two ways. First, they analysed as many spontaneous slips of the ear as they could find. An exploration of several collections of errors yielded 310 juncture misperceptions. These fell into the pattern predicted by the metrical segmentation strategy. Insertions before strong syllables (e.g. "analogy" → "and allergy") were more common than insertions before weak syllables ("effective" → "effect of"). Deletions before weak syllables ("my gorge is" → "my gorgeous") were more common than deletions before strong ("is he really" → "Israeli").

Secondly, juncture misperceptions were induced in the laboratory by presenting listeners with speech that was very faint, i.e. presented at a level (preset for each subject) at which only 50% of words could be correctly identified. Listeners heard six-syllable unpredictable utterances, with alternating patterns of strong and weak syllables, and their task was to write down what they thought each utterance was. Cutler and Butterfield examined the boundary misplacements (in only those responses which contained the correct number of syllables with the correct rhythmic pattern); as in the slips of the ear, there were significantly more boundary insertions before strong than before weak syllables, and significantly more boundary deletions before weak than before strong syllables.

Thus the segmentation errors that listeners make are strongly in accord with the predictions of the metrical segmentation strategy. Moreover, this strategy is well adapted to the structure of English. In an analysis of the MRC Database (a phonetically transcribed word-list based on the *Shorter Oxford English Dictionary*), Cutler and Carter (1987) found that nearly three-quarters of the sample began with strong syllables. Cutler and Carter's count included all word classes. However, as might be expected, the strong-initial tendency is particularly marked for English nouns: Cutler, McQueen, and Robinson (1990) report that nearly 85% of nouns in the *Longman Dictionary of Contemporary English* (Procter, 1975) begin with strong syllables. As nouns are among the least predictable parts of speech, the metrical segmentation strategy will work most efficiently of all where, in effect, it is most needed in speech recognition.

Even more unpredictable than nouns as a whole, perhaps, are proper names for people. Thus it is interesting that the same pattern was found when Cutler et al. (1990) examined the prosodic structure of English first names. However, this additional analysis revealed one intriguing asymmetry. Although names have the same overall pattern as nouns, male names have even fewer weak-initial syllables than nouns, whereas female names have rather more weak-initial syllables than nouns. This results in a significant difference between the two groups of names: Female names are significantly more likely to begin with a weak syllable than male names. This asymmetry was even more marked when frequently used names were considered alone. Lists of the most popular names in Britain and the United States include virtually no male names with weak initial syllables—in other words, not only are there very few such names, but those that exist are very rarely used (e.g. *Sebastian, Demetrius*). On the other hand, about

16% of frequently used female names begin with a weak syllable—so not only are there more weak-initial names for females, but some of these are in very common use (e.g. *Elizabeth, Michelle*). Speculations about the reasons for this asymmetry between male and female names, while fascinating, are outside the scope of this chapter (the reader is referred to Cutler et al., 1990, for such speculations, and for further asymmetries in the phonological structure of the two name classes). Here, the point at issue is that (irrespective of variations *within* the set) the most unpredictable set of words in the English language consists largely of items the onsets of which will be correctly located by the metrical segmentation strategy. Moreover, the more common the item, the more likely it is to have the predicted prosodic form.

Exactly this frequency effect also holds true of the English language in general. Cutler and Carter (1987) found that the mean frequency of the strong-initial content words (nouns, verbs, and adjectives) in the MRC Database was significantly higher than the mean frequency of the weak-initial content words. This predicts that in real speech samples, strong-initial content words will outnumber weak-initial ones to a much greater extent than they do in the vocabulary. Again, this is true. Cutler and Carter analysed a 200,000-word corpus of spontaneous speech (*A Corpus of English Conversation*, Svartvik & Quirk, 1980), and found that only 9.8% of content words began with weak syllables. This statistic suggests that a metrical segmentation strategy that assumes that content words begin with strong syllables will operate successfully over 90% of the time.

Nevertheless, not *all* content words begin with strong syllables; for instance, the preceding sentence alone contains *statistic, suggest, assume, begin* and *successful*. How problematic is it for the metrical segmentation stragegy that such words do occur? In a further exercise in lexical statistics, we attempted to address this issue. We examined all the weak-initial content words in the *Longman Dictionary of Contemporary English*. Consider words like *alert* and *assassin*. The metrical segmentation strategy will lead a listener to assume that the second (strong) syllable of a word of this type is the beginning of a new content word. If lexical access were to be initiated from the second syllable of these two words, however, no real words would be activated (that is, both *lert* and *sassin* are nonwords). If no real-word entry is mistakenly accessed, it can be assumed that the listener can readily recover from the misleading segmentation. However, some weak-initial words *do* contain strong-initial words embedded within them. For example, if we remove the initial syllable from prefixed weak-initial words such as *infrequent* and *displeasure*, we obviously obtain the words *frequent* and *pleasure*. But again, it is unlikely that the listener will experience much difficulty with this misleading segmentation either, because at least contact will have been made with a morphologically related lexical entry. Thus for both of these types of weak-initial word—the *alert* type and the *infrequent* type—no unrelated lexical competitors will be erroneously contacted via the operation of the metrical segmentation strategy.

The only words where the strategy would cause difficulty for the listener are those in which removing the initial, weak, syllable produces a totally unrelated strong-initial word. Presentation of such a word would, in effect, lead the listener up a lexical garden path, because a lexical entry would be activated that has nothing to do with the content of the actual utterance. Consider, for example, such words as *vermilion*, *informant* and *contributory*. It is unlikely that a listener's recognition of those words would be facilitated by contact with the lexical entries for *million*, *formant* and *tributary*. We computed, therefore (using the *Longman Dictionary of Contemporary English*), the proportion of the three types of weak-initial content word—the *alert* type, the *infrequent* type, and the *vermilion* type—in the English vocabulary.

Reassuringly, the results of this analysis suggest that lexical garden paths will be rare. As Fig. 2.2 shows, only 17.5% of weak-initial content words contain unrelated embedded words. We can combine this figure with those from Cutler and Carter's (1987) analyses to obtain an estimate of how often the metrical segmentation strategy will lead listeners up a garden path in average speech contexts. Cutler and Carter found that 41% of words in the *Corpus of English Conversation* were content words. Of these, as we mentioned earlier, only 9.8% began with weak initial syllables. From the present computation we can estimate that 17.5% of this weak-initial set were garden-path words. 17.5% of 9.8% of 41% is 0.7%—in other words, the garden-path words constitute less than 1% of words encountered in typical English speech. On this estimate the garden-path effect of words like *vermilion* under the metrical segmentation strategy would appear to be far less of a problem for spoken word recognition than that caused by lexical ambiguity (i.e. the multiple unrelated meanings of words such as *palm* and *bank*).

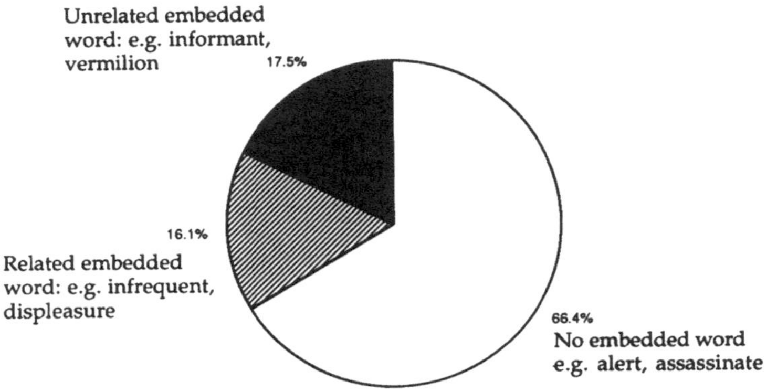

FIG.2.2 The proportion of weak-initial content words in the *Longman Dictionary of Contemporary English* with no embedded word beginning from the second syllable, with related words beginning from the second syllable, and with unrelated words beginning from the second syllable

This result highlights the fact that the metrical segmentation strategy will work very efficiently with the content words of the English language. As implied earlier, however, Cutler and Carter (1987) found that 59% of words in the spontaneous speech corpus were *not* content words. That is, a majority of words in typical English speech are function, or closed-class, words. How does the strategy deal with function words?

Because most function words are monosyllabic, lexical words counted for slightly more than half of the *syllables* in the corpus. Cutler and Carter computed the proportion of strong syllables that were initial or noninitial in both content and function words, and likewise for weak syllables. Nearly 75% of the strong syllables began (or were) content words; more than two-thirds of the weak syllables began (or were) function words. These statistics led them to suggest a refinement of the metrical segmentation strategy. The extended version of the strategy can be stated as follows: Assume that every strong syllable is the onset of a new content word, and also assume that weak syllables are the onsets of function words, but only when there are no other ongoing lexical hypotheses (that is, where the weak syllable must be an onset, assume the onset is of a function word). Cutler and Carter suggested a possible instantiation of this strategy in an algorithm that, given a strong syllable, attempts lexical look-up in a main lexicon of content words. In the absence of a strong syllable (i.e. with a weak syllable), the input is matched against a subsidiary lexicon, consisting of a list of function words.

Describing the segmentation strategy in this way leads to a further prediction for the data from the juncture misperception studies. This prediction concerns erroneous word boundary *insertions* only. Insertions before strong syllables should produce content words, but insertions before weak syllables should produce function words. Cutler and Butterfield (1992) confirmed this prediction, both for spontaneous and for laboratory-induced slips of the ear. When a word boundary was erroneously inserted before a strong syllable, the following word was significantly more likely to be a content word (e.g. *conduct ascents uphill* ➔ *the doctor sends her bill*) than a function word (e.g. *within reviewed results* ➔ *belief to who results*). When a word boundary was inserted before a weak syllable, however, subjects were more likely to misperceive the next word as a function word (*e.g. dusty senseless drilling* ➔ *thus he sent his drill in*) than as a content word (e.g. *an eager rooster played* ➔ *a new resolve again*).

To sum up so far, it appears that listeners use their accumulated knowledge of their own language in solving the lexical segmentation problem. The strategies they develop to make effective use of this knowledge are highly likely to be language-specific—the metrical segmentation strategy, for example, works well for English, but it would be of little use in a language with a markedly different prosodic distribution of content words, and of no use whatsoever in a language without rhythmic stress. In the next section, we consider a different question about how such strategies, exploiting listeners' knowledge of the distributional patterns within their vocabulary, might operate in speech recognition. Specifically, we consider the issue of whether the mental lexicon is directly involved in the operation of the segmentation process.

THE LEXICON AND SEGMENTATION

There appear to be two distinct ways in which the English vocabulary might be involved in segmentation for lexical access. First, the vocabulary, as instantiated in the mental lexicon of the listener, could be involved on-line in the segmentation process. As we consider the segmentation process to be pre-lexical, acting to initiate lexical access attempts, this amounts to an interactive approach to lexical segmentation. It could be instantiated in an interactive activation framework. The activation strength of the majority of the content words in the lexicon (those with strong initial syllables) could directly modify the segmentation process, increasing the likelihood that a strong syllable will be taken as the onset of a content word.

Secondly, lexical segmentation could be an autonomous process, not subject to on-line control from the lexicon. It is quite conceivable that the segmentation process could take advantage of the structure of the English vocabulary without the lexicon being directly involved in its operation. Listeners, as we have argued, would develop an heuristic such as the metrical segmentation strategy through exposure to the language. As a result, the strategy would exploit the prosodic distribution of the language, and hence involve the structure of the lexicon in each segmentation decision that was made. Nevertheless, the strategy, once developed, could operate pre-lexically and entirely autonomously, on the basis of bottom-up information from the speech signal alone.

There is little evidence that deals directly with this issue. Nevertheless, we favour the second alternative, for two reasons. These will be discussed in turn. First, it is our view that the weight of the evidence from tasks requiring phonetic decisions favours an autonomous view of speech processing (Burton, Baum, & Blumstein, 1989; Cutler, Mehler, Norris, & Segui, 1987; Frauenfelder, Segui, & Dijkstra, 1990; McQueen, 1991). Cutler et al. (1987) have argued that the variability of lexical involvement in the phoneme monitoring task can be more parsimoniously explained by an autonomous model of spoken word recognition than an interactive model such as the TRACE model of McClelland and Elman (1986). Frauenfelder et al. (1990) failed to find support for the interactive predictions that a model like TRACE makes for phoneme monitoring in nonwords. The model predicts that the top-down facilitation from the lexicon that speeds detection of, for example, /p/ in the word *olympiade* relative to /p/ in the matched nonword *arimpiako* should also have inhibitory consequences. Detection of /t/, for example, in the nonword *vocabutaire* should be inhibited, because the lexical entry *vocabulaire* should boost the activation of the /l/ phoneme-node, which in turn should inhibit the /t/ node (in the TRACE architecture, the phoneme-nodes compete). But Frauenfelder et al. found no difference between detection times for targets such as /t/ in *vocabutaire* and matched nonwords such as *socabutaire* (where there should be no top-down facilitation, and no resultant inhibition).

In addition to the phoneme-monitoring task, results from the phonetic categorisation task also favour an autonomous view of speech processing. Burton et al. (1989) found that the lexical shift in the phonetic categorisation of word-initial stops, originally reported by Ganong (1980), depends on the acoustic-phonetic quality of the materials. Listeners were asked to categorise a voice onset time (VOT) continuum ranging from /d/ to /t/, embedded in word–nonword (*duke–tuke*) and nonword–word (*doot–toot*) contexts. They were more likely to label ambiguous stops as /d/ when the voiced endpoint was a word (*duke*), and as /t/ when the unvoiced endpoint was a word (*toot*). But Burton et al. found that this lexical effect disappeared when the voicing continuum contained more acoustic-phonetic information. There was no lexical shift with a continuum where the burst and aspiration amplitude was manipulated in parallel with VOT. McQueen (1991) replicated this effect in word-final categorisation. Lexical effects should be larger and more robust word-finally because there is more time for lexical access before the final phoneme is heard. Listeners tended to label ambiguous fricatives in an /s/–/ʃ/ continuum according to the lexical status of the string: For example, ambiguous stimuli were more often categorised as /ʃ/ in the continuum *fish–fiss* than in the continuum *kish–kiss*. But this lexical shift only occurred when the fricatives were degraded by low-pass filtering.

As top-down processing in interactive models is considered to benefit speech perception, these demonstrations that lexical effects are not a mandatory feature of the perception of ambiguous phonemes (where one would predict top-down processing to be most in evidence) pose a problem for interactive models. McQueen (1991) also found that a specific reaction time prediction of the interactive TRACE model was not supported by the word-final categorisation data. Interactive models such as TRACE, which are based on activation, predict that top-down facilitation increases over time, as the evidence for a particular word accumulates. TRACE therefore predicts that the lexical shift in word-final categorisation should be larger for slower responses. Reaction times were split into three ranges, fast, medium, and slow, for each subject, following a procedure developed by Miller and Dexter (1988). Contrary to TRACE predictions, it was found that the lexical shift was largest in the fast RT range.

We have recently submitted these data to a more stringent test. Dividing each subject's overall data into three ranges ignores any variability in reaction time along the fricative continuum. Because responses to endpoint stimuli were faster than those to ambiguous region stimuli this range analysis will have tended, in the fast range, to increase the number of data points at the endpoints and decrease the number near the boundary. Conversely, in the slow range, there will have been relatively more data near the boundary and relatively less at the endpoints. Because the results suggest that there are lexical shifts in the fast range, and as these shifts are due to performance in the boundary region, it seemed important to attempt to

TABLE 2.1
Estimated 50% Crossover Points for Palatal Responses, as a Function of Reaction Time Range

Continua	*Fast Range*	*Medium Range*	*Slow Range*
Word–nonword	6.3	5.9	5.9
Nonword–word	5.9	5.7	5.7
Nonword–nonword	6.4	5.8	5.8

Note: The three ranges were based on each subject's data for each point along the continuum.
Source: Data from McQueen, 1991.

maximise the amount of data in the boundary region in the fast RT range. To this end, we performed the new RT range analysis. The data was again divided into three reaction time ranges for each subject, but now this analysis was performed separately for each of the nine fricatives along the continuum. This technique removes any variability in reaction time due to stimulus continuum position, and equates the amount of data contributing to each of the cells of the analysis.

Estimates of 50% crossover points were made by linear interpolation for each of the continuum types in each RT range. The means are given in Table 2.1. The percentages of palatal responses in the three RT ranges, with the data divided in this way, for each point along the continuum for each subject, are plotted in Fig. 2.3. The mean cut-off was 982msec (SD = 114msec) between fast and medium ranges and 1143msec (SD = 146msec) between medium and slow ranges.

The results replicated the original range analysis. There was a significant effect of continuum only in the fast range: $F(2, 42) = 8.79$, $p < 0.001$. This was partially due to a lexical shift. In an analysis comparing the word–nonword and nonword–word continua only, there were reliably more /ʃ/ responses when the palatal endpoint was a word than when this endpoint was a nonword: $F(1, 21) = 7.83$, $p < 0.05$. Combining the old and new analyses, it appears that the overall lexical shift is due to an effect that is largest in the fastest RT range and smallest in the slowest range. The shift is only statistically reliable in the fast range, whether the ranges are defined from each subject's overall response times or from each subject's responses to each of the nine fricatives.

This analysis therefore confirms that, irrespective of variability between average RTs to endpoint vs. ambiguous stimuli, it is the fast responses that show the greatest lexical shifts. As we pointed out earlier, TRACE would have predicted the opposite pattern of results. Thus McQueen's study joins the body of recent research that has demonstrated weakness in the interactive account of speech processing. On the other hand, McQueen's data do not challenge an autonomous model. Frauenfelder et al.'s data, likewise, are problematic for an interactive model, but not for an autonomous model, because autonomous theory predicts that the perception of nonwords should be insulated from lexical processing. The autonomous race model (Cutler & Norris, 1979; Cutler et al., 1987), as an example, predicts the pattern of RT range results that McQueen (1991) found for word-final categorisation. In this model, lexical and pre-lexical phoneme identification procedures are considered to race; the procedure which more rapidly produces an output on a particular trial will be responsible for the phonetic decision on that trial. Because in word-final categorisation the lexical route is faster on average

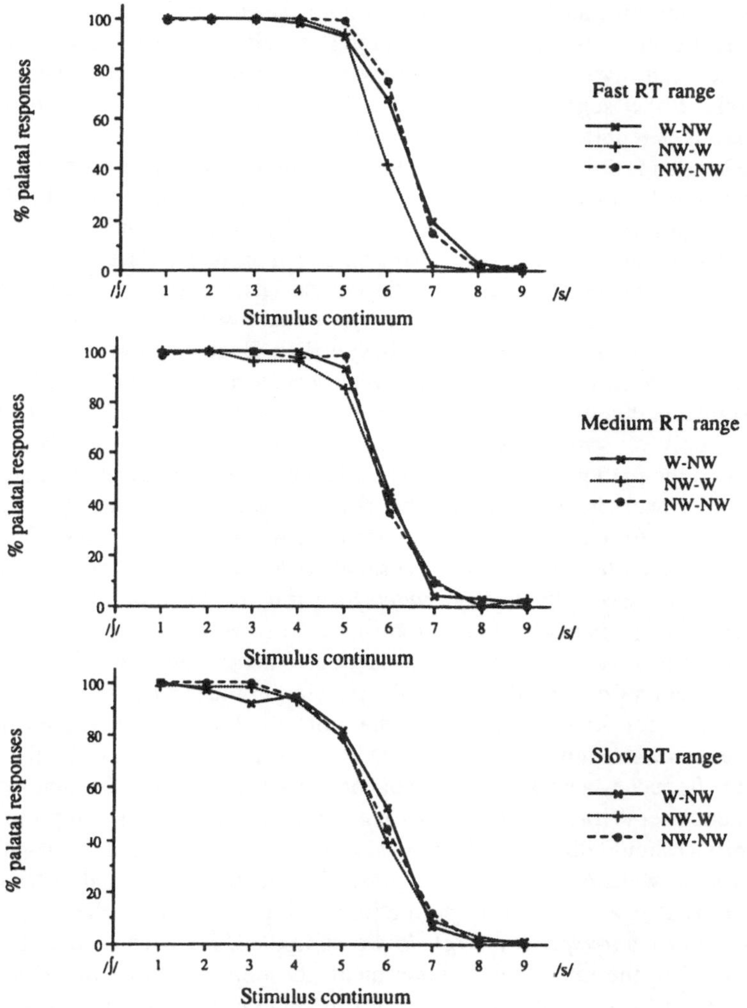

FIG.2.3 Percent palatal (/ʃ/) responses, divided into three reaction-time ranges: fast, medium, and slow, defined for each point along the continuum for each subject. The data are plotted, collapsed across the three vowel blocks, as the proportion of the total number of responses to each stimulus within each range (data from McQueen, 1991).

than the pre-lexical route, the responses producing the lexical shift (i.e. those made via the lexical route) will tend to be the faster responses.

On the basis of evidence from tasks requiring explicit phonetic decisions, then, it would appear that autonomous theories of speech processing are more plausible than interactive theories. This might suggest in turn that a strictly autonomous view of lexical segmentation should be preferred. The inference from the phoneme-monitoring and phonetic categorisation data to the normal segmentation of continuous speech is, however, not a strong one. Nevertheless, the second line of evidence that favours an autonomous view of segmentation is based on the operation of the segmentation process itself. We return to the juncture misperceptions reported by Cutler and Butterfield (1992).

If the lexicon is directly involved in lexical segmentation, its influence should be reflected in the boundary error data: Asymmetries in the vocabulary should be correlated with asymmetries in the errors. This hypothesis could be relatively easily tested, because of a particular characteristic of the materials used in the faint speech experiment described earlier. In these materials, it will be recalled, half the vowels were weak and half were strong. The weak vowels were mostly schwa, which indeed is usually the case for weak vowels in English. However, although the English phoneme repertoire contains over a dozen strong monophthong vowels, plus several diphthongs, the experimental materials were constrained such that they contained only six strong vowels (/ɛ, eI, ʌ, u, I, i/). Cutler and Carter's (1987) statistics on the predominance of strong initial syllables in English indicate that for *any* full vowel, there are likely to be more words with this vowel in a strong initial syllable (for example, with the vowel /ɛ/, words like *beg, chest, feather, residence, verisimilitude*) than with the same vowel in a strong second syllable, preceded by a weak syllable (e.g. *cadet, forgetful, suggestible, togetherness*). However, this ratio is likely to vary from vowel to vowel.

If the lexicon directly influences boundary placement, as an interactive account of speech recognition would suggest, then the larger the strong-initial to weak-initial ratio is for a particular vowel, the more likely a listener should be to misperceive a weak-initial word with that vowel as a strong-initial one. In other words, the frequency across vowels of boundary insertion errors in the faint speech experiment (i.e. errors in which a strong syllable is erroneously reported as word-initial) should directly reflect the size of the strong-initial to weak-initial ratio across vowels. A correlational analysis described in Cutler and Butterfield (1992) provided a test of this prediction. Using once again the *Longman Dictionary of Contemporary English*, we computed, for each of the six full vowels used in the faint speech experiment, the ratio of strong-initial words (*feather*, etc.) to weak-initial (*cadet*, etc). As predicted, this ratio was quite variable across the six vowels. We then computed the ratio of boundary insertions to boundary deletions before strong syllables containing each of these vowels. As Fig. 2.4 shows, the two ratios appeared to be quite uncorrelated (indeed, their relation was, if anything, in the wrong direction: $r(5) = -0.31$, $p > 0.5$).

An interactive account of the role of the lexicon in speech segmentation would also predict another correlation between lexical distribution and missegmentation frequency—this time for *deletion* errors. Deletion errors, it will be recalled, occur far more often before weak syllables than before strong ones—that is, boundaries before weak syllables tend to be overlooked. The effect of such a deletion error is, of course, to attach the weak syllable to a preceding strong syllable. If the lexicon is involved in boundary errors, such deletion errors should also reflect lexical distributions; specifically, they should be more common for those vowels that most often occur with a following weak syllable. We assumed that the ratio of words with each vowel in a penultimate syllable followed by a weak final syllable (e.g. *feather, forgetful*) to words with the vowels in a final strong syllable (e.g. *chest, cadet, comprehend*) would also vary across the six vowels; and again, we computed the relevant statistics using the *Longman Dictionary*, and found that it did. The prediction from the interactive account is that the larger this ratio is for a particular vowel, the more likely it should be that listeners will erroneously overlook a word boundary after that vowel. We performed a correlational analysis and again found that the correlation was not significant: $r(5) = 0.71$, $p < 0.1$. Figure 2.5 shows the data.

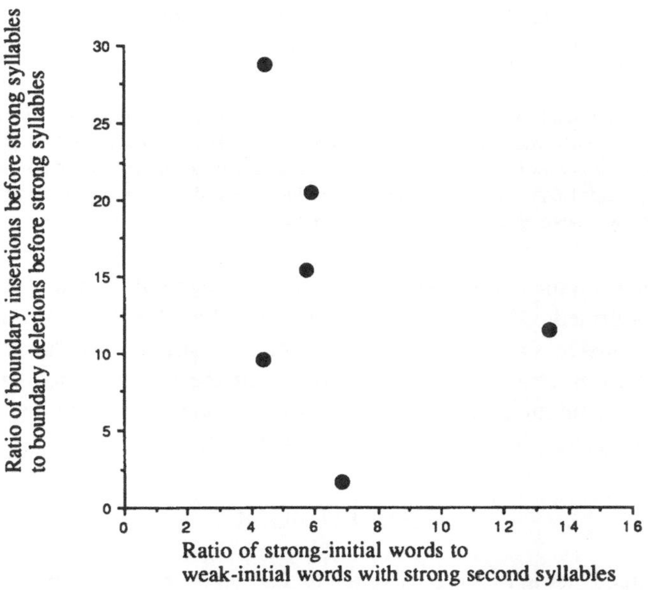

FIG.2.4 A scatter plot, for six vowels (/ɛ, eI, ʌ, u, I, i/). The ratios of words with each vowel in strong initial syllables to words with weak initial syllables followed by strong syllables containing the vowel are taken from the *Longman Dictionary of Contemporary English*. These are plotted against juncture misperception errors taken from Cutler and Butterfield (1992): The ratio of boundary insertions to boundary deletions before the strong syllables containing each of the six vowels.

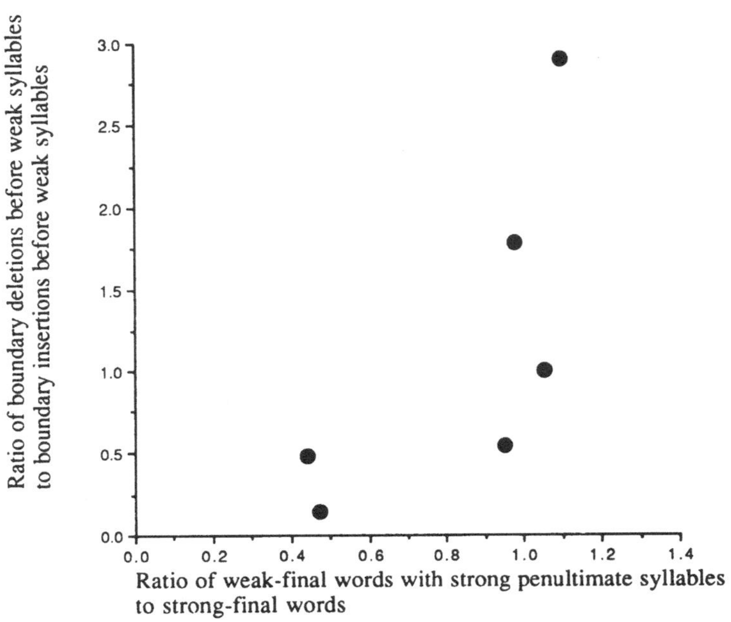

FIG.2.5 A scatter plot, for six vowels (ɛ, eI, ʌ, u, I, i/). The ratios of words with each vowel in penultimate strong syllables to words with final strong syllables containing the vowel are taken from the *Longman Dictionary of Contemporary English*. These are plotted against juncture misperception errors taken from Cutler and Butterfield (1992): The ratio of boundary deletions to boundary insertions before weak syllables following strong syllables containing each of the six vowels.

The predictions of an interactive view of lexical segmentation have, therefore, not been confirmed. Of course, these correlational analyses can not be held to provide conclusive support for an autonomous position. Nevertheless, these results, in combination with the findings from the phonetic decision tasks, indicate that an autonomous account of lexical segmentation may be in several respects more plausible than an interactive account.

CONCLUSIONS

We have argued that in order to solve the lexical segmentation problem, listeners make use of the structural properties of their language. In English, they exploit the distributional properties of the vocabulary, as indicated by lexical statistics. We have claimed that listeners adopt a metrical segmentation strategy. They assume that strong syllables are the beginnings of content words. If listeners have to take weak syllables as onsets, they treat them as the onsets of function words.

Estimates suggest that in typical English speech, the metrical segmentation strategy would cause misleading lexical entries to be accessed for less than 1% of words.

The continuous temporal nature of speech is best suited to a bottom-up analysis. Evidence from paradigms such as phonetic categorisation indicates that the lexicon does not influence pre-lexical processing. This suggests that the lexicon is not involved on-line in segmentation. Converging evidence for this claim comes from a correlational analysis of juncture misperceptions. What appears to be most plausible is that listeners learn to use a metrical segmentation heuristic through experience with their language, and that this process then operates pre-lexically.

ACKNOWLEDGEMENTS

We acknowledge financial support from the Joint Research Councils Initiative in HCI and Cognitive Science: Grant No. E304/148. We would also like to thank the Longman Group UK Inc. for allowing us to use a machine-readable version of the *Longman Dictionary of Contemporary English*.

REFERENCES

Burton, M.W., Baum, S.R., & Blumstein, S.E. (1989). Lexical effects on the phonetic categorization of speech: The role of acoustic structure. *Journal of Experimental Psychology: Human Perception and Performance, 15*, 567–575.

Cutler, A., & Butterfield, S. (1992). Rhythmic cues to speech segmentation: Evidence from juncture misperception. *Journal of Memory and Language, 31*, 218–236.

Cutler, A., & Carter, D. (1987). The predominance of strong initial syllables in the English vocabulary. *Computer Speech and Language, 2*, 133–142.

Cutler, A., McQueen, J., & Robinson, K. (1990). Elizabeth and John: Sound patterns of men's and women's names. *Journal of Linguistics, 26*, 471–482.

Cutler, A., Mehler, J., Norris, D., & Segui, J. (1987). Phoneme identification and the lexicon. *Cognitive Psychology, 19*, 141–177.

Cutler, A., & Norris, D. (1979). Monitoring sentence comprehension. In W.E. Cooper & E.C.T. Walker (Eds.), *Sentence processing: Psycholinguistic studies presented to Merrill Garrett*. Hillsdale, NJ: Lawrence Erlbaum Associates Inc.

Cutler, A., & Norris, D. (1988). The role of strong syllables in segmentation for lexical access. *Journal of Experimental Psychology: Human Perception and Performance, 14*, 113–121.

Frauenfelder, U.H., Segui, J., & Dijkstra, T. (1990). Lexical effects in phonemic processing: Facilitatory or inhibitory? *Journal of Experimental Psychology: Human Perception and Performance, 16*, 77–91.

Ganong, W.F. (1980). Phonetic categorization in auditory word perception. *Journal of Experimental Psychology: Human Perception and Performance, 6*, 110–125.

McClelland, J.L., & Elman, J.L. (1986). The TRACE model of speech perception. *Cognitive Psychology, 18*, 1–86.

McQueen, J.M. (1991). The influence of the lexicon on phonetic categorization: Stimulus quality in word-final ambiguity. *Journal of Experimental Psychology: Human Perception and Performance, 17*, 433–443.

Miller, J.L., & Dexter, E.R. (1988). Effects of speaking rate and lexical status on phonetic perception. *Journal of Experimental Psychology: Human Perception and Performance, 14*, 369–378.

Procter, P. (Ed.) (1975). *Longman Dictionary of Contemporary English*. London: Longman.

Svartvik, J. & Quirk, R. (1980). *A Corpus of English Conversation*. Lund: Gleerup.

3 On the Linguistic Module in Auditory Memory

Robert G. Crowder and Aimée M. Surprenant
Yale University, New Haven, CT, USA

INTRODUCTION

The penetration of language into various domains of human memory is not controversial. Compelling evidence supports the tendencies of people to describe their sensory experiences to themselves at the time they occur, and then, later, to remember those descriptions rather than the experiences themselves (for examples, see Conrad, 1964; Glanzer & Clark, 1963; Sperling, 1960). In many cases the schematic knowledge that structures our world, and therefore drives our memories, is probably linguistic in nature (see. e.g. Schank & Abelson, 1977). Vygotsky (1978) indeed argued that language is primary to memory in principle, because we cannot express many kinds of memory other than through words.

We shall focus on what once seemed a clear exception to this rule, auditory sensory memory. The evolution of this concept, in our laboratory at least, depended on two empirical phenomena in immediate memory for span-length series—the modality effect and the suffix effect—shown, respectively, in the two panels in Fig. 3.1. The upper curve in each panel shows idealised performance on lists of about nine unrelated characters or words, as spoken aloud for immediate ordered recall. Correct performance is shown as a function of the serial position occupied by each element in the list, from first to last. In the left panel this is compared to presentation conditions that are identical in all ways except that the characters are printed successively in the centre of a screen and read silently rather than heard aloud. Obviously the marked advantage of the auditory mode is located at the last few elements presented. This *recency effect* will be the one main signature of auditory memory in this chapter. In the right panel, exactly the same auditory control condition is compared with a suffix

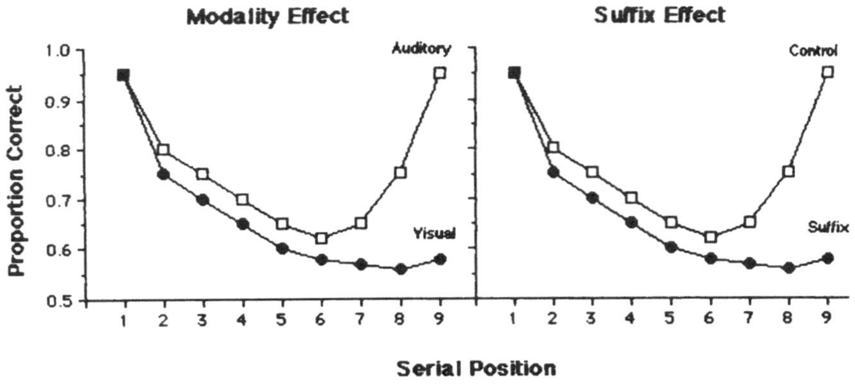

FIG.3.1 Idealised serial position curves illustrating the modality and suffix effects.

condition, in which an extra utterance is presented at the end of a spoken list, the same redundant utterance for every list in a session, therefore posing no additional load on memory. As Fig. 3.1 emphasises, this redundant suffix effectively removes the great advantage of auditory presentation over visual, the recency effect.

Crowder and Morton (1969) proposed that the findings illustrated in Fig. 3.1 were intimately related, theoretically, showing properties of a Precategorical Acoustic Storage system. The modality effect was to have been the contribution of a specialised sensory store associated with auditory processing, and not available from purely visual input. The suffix effect was thought to reflect the fact that subsequent auditory input could mask the contents of this store, leaving peformance more or less what it would have been without the auditory information in the first place. (See Crowder, 1976, for a detailed account of these data and ideas.)

The two classes of result most directly favourable to this hypothesis were that (1) the meaning, or categorical status, of a suffix item had no impact on the size of the suffix effect, and (2) its physical nature (voice quality, spatial location), on the other hand, did. Sensitivities of this sort were exactly what one would expect of a "pre-categorical" or pre-linguistic store, where of course these terms refer to a level of analysis and not a chronological history during perception (Morton, Crowder, & Prussin, 1971).

Attribution of the modality and suffix experiments to Precategorical Acoustic Storage was relatively undisturbed until experiments by Spoehr and Corin (1978) and by Campbell and Dodd (1980) showed, starkly, that the original hypothesis had been wrong. These authors demonstrated that silent lip-reading and related *silent* presentation modalities produced results nearly indistinguishable from spoken presentation and readily differentiated from the consequences of silently presented orthographic symbols (see also Greene & Crowder, 1984). Secondly,

Ayres et al. (1979) showed that the very same acoustic stimulus could produce different results as a suffix item depending on whether it was interpreted as human speech (a man saying "wa") or as a musical tone (a trumpet note using a "wa-wa mute"). We shall have more to say on this second disproof of the Crowder–Morton (1969) hypothesis later. For now, we can anticipate the major conclusion of our research effort, here, that both of these pieces of evidence, so problematic for pre-categorical acoustic storage, make sense if the data of Fig. 3.1 result from a specifically linguistic or phonetic processor rather than from a general property of auditory cognition.

One point of view had been that the immediate-memory experiments, with modality comparisons and suffixes, were only a convenient way of making manifest a set of mechanisms that were characteristic of auditory memory in general, and not uniquely relevant to speech. This attitude is implicit in Crowder's (1978) model for a "grid" representation of sound traces in memory, for example. The more linguistic point of view was probably first articulated by Liberman, Mattingly, and Turvey (1972) (see also Morton, Marcus, & Ottley, 1981). These authors supposed that recency results directly from the activity of a specialised processor for human speech, a module, and not from any general-purpose auditory information-processing mechanism.

Either hypothesis can accommodate all but the most recent evidence: For example, we know that a tone or buzzer after a spoken list of digits does not produce a suffix effect (Crowder, 1971a, Fig. 2, p. 330). On the general-auditory model, this is because a human voice is physically discrepant from a buzzer. On the modular speech account, it is because the buzzer does not qualify as speech.

The obvious test to choose between these positions is to use items that are not human speech as the memory stimuli. According to the auditory interpretation, if subjects must remember in order a series of buzzer-like sounds, for example, then we would expect a redundant speech stimulus to have no suffix effect, but another buzzer sound should cause a large one. Straightforward as this reasoning seems, our survey of the literature indicated that neither the recency effect characteristic of auditory presentation nor the suffix effect was unambiguous for nonspeech stimuli, including tonal sequences (Greene & Samuel, 1986; Foreit, 1976) and naturalistic sounds (Spoehr & Corin, 1978; Rowe & Rowe, 1976). Normal speech, on the other hand, was essentially *always* associated with the auditory-memory effects, and was effortless to show empirically, even with only a few minutes of class time.

We first set out to demonstrate this contrast between speech and nonspeech using reasonably uniform methods (list lengths, vocabulary sizes, presentation rates, response modes, and so on) in our own laboratory. In the first experiment, we wanted to capitalise on a research strategy that had been used before, and for related purposes, at Haskins Laboratories: The goal was to present identical sounds to two groups of subjects, one who would interpret those sounds as speech and the other who would interpret them as nonspeech noises (Remez,

Rubin, Pisoni, & Carrell, 1981). This contextual manipulation would then control for the many acoustic variables that separate the stimulus vocabularies used in immediate memory research, in order that we would be able to conclude with assurance that any obtained differences were due to recruitment of the speech processor. A successful demonstration of the importance of speech context would also replicate the important finding of the Ayres et al. (1979) experiment.

EXPERIMENT 1

A vocabulary of four "sinewave speech" stimuli (Remez et al., 1981) made up the memory stimuli, presented in lists of eight. One group of subjects was trained to hear these sounds as the digits one through four (from which they had indeed been derived) and the other group was given the names of naturalistic sounds to represent those same items. The question was whether the recency effect would appear and disappear for these stimuli depending on whether they were interpreted as speech or nonspeech, respectively.

Method

Stimuli. To construct stimuli permitting either interpretation (speech or nonspeech) we took tokens of a female pronouncing the digits one through four and degraded them by (1) reducing the centre bandwidth of each format until they were sinusoidal, and (2) further reducing cues for the second and third formants. We continued the second operation until the items sounded to us as if they could "go either way" perceptually.

Lists of eight items from this vocabulary of four were prepared by using each token twice, digitising them and recording them at a 2/second rate. Twenty seconds were allowed for recall between each list.

Procedure. Subjects listened to 98 lists and typed their responses on the z, x, c, and v keys of the same CRT terminal that controlled the experiment and recorded responses. The memory stimuli were presented through loudspeakers also controlled by the microprocessor.

The *speech* group of subjects was told that these were degraded versions of a female speaking the first four digits, and given practice until they could reliably press the key corresponding to each item, from a random series, 13 times in a row. For the nonspeech group, instructions suggested the names "bubbles, squeal, owl" and "whistle" for the same four sounds. (We made no suggestion that they had been derived from human speech.) These subjects, too, practised identification until they could press the corresponding key 13 times in a row from the same random series. The same computer keys were labelled with the four suggested names for them, rather than the four digit names.

Results

The main results are shown in Fig. 3.2, giving performance across serial position for the two groups. The result is easy to describe: Performance was completely unaffected by context, as manipulated here. However, we thought that this manipulation might not have been potent enough. Subjects might have been learning the test items in some way and then translating into either a speech or nonspeech code depending on their group, both translations unnatural for them.

EXPERIMENT 2

In the second experiment we tried to make the contextual interpretation of our sounds more convincing. We used a mixed-list procedure (Greene, 1989) in which more than one experimental condition of stimulus presentation was realised in the same eight-item list. The same two sinewave-speech items (the sinewave tokens of "two" and "four" used in Experiment 1) were present on every list heard by every subject. However, the remaining two items present in every eight-item list were different in the two groups: In the speech group, the remaining two items were the intact, undegraded, digits "one" and "three." In the nonspeech group they were the sounds of a telephone and a bell. Thus, in the former condition subjects were told they would hear four digits on every list, although two of them would be degraded. In the nonspeech condition, the sinewave speech

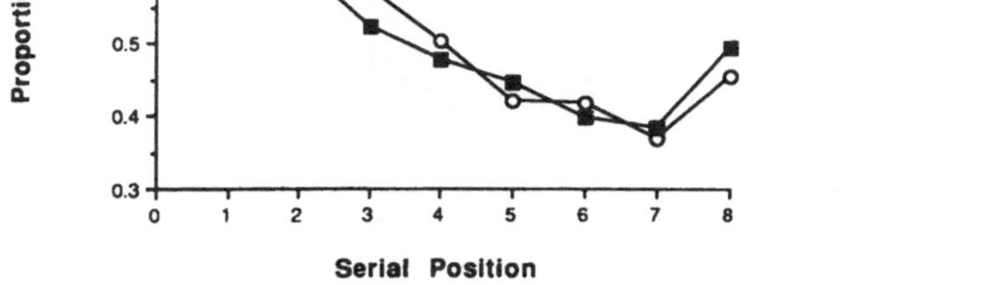

FIG. 3.2 Mean proportion correct as a function of speech and nonspeech descriptor conditions.

was identified as "bubbles" and "squeal" and they were told the other two would be "telephone" and "bell". In short, we thought the presence of companion items within lists in either the speech or nonspeech condition would provide a better context for perceiving the critical items than just instructions.

Method

The method matched that of Experiment 1 in all ways except for the following: Each list of eight items contained a random ordering of the four items assigned to the appropriate group (either the four digits—two degraded—or the four sounds—two acoustically identical to the sinewave digits).

Results

The results are shown in Fig. 3.3. Performance is given as a function of group and stimulus type. The sinewave digits and sinewave sounds represent performance on exactly the same two stimuli, acoustically, for the speech and nonspeech groups, respectively. The natural digits and natural sounds data are for the remaining two items within each stimulus set, which were intended to provide context.

We note again that context had no effect on the sinewave stimuli, even in this more powerful realisation of context. Independent checks indicated that this contextual manipulation had indeed been successful. What made a difference, as far as recency is concerned, was the presence of intact speech in the natural digits condition of Fig. 3.3. This conclusion matched our own reading of the

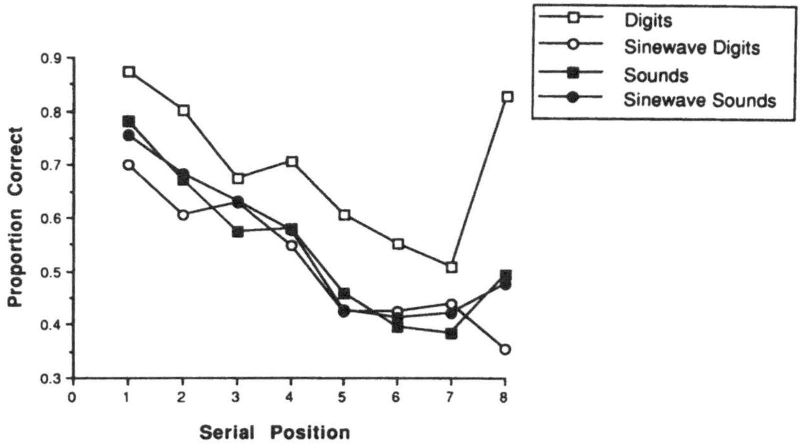

FIG. 3.3 Mean proportion correct as a function of the two digit (natural and sinewave) and sound conditions (natural and sinewave).

literature: For a large recency effect in immediate memory, the use of speech stimuli seem to be a necessary condition. This is not a sufficient condition, however, because many authors have shown that speech sounds that are difficult to discriminate (such as stop consonants) produce little or no recovery (Cole, 1973; Crowder, 1971b; Darwin & Baddeley, 1974).

What is it about natural speech that tends to promote the large recency effect in immediate recall? Following the model of Nairne (1988; 1990) for immediate recall—a position that may be identified as nonlinguistic according to our earlier distinction—we thought two main factors might be involved. Nairne proposed that *discriminability* and *familiarity*[1] were influential factors in producing recency in immediate recall. Without delving into the full model from which these formulations were derived, we can note immediately that human language stimuli are generally both very discriminable and very familiar, perhaps more so than alternative auditory stimuli that could be and have been used in immediate memory experiments. Furthermore, we already know that discriminability within the speech domain can control the amount of recency produced in recall (Cole, 1973; Crowder, 1971b; Darwin & Baddeley, 1974), so at first glance the facts favour Nairne's (1988; 1990) position. In our next experiments we looked for familiarity and discriminability effects, respectively.

EXPERIMENT 3

We examined the effects of familiarity by holding stimuli constant and varying the subject population. The stimuli were musical pitches and the subjects were either selected for extensive musical experience or selected so as to exclude appreciable musical experience. The former group had spent a good deal of their lives listening to and/or producing such tones, whereas the later group, albeit hardly completely innocent of musical sounds, had not listened analytically or extensively produced such sounds.

All memory lists were made up of eight tones in a series, presented as shown earlier. Discriminability was varied by comparing, for all subjects, vocabularies of closely spaced tones (narrow condition) with vocabularies of widely spaced tones (wide condition). In the limit, tones *too* closely spaced could not be discriminated at all, of course, so although our narrow condition employed four adjacent diatonic half steps—surely discriminable to all—we reasoned that a wider spacing would be more discriminable than a narrower spacing.

We thought discriminability might not have uniform effects across subject groups. For example, if the musicians were inclined to encode the series as melodies, then the narrow spacing of items might actually help them, for these items lie within a critical band and would favour assignment of items to a single auditory stream (Bregman, 1990). On the other hand, if the nonmusicians were not inclined to use a melodic encoding, then perhaps simple discriminability

[1] His term was *salience*.

would enhance performance. Thus, at least, an interaction between subject group and discriminability was expected.

Method

In most ways this experiment followed the methods used in the earlier ones, with the following exceptions:

Subjects. The eight musicians had reported at least six years of training on their instrument and were currently playing it on a regular basis. The eight nonmusicians reported no more than two years of training on any instrument, ever, and had not played that instrument for the past 10 years.

Stimuli. Two sets of four electronic piano notes were the stimulus vocabularies. In the narrow condition these notes were C4, C#4, D4, and D#4.[2] In the wide condition, the four pitches were C3, B3, A4, and G5, the same vocabulary used by Greene and Samuel (1986). The stimulus lists were eight items long, with each vocabulary item presented twice, all in random order. In both conditions the notes were labelled with the digits one through four, representing the notes from lowest to highest in pitch.

Procedure. The narrow and wide conditions were mixed randomly in the session (96 trials) for each subject. Before each trial, the vocabulary for that trial was presented rapidly, in ascending order, to indicate what interpretation (1, 2, 3, or 4) should be placed even on the first tone in the series when it occurred. After 1.5 seconds the eight-item series was presented, as in the earlier experiments. Eight practice trials preceded the test trials to accustom subjects to the experimental routine.

Results

The four conditions are shown in Fig. 3.4. The first salient aspect of the data is that none of the four treatment combinations produced much in the way of a recency effect. However, clearly both independent variables influenced performance overall, if not the recency effect: Performance of the musicians was substantially better than that of the nonmusicians. As these were different subjects, the result is strictly uninterpretable by itself as to whether it stems from subject differences or the specific familiarity of the tonal sequences. For the subjects altogether the wide condition was easier than the narrow condition, although this difference was larger by far for the unmusical group than for the musicians. Thus, our two independent

[2] In this range, a minor third lies just within a critical band.

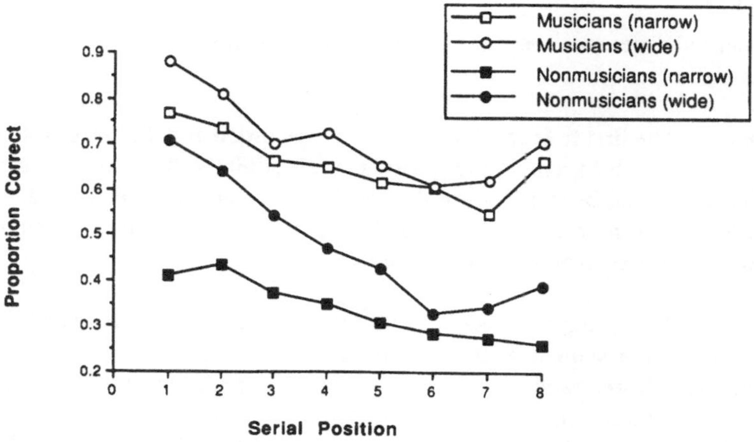

FIG. 3.4 Mean proportion correct as a function of type of subject (musician/nonmusician) and discriminability.

variables were effective in controlling performance overall, but they had no effect on recency.

In other experiments not described here, and in collaboration with Dr. Mark A. Pitt, we have tried in vain to replicate the Greene and Samuel (1986) result with musical stimuli. Thinking familiarity might have been the key, we went so far as to recruit graduate students in the Yale Music School who were studying violin or viola. In mixed lists, one of the sounds they had to remember was a bowed string note. We reasoned that a special mode of processing might exist for such sounds, given that they had been heard in abundance over a period of years within a few inches of the subject's ear. However, no substantial recency effect emerged for these items, as none had emerged in the data shown in Fig. 3.4.

EXPERIMENT 4

Next, we turned to a closer look at the factor of *discriminability* among items being remembered for ordered, immediate recall. The stimuli were entirely from the undegraded speech domain, the digits one through four, as before. However, within a list of eight, either one speaker pronounced all items (pure condition) or four different speakers presented the same list, alternating haphazardly (mixed condition). Thus the verbal properties of the stimuli were identical in the two main conditions, but acoustically the series in the mixed condition would, by any account, be more discriminable than those in the pure condition. We wanted to see whether this increased discriminability would enhance the recency effect, as expected by Nairne (1988; 1990).

Method

The essential differences between methodological points in this and in the earlier studies are:

Stimuli. The first four cardinal digits were recorded and digitised from four speakers: a male child, a male adult, another male adult (with an English accent), and a female adult. The stimuli were all about half a second in length. Lists allowed an interstimulus interval of 0.75 seconds and had to be increased in length to nine items in order to avoid ceiling effects.

Design and Procedure. Each of eight subjects received both pure and mixed series, in random sequence. In the former (pure) condition, one of the four speakers was chosen randomly and presented the entire nine-digit sequence on that trial. In the latter (mixed) condition, different voices pronounced the digits within the sequence. With a vocabulary of four digits and a list length of nine items, a given digit had to be repeated within a list, and in the mixed condition this was always by a different voice.

Results

Figure 3.5 shows the results of Experiment 4. As we have come to expect with uncorrupted speech, the recency effect was large in both conditions; however, it did not differ between them. If anything, the mixed-voices condition led to slightly worse performance overall, as it did in the work of Martin, Mullennix,

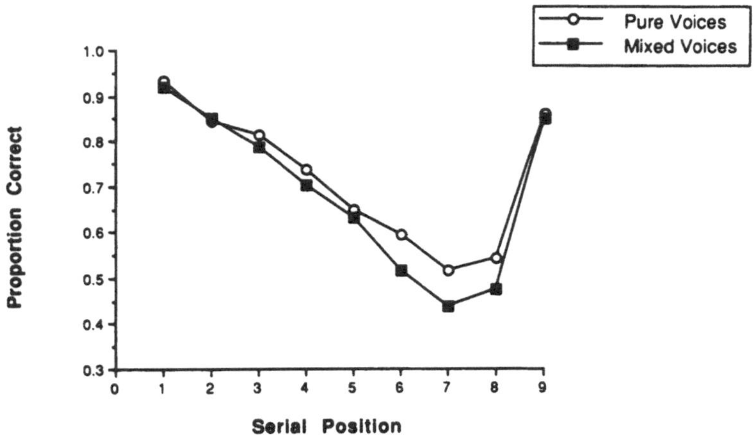

FIG. 3.5 Mean proportion correct as a function of pure and mixed voice trials.

Pisoni, and Summers (1989) and Greene (1991). We can attribute this *negative* effect of discriminability as an added requirement for something like speaker normalisation, as each digit in the list is presented. In any case, no support was found for the prediction that discriminability would have a positive effect on recency.

We were concerned that recency was so high in both conditions that little "room" remained for a difference between the pure and mixed conditions. Therefore we replicated the experiment using exactly the same stimulus items (in the experimental condition) but with instructions to remember the voices and to disregard the sequence of digits. In the pure condition, a single digit was spoken in a haphazard sequence of voices. In the mixed condition, both the digit identities and the talkers varied within a list. Although, as expected, performance was considerably worse (we had to reduce list length to eight items here), the size of the recency effect was not different between the pure and mixed conditions.

The experiments just described leave us with something of a puzzle: Discriminability, as defined by speech features, contributes significantly to the size of the recency effect (Cole, 1973; Crowder, 1971b; Darwin & Baddeley, 1974; see also Surprenant & Speer, 1990). However, when discriminability is defined the way we have here (spacing of four note vocabularies in Experiment 3, variability of speakers within lists in Experiment 4), recency stays uniform (absent in Experiment 3 and present in Experiment 4). We suggest a distinction between *phonetic discriminability* and *auditory discriminability* to cover this circumstance. Auditory discriminability does not appear to produce recency, on its own, unless it is correlated with differences in phonetic discriminability. This is as we would expect if the recency effect is all or largely produced within a specialised speech processor.

But making this assertion gives us concern again about why Experiments 1 and 2 did not show that engagement of the speech processor, either by instructions or by context, did not produce the large recency effect. Our explanation was that realistic speech sounds are a necessary condition for engaging the speech processor and that our sinewave tokens were not realistic enough. Experiment 5 was another attempt at finding ambiguous stimuli, capable of being heard either as speech or as naturalistic sounds.

EXPERIMENT 5

In this experiment we relied on the suffix effect rather than the recency effect, following the logic (and design) of Ayres et al. (1979). The stimulus sequences were nine-letter lists spoken aloud and the question was what suffix events would disrupt the recency effect known to result from such lists. The key comparison was between conditions with acoustically identical suffixes, designed to be interpreted by one group as a barnyard animal noise and by the other group as a nonsense syllable spoken by the same speaker who presented the lists.

Method

Stimuli. The memory stimuli were random sequences (without replacement) of nine letters from among the set C, G, H, J, K, L, X, R, S, T, U, and X, recorded by a male speaker and digitised. The letters were read aloud at a 2/second rate, with 15 seconds between trials.

Some suffix sound followed each list, including the following: For the control condition, a simple tone (1000Hz sinewave) was presented in the temporal position of a 10th item. The two animal suffixes were sounds transcribed from a sound-effects record of a dog barking and a cow mooing. The two human sounds were recordings of the same speaker as featured in the memory lists, saying "woof" or "moo" without trying in the least to imitate animal noises. The critical sound used as a suffix for all subjects was this same speaker pronouncing the syllable "baah" in such a way as to be ambiguous between the sound of a true animal and a human syllable.[3]

Design and Procedure. This ambiguous sound was used as a suffix on appropriately one-third of the trials within the main session of 45 trials. For the animal group the remaining two-thirds of the trials were followed by either the recording of the cow or of the dog, producing their characteristic noises (which we described as "moo" or "woof", respectively, in English). For the human group the remaining trials were followed by an unmistakeable human voice pronouncing the words "woof" and "moo". Both groups first went through a common block of 11 trials with the tone as a suffix. The first of these was discarded as practice and the remainder were used as a control condition to verify the comparability of the groups.

All subjects were first introduced to the immediate memory task. Then the animal group was told that after the ninth letter, "an animal noise" would indicate that the list was over and that they should begin their recall. The human group was told that after the ninth letter, the "same voice" would produce a "conventional animal sound" to indicate that the list was over and they should begin their recall. Following the practice block (tone suffix for all) the respective groups were reminded by an instruction on the screen that thereafter a human (or animal) sound would announce the end of each letter series. Recall was accomplished by clicking a mouse connected to the CRT display. With this recall method, the order of report *must* match the serial order of the items presented.

---

[3] We appreciate the help of Ian Neath in producing these sounds, especially the excellent sheep/human token.

Results

Figure 3.6 gives the results of Experiment 5. Note, first, that the two groups were quite comparable on the control trials with a tone suffix and, as expected, a tone had the least effect on recency of all suffixes tested, for both groups. Next, we can see that the true animal noises (Animals in Fig. 3.6) had a smaller suffix effect on performance than the verbal derivatives of these noises ("woof" and "moo"—Humans in Fig. 3.6). Finding a difference between these two conditions was a precondition for our interest in the ambiguous "baah".

The main result of the experiment was that this ambiguous sound had different effects on performance depending on whether it was interpreted as a human utterance (Human sheep) or an animal sound (Animal sheep) even though it was acoustically identical in the two cases. This result falsifies the model of Crowder (1976) in that it shows a nonacoustic factor responsible for interference among memories for auditory events. On the positive side, it replicates the experiment of Ayres et al. (1979) using the ambiguous "trumpet" sound. It also answers the question raised in Experiments 1 and 2, where we tried to get the same result using sinewave speech. What those experiments now seem to have shown is that realistic speech is a necessary condition for obtaining convincing auditory-memory effects. What Experiment 5 adds, now, is that the engagement of a speech processor is also a necessary condition, provided the stimuli allow for either speech or nonspeech interpretations. This conclusion is consistent with the assertion that recency (and suffix effects) result from activity in a speech processor.

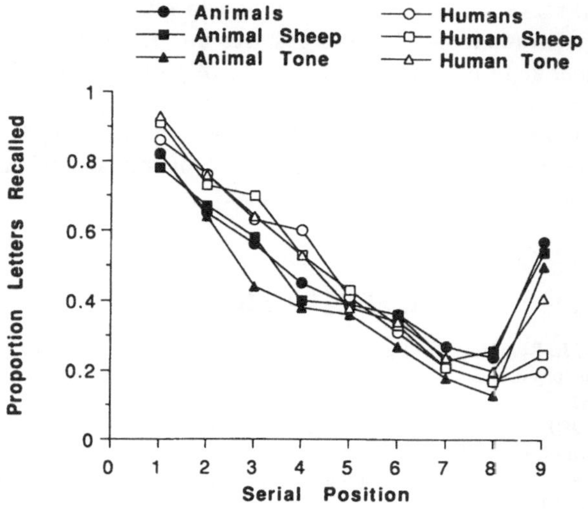

FIG. 3.6 Mean proportion correct as a function of suffix type.

CONCLUDING COMMENT

The results of the five experiments reviewed here are bewildering from the stance that the recency-suffix results derive from the way the auditory information is processed, in general, independently of its source. These results make sense, however, on the assumption that the recency and suffix phenomena are consequences of activity within a phonetic (speech) processor, or module. The target category states of such processing would presumably be phonetic gestures (Liberman & Mattingly, 1985) and not momentary energy configurations. Because the most distinctive speech gestures unfold during a non-negligible time span, it follows that this should be a long-lasting procedural residue (store, in the older sense).

If auditory memory is associated with the recovery of phonetic gestures, the data on lip-reading and mouthing fall into place as well. Remember, the puzzle was why these *silent* modes of processing produce memory results typical of auditory, and not visual, presentation. The essential point is that the reflection of light and sound from body (articulatory) surfaces are two logically comparable ways of recovering those same gestures. This is the central meaning of the motor theory of speech perception (Liberman & Mattingly, 1985). For a gesture like lip protrusion or rounding, seeing reflected light is approximately as good as hearing reflected sound. With more concealed articulatory gestures (glottal, palatal, and so forth) reflected sound is a much better way of perceiving the changing surfaces than light, so that the auditory mode is the more indispensable mode in speech perception. But *both* ways of perceiving phonetic gestures are quite unlike reception of information that depends on an orthographic code. To some extent these same gestures become *available* to a fluent reader, who, after all, can read new words aloud, but the gestures are not themselves directly perceived by either sight or sound. Another way of putting this is that the so-called speech module is not immediately engaged by reading, but it is by either lip-reading or by vocal speech sounds. Therefore, the memory results sort themselves out according to presence or absence of this specialised speech processing, not the acoustic nature of the sounds.

REFERENCES

Ayres, T.J., Jonides, J., Reitman, J.S., Egan, J.C., & Howard, D.A. (1979). Differing suffix effects for the same physical suffix. *Journal of Experimental Psychology: Human Learning and Memory*, *5*, 315–321.

Bregman, A.S. (1990). *Auditory scene analysis: The perceptual organisation of sound.* Cambridge, MA: Bradford Books (MIT Press).

Campbell, R., & Dodd, B. (1980). Hearing by eye. *Quarterly Journal of Experimental Psychology*, *32*, 85–99.

Cole, R.A. (1973). Different memory functions for consonants and vowels. *Cognitive Psychology*, *4*, 39–54.

Conrad, R. (1964). Acoustic confusions in immediate memory. *British Journal of Psychology, 55*, 75–84.

Crowder, R.G. (1971a). The sound of vowels and consonants in immediate memory. *Journal of Verbal Learning and Verbal Behavior, 10*, 587–597.

Crowder, R.G. (1971b). Waiting for the stimulus suffix: Decay, delay, rhythm, and readout in immediate memory. *Quarterly Journal of Experimental Psychology, 23*, 324–340.

Crowder, R.G. (1972). Visual and auditory memory. In J.F. Kavanagh & I.G. Mattingly (Eds.), *Language by ear and by eye; The relation between speech and learning to read*. Cambridge, MA: MIT Press.

Crowder, R.G. (1976). *Principles of learning and memory*. Hillsdale, NJ: Lawrence Erlbaum Associates Inc.

Crowder, R.G. (1978). Mechanisms of auditory backward masking in the stimulus suffix effect. *Psychological Review, 85*, 502–524.

Crowder, R.G., & Morton, J. (1969). Precategorical acoustic storage (PAS). *Perception and Psychophysics*, 5, 365–373.

Darwin, C.J., & Baddeley, A.D. (1974). Acoustic memory and the perception of speech. *Cognitive Psychology, 6*, 41–60.

Foreit, K.G. (1976). Short-lived auditory memory for pitch. *Perception and Psychophysics, 19*, 368–378.

Glanzer, M., & Clark, W.H. (1963). The verbal loop hypothesis: Binary numbers. *Journal of Verbal Learning and Verbal Behavior, 2*, 301–309.

Greene, R.L. (1989). Immediate serial recall of mixed-modality lists. *Journal of Experimental Psychology: Learning, Memory and Cognition, 15*, 266–274.

Greene, R.L. (1991). Serial recall of two-voice lists: Implications for theories of auditory recency and suffix effects. *Memory and Cognition, 19*, 72–78.

Greene, R.L., & Crowder, R.G. (1984). Modality and suffix effects in the absence of auditory stimulation. *Journal of Verbal Learning and Verbal Behavior, 23*, 371–382.

Greene, R.L., & Samuel, A.G. (1986). Recency and suffix effects in serial recall of musical stimuli. *Journal of Experimental Psychology: Learning, Memory and Cognition, 12*, 517–524.

Liberman, A.M., & Mattingly, I.G. (1985). The motor theory of speech perception revised. *Cognition, 21*, 1–36.

Liberman, A.M., Mattingly, I.G., & Turvey, M.T. (1972). Language codes and memory codes. In A.M. Melton & E. Martin (Eds.), *Coding processes in human memory*. Washington, DC: Wiley.

Martin, C.S., Mullennix, J.W., Pisoni, D.B., & Summers, W.V. (1989). Effects of talker variability on recall of spoken word lists. *Journal of Experimental Psychology: Learning, Memory and Cognition, 15*, 676–684.

Morton, J., Crowder, R.G., & Prussin, H.A. (1971). Experiments with the stimulus suffix effect. *Journal of Experimental Psychology: Monographs, 91*, 169–190.

Morton, J., Marcus, S.M., & Ottley, P. (1981). The acoustic correlates of "speechlike": A use of the suffix effect. *Journal of Experimental Psychology: General, 110*, 568–593.

Nairne, J.S. (1988). A framework for interpreting recency effects in immediate serial recall. *Memory and Cognition, 16*, 343–352.

Nairne, J.S. (1990). A feature model of immediate memory. *Memory and Cognition, 18*, 251–269.

Remez, R.F., Rubin, P.E., Pisoni, D.B., & Carrell, T.D. (1981). Speech perception without traditional speech cues. *Science, 212*, 947–950.

Rowe, E.J., & Rowe, W.G. (1976). Stimulus suffix effects with speech and nonspeech sounds. *Memory and Cognition, 4*, 128–131.

Schank, R.C., & Abelson, R.P. (1977). *Scripts, plans, goals, and understanding*. Hillsdale, NJ: Lawrence Erlbaum Associates Inc.

Sperling, G. (1960). The information available in brief visual presentations. *Psychological Monographs, 74*, (whole No. 498).

Spoehr, K.T., & Corin, W.J. (1978). The stimulus suffix effect as a memory coding phenomenon. *Memory and Cognition, 6*, 583–589.

Surprenant, A.M., & Speer, S.R. (1990). *The influence of segmental sonority in immediate memory for syllables.* Poster presented at the 31st Annual Meeting of the Psychonomic Society, New Orleans, LA.

Vygotsky, L.S. (1978). In M. Cole, V. John-Steiner, S. Scribner, & E. Souberman (Eds.), *Mind in Society.* Cambridge, MA: Harvard University Press.

4 Gestures, Features and Segments in Early Child Speech

Michael Studdert-Kennedy and Elizabeth Whitney Goodell
Haskins Laboratories, New Haven, CT, USA

INTRODUCTION

Preliminary

That an alphabetic orthography represents speech at the level of the phoneme seems to be generally agreed. But the definition of the phoneme and even its functional status are still matters of contention among linguists. We do not propose to join the linguistic argument here. We take the facts of reading and writing to be sufficient evidence for the functional reality of the phoneme as a perceptuomotor control structure representing a class of phonetic segments (cf. Studdert-Kennedy, 1987). We assume, further, that phonetic segments (consonants and vowels) are not the irreducible elements of which speech is composed. Rather, segments are complex structures, implicit in the gestural patterns of speech, that gradually emerge and take on their perceptuomotor functions over the first few years of life. This chapter attempts to justify this claim by applying a developing theory of articulatory phonology (Browman & Goldstein, 1986; 1989) to a small set of data drawn from the utterances of a 2-year-old child.

Background

A child, learning to talk, often says the same word in several different ways. Indeed, variability of phonetic form has been a commonplace of child language studies since their inception (e.g. Albright & Albright, 1956; 1958; Cohen, 1952; Leopold, 1953). On the other hand, a child, learning to talk, often says several different words in the same way, and this homonymy is also a commonplace of child language studies (see Vihman, 1981, for review). While variability and homonymy may reflect many factors, including the communicative situation, whether the utterance is spontaneous or imitated, its meaning, phonetic structure, phonetic context and so on (Schwartz, 1988), none of these factors would matter, if it were not that ". . . a child's phonemic system is in the process of development, and the sound patterning is probably less regular than that of adult speech" (Albright & Albright, 1956, p. 382). But what, in fact, is developing, and what is the nature of the irregularity? What varies in the execution of a target word from one occasion to another? What does the child find that different words have in common?

Let us begin with the observation, now supported by a variety of evidence, that the unit of phonological contrast, and therefore the unit of articulatory organisation, in early child speech is the whole word or phrase rather than the segment (Ferguson, 1963; 1986; Ferguson & Farwell, 1975; Macken, 1979; Menn, 1983; Menyuk, Menn, & Silber, 1986; Nittrouer, Studdert-Kennedy, & McGowan, 1989; Waterson, 1971). To say that a child utters a word as a "whole", or Gestalt, cannot mean, however, that the child has not broken the word into at least some of its parts, because even a partly correct utterance requires co-ordination of independent, or partially independent, actions of lips, tongue, jaw, velum, and larynx. Accordingly, while the word may be the domain over which a child organises its articulations, it cannot be the basic unit of production (or, *a fortiori*, of perception). Nor, as the segment is no less compounded of independent articulatory actions than the word, can the basic unit be the segment itself.

The standard unit adopted in studies of child phonology is, of course, the feature. By this we cannot mean the abstract feature of generative phonology, a relational property fulfilling the linguistic function of contrast across a phonological system, because we are dealing with a child for whom such a system does not yet exist. We must therefore mean the concrete feature, an absolute property located ". . . within the speech sounds, be it on their motor, acoustical, or auditory level" (Jakobson & Halle, 1956, p. 8). However, at least two facts make this proposal unacceptable. First, the feature has no independent existence: It is a property of a larger unit and is carried into existence on that unit, as an adjective, not a noun (cf. Fowler, Rubin, Remez, & Turvey, 1980). This fact is implicit in the adjectival terminology of all feature theories: grave, acute, compact, coronal, nasal, strident, and so on.

A second, closely related objection is that the properties to which featural terminology customarily refers are purely static, devoid of temporal extension, and therefore intrinsically unfit to define the dynamic properties of speech either as a motor act or as an acoustic signal. Not surprisingly, none of several sets of acoustic and articulatory definitions of phonological features (e.g. Chomsky & Halle, 1968; Jakobson, Fant, & Halle, 1952/1963; Stevens, 1972; 1975; 1989) has proved precise or full enough to support a procedure for speech synthesis or speech recognition by machine, let alone a theory of speech production or speech perception.[1] The "autonomous features" of autosegmental and other forms of nonlinear phonology (e.g. Clements, 1985; Goldsmith, 1990; McCarthy, 1988; cf. Menn, 1978) might seem to promise a solution. However, these features are abstract units, the temporal analogs of points in Euclidean space, admitting of sequence, but not of extension. In short, as Ladefoged (1980, p. 485) has remarked, ". . . phonological features are certainly not sufficient for specifying the actual sounds of a language". They can hardly therefore help a child striving to learn how to perceive and produce those sounds.

Very much the same holds for the informal, and perhaps intuitively more appealing, phonetic features adopted by, for example, Waterson (1971, p. 183; cf. Ferguson & Farwell, 1975; Macken, 1979). She analyses a child's word forms into: "Various features of articulation, such as nasality, sibilance, glottality, stop (complete closure), continuance, frontness, backness, voicing, voicelessness, labiality, rounding, non-rounding." Waterson goes on to group the child's forms into "structures" or "schemata", corresponding to the adult "prosodic" patterns in which features are distributed over a word. She shows how in a child's utterance the "prosody" may be disrupted, so that features lose their temporal order and recombine into patterns quite unlike the adult model. In this respect, Waterson's work has stimulated the approach taken in this chapter. None the less, her schemata are purely descriptive, indications of, but certainly not specifications for, the spatio-temporal pattern of movements by which a speaker, child or adult, executes a word. They offer, at most, a sketch of the high points of a word, rendered in the familiar language of traditional articulatory phonetics. We conclude that, despite the utility of the feature as a descriptive and classificatory element in phonetic theory, it cannot guide a child into speech.

In fact, what a child quite evidently needs, to imitate an adult word, is a grasp on which articulators to move where and how, and on when to move them. And what we, for our part, need, to understand the child's attempts, is a description of the target word in terms of the units of articulatory action, and their relative timing, necessary to utter it. No generally agreed upon set of articulatory units exists, although several have been proposed. Ladefoged (1980), for example, offered a tentative list of 17 "articulatory parameters" that he judged necessary and sufficient to specify the sounds of a wide range of languages, but he did not develop them into a functional model. Here we adopt the framework of the most explicit model of speech production currently available, the gestural phonology being developed by Browman, Goldstein, Saltzman and their colleagues at Haskins Laboratories (Browman & Goldstein, 1986, 1987, 1989, 1990; Saltzman,

[1]Fant (1962, p. 4) remarked many years ago concerning the theory of Jakobson, Fant and Halle (1952/1963): ". . . its formulations are made for the benefit of linguistic theory rather than for engineering or phonetic applications. Statements of the acoustic correlates to distinctive features have been condensed to an extent where they retain merely a generalised abstraction insufficient as a basis for practical applications." The same is true of subsequent attempts to formulate acoustic and articulatory correlates of the features.

1986; Saltzman & Munhall, 1989), in which the basic phonetic and phonological unit is the gesture. We illustrate the approach with a small set of data, drawn from the utterances of a 21–25-month-old girl, learning American English. But before we come to the data we must give a brief sketch of the gestural framework.

Gestures as Basic Units of Articulatory Action

If we watch, or listen to, someone speaking, we see, or hear, the speaker's mouth repeatedly closing and opening, forming and releasing constrictions. In the framework of gestural phonology, each such event, each formation and release of a constriction, is an instance of a gesture. Constrictions can be formed within the oral, velic or laryngeal articulatory subsystems; within the oral subsystem, they can be formed by the lips, the tongue tip (blade) or the tongue body. The function of each gesture, or act of constriction, is to set a value on one or more vocal tract variables that contribute to the shaping of a vocal tract configuration, by which (in conjunction with pulmonic action) the flow of air through the tract is controlled, so as to produce a characteristic pattern of sound. Presumably, this pattern of sound specifies for a child (or an adult) the gestures that went into its making.

Figure 4.1 displays the tract variables and the effective articulators of a computational model for the production of speech, at its current stage of development (Browman & Goldstein, 1990). The inputs to the model are the parameters of sets of equations of motion for gestures. A gesture is an abstract description of an articulator movement,[2] or of a co-ordinated set of articulator movements, that unfolds over time to form and release a certain degree of constriction at a certain location in the tract. Settings of the parameters permit constriction degree to vary across five discrete values (closed, critical, narrow, mid, wide), and constriction location for oral gestures to vary across nine values (protruded [lips], labial, dental, alveolar, post-alveolar, palatal, velar, uvular, pharyngeal).[3] The reader may observe that the degree and location of an oral constriction roughly correspond to the manner and place of articulation of a segment in standard terminology.

The gestures for a given utterance are organised into a larger co-ordinated structure, represented by a gestural score. The score specifies the values of the dynamic parameters for each gesture and the period over which the gesture is active. Figure 4.2 schematises the score for the word *nut* ([nʌt]), as a sequence

---

[2]In what follows we use the term "gesture" to refer either to an underlying abstract control structure, or to a concrete instance of a gesture activated by this structure, relying on context to make clear which is intended.

[3]These categorical values, axiomatic within gestural phonology, may have emerged evolutionarily, and may still emerge ontogenetically, through auditory and articulatory constraints on individual gestures (Stevens, 1989), and on the entire set of gestures within the child's developing lexicon (Lindblom, 1986; Lindblom et al., 1983).

	tract variable	articulators involved
LP	lip protrusion	upper & lower lips, jaw
LA	lip aperture	upper & lower lips, jaw
TTCL	tongue tip constrict location	tongue tip, tongue body, jaw
TTCD	tongue tip constrict degree	tongue tip, tongue body, jaw
TBCL	tongue body constrict location	tongue body, jaw
TBCD	tongue body constrict degree	tongue body, jaw
VEL	velic aperture	velum

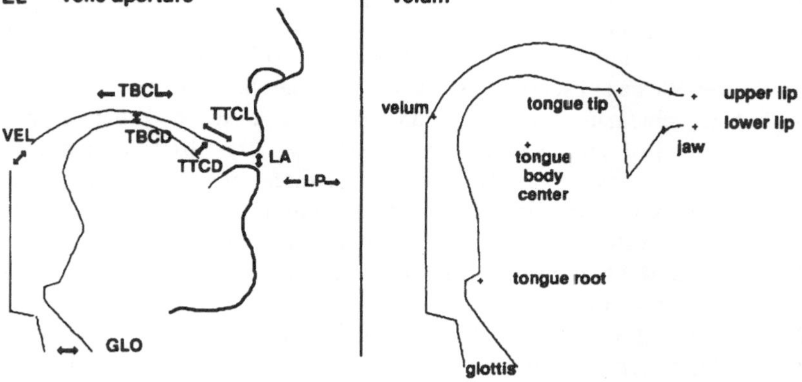

FIG.4.1 Tract variables and associated articulators used in the computational model of phonology and speech production discussed in the text (adapted from Browman & Goldstein, 1990).

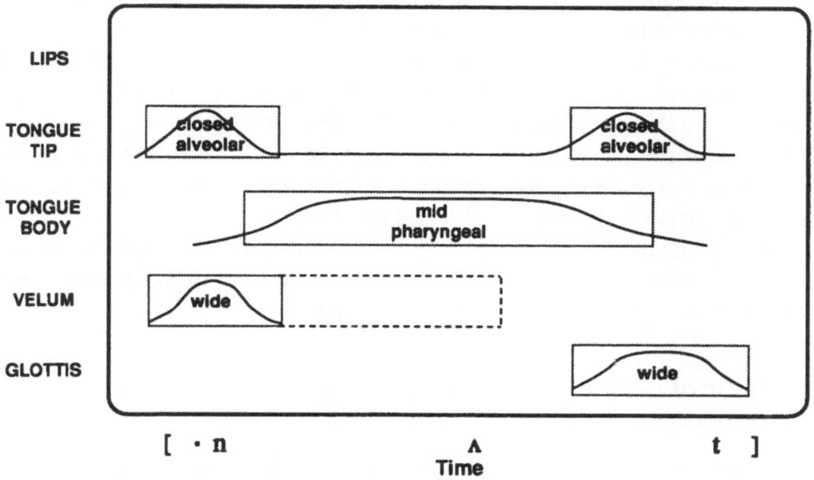

FIG.4.2 Schematic gestural score for the word *nut* [ˈnʌt). The boxes indicate the activation intervals called for by the score, the solid lines the tract variable changes over time. The extension of the velic activation interval by dashed lines indicates possible free variation in the duration of the velic gesture.

of partially overlapping gestural activation intervals with the generated tract variable motions superimposed; possible free variation in the duration of the velic gesture, and the resulting nasalisation of the vowel, is indicated by extending the velic activation interval with a dashed line.

We cannot here go into detail on the workings of the model (for which the reader is referred to the papers cited earlier). We note only the following further points that, taken with the preceding sketch, may suffice for an intuitive grasp of how a gestural framework can contribute to an understanding of the nature and origin of irregularities in a child's early words.

1. An instance of a gesture is an objective, observable event. We can observe a gesture by ear, and this is the usual basis of both imitation and phonetic transcription. We can observe a gesture by eye, either unaided, as in lip-reading, or with X-ray cinematography. We can observe a gesture by touch, as in the Tadoma method of speech perception. Finally, we can observe a gesture by sensing our own movements. However, if gestures drawing on the same, or closely neighbouring, neuromuscular sets overlap in time (as, for example, in certain lingual gestures for the consonantal onset and vocalic nucleus of a syllable), the individual gestures may merge, so that we can observe only the resultant of their vectors.

2. The articulator sets and their dimensions given earlier are not exhaustive. For example, the tongue root must ultimately be included in the model to handle variations in pharynx width. Also, constriction shape will have to be included, to handle the tongue bunching, narrowing or hollowing, necessary in the formation of certain complex gestures (cf. Ladefoged, 1980). Even the definition of the gesture itself may have to be revised to permit independent control of the formation and release of a constriction.

3. A gesture is larger than the properties of constriction location, degree, and shape that describe it, but smaller than the segment. Several independent gestures are required to form a segment, syllable, or syllable string.

4. Each gesture has an intrinsic duration that varies with rate and stress. Correct execution of an utterance requires accurate timing of the gesture itself, and accurate phasing of gestures with respect to one another.

5. By adopting the gesture as a primitive of articulatory action we can predict what types of errors children are likely, or not likely, to make in their early attempts at adult words. This topic we now discuss.

The Gestural Origins of Errors in a Child's Early Words

Phonetically, speech emerges over the first year of life from the lip smacks, tongue clicks, and pops associated with the vegetative processes of eating and breathing, combined with the stereotyped vocalisations of cries and comfort sounds (Stark, 1986), through the reduplicated syllables of canonical babble, into the brief strings of phonetically contrastive elements that make up early words. Articulatorily, the progression is a cyclical process of differentiation and integration by which the child moves toward finer modulation of individual gestures and more precise phasing of their sequence. (For a fuller account of the hypothesised developmental course, see Studdert-Kennedy, 1991 a, b.)

Here, two steps are of interest. The first is the shift in gestural timing associated with the integration of pre-babbling oral and laryngeal gestures into the canonical syllable, usually around the seventh month (Holmgren et al., 1986; Koopmans van Beinum & van der Stelt, 1986). Earlier vocalisations, termed "marginal babble" by Oller (1980), are commonly longer than adult syllables, but display adult-like properties of resonance, intensity, and fundamental frequency contour. Canonical babble is marked by integration of a resonant nucleus with rapid (25–120msec) closing gestures at its margins to form a syllable with adult-like duration (100–500msec) (Oller, 1986). The canonical syllable is the first step in the emergence of two major classes of oral gesture: the narrow or complete constriction of consonants and the wider constriction of vowels (cf. MacNeilage & Davis, 1990).

The early canonical syllable is often, although not always, one of a rhythmic, reduplicated string of identical syllables. Reduplication indicates first that the child may lack independent control of the closing constriction at the margin and the wider constriction at the nucleus of a syllable; second, that the child cannot easily switch gestures in successive syllables. The tendency to reduplicate may continue for many months, or even years, as evidenced by the commonly reported harmony in early words between consonants (Vihman, 1978) and vowels, and even within consonant–vowel sequences. The last is revealed, for example, by certain children's preference for high front vowels after alveolar closures, and for low back vowels after the relatively extensive jaw-lowering release of labial closures (Davis & MacNeilage, 1990; cf. Jakobson, 1941/1968, pp. 29, 50).

Integration of pre-babbling gestures into the canonical syllable is a necessary condition of a second step: differentiation of the syllable into independent gestural components. Differentiation gives rise to what Oller (1980) terms "variegated babble" in which the consonant-like syllable onset and the vowel-like nucleus, or both, differ in successive syllables. The process may begin soon after, or even at the same time as, the onset of canonical babble, but typically comes to predominate in the fourth quarter of the first year, and continues over many months in both babble and early words (Davis & MacNeilage, 1990; Vihman et al., 1985).

Before we consider the types of error that a child may make we should note that, although we shall appeal to similarity among gestures as the basis of a child's confusions, we will not spell out the dimensions of similarity. In fact, we shall deliberately avoid the question of whether those confusions reflect an incomplete percept (under which we may include incomplete storage of the percept in memory) or inadequate articulatory control (under which we may include failure to recover stored motor commands from memory). Perhaps, indeed, there is no general answer to this question: Similar errors may reflect different processes in different words and in different children. Here we adopt a neutral stance. We suppose that learning the phonology of a language is a matter both of learning to perceive the acoustic pattern that specifies a talker's gestures, and of learning to plan and produce that pattern oneself. Both these processes can be a source of error.

Differentiation itself has two aspects, each open to characteristic forms of error. The first is paradigmatic differentiation among individual gestures. Possible errors here follow from failure to identify or execute the location, shape, or degree of a gesture; in the limit, an error of degree (or amplitude) may yield complete omission. The second aspect is syntagmatic differentiation among gestures in a particular utterance. Possible errors here include gestural reduplication (harmony), errors of timing (duration and relative phasing, including metathesis), and errors of amplitude or degree. The consonant–vowel (or vowel–consonant) harmony noted earlier may be viewed as a syntagmatic error arising from incomplete differentiation of the syllable into its component consonantal and vocalic gestures. Our purpose in what follows is to illustrate how the erroneous forms of a child's early words can be perspicuously described as arising from gestural errors such as these.

METHOD

The subject "Emma" is a second child, born in Connecticut, USA, to parents who had moved there from Vancouver, British Columbia. Emma's mother was the full-time caregiver for the child. The second author of this chapter (E.W.G.) lived with the family before and during the study and spent several hours a day observing Emma at meals, watching her play with her older brother and interact with her parents, and occasionally looking at picture books with her. One of these books (*Richard Scarry's Best Word Book Ever*) was a rich source of new words (Scarry, 1980).

Audio recordings began when Emma had a vocabulary of about 100 words, mostly monosyllables understood primarily by her mother and brother. The size of her vocabulary was assessed with the MacArthur Communicative Development Inventory for Toddlers, and by maternal report. In the 91st week her mean length of utterance (MLU) was 1.00 and at the end of the study (week 106), 1.15. For the weekly audio taping sessions, lasting from 30 minutes to an hour, she wore a wireless 831 Audio Technical lapel microphone concealed in a vest. E.W.G. was present at all sessions and kept a diary of the subject's phonological development to supplement the recordings.

To facilitate the transcription and analysis of Emma's utterances, recordings of the sessions were digitised on a VAX 780 computer, at a 20kHz sampling rate, to yield a total of some 950 utterances of which the experimenter and a colleague independently transcribed roughly 250. Transcription followed the principles of the International Phonetic Association (1989), with some elaborations according to the Stanford system for transcribing consonants in child language (Bush et al., 1973). Each utterance was coded as either spontaneous or imitated; an utterance was assumed to be spontaneous, unless it immediately followed the adult target; all the examples reported in this chapter were spontaneous, unless otherwise indicated. We report only utterances on which the two transcribers independently agreed. The transcriptions will be given in square brackets, following the convention for adult phonetic segments. We emphasise that our use of phonetic symbols does not imply that segments were already established in the child as discrete units of perception and production. A phonetic symbol is simply a convenient shorthand for combinations of laryngeal, oral or velic gestures.

RESULTS AND DISCUSSION

Many researchers have described how a child, making the transition from reduplicated babble to variegated speech, discovers a pattern that roughly fits a fair number of adult words, and so can serve as a bridge into the lexicon. These patterns, variously termed prosodic schemata (Waterson, 1971), canonical forms (Ingram, 1974), articulatory routines, programs, templates (Menn, 1978; 1983), word patterns (Macken, 1979), or vocal motor schemes (McCune & Vihman, 1987) will be treated here as routinised gestural scores. (Much of our analysis will indeed follow the lead of Waterson, 1971, Macken, 1979, and, particularly, Menn, 1978; 1983, whose attention to the articulatory organisation of a child's utterances anticipates our own). Gestural routines support both stereotypy (including homonymy) and variability in a child's early attempts at words; they are of interest because the gestural properties common to a particular score and to the different target words for which it is used reveal the scope of a child's gestural conflations.

Stereotypy

Gestural Routines in Babble and Word Play. During the sessions themselves Emma did not babble much, but diary entries from the first month of the study (weeks 91–94) often record Emma's babbles while quietly playing. For example:

(1) [ɑ'biːn'ɑ'biːn'ɑ'biːn]

(2) ['beː'də'beː'də'beː'də'beː'də]

These utterances happen to consist of repetitions of one of Emma's forms for *elephant* ('ɑ'bin]) and *playdough* ('beː'də]), but she chanted the sequences in a sing-song, with no apparent communicative intent. Both utterances contain the alternating sequence of constrictions at the lips and at the alveolar arch that proved to be Emma's most productive gestural routine. (For an example of another child, learning Mexican Spanish, with a similar routine, see Macken, 1979).

Strings of similar alternations occasionally occurred in taping sessions over the same period:

(3) ['mʌtʃː'mʌtʃː'mʌtʃː]
(4) ['ɑ'buː'diː'ɑ'buː'diː'ɑ'buː'kuːkiː]
(5) ['weː'da'wiː'da'meː'na'miː'nə'muː'niː'miː'niː'miː'niː]

Emma repeatedly produced (3) in weeks 92 and 93, elongating the final frication, as though savoring the flow of air, and with no apparent referent. (4) contains two of Emma's words (see Table 4.1 for ['a'buː'diː]), while (5) is a mixture of apparent nonsense syllables and word forms (see Table 4.2), but none of the objects to which the words refer was present. In (4) she abruptly broke off her labial-alveolar chant when a cookie came into view. In (5) she seemed to be playing with the location and degree of labial constriction ([w]–[m]), the degree of accompanying velic constriction ([w]–[m], [d]–[n]), and (in an apparent instance of vowel–consonant harmony), the front–back location of narrow constrictions at the syllable nucleus before an alveolar constriction ([iː]–[eː]–[uː]).

These examples illustrate the emergence of gestural stereotypy in babble and word play. They also illustrate the familiar, but important fact that a listener often cannot distinguish, by phonetic form alone, between syllables that are babbles and syllables that should count as a word.[4] Despite the discontinuity of function that Jakobson (1941/1968) noted many years ago, babble and speech are formally continuous.[5] An adequate account of the shift in function must therefore posit units of action that can be comfortably engaged by both babble and speech. Phonemes, phonetic segments, and features are unsuited to this task: They cannot properly be adopted for prelinguistic babble because they are defined in terms of language and speech. Moreover, as already noted, segments are complex units, customarily

---

[4]The problem and criteria for its solution are thoroughly discussed by Vihman and McCune (in press).

[5]Much of the controversy over the issue of continuity between babble and speech has arisen, in our view, from a misreading of Jakobson's claims, and from a failure to distinguish between phonetic form and phonetic function. Jakobson himself drew this distinction quite clearly. Although he believed that ". . . a short period may sometimes intervene . . . in which children are completely mute", he also recognised that: "For the most part . . . one stage merges unobtrusively into the other, so that the acquisition of vocabulary and the disappearance of the pre-language inventory occur concurrently" (Jakobson, 1941/1968, p. 29). In fact, he assumed what later studies have conclusively demonstrated (e.g. MacNeilage, Hutchinson, & Lasater, 1981; Oller, Wieman, Doyle, & Ross, 1976; Vihman et al., 1985) that listeners often cannot distinguish, by phonetic form alone, a "child's embryo-words from the pre-language residue" (Jakobson, 1941/1968, p. 29). The discontinuity that Jakobson (correctly) posited was a discontinuity of function, not of form.

TABLE 4.1
Active Use of the Labial-alveolar Routine as a Bridge into the Lexicon

New Words	*Adult Target*	*Emma's Attempts*
Cranberry	['krænbɛri])	['beː'bi] ['boː'beː'bi] ['ɑ'buː'diː]
Red Lights	['rɛd'lɑɪts]	['weː'jɑɪ] ['bɛ'tθɑɪts]
Hippopotamus	['hɪpə'pɑtəmʌs]	['ɑ'pɪnz] ['hɪpɑs]

analysed into their featural predicates, whereas features have no existence independently of the syllables and segments they describe. By contrast, the posited gesture is an integral unit of action that can serve equally as a primitive unit of both babble and speech.

Gestural Routines as Bridges into the Lexicon. A child who has discovered a gestural routine, such as the labial-alveolar sequence described above, will often extend it to a surprisingly diverse collection of new words in which it recognises the appropriate pattern (Macken, 1979)—in Emma's case words as diverse as *cranberry*, *red lights*, and *hippopotamus* (see Table 4.1). Thus in the recording session of week 92, Emma's mother showed her a cranberry for the first time, repeated the word and asked her to say it. First Emma attempted the word with gestural harmony, repeating the labial closure of the second syllable, ['beː'biː], then she perfected the number of syllables, ['boː'beː'biː], finally she reverted to a three-syllable labial-alveolar routine, ['a'buː'diː], transposing the post-alveolar retroflex constriction of [r] into the alveolar closure of [d]. She used this form for *cranberry* for approximately the next two months. (We may note, incidentally, that Emma here adopted a tactic that recurred in her attempts at several other words, usually words of three or more syllables. She lowered her jaw and substituted the wide vocalic gesture of [ɑ] as a sort of place-holder for the initial syllable or syllables.)

In week 95, hearing her mother point out the red lights on the tape recorder, Emma spontaneously attempted *red lights* as ['weː'jɑɪ], and seconds later, without correction, as ['bet'θɑɪts]. Here, for [r], she first picked up the narrow constriction at the protruded lips, but omitted the accompanying post-alveolar retroflexion, giving [w], then fell back on full labial closure, giving [b]. The alveolar closure for [d] she omitted on the first attempt, while successfully executing the nearby palatal glide of [j] in place of [l]—a common shift in the exact location and shape of the gesture for [l] in early speech (e.g. Vihman & Velleman, 1989). On the second attempt she achieved full alveolar closure, but anticipated the glottal opening and critical fricative constriction of final [ts], giving the sequence [tθ] instead of [dl].

A final, more complicated example occurred in week 101. Seeing a familiar picture of a hippopotamus, Emma spontaneously pronounced ['ɑpɪnz]. Here she substituted her favoured wide vocalic constriction for the first one or two syllables. The remaining three or four syllables she collapsed into one, built around her labial-alveolar routine. For this she correctly executed the labial closure and glottal opening of [p], as well as the alveolar constrictions of medial [t] and final [s]. But she omitted the labial closure of [m] and the glottal openings of [t] and [s]; she roughly harmonised the syllable nucleus to the following alveolar closure; and she erroneously synchronised alveolar closure for [t] with velic opening for [m]. The outcome of these manoeuvres was [pɪnz], a syllable composed of four apparent segments, three of which do not occur in the target word—a result difficult to understand if we assume segmental primitives, but readily intelligible in gestural terms.

To Emma's spontaneous ['ɑpɪnz] E.W.G. replied: "Oh, hippopotamus", eliciting a form that Emma had used on previous occasions: ['hɪpɑs], repeated four times. Here, with the model freshly in mind, Emma recaptured the first syllable, but omitted the second, as well as the medial alveolar and velic gestures of the final three syllables, which she collapsed into the bare routine of initial labial and final alveolar gestures.

These three examples illustrate Emma's active use of a routinised gestural score as an armature, or skeleton, around which to construct her articulation of words presumably otherwise too difficult, whether perceptually or motorically, to attempt. We have characterised the routine in terms of rough gestural location, disregarding differences in precise location and in degree or shape. Thus, we

TABLE 4.2
Words Attempted by Means of the Labial-alveolar Routine in Weeks 91–94

Emma's Attempts	*Adult Targets*
['buː'di]*	berry, bird, booster
['beː'də]*	pillow, playdough
['beː'diː]	umbrella
['peː'də]	peanut
['pə'tə]	puppet
['meː'nə]	tomato
['meː'niː]	medicine
['muː'niː]	money
['weː'də]	playdough
['weː'diː]	raisin
['ɑ'miːn]*	elephant, airplane
['ɑ'biːn]	elephant
['ɑ'piːn]	airplane
['ɑ'buː'diː]*	Happy Birthday, cranberry, raspberry

*Homonyms

have treated [b/p/m] and [w] as equivalently labial in Emma's utterances, [d/t/n], [j], [r], and [s] as equivalently alveolar. These equivalences are justified by Emma's gestural alternations both in the examples given earlier and in her other uses of the labial-alveolar routine, to which we now turn.

A Gestural Routine as a Source of Homonyms. Table 4.2 lists the entire set of recorded words to which Emma applied the labial-alveolar routine. Some of these were in Emma's repertoire before the study began (according to maternal report) and, with the exception of ['ɑ'min], *elephant*, all were recorded during the first month of the study. We have grouped them according to the similarity of their phonetic patterns, making clear that in addition to the actual sets of homonyms, marked with asterisks, there are several sets of near-homonyms (Emma's forms for *pillow* and *umbrella*, *tomato* and *medicine*, *playdough* and *raisin*, where each member of a pair differs from the other only in its final vocalic gesture). These homonymous groups, clearly not semantically based, validate the proposed routine as a functional process in Emma's attack on the lexicon, by drawing attention to gestural similarities among target words that, at first glance, are quite dissimilar (cf. Vihman, 1981). Thus, we find alveolar [d] for [r] in *berry*, for [st] in *booster*, for [l] in *pillow* and *umbrella*, for [s] in *raisin*. At the same time, the labial grouping is justified by Emma's own use of [b] and [w] for [pl] in *playdough*, of [p] and [m] for [pl] in airplane, of [w] for initial [r] in raisin, of [m] and [b] for [f] in *elephant*.

Several of these substitutions can, of course, be interpreted in featural terms. However, substitution of the narrow labial constriction of [w] for [r] in initial position, but of full alveolar closure for [r] in medial position, would not be expected on a featural account, because a given segment carries the same featural predicates regardless of context, and so should be subject to the same perceptual or motoric confusions.[6] A gestural account, on the other hand, predicts such syntagmatic errors precisely because it views the task of learning to talk as quite largely one of learning to co-ordinate gestures that may differ in their articulatory compatibility (cf. Menn, 1983). We shall see further examples of contextual effects in our discussion of variability.

Finally, we must remark on another process, difficult for a featural account, and important to our later discussion: The tendency for gestures to "slide" along the time line (Browman & Goldstein, 1987) into misalignment with other gestures, often giving rise to apparent segments not present in the target word. We have already noted this process in Emma's ['ɑpɪnz] for hippopotamus. Here (Table 4.2) we find it in ['meː'nə], *tomato*, where velic lowering for [m] extends into the alveolar closure for [t], yielding [n]; and in ['ɑ'miːn], *elephant*, *airplane*, where velic lowering for [n] slides into alignment with labial closures for [f] or

[6]We thank Susan Brady for pointing this out to us.

[pl], yielding [m]. In these examples the effect is of gestural harmony, and so may be due not only to an error of gestural phasing, but also to "... the difficulty in planning and production of rapid changes of articulation in a short space of time" (Waterson, 1971, p.13, cited by Menn, 1983, p. 30). Of course, this too is a form of timing error.

Variability

Spontaneous Variations. Although a gestural routine may afford a child initial access to difficult words of similar gestural pattern, it cannot solve all the problems of gestural selection and phasing with which the child must contend in moving toward an acceptable pronunciation. Variability within the constraints of the routine is an important part of this process.

For example, Emma's attempts at *elephant* in a single session in week 91 included: ['ɑm'bin], ['ɑ'min], ['ɑ'fin], and ['ɑ'pin), all of which are formed by combining her initial vocalic place-holder and her labial-alveolar constriction routine with her favoured medial vowel–consonant harmony. Yet within these limits she seemed to be trying to hit upon the exact location of the gesture for labial [f], and the relative phasing of glottal opening for [f] and velic lowering for [n]. She experimented with the timing of velic action again in her forms for *raisin*: ['we:'ni], ['weːn'di], ['weː'di]. And in ['beː'də], ['weː'də], *playdough*, she seemed to be trying to simulate the labial alveolar sequence in the cluster [pl] by playing with the exact location and degree of labial constriction.

Further examples of variability within the constraints of a stereotyped routine come from Emma's attempts to execute the syllable ['nʌt] in the words *doughnut* and *peanut*. We might have expected these words to be relatively easy, the first because it calls for three harmonious alveolar gestures, the second because it fits Emma's labial-alveolar routine, already well established when she met the word. But in fact they proved to be quite difficult, both overall and in their identical final syllable in particular. This syllable elicited very different patterns in the two contexts—a type of result, as we have already remarked, readily intelligible on a gestural, but not on a featural account of her errors.

Doughnut was introduced in week 92. Emma's first attempts were ['duː'dʌtʃ] and ['doː'dʌts]. The final critical alveolar constrictions added apparent segments not present in the model. They were not attempts at the plural, because she was given only part of a doughnut to eat and only heard the word in the singular. Rather, they seem to have resulted from a relatively slow release of [t], making the fricative portion of the release (Fant, 1973, p. 112) more salient. Steriade (1989) offers a similar analysis for derived affricates, proposing that they "... differ from stops in the quality of their release". Over the next 10 weeks Emma's attempts at this word varied over forms as diverse as ['duː'də] and ['du:n'dʌnt]. The latter seems to result from prolongation of the alveolar closure for medial [n] after velic release, giving an unwanted [d], combined with prolongation of the alveolar closure for final [t] and a shift in (or harmonious repetition of) the medial velic gesture, giving the unwanted final cluster. Figure 4.3 (top) displays a schematic gestural score illustrating the timing errors required to make the shift from ['nʌt] (Figure 4.3 [middle]) to ['dʌnt], and Table 4.3 lists in chronological order some of the variations on *nut* in *doughnut* for comparison with those elicited by *peanut*.

Emma encountered a peanut in a picture book in week 94. Drawing appropriately on her labial-alveolar routine, she first tried ['peː'də], omitting velic action, and later that week, ['pe:n'tə], where prolongation of the medial alveolar closure, combined with a shift in the timing of the final glottal opening, relative to velic closure and the tongue body gesture, gives rise to an apparent shift in the ordering of the target consonant-vowel-consonant sequence—a result difficult to explain in either segmental or featural terms. In week 96 she offered ['pi:'pʌp], omitting the velic gesture and succumbing to labial harmony, and ['pe:m'pump]. The latter, formally analogous to ['du:n'dʌnt], *doughnut*, with its velic harmony, mistimed velic action, and resulting unwanted segments, is further complicated by the substitution of harmonised labial closures for the alveolar closures called for by the target, and proper to her routine. Figure 4.3 (bottom) illustrates the errors of gestural location and timing required to make the shift from ['nʌt] to ['pʌmp].

Other examples of Emma's errors, evidently due to a variety of gestural processes, including harmony and the slow release of alveolar closures, include: ['du:'dᵊtʃiz], ['doːnʌ'tʃfiz], *doughnut please*, and ['sɛlzɛ'tʃiz], ['sɛpᵊ'piz], *seltzer please*. As isolated forms for both *seltzer* and *please* occurred in Emma's repertoire, the last example nicely illustrates a child

TABLE 4.3
Spontaneous Variability Within and Between Words:

Nut as in *Doughnut* and *Peanut*

Doughnut ['dO:nʌt]	→	*Nut*	*Nut*	←	*Peanut ['pi:ŋʌτ*
['duː'də]		də	də		['peː'də]
['duːn'dʌnt]		dʌnt	tə		['peːn'tə]
['doː'diːdʌt]		dʌt	de:		['peː'deː)
['duː'dʌtʃ]		dʌtʃ	pʌmp		[peːm'pʌmp
['duː'dʌts		dʌts	pʌp		['piː'pʌp]
['doː'nʌt]		nʌt	nʌt		['piː'nʌt]

Note: The same target syllable executed differently in different phonetic contexts and on different occasions. The utterances are listed chronologically, but the columns for doughnut and peanut are not synchronised.

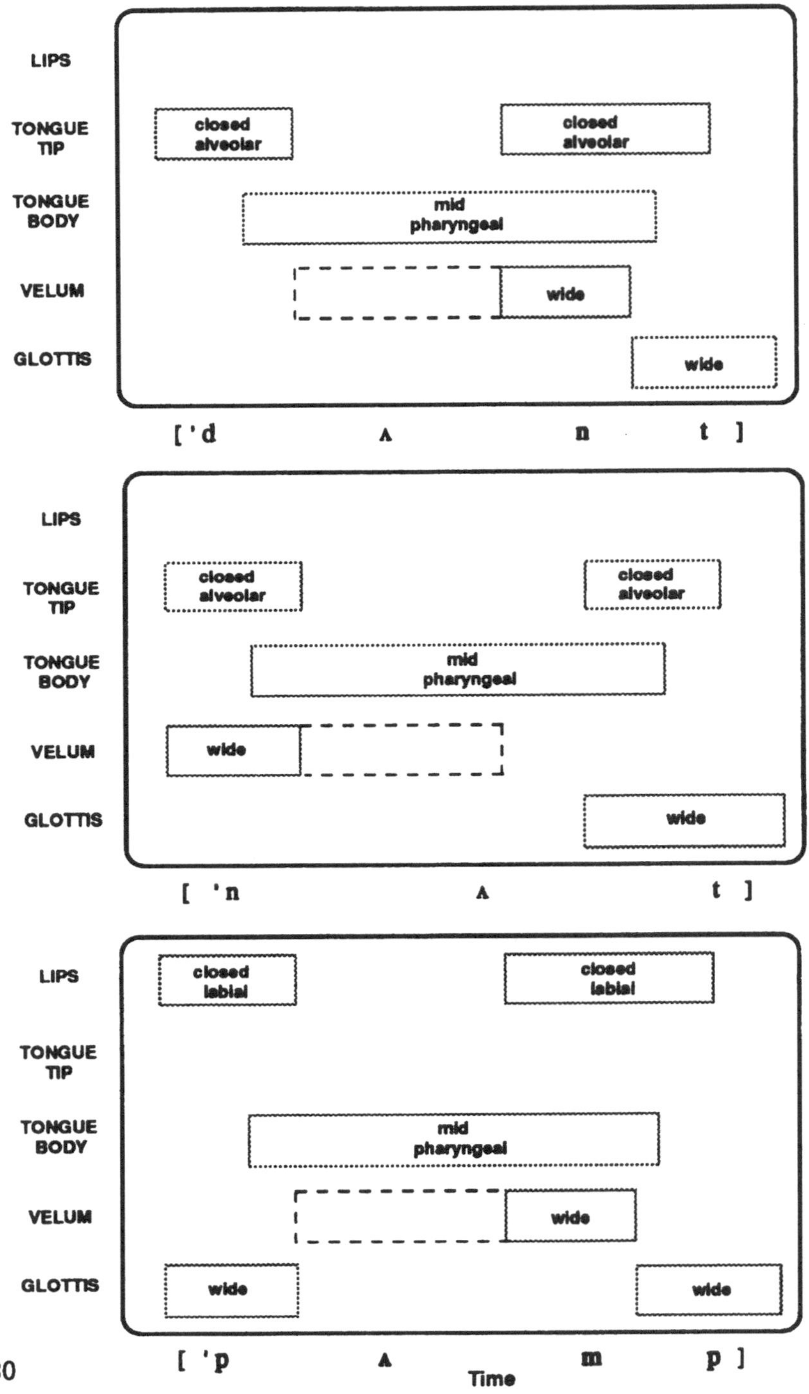
LIPS
TONGUE TIP
TONGUE BODY
VELUM
GLOTTIS
closed alveolar
closed alveolar
mid pharyngeal
wide
wide
['d ʌ n t]
LIPS
TONGUE TIP
TONGUE BODY
VELUM
GLOTTIS
closed alveolar
closed alveolar
mid pharyngeal
wide
wide
['n ʌ t]
LIPS
TONGUE TIP
TONGUE BODY
VELUM
GLOTTIS
closed labial
closed labial
mid pharyngeal
wide
wide
wide
['p ʌ m p]
Time

organising its articulations over a phrase of several syllables (cf. the "coalesced word patterns" of Macken, 1979).

Variability in Imitations. As a final example, let us consider six of Emma's repeated attempts to imitate a word that did not lend itself either to gestural harmony or to the labial-alveolar routine: *apricot*, ['æpri'kɑt]. (All these examples were recorded in week 95, except for the third which was recorded in week 105.) The word is challenging because it calls not only for three different locations of gestural closure, irregularly ordered (labial, velar, alveolar), but also for an alternating pattern of glottal closure and release.

Table 4.4 lists Emma's attempts. With several exceptions she captures certain properties of the word quite accurately: the number of syllables (2–6), the stress pattern (1, 4), an initial vocalic gesture (1–4), the constriction degree of the final vowel (1, 3–6), the rough location of at least two out of three consonantal constrictions (2–6), and, omitting the initial velar intrusions of 5 and 6, the labial-lingual sequence of these constrictions. Yet every attempt contains at least one apparent segment not present in the model: [b], [g], [f], [ts], or [ŋ]. With the exception of [f] (an error in the exact location and degree of the word's labial constriction), all these errors arise from a failure of gestural timing or co-ordination: for [b], [g], and [ŋ], a failure to open the glottis during oral closure; for the affricate [ts] (in 4), a relatively slow release of [t], as in the earlier examples. Other indications that Emma had difficulty in managing the alternating pattern of glottal action in the word come from the brief periods of aspiration (superscript [h]) inserted in 1, 4, and 6. Finally, the whispered initial vowel of 2 presumably reflects a delay in glottal closure, whereas the initial velar nasal

TABLE 4.4
Imitation: Within-word Variability in Emma's Attempts at *apricot*.

Adult Target	*Order of Closure Constrictions*	*Emma's Imitations*	*Consonantal Constrictions*
['æprɪkɑt]	Labial—Velar—Alveolar	1. ['aɪbə^{w}ɑ^{h}ɑː]	L
		2. ['ɑpə'gʌ]	L—V
		3. ('ə'fu'kɑː]	L—V
		4. ['^{h}ʌfə'tsɑː]	L—A
		5. ['gɛl'gʌ'pɑː]	V—V—L
		6. ('ɥə'^{h}ɑp^{w}ə't^{h}ɑː]	V—L—A

Note: Apparent consonantal segments in Emma's responses not found in adult target: [b], [g], [f], [ts], [ɥ].

FIG. 4.3 *Opposite*: Schematic gestural scores for the target word *nut*, ['nʌt] [centre], and for *nut* as spoken by Emma in *doughnut*, ['dʌnt] (top), and *peanut*, ['pʌmp] (bottom). The extensions of the velic activation intervals by dashed lines indicate possible free variation in the duration of the velic gestures.

of 6 reflects a delay in velic closure, as the child moves from silent breathing to speech. Thus, the principal source of error (apart from errors in the location and degree of vocalic constrictions) was gestural phasing. No doubt we could construct a set of "rules" relating the observed segments to the supposed underlying forms of the target utterance. But the task would be laborious, and completely *ad hoc*. A gestural account, by contrast, is simple and readily intelligible.

GENERAL DISCUSSION

The Relation of Gestures to Features and Segments

We have tried to show how a child's errors in early words can arise from paradigmatic confusions among similar gestures in a child's repertoire and from syntagmatic difficulties in co-ordinating the gestures that form a particular word. Yet a reader accustomed to think in terms of features and segments may see little difference between our approach and those of previous researchers. For example, Waterson (1971, p.181) proposes that ". . . a child perceives only certain of the features of the adult utterances and reproduces only those that he is able to cope with"; Macken (1979, p. 29) writes of a child's ". . . tendency to combine features from different segments of the adult word"; Ferguson and Farwell (1975, p. 426), commenting on a child's diverse forms for a single word, suggest that the child ". . . seems to be trying to sort out the features of nasality, bilabial closure, alveolar closure, and voicelessness."

What is missing in all these formulations is an explicit statement of how a percept is linked to its articulation. Their implicit conception of the link seems to be close to that of K.N. Stevens who answered a conference question on this matter as follows: "I would say that the lexicon is represented in abstract units that are neither directly articulatory nor directly acoustic. A relation projects these abstract units both to the acoustics and to the articulation. As you can see, I am taking the view of Jakobson, originally postulating something like features which have both acoustic correlates and articulatory correlates and must have both" (Mattingly & Studdert-Kennedy, 1991, p. 194).

We have already stated the key objection to this position: A feature is a property, not an entity. Phonetic features are not like facial features—eyes, nose, mouth—each of which can, at least in principle, be removed from one face and transferred to another. Rather, phonetic features are like the size and shape of a nose. We cannot remove either without removing the nose in which they are embodied. In short, features are attributes, not substantive components.

Of what substantive object or event, then, is the feature an attribute? The customary answer, the phonetic segment or phoneme, will not do, because segments are defined by their features: The answer is circular as long as we have no independent (and no substantive) definition of a segment. We propose, instead, that a feature is an attribute of a gesture. We assume that gestures, like Jakobson's features, "... have both acoustic correlates and articulatory correlates and must have both." Because these two sets of correlates are necessarily isomorphic, the gesture is the link between a speech percept and its articulation. In this respect, speech gestures resemble every other imitable act: Their perceptual representation specifies their motor form.

Adopting the gesture as a vehicle for the feature also permits an independent and substantive definition of the segment. We noted earlier that the canonical syllable was the first step toward differentiation of two major classes of oral gesture: vocalic and consonantal. Let us now note, further, that although consonant and vowel gestures may interact (as in Emma's preferences for particular consonant–vowel combinations) they are not interchangeable: we do not find a child (or an adult) making the mistake of replacing a narrow/mid/wide vocalic gesture with a closed/critical consonantal gesture, or vice versa. No doubt such errors are blocked by the biophysical structure of the syllable, that is, by its alternating pattern of opening and closing the mouth. In any event, we view differentiation of the syllable into its closed and open phases as a move toward the formation of gestural routines with a narrower domain than the word, namely, the encapsulated patterns of precisely phased laryngeal, velic, and oral gesture that we term segments (cf. Menn, 1986; Studdert-Kennedy, 1987).

The Emergence of Segments

The emergence of segments as elements of word formation in a child's lexicon seems, then, to have two aspects. The first is the grouping of all instances of a particular sound-gesture pattern into a single class, presumably on the basis of their perceptuomotor, or phonetic, similarity (e.g. grouping the initial or final patterns of *dad*, *dog*, *bed*, etc. into the class /d/). The second is the distributional analysis and grouping of these gesture-sound patterns into higher order classes (consonants, vowels) on the basis of their syllabic functions (onset, nucleus, coda).

Two possible selection pressures may precipitate formation of these categories. One pressure is toward economy of storage. As the lexicon increases, words may organise themselves according to their shared gestural and sound properties. Recurrent patterns of laryngeal and supralaryngeal gesture would thus form themselves into classes of potential utility for recognition or activation of lexical items (Lindblom, 1989; Lindblom, MacNeilage, & Studdert-Kennedy, 1983).

A second pressure may be toward rapid lexical access in the formation of multiword utterances. Several authors (e.g. Branigan, 1979; Donahue, 1986) have reported evidence that the form of early multiword combinations may be limited by the child's ability to organise the required articulatory sequences. Donahue, for example, reports her son's "adamant refusal" to attempt two successive words with different initial places of articulation. Such findings imply that the integration of gestures into independent phonemic control structures, or articulatory routines (Menn, 1983), may serve to insulate them from articulatory competition with incompatible gestures, and so facilitate their rapid, successive activation in multiword utterances.

SUMMARY

We have presented three lines of evidence for a gestural model of phonological development that can deal coherently with (1) the continuous transition from babbling to speech, and (2) the word as the contrastive unit of early phonology. For the transition from babbling to speech, details of the developmental course may vary from child to child: Not every child displays gestural harmony, not every child who does so escapes from harmony into the lexicon by a nonharmonious gestural routine. None the less, every child does have to find a path from babbling to speech. We have argued from one child's path that the gesture, with its roots in the child's pre-linguistic mouthings and vocalisations, is a more valid unit of linguistic function than the feature with its roots in the formalisms of adult phonology.

With regard to the word as the contrastive unit of early phonology, we have reviewed two lines of evidence that the gesture, rather than the feature, is the basic unit of a word's articulatory organisation. First, the same syllable may take different forms as a function of the target word, or phonetic context, in which it appears. A featural account would not predict this outcome, because a given segment carries the same featural predicates regardless of context; a gestural account, on the other hand, with its emphasis on the syntagmatic processes of articulatory action, finds the outcome natural. Second, in our subject's attempts to articulate a word with a pattern of alternating glottal gestures and a varied sequence of oral constrictions, the attempts were so diverse, so variable from occasion to occasion, that a featural account of the child's utterances would be little more than a list of arbitrary deletions, additions, and substitutions. By contrast, the present approach attributing the child's errors to imprecise execution and timing of the gestures that form the target word offers a simple and perspicuous account.

Finally, we have argued that the feature can be ruled out as a basic unit of either speech perception or speech production on rational grounds because it is, by definition, an attribute that has no existence independently of the object or event that it describes. We reject the segment as the primary vehicle of the feature because a segment is (circularly) defined by its features. We propose instead that a feature be viewed as an attribute of a gesture, and that segments be defined, superordinate to the gesture, as emergent structures, comprising recurrent, spatiotemporally co-ordinated, gestural routines.

ACKNOWLEDGEMENTS

Some of the data reported here were first presented at the Fifth International Congress for Child Language, Budapest, July 1990. We thank "Emma" and her family for their cheerful co-operation; Cathe Browman, Charles Ferguson, Louis Goldstein, Marlys Macken, Lise Menn, Elliot Saltzman, Marilyn Vihman, and Natalie Waterson for the insights we have gained from their papers; Catherine Best, Cathe Browman, Ignatius Mattingly, and Natalie Waterson for their instructive comments; and Zefang Wang for assistance with the figures. The research and the preparation of this paper were supported, in part, by NIH grants to Haskins Laboratories, HD–01994 and NS–24655.

REFERENCES

Albright, R.W., & Albright, J.B. (1956). The phonology of a two-year-old child. *Word, 12*, 282–390.

Albright, R.W., & Albright, J.B. (1958). Application of descriptive linguistics to child language. *Journal of Speech and Hearing Research, 1*, 257–261.

Branigan, G. (1972). Some reasons why successive single word utterances are not. *Journal of Child Language, 6*, 411–421.

Browman, C.P., & Goldstein, L. (1986). Towards an articulatory phonology. *Phonology Yearbook, 3*, 219–252.

Browman, C.P., & Goldstein, L. (1987). Tiers in articulatory phonology, with some implications for casual speech. In J. Kingston & H.E. Beckman (Eds.), *Papers in Laboratory Phonology*, I. (pp. 341–376). New York: Cambridge University Press.

Browman, C.P., & Goldstein, L. (1989). Articulatory gestures as phonological units. *Phonology, 6*, 151–201.

Browman, C.P., & Goldstein, L. (1990). Gestural specification using dynamically defined articulatory structures. *Journal of Phonetics, 18*, 299–320.

Bush, C.N., Edwards, M.L., Edwards, J.M., Luckau, C.M., Macken, M.A., & Peterson, J.D. (1973). *On specifying a system for transcribing consonants in child language.* Stanford Child Language Project. Stanford, CA: Department of Linguistics, Stanford University.

Chomsky, N., & Halle, M. (1968). *The sound pattern of English.* New York: Harper & Row.

Clements, G.N. (1985). The geometry of phonological features. *Phonology Yearbook, 2*, 225–252.

Cohen, M. (1952). Sur l'étude du language enfantin. *Enfance, 5*, 181–249.

Davis, B.L., & MacNeilage, P.F. (1990). Acquisition of correct vowel production: A quantitative study. *Journal of Speech and Hearing Research, 33*, 16–27.

Donahue, M. (1986). Phonological constraints on the emergence of two word utterances. *Journal of Child Language, 13*, 209–218.

Fant, G. (1962). Descriptive analysis of the acoustic aspects of speech. *Logos, 5*, 3–17.

Fant, G. (1973). *Speech sounds and features.* Cambridge, MA: MIT Press.

Ferguson, C.A. (1963). Contrastive analysis and language development. *Georgetown University Monograph Series, 21*, 101–112.

Ferguson, C.A. (1986). Discovering sound units and constructing sound systems: It's child's play. In J.S. Perkell & D.H. Klatt (Eds.), *Invariance and variability in speech processes* (pp. 36–51). Hillsdale, NJ: Lawrence Erlbaum Associates Inc.

Ferguson, C.A., & Farwell, C.B. (1975). Words and sounds in early language acquisition. *Language, 51*, 419–439.

Fowler, C.A., Rubin, P.E., Remez, R., & Turvey, M. (1980). Implications for speech production of a general theory of action. In B. Butterworth (Ed.), *Language production* (pp. 373–420). New York: Academic Press.

Goldsmith, J.A. (1990). *Autosegmental and metrical phonology*. Oxford: Basil Blackwell.

Holmgren, K., Lindblom, B., Aurelius, G., Jalling, B., & Zetterström, R. (1986). On the phonetics of infant vocalisation. In B. Lindblom & R. Zetterström (Eds.), *Precursors of early speech* (pp. 51–63). New York: Stockton.

Ingram, D. (1974). Fronting in child phonology. *Journal of Child Language, 1*, 233–241.

International Phonetic Association (1989). Report on the 1989 Kiel Convention. *Journal of the International Phonetic Association, 19*, 67–80.

Jakobson, R. (1941/1968). *Child language, aphasia and phonological universals*. [Trans. of *Kindersprache, Aphasie und allgemeine Lautgesetze*. Uppsala: Almqvist & Wiksell, 1941]. The Hague: Mouton.

Jakobson, R., Fant, G., & Halle, M. (1952/1963). *Prelimaries to speech analysis: The distinctive features and their correlates*. Cambridge, MA: MIT Press.

Jakobson, R., & Halle, M. (1956). *Fundamentals of language*. The Hague: Mouton.

Kent, R.D., & Bauer, H.R. (1985). Vocalizations of one year olds. *Journal of Child Language, 12*, 491–526.

Koopmans, van B., Florien, J., & van der Stelt, J.M. (1986). Early stages in the development of speech movements. In B. Lindblom & R. Zetterström (Eds.), *Precursors of early speech* (pp. 37–50). New York: Stockton.

Ladefoged, P. (1980). What are linguistic sounds made of? *Language, 56*, 485–502.

Leopold, W.F. (1953). Patterning in children's language learning. *Language Learning, 5*, 1–14.

Lindblom, B. (1986). Phonetic universals in vowel systems. In J.J. Ohala & J.J. Jaeger (Eds.), *Experimental phonology* (pp. 13-44). New York: Academic Press.

Lindblom, B. (1989). Some remarks on the origin of the "phonetic code". In C. von Euler, I. Lundberg, & G. Lennerstrand (Eds.), *Brain and reading* (pp. 27–44). Basingstoke, UK: Macmillan.

Lindblom, B., MacNeilage, P., & Studdert-Kennedy, M. (1983). Self-organising processes and the explanation of phonological universals. In B. Butterworth, B. Comrie, & Ö. Dahl (Eds.), *Language universals* (pp. 181–203). The Hague: Mouton.

MacArthur Communicative Development Inventory: Toddlers (1989). Center for Research in Language, UCSD C–008, San Diego, CA 92093.

Macken, M.A. (1979). Developmental reorganization of phonology: A hierarchy of basic units of acquisition. *Lingua, 49*, 11–49.

MacNeilage, P.F. & Davis, B.L. (1990). Acquisition of speech production: Frames, then content. In M. Jeannerod (Ed.), *Attention and performance, Vol. XIII: Motor representation and control*. (pp. 452–476) Hillsdale, NJ: Lawrence Erlbaum Associates Inc.

MacNeilage, P.F., Hutchinson, J., & Lasater, S. (1981). The production of speech: Development and dissolution of motoric and premotoric processes. In J. Long & A. Baddeley (Eds.), *Attention and performance* (Vol. IX, pp. 503–520). Hillsdale, NJ: Lawrence Erlbaum Associates Inc.

Mattingly, I.G., & Studdert-Kennedy, M. (1991) (Eds.). *Modularity and the motor theory of speech perception*. Hillsdale, NJ: Lawrence Erlbaum Associates Inc.

McCarthy, J.J. (1988). Feature geometry and dependency: A review. *Phonetica, 43*, 84–108.

McCune, L., & Vihman, M.M. (1987). Vocal motor schemes. Papers and reports in *Child Language Development, 26*.

Menn, L. (1978). Phonological units in beginning speech. In A. Bell & J. Hooper (Eds.) *Syllables and segments* (pp. 157–171). Amsterdam: North-Holland.

Menn, L. (1983). Development of articulatory, phonetic and phonological capabilities. In B. Butterworth (Ed.), *Language production* (pp. 3–50). London: Academic Press.

Menn, L. (1986). Language acquisition, aphasia and phonotactic universals. In F.R. Eckman, E.A. Moravcsik, & J.R. Wirth (Eds.), *Markedness* (pp. 241–255). New York: Plenum Press.

Menyuk, P., Menn, L., & Silber, R. (1986). Early strategies for the perception and production of words and sounds. In P. Fletcher & M. Garman (Eds.), *Language acquisition* (2nd ed., pp. 198–222). New York: Cambridge University Press.

Nittrouer, S., Studdert-Kennedy, M., & McGowan, R.S. (1989). The emergence of phonetic segments: Evidence from the spectral structure of fricative-vowel syllables spoken by children and adults. *Journal of Speech and Hearing Research, 32*, 120–132.

Oller, D.K. (1980). The emergence of the sounds of speech in infancy. In G.H. Yeni-Komshian, J.F. Kavanagh, & C.A. Ferguson (Eds.), *Child Phonology, Vol. 1: Production* (pp. 93–112). New York: Academic Press.

Oller, D.K. (1986). Metaphonology and infant vocalizations. In B. Lindblom & R. Zetterström (Eds.), *Precursors of early speech* (pp. 21–35). New York: Stockton.

Oller, D.K., Wieman, L.A., Doyle, W., & Ross, C. (1975). Infant babbling and speech. *Journal of Child Language, 3*, 1–11.

Saltzman, E. (1986). Task dynamic coordination of the speech articulators: A preliminary model. Generation and modulation of action patterns. In H. Heur & C. Fromm (Eds.), *Experimental Brain Research Series, 15*, (pp. 129–144). New York: Springer-Verlag.

Saltzman, E., & Munhall, K. (1989). A dynamical approach to gestural patterning in speech production. *Ecological Psychology, 1*, 333–382.

Scarry, R. (1980). *Richard Scarry's Best Word Book Ever*. New York: Western Publishing Company.

Schwartz, R.G. (1988). Phonological factors in early lexical acquisition. In M.D. Smith & J.L. Locke (Eds.), *The emergent lexicon* (pp. 185–222). New York: Academic Press.

Stark, R.E. (1986). Prespeech segmental feature development. In P. Fletcher & M. Garman (Eds.), *Language acquisition* (2nd ed., pp. 149–173). New York: Cambridge University Press.

Steriade, D. (1989). *Affricates*. Paper read at Conference on Feature and Underspecification Theories, Massachusetts Institute of Technology, 7th–9th October.

Stevens, K.N. (1972). The quantal nature of speech: Evidence from articulatory-acoustic data. In E. & E. David B. Denes (Eds.), *Human communication: A unified view* (pp. 51–66). New York: McGraw-Hill.

Stevens, K.N. (1975). The potential role of property detectors in the perception of consonants. In G. Fant, & M.A.A. Tatum (Eds.), *Auditory analysis and perception of speech* (pp. 303–330). New York: Academic Press.

Stevens, K.N. (1989). On the quantal nature of speech. *Journal of Phonetics, 17*, 3–45.

Studdert-Kennedy, M. (1987). The phoneme as a perceptuomotor structure. In A. Allport, D. MacKay, W. Prinz, & E. Scheerer (Eds.), *Language perception and production* (pp. 67–83). London: Academic Press.

Studdert-Kennedy, M. (1991a). A note on linguistic nativism. In R.R. Hoffman & D. Palermo (Eds.), *Cognition and the symbolic processes* (pp. 39–58). Hillsdale, NJ: Lawrence Erlbaum Associates Inc.

Studdert-Kennedy, M. (1991b). Language development from an evolutionary perspective. In N.A. Krasnegor, D.M. Rumbaugh, R. Schiefelbusch, & M. Studdert-Kennedy (Eds.), *Biological and behavioral determinants of language development* (pp. 5–28). Hillsdale, NJ: Lawrence Erlbaum Associates Inc.

Vihman, M.M. (1978). Consonant harmony: Its scope and function in child language. In J. Greenberg (Ed.), *Universals of human language, Vol. 2: Phonology* (pp. 282–334). Stanford: Stanford University Press.

Vihman, M.M (1981). Phonology and the development of the lexicon: Evidence from children's errors. *Journal of Child Language, 8*, 239–264.

Vihman, M.M., Macken, M., Miller, R., Simmons, H., & Miller, J. (1985). From babbling to speech: A re-assessment of the continuity issue. *Language, 61*, 397–445.

Vihman, M.M. & McClune, L. (in press). When is a word a word? *Journal of Child Language*.

Vihman, M.M., & Velleman. S. (1989). Phonological reorganisation: A case study. *Language and Speech, 32*, 149–170.

Waterson, N. (1971). Child phonology: A prosodic view. *Journal of Linguistics, 7*, 179–211.

II Speech and Reading in Different Modalities

5 Language by Touch: The Case of Braille Reading

Paul Bertelson
Université Libre de Bruxelles, Belgium

MODES OF LANGUAGE INPUT

Language can be conveyed through several input modes. For the majority of people through most of human history, the principal mode was speech, with the deaf and some other little-documented minorities using visible gestures.[1] A third mode appeared with the somewhat recent invention of writing. Still more recently, systems of tangible typography, allowing the tactile identification of written symbols, have been developed for the sake of the blind.

The existence of partially equipotential modes[2] transmitting similar information would seem to offer interesting opportunities for a comparative approach to the study of linguistic communication. So far, however, rather little advantage has been taken of these opportunities.

In linguistics, the majority of 20th-century theorists have focused their attention quasi exclusively on speech. This tendency was of course partly in reaction to the earlier concentration on written material. Interest in the linguistic

---

[1]It is now generally assumed that the emergence of speech was preceded by a period during which gestures were the main human mode of communication (Corballis, 1992). No evidence is of course available regarding the form of this early gestural language, nor about its relation to speech and to contemporary sign language.

[2]It is necessary to distinguish input modes from sensory modalities. Contrary to what the three examples of speech, print, and braille, which at first sight address respectively audition, sight, and touch, might suggest, there is no one-to-one matching between modes and modalities. Sight of facial movements plays a substantial role in face-to-face speech communication. Thus vision serves at least three linguistic communication modes: speech, reading, and sign language. Touch is used for tactile reading, and also in some forms of speech communication for the deaf-blind.

nature of the various forms of written representation has been restricted to a relatively small group of linguists and paleographers (e.g. DeFrancis, 1989; Gelb, 1963; Sampson, 1985) and of cognitive psychologists studying reading (Gleitman & Rozin, 1977; Henderson, 1982).

In psycholinguistics, on the other hand, work on language comprehension has for several decades been conducted mainly with written material. One undoubted reason was expediency: At a time when speech editing facilities were not available, it was much easier to present text than speech under controlled conditions. As a consequence, research on speech perception was mostly limited to short infralexical fragments like syllables, whereas word or sentence recognition was studied using printed material. The tradition carried the more or less implicit assumption that the processes involved in comprehension are not much influenced by the specific features of visual presentations (Bradley & Forster, 1987). Contemporary work on speech recognition (Altmann & Shillcock, 1994; Frauenfelder & Tyler, 1987; Marslen-Wilson, 1990) has provided many demonstrations that the assumption is not tenable. For instance, one of the most difficult problems regarding the recognition of ongoing speech concerns the identification of word boundaries (Cutler, in press), which in print are simply indicated by blank intervals.

Thus, it seems clear that systematic comparisons of the effects of the two types of inputs are necessary to avoid all sorts of unwarranted generalisations. But limiting ourselves to the two cases of speech and print would, on the other hand, leave us with considerable confounding between several important differences: Reading is much more recent than speech in the history of the species; it proceeds by discrete fixations, whereas speech is basically sequential; and it is self-paced, whereas speech is speaker-paced. Obviously, to interpret any processing difference between the two cases, it will be necessary to deconfound the effects of these different factors. Help could come from consideration of other existing input modes, such as lip-reading, cued speech (Alegria, Leybaert, Charlier, & Hage, 1992), or tactile reading.

This chapter is focused on the opportunities offered by the study of braille reading, the most common form of tactile reading.

THE BRAILLE SYSTEM

Braille is a typography identifiable by touch in which each character is a pattern of up to six raised dots in a 2×3 matrix. When it is used to represent alphabetic text, each of the 63 possible patterns stands for a letter, a digit, a punctuation sign, or (in "abbreviated" or "grade-2" braille) a language-specific abbreviation. The spatial layout of braille characters reproduces that of letters in text, i.e. they follow each other from left to right, and there are spaces between words. With other mapping principles, braille can also be used to represent nonalphabetic orthographies, music, and mathematics.

The system was designed about 1825 by Louis Braille, a young man who had lost his sight in childhood through an accident and who was a student at L'Institution Royale des Jeunes Aveugles in Paris, the first established school for the blind, founded in 1784 by Valentin Haüy.

The notion of using the haptic system of blind people for written communication had inspired many attempts through the ages. Most had involved the use of tangible three-dimensional models of visible letters in wood, clay, wax or metal or, in the system taught at the Institution Royale in Braille's time, raised paper. These attempts had been largely unsuccessful. To be identifiable by touch, the letters had to be large. They required *contingent exploration movements*, i.e. movements dependent on the particular shape of each letter. Finally, even if they allowed some kind of reading, these systems did not allow writing. In contrast, the dot patterns used by Braille could be identified through continuous noncontingent horizontal rubbing with the pulp of the finger. They could be produced using a cheap device, consisting of a punch and a metal slate with holes at the place of the dots.

The critical step that Braille accomplished consisted of rejecting any constraint from existing visual characters. He could thus concentrate on attempting, by trial and error, to obtain tactile patterns easily identifiable by touch. The principle of raised dots he borrowed from a notation system designed by an artillery officer, Charles Barbier, to allow the taking of notes and their reading during night operations. Barbier's system was, however, too complicated to become a workable typography.

According to Henri (1952), Braille's system was adopted enthusiastically by the students of the school. After being taught for some time side-by-side with raised roman letters, it was officially endorsed by the authorities, and during the second half of the century spread to the rest of France and then to other European countries and to America. The movement met with resistance from defenders of raised letters, whose main argument was that braille might isolate blind readers from the rest of society. On the other hand, local versions of braille, adapted to peculiarities of the language—taking account, for instance, of the frequency of occurrence of the different letters—were sometimes preferred to the original French version, but after several strong controversies considerations of standardisation finally led to the nearly universal adoption of forms of that version (Mackenzie, 1954). The only alternative tactile typography still in use, the Moon alphabet, consists of linear simplified raised roman letters. According to its proponents, it is indicated for people going blind in later life who find learning braille too difficult.

One reason why braille was successful where tangible letters failed was put in evidence recently, through the work of Loomis (1981). This author started from the notion that the main bottleneck for tactual information input is the fact that the haptic system can only pick up the lower frequency components of spatial patterns. He showed that sighted subjects, when instructed to identify printed representations of both braille and roman letters, submitted to low-pass filtering (i.e. blurred) did better with braille characters. That would mean that in the spatial frequency range that the skin transmits, braille patterns are more discriminable than letters of the alphabet.

THE EXPLORATION OF BRAILLE TEXT

A prerequisite to any discussion of the processes of braille reading is a knowledge of the patterns of hand movements used to explore the page. On these patterns depends, of course, the type of input which must be processed. Curiously, at the time our original work started, only sketchy descriptions were available (Bürklen, 1917; Davidson, Wiles-Kettenmann, Haber, & Appelle, 1980; Kusajima, 1974).

The study we reported some years ago (Bertelson, Mousty, & D'Alimonte, 1985; Mousty, 1986; Mousty & Bertelson, 1985) consisted of recording on video the hands of blind adults reading aloud different types of text—prose, scrambled words, and statistical approximations—printed in unabbreviated braille. Each subject read texts of these three categories with either hand alone, and with the two hands, using his preferred procedure. The analysis of the data involved tedious frame by fame monitoring of the recordings. Since then, an automatic recording system has been developed. A small diode in which a flash is produced every 40msec is pasted to the nail of each reading finger. The flashes are recorded by a solid state camera and the numerical values corresponding to the horizontal and vertical location of each flash are computed by a specially designed processing unit (Noblet, Ridelaire, & Sylin, 1985) and stored in a microcomputer. Several parameters of exploration activity can be obtained from these data, and one can, for instance, construct *actograms*, giving the position of each reading finger on successive recording cycles. With that new device, we have analysed the exploration movements of six representative readers for a material much more important than in the original study (Mousty, 1986). The new results have essentially confirmed the previous ones. The following description is based on the cumulative data from the two studies.

Braille is read either with one hand or with the two together. Most skilled readers use two hands, but can also read with one hand alone, as for example when they take down notes with the slate or with a braille typewriter. In that case, they write with one hand, and read with the other.

Our subjects used only the index finger to scan the line of text. Other fingers were occasionally seen to touch the page, mostly out of the text line. This practice might possibly be useful for locating the line, but we have no specific data to confirm this.

In one-handed reading, the reading finger scans the line from left to right, then returns to the following line. The scanning movements of skilled readers are smooth, with few variations in speed. As the example in Fig. 5.1, frame a, shows, they are sometimes interrupted by *regressions* to a region that has already been explored. One also observes brief stops, during which the finger often engages in sagittal palpation. One striking feature of exploration behaviour is that the reading finger keeps permanently in contact with the paper, even during return sweeps. We never observed jumps over particular words or passages such as constructivist views of the reading process (Goodman, 1967) would predict. As far as one can generalise from our data, braille reading involves exhaustive exploration of the line of text.

In two-handed reading, a variety of patterns of two-handed exploration can be observed. Some readers practise throughout scanning and return sweep *conjoint exploration*, a pattern in which the two indexes move continuously side-by side (Fig. 5.1, frame b). This operating mode is rare, and occurs mostly in slow, presumably inexperienced readers. In other readers, some *dissociation* between the hands is observed. Conjoint exploration occurs only on some central region of the line (Fig. 5.1, frame c). It is interrupted when the left hand starts moving towards the beginning of the next line, letting the right hand complete scanning of the current line. Upon completion of its return movement, the left hand starts scanning the new line, and is met by the returning right hand somewhere during its forward movement. In such *disjoint exploration* patterns, each line is thus divided into three segments explored respectively by the left hand alone, the two hands conjointly and the right hand alone. The respective sizes of the three segments vary considerably among readers. For instance, in our population, the relative size of the central bimanual segment ranged from 90% to less than 10%.

There is a strong correlation between degree of hand dissociation and reading speed: The fastest readers are also those who use the hands independently to the

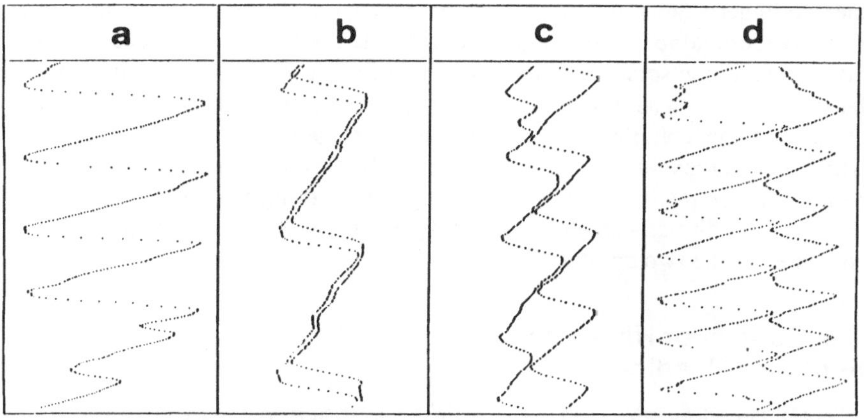

FIG. 5.1 Actograms showing lateral position of finger(s) (abcissa) for successive cycles (ordinate) of the video recording system during reading of easy prose (detective story). a: One-handed reading. b: Two-handed reading with conjoint exploration pattern, in a slow reader. c: Two-handed reading with moderate hand dissociation. d: Two-handed reading with strong dissociation, in a very fast reader. Lines are always 40 cells long. Differences in horizontal extent result simply from different settings of printer parameters.

largest extent. The correlation, it must be noted, is observed not only for two-handed reading but also for one-handed reading, and thus cannot be attributed to a specific advantage of dissociation. A more plausible hypothesis is that to dissociate the hands effectively, one must be able to read fast and reliably with each hand separately.

It thus appears that the various patterns of two-handed exploration result from the combination of several basic configurations of hand co-operation: conjoint exploration, in which the two reading fingers scan the same passage side-by-side and three forms of disjoint exploration. In two of these, either the left or the right finger alone is scanning the text, while the other finger is returning to the line. The third form is observed when the left hand, on completion of its return sweep, starts scanning the line while the right hand is still busy on the end of the preceding line. In such cases, a period of *simultaneous disjoint exploration* occurs, during which the fingers scan in parallel different passages of text. Some examples of that operating mode appear in Fig. 5.1, frames c and d.

Simultaneous disjoint exploration is certainly one of the most intriguing aspects of skilled braille reading. In the majority of our subjects, it occurred for prose reading on nearly every line transition. Detailed analysis of scanning speed during the different phases of line exploration showed that in fast readers there was no slowing down of forward movement during the phase of simultaneous exploration (Bertelson et al., 1985; Mousty, 1986). Thus, during these phases which last on average about 0.5 seconds per line, twice as much text information is input as during the other phases.

Conjoint exploration also appears to involve parallel information intake by the two fingers. Several data suggest that this operating mode is advantageous. First, readers adopt more conjoint two-handed patterns when reading more difficult text, e.g. scrambled words instead of prose. On the other hand, in a so far unpublished experiment with a sentence verification task, in which the use of several finger combinations was imposed, all subjects were found to read faster with the two index fingers side-by-side than with their best finger alone (Mousty, 1986). Finally, measurements of scanning speed during the different phases of line exploration has revealed a slight acceleration during the conjoint phase, compared to the two one-handed phases.

The Control of Hand Movements During Sentence Reading

In optical reading, the reader can adjust his or her ocular exploration to the demands of comprehension to a considerable degree. For instance, in reading sentences with temporary local ambiguities, so-called "garden path effects" in the form of rapid modifications of exploration speed can be detected as soon as the eye reaches the disambiguating word (e.g. Frazier & Rayner, 1982). On the other hand, work with contingent presentation procedures has shown that parameters such as fixation duration and amplitude of the following saccade can be influenced by information available during the fixation itself (Rayner & Pollatsek, 1989, pp. 153–180).

One result of the analyses of the movements of the hands during braille reading, which were described in the preceding section, was that the speed of forward scanning was very stable during exploration of each line. Of course, overall speed depended on text difficulty: It was faster for prose reading than for reading of scrambled word-lists, but there was little evidence of short-term variations of scanning speed that might result from local variations in text difficulty. On the other hand, the relative incidence of regressions was strongly correlated with reading difficulty, being, for instance, higher in slow than in fast readers and higher for scrambled words than for prose (Mousty, 1986). These observations suggested that scanning speed cannot be adapted easily to local changes in processing load, and that as a consequence regressions become the main repair device available to the reader.

One way to explore these possibilities further was to examine how the hand exploration pattern of braille readers would be affected by a form of local change in processing load known to affect eye movements in optical reading. A situation which might fulfil that condition was provided by a well-known study by Rayner, Carlson, and Frazier (1983, Experiment 2). They recorded the eye movements of subjects reading syntactically ambiguous sentences like:

(A) The spy saw the cop with binoculars, but the cop did not see him.
(B) The spy saw the cop with the revolver, but the cop did not see him.

These sentences are ambiguous because the prepositional phrase (PP) ("with binoculars/with the revolver") can be attached either to the verb (saw), or to the noun (cop). The ambiguity is released in (B) by the semantic/pragmatic content of the PP ("with the revolver"), which is not compatible with attachment to the verb. In (A), both interpretations remain possible. The sentences were designed to test the "minimal attachment" principle, according to which the syntactic parser initially assigns the ambiguous beginning to the tree structure with the fewer nodes, in this case the structure with verb attachment. In (B), when "revolver" arrives, a new structure must be calculated, which, according to the model, would take a detectable time.

The recordings showed that overall reading time was effectively longer for type (B) sentences. Moreover, the slowing down resulted essentially from lengthening of the three fixations following immediately that on the critical word.

In our study, skilled blind readers read unimanually, with their preferred hand, French sentences constructed following the same principles as Rayner et al.'s (1983) material. Each sentence had two versions, one favouring verb-phrase attachment of the PP (VPA sentences), the other noun-phrase attachment (NPA sentences). The movement of the reading finger was recorded using the video system described in the preceding section. Mean scanning time per character was calculated for four regions of each sentence, the two critical regions being the ambiguous post-verbal noun phrase ("the cop with") and the disambiguating PP region ("binoculars/the revolver").

The results were fairly clear. Mean time per character was longer for noun-phrase attachment (NPA) sentences than for VPA sentences in the disambiguating region, and there was no difference in the other regions. This pattern resulted in an interaction between type of sentence and region that was significant by subjects, but not by items, a point we shall return to. To see what aspect of hand activity produced the critical slowing down, the time spent by the finger in each of the four regions of each sentence was further divided into two parts occupied respectively by first-pass scanning and by regressing. The result was that the speed difference between NPA and VPA sentences observed in the disambiguation region originated entirely in more time being spent regressing on the NPA sentences. No differences whatever was observed at the level of first-pass scanning. So, it appeared that the response to the garden path situation consisted exclusively in increased recourse to regressions.

It was unfortunately not possible to consider this interesting conclusion as fully established because the critical sentence type by region interaction was not significant by items. One possible reason for that failure could be that minimal attachment, the factor on which the construction of the material was based, was not the only source of garden path effects. Taraban and McClelland (1988) asked judges to rate the predictability of the eventual syntactic structure in the sentences used by Rayner et al. (1983) and found that in general VPA was expected more than NPA. Moreover, using a self-paced presentation task, they showed that the relative time spent on the different regions was inverted in sentence pairs in which the NPA structure was more expected. It was thus possible that uncontrolled variations in structure expectation prevented the garden path effect from occurring reliably in the NPA sentences of our material. This notion led us to carry out a new analysis of the results, taking account of predictability ratings applied to the sentence pairs. It appears that a clear garden path effect on the NPA version occurred only in those sentence pairs in which the VPA structure was the more expected one. For these pairs, the pattern observed at the level of the whole material—i.e. that disambiguation affected only regressions and not first-pass scanning—was confirmed, as is shown in Table 5.1. Moreover, the sentence type by region interaction in the analysis of the time spent regressing was here significant both by subjects and by items.

Taken together with the data from observation of hand movements, the present results support the notion that short-term changes of scanning speed are not available to the braille reader as devices to adapt to local changes in processing load. Hence, in case of overload the reader would have to rely on regression to the difficult passage. Forward scanning would be programmed at the beginning of a passage and would proceed at the chosen rate until an unexpected difficulty imposes a regression.

TABLE 5.1
Scanning Time (msec/cell) as a Function of Region and Sentence Type (VPA vs. NPA*) for Sentences with Expectation of VPA (N =10)

Region	*Sentence Type*	*First-pass*	*Regression*	*Total*
Disambiguating	VPA	101.1	11.7	112.8
(binoculars/revolver)	NPA	107.2	59.2	166.4
Other regions	VPA	103.0	6.0	109.0
	NPA	100.6	4.6	105.2

*VPA = verb-phrase attachment; NPA = noun-phrase attachment.

One possible reason for this state of affairs might be that speed is a critical dimension of the braille access code, and that changes resulting from decelerations of scanning would cause distortions and hinder interpretation. In visual reading, scanning can be speeded up or down to important extents without effects on signal identifiability, thanks to the principle of fixations and saccades. Experiments in which the text was masked at several time intervals after saccade end (Rayner et al., 1981) have shown that only a short part of the normal fixation duration, of the order of 50msec, is necessary to allow normal reading speed.

BRAILLE WORD RECOGNITION

The most characteristic aspect of the braille input that results from the description of reading-hand movements is that it is continuous and sequential. This is most clearly the case for one-handed reading and for the one-handed exploration phases of two-handed reading: The reading finger scans the characters from left to right in a strict succession that is interrupted only by regressions. The situation is somewhat more complicated for conjoint exploration and for simultaneous disjoint exploration, both of which involve parallel intake of text information by two different fingers, but even in these cases, the input is sequential at the level of each reading finger.

That sequential character of the sensory datum distinguishes braille reading from optical reading, in which on each fixation a window of text is made available simultaneously for perceptual analysis. Braille reading is thus closer to listening to speech, in which the input is also basically sequential, but with two important differences. First, the listener has no direct control on input rate, while the braille reader, despite the limitations on short-term modifications of first-pass scanning discussed in the preceding section, can achieve some adaptation of that rate through regressions and the choice of an adequate long-term speed. Second, braille words are, like printed words, separated by empty spaces which, as noted already, have no equivalent in the speech flow. Finally, the arrival of braille information is strictly serial, letter by letter, whereas for speech, co-articulation results in overlap within the syllable of acoustic data relevant to successive segments

(Liberman, 1970). Thus, braille reading might well be the most strictly serial mode of access to linguistic data.

Our present knowledge of word recognition processes is based essentially on data obtained with visual presentations. It has led to models that, of course, make no provision for progressive obtaining of the sensory evidence. Some research with braille has been aimed at examining if some of the typical phenomena of the visual word literature can be reproduced with braille words. For instance, Krueger (1982) found that letter search through common words is similarly (about 10%) accelerated, relative to nonwords, for braille readers exploring braille text as for sighted subjects exploring print. This result suggests that, contrary to an often quoted claim (Nolan & Kederis, 1969[3]), the usual word-superiority effect occurs in braille text processing. Another example is a study by Pring (1985) who, using the lexical decision task, did not obtain for braille readers the classical pseudo-homophone effect (slower "no" reaction time for pseudowords that are homophones of existing words than for nonhomophonic ones), which her sighted control subjects duly replicated with visual presentations of the same material. Although such data are certainly useful for the constraints they put on future theorising, their interpretation would require models that take account of the sequential character of the braille input.

It might be the case that with sequential inputs, the process of selecting a lexical interpretation is started before all the evidence relevant to the presented word has been obtained. This notion of *on-line processing* has been entertained for some time in the case of spoken words.

A very simple on-line mechanism was considered by Marslen-Wilson and Welsh (1978) in their "cohort model". They proposed that when a word is heard, a short-list, or cohort, of lexical interpretations sharing its early sounds is activated, and is subsequently submitted to a process of selection through which members inconsistent with later arriving batches of acoustic data are progressively eliminated. Recognition would occur at the time cohort size comes down to one.

The mechanism considered in the original cohort model was, of course, not the only possible on-line process, for it incorporated several arbitrary assumptions, like viewing activation as an all-or-none variable. Several authors have noted that the all-or-none assumption implied that a word affected by noise

---

[3]Nolan and Kederis (1969) measured *recognition thresholds* for both isolated letters and familiar words, using an apparatus, the *tachistotachometer*, which allowed the presentation of windows of braille text for a controlled duration (thus, mimicking the tachistoscope). They claimed that the recognition thresholds for words were longer than the sum of the thresholds for all the letters composing those words. However, different criteria for defining the threshold were used for respectively letters (duration at which three correct responses are obtained for four successive presentations) and words (duration at which first full recognition occurs), making the critical comparison at least dubious. On the other hand, the relation of recognition threshold to duration of identification processes is not self-evident.

or by an error of pronunciation or of perception (e.g. "shigarette") could never be recognised (McClelland & Elman, 1986; Norris, 1986). Alternative theoretical proposals have been developed that, although maintaining the central notion of on-line processing, admit variable levels of activation (Marslen-Wilson, 1987; McClelland & Elman, 1986; Taft & Hambly, 1986).

Several types of data have been presented as supporting the notion of on-line processing for spoken utterances. Word recognition responses sometimes occur before the whole word has been delivered (Marslen-Wilson & Welsh, 1978; Radeau, Mousty, & Bertelson, 1989). Pronunciation errors are detected more efficiently when they occur late in a word than in the early part (Cole, 1973). More recently, it has been claimed that spoken primes that share their beginning with a word probe are more effective than those that share a later fragment (Marslen-Wilson & Zwitserlood, 1989; Zwitserlood, 1989). The data that have been cited most often as favouring some kind of the on-line view, however, are the effects on response latency of the time at which all the information theoretically necessary to make a particular decision has been delivered. Such points are called *recognition points*. For word recognition, the recognition point is the *uniqueness point*. It is the point from which only one known word is compatible with the acoustic data obtained up to then. Effects of the location of the uniqueness point on reaction time have been obtained with different word recognition tasks: phoneme detection (Marslen-Wilson, 1984; Frauenfelder, Segui & Dijkstra, 1990), lexical decision (Taft & Hambly, 1986), gender classification, i.e. deciding if a presented French noun is feminine or masculine (Radeau, Mousty, & Bertelson, 1989), and word repetition (Radeau & Morais, 1990). For nonword responses in the lexical decision task, the recognition point is the *deviation point*, i.e. the point from which no existing lexical item matches the input. Effects of location of the deviation point on nonword reaction time have been demonstrated in several studies (Marslen-Wilson, 1984; Huttenlocher & Goodman, 1987).

We wanted to know if similar evidence can be obtained for braille reading. In a study which was described in more detail elsewhere (Bertelson, Mousty, & Radeau, 1992), we have examined if the speed of recognition of isolated braille words is influenced by the location of the uniqueness point. Because the time it takes the finger to reach that point depends on scanning speed, and thus varies between subjects and between trials, it was necessary to record the scanning movement for each individual trial. These recordings were performed using the video system described earlier. The experimental situation involved an "active line" controlled by a microcomputer. On an active line, plastic styluses protruding at the surface of a metal plate form braille characters. On each trial, the subject first put the preferred reading finger, with the flash-emitting diode attached, on a starting position. A word was displayed to the right of that position, and a tone informed the subject that they could start scanning. The system recorded automatically the time of passage past the first letter, past the uniqueness point and past the last character of the word, as well as response time. Instructions were to respond as fast as possible after starting scanning the word.

In a first experiment, the effect of the location of the uniqueness point on response latency was examined for two different word recognition tasks, gender classification and pronunciation. The gender classification task has allowed the demonstration of significant effects of uniqueness point location in the study with spoken presentations that was cited earlier (Radeau et al., 1989). Word pronunciation was used on the other hand partly to check on the generality of the results obtained with gender classification, partly because it has been used so extensively in work on printed word recognition (e.g. Frost, Katz, & Bentin, 1987; Monsell, Doyle, & Haggard, 1989).

Two subsets of 84 nouns, half feminine and half masculine, 8 to 10 letters long, were chosen using the BRULEX lexical database, which contains about 30,000 frequent French words (Content, Mousty, & Radeau, 1990). Half the words in each subset had an early uniqueness point (2nd to 5th letter, mean 3,95) and the other a late uniqueness point (7th to 10th letter, mean 8,95) and the two halves were paired as to usage frequency. The subject responded orally, by saying "féminin" or "masculin" for gender classification, or by saying the word aloud in the pronunciation task. In both cases, the beginning of the response activated a voice key that stopped the timer.

Reaction time, measured from start of word scanning, was for each task significantly faster for the words with early uniqueness point. That result indicates some degree of on-line processing for braille words.

The latency of a response to a braille word depends on two logically distinct factors: The speed at which the word is scanned by the reading finger and the speed of processing the obtained tactile input. The recordings offered the opportunity to measure mean scanning time per character before and after the

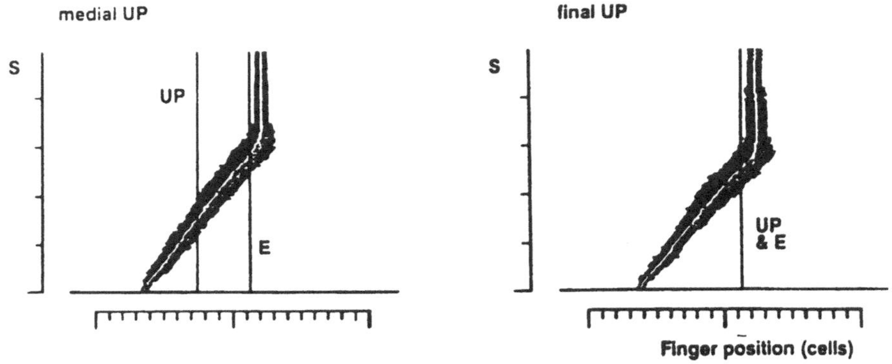

FIG. 5.2 Finger movement during single word exploration: Mean actograms of one typical subject, showing mean lateral position (white line) on successive cycles of the recording, with two standard deviation intervals (black area). Abcissa = lateral position of finger in braille cell units; ordinate = time in seconds; UP = uniqueness point; E = end of word.

uniqueness point, at least for items with an early uniqueness point, which provided a sufficiently large post-uniqueness-point space. Mean values of 215msec per character before the uniqueness point and 238msec after were obtained for gender classification, and of respectively 230 and 255msec for pronunciation. None of these differences reached significance. These results were confirmed in a specially devised study, in which the cycle-by-cycle progression of the finger was recorded for each word. A great uniformity of scanning speed across each word, unaffected by uniqueness point location, was observed (see Fig. 5.2). Thus, it would seem that the uniqueness-point effect originates entirely in processing speed. On the other hand, these results add to the corpus of data (see the previously discussed findings for reading ambiguous sentences) showing that first-pass scanning speed is largely insensitive to local changes in processing load.

The mean difference in RT between items with respectively late and early uniqueness point was 208msec for gender classification and 117msec for pronunciation. These effects are smaller than the corresponding differences in mean scanning time necessary to reach the uniqueness point, which were respectively 1185 and 1229msec for the two tasks. Thus, the effects on RT of changes in uniqueness point location are much smaller (17% and 9%, respectively) than the effects on time to uniqueness point. This aspect of the results is inconsistent with one prediction of the original cohort model for which, because recognition occurred exactly at recognition point, the trade-off function between temporal location of that point and RT had to be 100%. That prediction, however, has been supported for the case of speech only in two experiments reported very briefly by Marslen-Wilson (1984), one with a phoneme detection and the other with a nonword detection task. The other studies that provided some of the necessary quantitative data showed substantial discrepancies with the prediction (Huttenlocher & Goodman, 1987; Radeau et al., 1989; Taft & Hambly, 1986).

The trade-off function of 17% obtained for gender classification of braille words was inferior to those obtained by Radeau et al. (1989) for the same task applied to spoken words (31% and 38% respectively). The difference, however, could have resulted from a number of causes: different subjects (blind vs. sighted), different materials, different input modalities. To sort out these possibilities, in another experiment we had blind subjects perform gender classification with the same words presented auditorily and in braille. Mean trade-off functions were 18% for auditory presentation and 19% for braille presentation. Thus the effect of uniqueness-point location is as strong with braille as with spoken words. That the blind subjects showed weaker effects than the sighted might be linked to the amount of linguistic experience enjoyed by the two populations—a speculation that would, of course, still need independent empirical support.

The fact that comparable effects of uniqueness-point location were observed with braille and with spoken words shows clearly that on-line processing is not part of the innate endowment of speech. It opens the possibility that sequential delivery of input would be a sufficient condition for on-line lexical access. Some evidence bearing on that possibility has been obtained in the visual modality. It is possible to achieve a sequential orthographic input by displaying the letters of a written word progressively on a computer screen. Blosfelds (1981), working with Bradley and Forster (1987), found that subjects could easily identify words presented following a procedure in which the word was displayed incrementally on the screen, starting with the left-most letter, the other letters being added one by one in their normal place. Radeau et al., (1992) had subjects perform gender classification on words with uniqueness point in different locations—those used previously in the auditory experiments (Radeau et al., 1989)—presented following the incremental method. The speed of presentation was such that the time necessary to display fully each word was equal to the duration of its pronunciation in the auditory experiments. The mean RT difference between words with late and early uniqueness point (109msec) was virtually identical to those (133 and 110msec in two separate experiments) obtained with auditory presentations of the same material by Radeau et al. (1989).

One obvious limitation of the present studies is their reliance on the rather crude indexes of on-line processing provided by the effects of recognition-point location. Once the simple all-or-none mechanism of the early cohort model is abandoned for that of a network of lexical units with varying levels of activation, other factors become susceptible of influencing decision speed. Candidate factors are number of competitors, or "neighbourhood density", at different temporal locations relative to the decision point, and their respective frequencies of occurrence, relative to the leading unit. Recent work on printed word recognition (e.g. Grainger, 1992; Segui, 1994) has shown that the existence of at least one higher-frequency neighbour is a powerful determinant of word recognition speed. Systematic studies of the effects of such variables with sequential presentation modes are necessary to achieve a more promising description of on-line processing.

SUMMARY

The braille typography, in which characters consist of patterns of raised dots, is today still the most efficient system of written communication available to the blind. The reason it succeeded, where systems based on tangible tokens of letters of the alphabet failed, is probably, as the work of Jack Loomis has shown, the higher discriminability of braille patterns in the low-frequency spatial band width that the skin principally picks up. As a consequence, the trained braille reader can recognise sequences of braille characters by a continuous noncontingent lateral scan with the tip of the finger.

There are several reasons for studying braille reading, of which the most obvious one is improving communication for blind people. In this chapter, the focus is on the possible contribution of data regarding braille reading performance to a comparative approach to language comprehension.

After a short description of the braille system and of its historical origins, the types of hand movements used by expert readers were briefly examined. Most readers can read with either hand alone or with the two hands. From the viewpoint of this chapter, the main aspect of exploration movements is that the reading finger (nearly always one of the index fingers) scans the line from left to right, keeping continuous contact with the page and at a rather constant speed. The scan is occasionally interrupted by regressions to a previously explored passage. In two-handed reading, different parts of each line are generally read by the left finger alone, the two fingers side-by-side and the right finger alone. But here also, the exploration is for each segment carried out at constant speed.

One important question to ask about exploration movements concerns the degree to which they are controlled by ongoing comprehension processes. In work on visual reading, relevant evidence has been obtained by recording the eye movements of subjects reading temporarily ambiguous sentences. Typically, the fact of reaching the region which allows resolution of the ambiguity resulted in a "garden path effect" manifesting itself under the form of slower exploration. Using one of the classical garden path situations, we have found that braille readers similarly slow down sentence exploration on reaching the disambiguation region. However, in the case of braille, the effect consisted wholly of increased incidence of regressions, whereas first-pass scanning was not affected by disambiguation. The finding concurs with our earlier observations concerning the relative constancy of scanning speed across lines of texts in suggesting that, for some reason that further research should elucidate, short-term adjustments of scanning speed are less available to the braille reader than to the visual reader.

Another question that we asked regarding braille reading is whether word recognition processes reflect the sequential character of the input. More specifically, is the process of reducing the set of lexical units compatible with the sensory input started on-line on the basis of partial early information, as so-called cohort theories assume, or is it delayed until all information regarding the word has been delivered? By manipulating the location in braille words of the recognition point—the point from which all the information is available that is theoretically necessary to make the decision implied by the experimental task—evidence favourable to the on-line viewpoint was obtained. Moreover, the relative effect of recognition-point location was of comparable relative size with braille and with spoken presentation, a result suggesting that on-line processing might occur whenever the input is sequential. Some support for this notion was obtained in a task with incremental left-to-right presentation of the letters of a printed word. Finally, although lexical selection appears to be started on-line during braille word exploration, it does not influence finger scanning speed: The latter is not influenced by reaching the recognition point. The finding is consistent with other data showing little effects of ongoing comprehension processes on scanning speed.

REFERENCES

Alegria, J., Leybaert, J., Charlier, B., & Hage, C. (1992). On the origin of phonological representations in the deaf: Hearing lips and hands. In J. Alegria, D. Holender, J. Junça de Morais, & M. Radeau (Eds.), *Analytic approaches to human cognition* (pp. 107–132) Amsterdam: North-Holland.

Altman, G.T.M., & Shillcock, R. (1994). *Cognitive models of speech processing*. Hove, UK: Lawrence Erlbaum Associates Ltd.

Bertelson, P., Mousty, P., & D'Alimonte, G. (1985). A study of braille reading. 2. Patterns of hand activity in one-handed and two-handed reading. *The Quarterly Journal of Experimental Psychology, 37*, 235–256.

Bertelson, P., Mousty, P., & Radeau, M. (1992). The time course of braille word recognition. *Journal of Experimental Psychology: Learning, Memory and Cognition, 18*, 284–297.

Blosfelds, M. (1981). *Visual and auditory word recognition*. Unpublished honors thesis, Monash University.

Bradley. D.C., & Forster, K. (1987). A reader's view of listening. *Cognition, 25*, 103–134.

Bürklen, K. (1917). Das Tastlesen der Blinden-Punktschrift. *Beiheft zur Zeitschrift für Angewandte Psychologie, 16*, 1–66.

Cole, R.A. (1973). Listening for mispronunciations: A measure of what we hear during speech. *Perception and Psychophysics, 13*, 153–156.

Content, A., Mousty, P., & Radeau, M. (1990). BRULEX: Une base de données lexicales informatisée pour le français écrit et parlé. *L'Année Psychologique, 90*, 551–566.

Corballis, M.C. (1992). On the evolution of language and generativity. *Cognition, 44*, 197–226.

Cutler, A. (in press). Prosody and the word boundary problem. In J. Morgan & K. Denneth (Eds.), *Signal to syntax*. Hillsdale, NJ: Lawrence Erlbaum Associates Inc.

Davidson, P.W., Wiles-Kettenman, M., Haber, R.N., & Appelle, S. (1980). Relationship between hand movements, reading competence and passage difficulty in braille reading. *Neuropsychologia, 18*, 629–635.

DeFrancis, J. (1989). *Visible speech*. Honolulu: Hawaii University Press.

Frauenfelder, U.H., Segui, J., & Dijkstra, T. (1990). Lexical effects in phonemic processing: Facilitatory or inhibitory? *Journal of Experimental Psychology: Human Perception and Performance, 16*, 77–91.

Frauenfelder, U.H., & Tyler, L.K. (Eds.) (1987). *Spoken word recognition*. Cambridge, MA: MIT Press.

Frazier, L., & Rayner, K. (1982). Making and correcting errors during sentence comprehension: Eye movements in the analysis of structurally ambiguous sentences. *Cognitive Psychology, 14*, 178–210.

Frost, R., Katz, L., & Bentin, S. (1987). Strategies for visual word recognition and orthographical depth: A multilingual comparison. *Journal of Experimental Psychology: Human Perception and Performance, 13*, 104–114.

Gelb, I.J. (1963). *A study of writing*. University of Chicago Press.

Gleitman, L., & Rozin, P. (1977). The structure and acquisition of reading I: Relations between orthographies and the structure of language. In A.S. Reber & D.L. Scarborough (Eds.), *Towards a psychology of reading*. Hillsdale, NJ: Lawrence Erlbaum Associates Inc.

Goodman, K.S. (1967). Reading: A psycholinguistic guessing game. *Journal of the Reading Specialist, 6*, 126–135.

Grainger, J. (1992). Orthographic neighborhoods and visual word recognition. In R. Frost & L. Katz (Eds.), *Orthography, phonology, morphology and meaning* (pp. 131–146). Amsterdam: North-Holland.

Henderson, L. (1982). *Orthography and word recognition in reading*. London: Academic Press.

Henri, P. (1952). *La vie et l'oeuvre de Louis Braille*. Paris: Presses Universitaires de France.

Huttenlocher, J., & Goodman, J. (1987). The time to identify spoken words. In A. Allport, D. Mackay, W. Prinz, & E. Scheerer (Eds.), *Language perception and production: Relationships between listening, speaking, reading and writing* (pp. 431–444). London: Academic Press.

Krueger, L.E. (1982). A word-superiority effect with print and braille characters. *Perception and Psychophysics, 31*, 345–352.

Kusajima, T. (1974). *Visual reading and braille reading: An experimental investigation of the physiology and the psychology of visual and tactual reading*. New York: American Foundation for the Blind.

Liberman, A.M. (1970). The grammars of speech and language. *Cognitive Psychology, 1*, 301–323.

Loomis, J. (1981). Tactile pattern perception. *Perception, 10*, 5–27.

Mackenzie, C.N. (1954). *World braille usage: A survey of efforts towards uniformity of braille notation*. Paris: Unesco.

Marslen-Wilson, W.D. (1984). Function and process in spoken word recognition. In H. Bouma & D.G. Bouwhuis (Eds), *Attention and performance, Vol. X: Control of language processes* (pp. 125–150). Hillsdale, NJ: Lawrence Erlbaum Associates Inc.

Marslen-Wilson, W.D. (1987). Functional parallelism in spoken word-recognition. *Cognition, 25*, 71–102.

Marslen-Wilson, W.D. (1990). Activation, competition, and frequency in lexical access. In G.T.M. Altmann (Ed.), *Cognitive models of speech processing: Psycholinguistic and computational perspectives* (pp. 148–172). Cambridge, MA: MIT Press.

Marslen-Wilson, W.D., & Welsh, A. (1978). Processing interaction and lexical access during word recognition in continuous speech. *Cognitive Psychology, 10*, 29–63.

Marslen-Wilson, W.D., & Zwitserlood, P. (1989). Accessing spoken words: The importance of word onsets. *Journal of Experimental Psychology: Human Perception and Performance, 15*, 576–585.

McClelland, J.L., & Elman, J.L. (1986). The TRACE model of speech perception. *Cognitive Psychology, 18*, 1–86.

Monsell, S., Doyle, M.C., & Haggard, P.N. (1989). Effects of frequency on visual word recognition tasks: Where are they? *Journal of Experimental Psychology: General, 118*, 43–71.

Mousty, P. (1986). *La lecture de l'écriture braille: Patrons d'exploration et fonctions des mains*. Unpublished doctoral dissertation. Bruxelles: Université Libre de Bruxelles.

Mousty, P., & Bertelson, P. (1985). A study of braille reading: 1. Reading speed as a function of hand usage and context. *The Quarterly Journal of Experimental Psychology, 37A*, 217–233.

Mousty, P., & Bertelson, P. (1992). Finger movements in braille reading: The effect of local ambiguity. *Cognition, 43*, 67–84.

Noblet, A., Ridelaire, H., & Sylin, G. (1985). Equipment for the study of operating processes in braille reading. *Behavior Research Methods, Instruments and Computers, 17*, 107–113.

Nolan, C.Y., & Kederis, C.J. (1969). *Perceptual factors in braille word recognition*. New York: American Foundation for the Blind.

Norris, D. (1986). Word recognition: Context effects without priming. *Cognition, 22*, 93–136.

Pring, L. (1985). Processes involved in braille reading. *Journal of Visual Impairment and Blindness, 79*, 252–255.

Radeau, M., & Morais, J. (1990). The effect of the uniqueness point in shadowing spoken words. *Speech Communication, 9*, 155–164.

Radeau, M., Morais, J., Mousty, P., Saerens, M., & Bertelson, P. (1992). A listener's investigation of printed word processing. *Journal of Experimental Psychology: Human Perception and Performance, 18*, 861–871.

Radeau, M., Mousty, P., & Bertelson, P. (1989). The effect of the uniqueness point in spoken-word recognition. *Psychological Research, 51*, 123–128.

Rayner, K., Carlson, M., & Frazier, L. (1983). The interaction of syntax and semantics during sentence processing: Eye movements in the analysis of semantically biased sentences. *Journal of Verbal Learning and Verbal Behavior, 22*, 358–374.

Rayner, K., Inhoff, A.W., Morrison, R.E., Slowiaczek, M.L., & Bertera, J.H. (1981). Masking of foveal and parafoveal vision during eye fixations in reading. *Journal of Experimental Psychology: Human Perception and Performance, 7*, 167–179.

Rayner, K., & Pollatsek, A. (1989). *The psychology of reading*. Englewood Cliffs, NJ: Prentice Hall.

Sampson, G. (1985). *Writing systems: A linguistic introduction*. London: Hutchinson.

Segui, J. (1994). Language perception in the visual and auditory modalities: Analogies and differences. In G. d'Ydewalle, P. Eelen, & P. Bertelson (Eds.), *International perspectives on psychological science: The state of the art* (pp. 119–134). Hove, UK: Lawrence Erlbaum Associates Ltd.

Taft, M., & Hambly, G. (1986). Exploring the cohort model of spoken word recognition. *Cognition, 22*, 259–282.

Taraban, R., & McClelland, J.L. (1988). Constituent attachment and thematic role assignment in sentence processing: Influences of content-based expectations. *Journal of Memory and Language, 27*, 597–632.

Zwitserlood, P. (1989). The locus of the effects of sentential-semantic context in spoken-word processing. *Cognition, 32*, 25–64.

6 Pre-lingual Deafness and Literacy: A New Look at Old Ideas

Ruth Campbell and Vivian Burden
Goldsmiths' College, London, UK

INTRODUCTION

People born with profound hearing loss are disadvantaged in their phonological development: The intelligibility of speech that can only be seen on the lips of the speaker is minimal (Campbell, 1989; Summerfield, 1991), and the useful speech of most born-deaf people is often limited and is usually understood only by close associates and carers. Despite this, the deaf can show normal rather than deviant patterns of general phonological development in their own speech, although these are invariably developmentally delayed and extended in time (Dodd, 1976; Oller & Kelly, 1974). However slowly or quickly their phonological skills develop, for the deaf there will always be a problem in specifying some of the phonological aspects of the word, for it is simply impossible to see or otherwise (naturally) perceive all the heard phonemic contrasts available to the ear. Thus it is very likely that phonological representations are *underspecified* for the deaf—although there will be great variability in the extent of such underspecification both across people and within the individual. Such representations are the basis for the development of literacy in the hearing child for they are the target of the exercise of learning which letters map to words known by ear.

Two skills are paramount in the acquisition of literacy: One is decoding skill, namely mapping the "new" written word form to the word known by ear and by speech. If the target phonological form is variable and underspecified, then this should be expected to have a detrimental effect on acquiring such decoding. The other is contextual skill, the ability to bring all linguistic and pragmatic (inferential) abilities to bear on the written text in order to understand it. There is ample evidence that many of the deaf have impaired skills in this domain. The two skills are functionally independent but normally interactive in development (Stanovitch, 1986). If in people born deaf both these component skills are underdeveloped, literacy will be drastically affected because decoding and contextual skill work interactively. The deaf are, indeed, poor readers, typically leaving full-time education in their late teens with the reading abilities of a 10-year-old.

Is this failure a simple reflection of a catastrophic interaction between the two critical reading skills or is the picture more complicated? If the deaf cannot hear (or lip-read or say) the difference between "bore" and "more" then they should be disadvantaged in trying to learn about the mappings between the speech form and the corresponding letter forms in the written word. They might then be expected to behave as if reading English (or any other alphabetic language) were like reading Chinese (but see Chapter 11): They need to acquire a mapping between a spoken form (which may be homophonous with several others) and a discrete written form where there is little perceived correspondence between the characters and the components of the speech-form. They should not be sensitive to *regularity of letter–sound mappings* in their processing of the written word. In this chapter we suggest that some profoundly congenitally deaf school-leavers, with low reading ages measured by comprehension tests, can show surprisingly good word decoding skills in spelling and in reading. In spelling they showed marked sensitivity to the mapping between sounds and letters in English (alphabetic regularity effects). However, their sensitivity to orthographic regularity in reading may not be quite as marked as in most normal hearing youngsters of similar reading age. Such a pattern has been reported before for deaf college-educated readers in the United States (Hanson, Shankweiler, & Fischer, 1983), but not, as far as we know, in a less skilled sample of young deaf adult readers. This pattern of differential sensitivity to the sounds of letters in spelling and in reading tasks might suggest that different strategic skills are used by deaf and hearing children in reading and spelling.

We systematically examined written-word decoding skill in a population of English born-deaf school leavers (16–18 years) and two control groups, real-age matched youngsters and youngsters matched on SPAR and GAP reading test scores to the deaf group. The reading-age matched group was around 10 years old. We investigated spelling to dictation, using picture stimuli, and lexical decision, using manual response in a computer-controlled word-presentation task.

The systematic use of carefully selected stimuli was the most important aspect of this study. Word frequency was controlled independently of word regularity. We examined three classes of words: *regular* words such as FIRE, *exception* words including mildly irregular and more obviously irregular words, including members of word-ending families like *love* (*stove, rove*) and *strange* words which have unique sound–letter spelling patterns (*soap, choir*). Words such as *aisle* are also orthographically strange in terms of English bigram positional frequency, as well as having idiosyncratic pronunciations and these were included in the *strange* category, too. All the nonwords in this study followed the orthographic constraints of acceptable English. Thus we did not include items like *zwav*—although this is a pronouncable string, these particular letters in these positions do not occur in English.

For hearing English readers lexical decision is often sensitive to regularity and to word frequency and these interact with the level of reading proficiency. In less proficient, younger readers regular words are more efficiently processed than exception or strange words. With reading experience the regularity effect becomes tempered by word frequency: High-frequency words are processed more efficiently whatever their orthography, but regularity still exerts an influence on low-frequency words in lexical decision and naming tasks (Besner & McCann, 1987; Seidenberg, 1985; Seidenberg, Waters, Barnes, & Tanenhaus, 1984; Waters, Bruck, & Seidenberg, 1985; Waters & Seidenberg, 1985). A similar pattern can be described for spelling (Bruck & Waters, 1990), though typically word spelling shows more marked regularity effects, for a longer developmental period, than word recognition (Frith, 1985; Seymour, 1992).

EXPERIMENT 1: SPELLING

The experiment tested 15 deaf school leavers (all with profound deafness from birth and no other handicap) who were about to leave their special schools for the deaf in Hertfordshire and Cambridgeshire, England. They were 16 to 18 years old. Their reading age was assessed by SPAR and GAP test (reading for content and context). Their mean reading age was 9–10 years on these tests. Fifteen hearing children of similar real age and fifteen 9–10-year-olds were matched against the deaf group.

The subjects were asked to spell the name of an object presented in a picture by writing it down. The words corresponding to the pictured objects varied systematically in regularity and frequency as already described. Half the words were of high frequency (more than $76/10^6$) and half were low frequency ($4/10^6$ or less). Within each frequency group were words of three levels of regularity of spelling: regular words, irregular (or exception) words, and strange words. Twenty words were written for each condition.

After pre-testing the line drawings to make sure that they were unambiguously named by children at even the youngest age, we showed the pictures on cards to the subjects and asked them to write down the name of the object shown. Subjects were seen one at a time and the pictures were shown in random order. All subjects could do the task properly—that is fewer than 2% of responses were errors of naming or omissions. But they made spelling errors. Figure 6.1 shows that both regularity and frequency had very marked effects on spelling accuracy—at all levels and ages. The deaf were significantly worse than their real-age matches and significantly better than their reading-age matches in terms

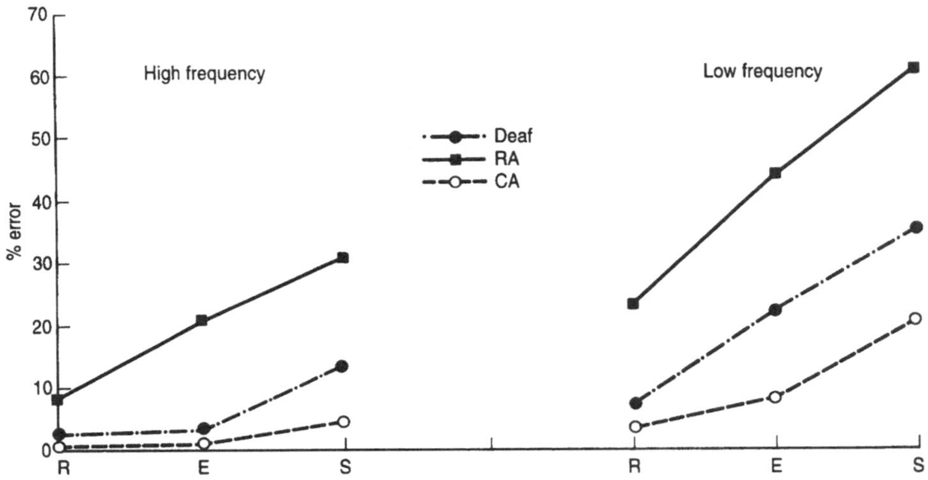

FIG. 6.1. Spelling accuracy as a function of regularity and frequency in deaf and hearing subject. $N = 15$ deaf, $N = 15$ reading-age match (ra), $N = 15$ chronological-age match (ca). R, regular words, E, exception words; S, strange words.

of accuracy. So our first conclusion is that these (normal) deaf children are better spellers than is predicted by their reading-age scores. This conclusion has been arrived at before, for instance by Gates and Chase (1926). They thought that good spelling in the deaf reflected relatively better irregular word spelling (see also Dodd, 1980; Dodd & Cockerill, 1985). But this was not found in our study. The deaf were highly sensitive to spelling regularity. It was *not* the case that their spelling superiority arose through good spelling of irregular words; quite the contrary. They were worst at spelling strange words and poor at exception words. In this pattern they were indistinguishable from the hearing youngsters. In a general ANOVA in which the between-subjects (group) factor was age and/or hearing status and the within-subject factors were frequency and the three levels of regularity, there was no interaction between the group factor and either regularity, frequency, or their interaction. Each of the within-subject factors, and their interaction, had a significant effect on error rate. Moreover, the pattern of the deaf subjects' spelling errors confirmed this highly "alphabetic" pattern. All of their errors were admissable as (lip-read) approximations to the spoken word and a number were very close indeed: *skwrl* for *squirrel*, *iorn* for an *iron*, *Sponch* for *sponge*, were actual errors produced by these deaf youngsters, but were also seen in hearing children's spellings and are clearly based on how the word is spoken rather than the pattern of its letters. It should be noted that these errors do not follow the orthographic constraints of English (*kwr* is an inadmissable tri-graph)—but this was also true for the younger, hearing readers tested.

This pattern of results, moreover, is not due simply to a few "phonologically skilled" deaf students. It held for all of them—even those with unintelligible speech and who were said by their teachers to have "poor lip-reading". There is a general and robust spelling pattern in these deaf youngsters: They are much better at spelling than their reading-age-matched cohort and their spelling accuracy is governed by regularity of sound–letter correspondence and by word frequency in a similar way to hearing people.

Hanson et al. (1983) also found sensitivity to regularity in word-spelling in a group of born-deaf readers. These were college-level, profoundly pre-lingually deaf young adults of varied educational background. They were much better readers than our group, reading at 10th-grade level (reading age 15–16 years). Hanson et al. used a sentence-frame procedure to test spelling, in which students had to complete a written sentence with the missing word. Despite these differences in subject skill and in procedure, their findings were very similar to ours. The deaf were as sensitive to regularity in spelling as were chronological controls despite the fact that, in that study, the deaf group were poorer spellers overall, than the hearing controls. In fact, the deaf group studied by Hanson et al. seemed to have reading skills that were in line with their overall spelling ability.

By contrast, in our deaf school-leavers spelling was not only more sensitive to letter–sound regularity, but also significantly better than reading ability predicted. One possibility is that in these deaf youngsters, reading and spelling failed to develop interactively as cognitive tasks. They may have failed to connect. In normal children there is good evidence that skill in one decoding task informs and "bootstraps" developing ability in the other (see e.g. Seymour, 1992). We needed to examine word-decoding skills in a reading task to establish whether this was the case.

EXPERIMENT 2: LEXICAL DECISION

The effects of regularity on lexical decision have been explored in detail in deaf Canadian youngsters by Waters and Doehring (1990). The deaf in their study showed no regularity effects whatever, at any of three tested age levels between 7 and 20 years. Similarly, in a test of spelling *recognition*, where subjects had to distinguish correct spellings (of words they had previously written down) from incorrect ones, the deaf in Hanson et al.'s (1983) study made relatively fewer errors for the less regular words. That is, they were somewhat less dependent on letter–sound mappings (at least for the less regularly spelled words) than hearing youngsters.

Because our first experiment indicated that regularity effects were marked in deaf youngsters' spelling, it was clear that we needed to replicate Waters and

Doehring's results with our subjects. We used a slightly different stimulus list than Waters and Doehring (see Discussion), but in other respects our experiments were the same. We tested 14 profoundly congenitally deaf school-leavers from the same institutions as in Experiment 1. Once again we matched them with students who had normal hearing on both reading age (SPAR and GAP tests) and chronological age. Once again we tested them with words of controlled frequency and regularity level that fell within orthographic constraints of English. Figures 6.2 and 6.3 summarise the results.

The interpretation of these data is more contentious than that for the spelling study, for the data tell an ambivalent story. Reaction time and error rates will be discussed together because the ambivalence extends to both and, in any case, there is no speed error trade-off in these results. First, separate overall ANOVAs for high- and for low-frequency words, in which group and regularity were entered as independent variables, revealed both a main effect of group entirely due to the poorer performance of the reading-age-matched group, and a main effect due to regularity of spelling. There were no further group-by-condition interactions. This was the pattern both for RTs and for errors.

However, separate within-group ANOVAs suggested a slightly different story. While the younger hearing group showed sensitivity to regularity at all levels in their RTs for low-frequency words, the deaf and the older hearing readers only showed an overall effect: Strange words were detected poorly compared with regular words (R < S, but R = E and E = S). The deaf showed more marked sensitivity to regularity in error analysis, however, with significantly more errors for strange than for other classes of word (S > E = R). Only the reading-age-matched group showed the full regularity effect (S > E > R).

Thus, it appears that the deaf are not particularly sensitive to regularity in a reading-related task, but then neither are their hearing peers of the same age. Moreover, in this study the deaf were indistinguishable in speed and accuracy from their real-age peers, rather than falling between the real-age and reading-age controls in the spelling study. What best describes what they are doing? To clarify this it is necesary to recapitulate earlier findings on lexical decision tasks. Although regularity effects can be found in many studies of lexical decision with adults (at least for low-frequency words), this is not always the case. Waters and Seidenberg (1985) discovered one reason for the discrepancy. Where words such as *aisle* and *choir* (strange words of low orthographical regularity and also of low frequency of occurrence) were in the stimulus set, regularity effects were apparent that disappeared when the stimulus set comprised a more limited set of only regular and exception words and the nonwords were all pronounceable. Their rationale for this changing pattern was as follows: The presence of strange words in the stimulus set makes the word/nonword decision more difficult. Without the presence of such items, subjects can make a decision based on orthographic wordlikeness (i.e. the precise visual letter sequences)—the nonwords in the lexical decision task are orthographically least word-like. The

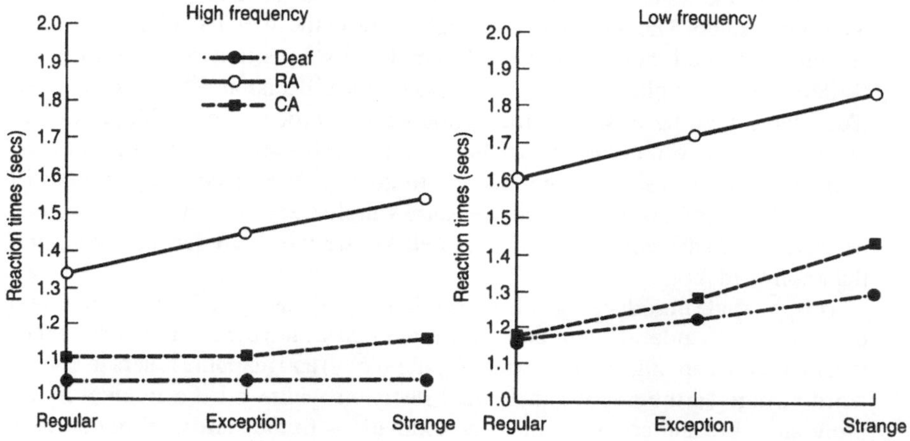

FIG. 6.2. Lexical decision: Reaction times for correct responses as a function of regularity and frequency in deaf and hearing subjects. $N = 15$ deaf, $N = 14$ reading-age match (ra), $N = 15$ chronological-age match (ca). R, regular words; E, exception words; S, strange words.

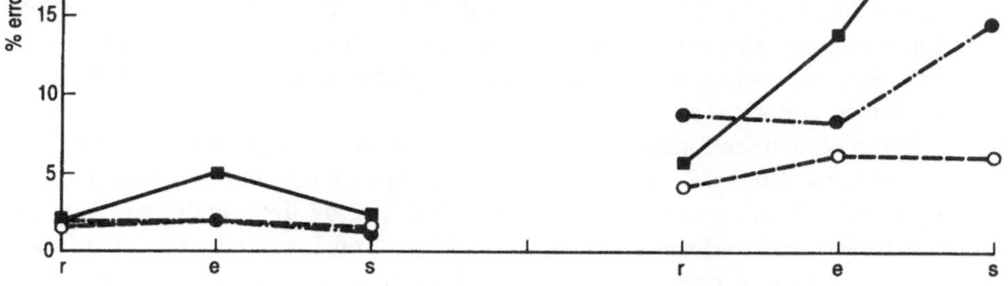

FIG. 6.3. Lexical decision: Errors as a function of regularity and frequency in deaf and hearing subjects. $N = 15$ deaf, $N = 14$ reading-age match (ra), $N = 15$ chronological-age match (ca). R, regular words; E, exception words; S, strange words.

presence of *strange* words forces the subject to use a different tactic because such words are, by definition, not orthographically as constrained as the other material. The only basis on which subjects could then make their decision is the pronunciation of the item—it is the phonology of *choir* or *aisle* that reveals it to be a word (it has a semantic entry), but *nust* or *bove* can be judged to be nonwords on this basis, too. The presence of strange words in the lexical decision-stimulus set where all the other items are orthographically constrained thus moves the skilled reader to a phonological strategy in lexical decision. The task becomes like a word-naming task for which phonological processing is obligatory and where regularity effects are invariably found. This rationale holds only for low-frequency words in sets of high and low frequency: High-frequency words will show reduced effects of regularity because simple frequency of occurrence can be sufficient to drive lexical decision (well-known words are far more common than nonwords).

This rationale introduces the idea that relative proficiency at the different levels of regularity (regular, exception, and strange) may indicate relative differences in reliance on mapping letters to sounds (phonology) and mapping letters to known word-strings (orthography) in lexical decision where all the nonwords are pronounceable and are word-like approximations to the statistical regularities of written English. A reader who "sounds out" in order to make a lexical decision will be fastest at regular words and less fast at irregular and strange words because neither conform to the simplest mapping rules. That is, the reader will be characterised by a pattern of performance in which R < E = S. In contrast, the orthographic reader, relying on the apparent wordlikeness of the letter string in terms of the position of the constituent letters, will be particularly perturbed by the strange words (by definition many are "unwordlike" in terms of orthographic constraints) and will show a R = E < S pattern, as well as more errors for nonwords.

Waters and Doehring's (1990) study examined deaf children in three age groups using words of high frequency. They found no regularity effects in RT for any group, suggesting the deaf were not using phonology in the task. The words may have been judged simply on the basis of the familiarity of the written form. Tantalisingly, Waters & Doehring report that they repeated the study with low-frequency words and that similar (null) results were obtained but they give no data to support this.

Following the rationale already outlined, the pattern of performance reported in detail by Waters & Doehring still leaves open the possibility that the deaf may code phonologically in lexical decision for (low-frequency) words when the following conditions are met: (1) High- and low-frequency words are presented within one stimulus set, (2) some of the words seen are more unwordlike in terms of orthographic structure (positional bigram frequency in English) than some of the nonwords, and (3) all the nonwords are pronounceable. These conditions are met in the present study and, rather than *no* evidence, we found *ambivalent* evidence for phonological coding in lexical decision in the deaf. (Regular words were processed faster than strange ones, but with not much difference between regular and irregular nor between irregular and strange). A further point is indicated by these results. The pattern of performance shown by the deaf, in which strange words are particularly error-prone, suggests that the deaf tended to make their decision on the basis of orthographic structure (word-likeness) more than anything else. If this were so, they might be expected to make errors on nonwords to a greater extent than the other two groups, for the nonwords are orthographically constrained in this study. Although we did not record nonword reaction times, nonword *errors* failed to confirm this interpretation. There was no difference between groups for errors on nonwords. Deaf youngsters may be using both orthographic and phonological regularities in this task.

DISCUSSION

In an important study of spelling by deaf people, Dodd (1980) reports that the deaf spelled irregular words well, but she also showed that they could spell lip-read nonwords. Thus they understand the need for alphabetic mapping skills and are able to perform the necessary segmentation and blending operations when these are required. It is clear from Experiment 1 that sensitivity to regularity in word spelling need not be abnormal in the deaf. It may have appeared to Dodd and to others, including Gates and Chase, that the deaf might be particularly good at spelling irregular words, but as this is a developing skill in normal readers and writers, it is important to contrast them with appropriate control groups and with appropriate (frequency-controlled) stimuli. When matched in this way, as in our study, we see that the deaf perform very similarly to hearing readers who are slightly younger than they are, rather than much younger readers matched precisely for reading age. Such young readers are very much more likely to regularise their spellings than older readers. Our conclusion is that deaf youngsters may regularise their spellings, too. This conclusion is at apparent odds with other findings with the deaf (e.g. Dodd & Cockerill, 1985), yet may not be so problematic when these methodological points of comparison are taken into account. Moreover, in Hanson et al.'s (1983) study, skilled deaf readers (better than those in our study by several reading years) showed very similar patterns of sensitivity to regularity in spelling to those we report here. Spelling, like other language tasks, is delayed in the deaf. Nevertheless, it follows an essentially normal pattern with respect to its reliance on letter–speech-sound coding. The normal pattern is for very marked regularity effects to be seen in the early stages that gradually lessen with reading skill—and as function of familiarity with the written words seen.

Nor is this isolated evidence for reliance on phonological skills underpinning some aspects of literacy in the deaf. As far as reading skills go, at least two recent studies show inner speech in action. Leybaert and Alegria (1993) shows that born-deaf people are susceptible to Stroop effects in colour naming that follow the same gradient of interference as that for hearing children (from unpronounceable to pronounceable nonwords, to nonrelated words to colour words) whether manual or spoken responses were required. Furthermore, both groups showed marked interference in naming the colour carrier when it was a homophone of a colour word. Hanson and Fowler (1987) reported that deaf college students, like hearing controls, were sensitive to rhyme structure in a paired lexical decision task. Thus, they were faster at deciding that two words were displayed when those words rhymed (*hare pair*) than when they did not (*are pair*). Care was taken to control for orthographic similarity in this study. This study also revealed that these same students failed to show much sensitivity to rhyme in an overt task of rhyme judgement, where they were often confused by orthographical similarity. That is, a distinction between overt phonological ability (the rhyme task) and covert reliance on phonology (the paired lexical decision task) seemed to be indicated by this study.[1]

However, it would be wrong to conclude that the deaf are dependent on speech sound mappings in all aspects of word decoding. Whereas we did not find flat regularity functions in lexical decisions in the deaf, we did find far less evidence for reliance on letter–sound mappings in their reading than in their spelling. Coupled with their lexical decision speed and accuracy (indistinguishable from age-matched hearing subjects) this lends some support to the notion that spelling and reading might develop in a disconnected fashion in the deaf. We would not expect such (relatively) poor spelling from people who are fast, skilled word readers. Other adult poor spellers who are good readers (Burden, 1990) are rather poor, slow and regularity-prone in their lexical decisions. Qualitatively (spelling "by ear", recognising "by eye") and quantitatively (spelling better than reading-age, but recognising as good as chronological-age) the deaf suggest that the mastery of word-decoding progresses in a fashion where, although the components are essentially normal, the meshing of those components may not be.

Orthographic (Abstract) Regularity and PDP

Seidenberg and McClelland (1989) have described a parallel distributed processing model for learning the relationships between written and spoken words. The model specifies mappings, through a hidden unit layer, between orthography (letters) and phonology (from speech sounds). It does not include

[1]It should be noted that Waters and Doehring's (1990) students, who showed no regularity effects in lexical decision, also failed to show sensitivity to rhyme in the paired lexical decision task of Hanson and Fowler (1987). This was attributed, provisionally, to the lower literacy of Waters and Doehring's subjects compared with Hanson and Fowler's college students. However, as our British subjects, with pre-teen reading ages, showed regularity effects in lexical decision, this may not be the right explanation for the discrepancy.

a lexical level of representation, although words are the form of input to the system: spoken words for phonological representations and written words for orthographic ones. It does not instantiate, directly, any particular set of rules concerning which letters map to which sounds. Such regularity emerges from the model by virtue of feedback (from the hidden units) on specific weighting patterns. Because the mappings are distributed across the net of correspondences, such learning becomes sensitive to regularities in the system as a whole. What we have termed phonological regularity does not, in this type of model, constitute a set of specific letter-to-sound rules, but rather the emergence of the most systematic mappings within a multiply interconnected network. Among the many ways in which the model fits the experimental data, it shows "normal" patterns of sensitivity to regularity in lexical decision for (low-frequency) written words that vary in their degree of regularity. The model has not been used to simulate spelling, nor the interaction of spelling and reading in normal development.

To simulate deafness in the model it would be necessary to break the links between speech input (or output) and the phonetic representations—the targets for orthographic mapping. The break would not need to be complete. We have suggested that the deaf have underspecified phonological representations of words, not that such representations are absent (although they may be fewer than in the reported simulation of written-word learning). Given the parallel, interconnected nature of the model the two interesting questions are, first, whether such a break need impair the acquisition of regularity sensitivity in reading and writing and, secondly, whether phonological specifications could be "educated" by exposure to orthographic material. The data from our deaf study suggest a reasonably positive answer to the first question. If all other components of the model are functional (in particular, if the hidden layer unit is functioning effectively), then, because orthographic learning will occur, phonological and orthographic regularity effects may also emerge. It may be sufficient that distinctive *orthographic* representations map onto different meanings (as for homophones). In answer to the second question, it may be possible that, as a result of exposure to written words, regularities might emerge that could in turn "educate" the phonological level of representation into more detailed, better-specified representations.

There seems to be nothing intrinsically unworkable in this type of adjustment to the model if one considers it to be driven not just by well-specified phonological representations in the first place but (potentially) by a combination of orthographically well-specified inputs (letters in written words) and some consistent, if underspecified, level of representation in the phonological domain. Our provisional claim is that it is exposure to written words that has led to the improvement in specification of phonological representations in the deaf, despite the isolation of such representations from speaking or hearing. In the deaf youngsters we have tested it seems that sensitivity to orthographic structure is very marked in lexical decision and we surmise that (as in younger hearing readers) the deaf are not yet able to capitalise on this sensitivity in their spelling, which is based on simpler, alphabetic mappings. In other words, the pattern presented by the deaf in this study is primarily of developmental delay rather than deviance, although with evidence of less connection between their spelling and reading decoding skills than is found in hearing youngsters. The deaf youngsters' wrong spellings were generally phonologically acceptable following a broad criterion, namely that these spellings would be lip-read as the target. But their spellings did not always obey orthographic constraints in English. In this, these deaf youngsters resembled younger hearing children who may attempt any alphabetic spelling for a word they do not know. One could call these spellings orthographically unsophisticated. Orthographic sensitivity in lexical decision seems not yet to have improved the deaf youngsters' spellings to the level reached by their chronologically age-matched peers (remember that their lexical decision skills were equivalent to those of chronologically aged-matched students).

A PDP model applied directly to spelling might indicate more orthographic regularity in output, mirroring that for input, for all people who can read. Clearly further processes are indicated to account for the highly alphabetic (simple sound-to-letter mappings) spellings that are generated by most people (including our deaf subjects) in the pre-teen and often teen years (Burden, 1990). However, we emphasise here that these deaf youngsters do have a phonological (alphabetic) strategy for spelling words which must be based on the skill of phonological segmentation.

In our view, the general properties of a PDP system that allow for orthographic and phonological regularities to develop as emergent properties of a system trained to map (meaningful) orthographic strings to phonological forms appear to be on the right track in explaining many phenomena in reading and writing and its development in the deaf as in other people. Through intense efforts by therapists and carers to improve speech quality the young deaf child often develops metalinguistic, phonological awareness on an underdeveloped phonological system. When this makes contact with a systematic orthography there is potential for further refinement of phonological representations (see Morais & Kolinsky, Chapter 15).

The sort of pattern of response to written words that we have described for the deaf would not be predicted from a model of the relationship between phonological abilities and developing literacy in which literacy depended directly on phonological *ability*. Even though the deaf may have good phonological *awareness*, in the sense that they are often drilled ostensively in phonemic tasks as they approach the school years, this cannot make contact with properly specified phonological representations, for (by definition) these do not exist for the deaf. Only when they are confronted with an alphabetic orthography will some of the phonetic contrasts they cannot "hear", and which will thus be perceived as homophones in interpreting speech, become clear. Such clarifications may become instantiated both as orthographic *and* phonological realities. That they might develop in this way might be illustrated by analogy. Several years ago I (the first author) wondered why it was that the Indian Independence leader and the two prime-ministers who shared his name had that name so consistently misspelled by English people. They spell it *Ghandi* (Campbell & Coltheart, 1984). It was because that particular letter string more closely fitted the orthographic constraints of English than the correct spelling, *Gandhi*. For English speaker/hearers the spellings are homophonous. A speaker of Indian languages explained to me that written *gh* and *dh* represent phonemes distinct from *g* and *d* and she showed me the differences by speaking words with the different phonemes in them. I could neither reliably pronounce nor (quite) hear them. Yet the distinction is a phonological fact and one which I know as such, despite my poor production and perception of it. Because of this I know that other apparently homophonous Indian words may be distinguished in this way. Even if this knowledge is realised in a partial fashion (by unreliable discrimination or production), it will still be of specific use. I am suggesting that, in the deaf people we have studied, exposure to English written language enlightens in this way, but through covert sensitivity rather than overt instruction.

In this chapter we have striven towards an explanation of reading and writing decoding skills in a group of orally trained English deaf school-leavers. We have shown the component skills to be (essentially) normal, both quantitatively and qualitatively, and in this we are at odds with other researchers who find evidence for a lack of phonological recoding in the deaf on these tasks, but in agreement with others who do find such evidence. This suggests to us that not only are there likely to be sampling differences (schooling methods in particular) behind these differences but, more importantly, that there is no very strong evidence that the deaf *cannot* apply phonological strategies to such tasks, although sometimes they *may* not. We have put to one side the most important fact that despite such relatively good decoding skills these youngsters are very poor indeed at reading and writing texts. The simplest and most likely explanation for this is that they lack the broader psycholinguistic contextual abilities, including those of syntactic, semantic, and pragmatic inference, that are needed and used by readers. This has been pointed out before, and shows very consistently in studies on cognition in the deaf (Quigley & Paul, 1984; Rodda & Grove, 1987; Wood, Wood, Griffiths, & Howard, 1986). However, it is possible that the results reported here are suggesting a further, general problem. This is that although subcomponents of reading can be trained separately and effectively in the deaf, they may not necessarily interconnect in a natural and useful way. We have observed relatively normal reading and spelling of single words, but this seems to be a little "out of phase" in the deaf compared with normal readers. Good, separate recoding skills cannot bootstrap each other and cannot support effective literacy on their own. Could such general and "isolating" effects of apparent language deprivation in the deaf be moderated by literacy? Or will we continue to find that by the time they leave school many deaf people are essentially "hyperlexic"—relatively good at reading and writing words, but unable either to use good word recognition to improve their spelling or to contextualise this word knowledge in reading text? For deaf youngsters, the research imperative must be to determine whether, how, and to what extent contextual language abilities can be improved through and with reading and spelling, now that we are more sure that the decoding aspect of their reading and spelling is relatively secure and, in most respects, "normal".

REFERENCES

Besner, D., & McCann, R.S. (1987). Word frequency and pattern distortion in visual word identification and production: An examination of four classes of models. In M. Coltheart (Ed.), *Attention and performance, Vol. XII: The psychology of reading*. Hillsdale, NJ: Lawrence Erlbaum Associates Inc.

Bruck, M., & Waters, G.S. (1990). An analysis of the component reading and spelling skills of goodreaders-goodspellers, goodreaders-poorspellers and poorreaders-poorspellers. In T. Carr & B.A. Levy (Eds.), *Reading and its development: Component skills approaches*. New York: Academic Press.

Burden, V. (1990). D. Phil. thesis, Cambridge University.

Campbell, R. (1989). Lipreading. In A.W. Young & H.D. Ellis (Eds.), *Handbook of research on face processing* (pp. 187–234). Amsterdam: Elsevier.

Campbell, R., & Coltheart, M. (1984). Ghandi: The non-violent route to spelling reform? *Cognition, 17*, 185–192.

Dodd, B. (1976). The phonological systems of deaf children. *Journal of Speech and Hearing Disorders, 41*, 185–198.

Dodd, B. (1980). The spelling abilities of profoundly deaf children. In U. Frith (Ed.), *Cognitive processes in spelling*. London: Academic Press.

Dodd, B., & Cockerill, H. (1985). Phonological coding deficit: A comparison of spelling errors made by deaf, speech-disordered and normal children. *Beiträge zur Phonetik und Linguistik, 48*, 405–415.

Frith, U. (1985). Beneath the surface of surface dyslexia. In K. Patterson, J.C. Marshall, & M. Coltheart (Eds.), *Surface dyslexia*. London: Lawrence Erlbaum Associates Ltd.

Gates, A.I., & Chase, E.H. (1926). Methods and theories of learning to spell tested by studies of deaf children. *Journal of Educational Psychology, 17*, 289–300.

Hanson, V.L., & Fowler, C. (1987). Phonological coding in word reading: Evidence from hearing and deaf readers. *Memory and Cognition, 15*, 199–207.

Hanson, V.L., Shankweiler, D., & Fischer, F.W. (1983). Determinants of spelling ability in deaf and hearing adults: Access to linguistic structure. *Cognition, 14*, 323–344.

Leybaert, J., & Alegria, J. (1993) Is word processing involuntary in deaf children? *British Journal of Psychology*.

Oller, D.K., & Kelly, C.A. (1974). Phonological substitution processes of a hard-of-hearing child. *Journal of Speech and Hearing Disorders, 39*, 65–74.

Quigley, S.P., & Paul, P.V. (1984). *Language and deafness*. London: Croom Helm.

Rodda, M., & Grove, C. (1987). *Language, cognition, and deafness*. Hillsdale, NJ: Lawrence Erlbaum Associates Inc.

Seidenberg, M.S. (1985). Constraining models of word recognition. *Cognition, 20*, 169–190.

Seidenberg, M.S., Waters, G.S., Barnes, M.A., & Tanenhaus, M.K. (1984). When does irregular spelling or pronunciation influence word recognition? *Journal of Verbal Learning and Verbal Behavior, 23*, 383–404.

Seidenberg, M.S., & McClelland, J.L. (1989). A distributed, developmental model of word recognition and naming. *Psychological Review, 96*, 523–568.

Seymour, P.H.K. (1992). The psychology of spelling: A cognitive approach. In C. Sterling & C. Robson (Eds.), *Psychology, spelling and education* (pp.50–62). London: Multilingual Matters.
Stanovich, K. (1986). Matthew effects in reading: some consequences of individual differences in the acquisition of literacy. *Reading Research Quarterly, 4*, 360–406.
Summerfield, A.Q. (1991). The visual perception of phonetic gestures. In I.G. Mattingley & M. Studdert-Kennedy (Eds.), *Modularity and the motor theory of speech perception: Proceedings of a conference to honor Alvin M. Liberman*. Hillsdale, NJ: Lawrence Erlbaum Associates Inc.
Waters, G.S., & Doehring, D. (1990). The nature and role of phonological information in reading acquisition: Insights from congenitally deaf children who communicate orally. In T. Carr & B.A. Levy (Eds.), *Reading and its development: Component skills approaches*. New York: Academic Press.
Waters, G.S., Bruck, M., & Seidenberg, M.S. (1985). Do children use the same processes to read and spell words? *Journal of Experimental Child Psychology, 39*, 511–530.
Waters, G.S., & Seidenberg, M.S. (1985). Spelling-sound effects in reading: Time course and decision criteria. *Memory and Cognition, 13*, 557–572.
Wood, D., Wood, H., Griffiths, A., & Howard, I. (1986). *Teaching and talking with deaf children*. Chichester, UK: Wiley.

7 Memory Deficits for Heard and Lip-read Speech in Young and Adult Poor Readers

Beatrice de Gelder and Jean Vroomen
Tilburg University, The Netherlands

INTRODUCTION

The notion that reading acquisition difficulties are associated with poor memory for verbal material seems well established in studies using a variety of tasks examining short-term memory for letter names, words, or sentences (e.g. Gathercole & Baddeley, 1990; Shankweiler et al., 1979; see Wagner & Torgesen, 1987, for an overview). This wealth of data contrasts with the persisting uncertainty about the actual nature of the relationhip between reading difficulties and memory impairments. Another aspect that is equally unclear concerns the persistence of these memory impairments over time. This chapter focuses on the memory problems of disabled readers, this time by introducing two somewhat novel dimensions. The issue is approached by comparing memory performance across two input modalities for speech; an auditory-based one, where the materials are heard, and an input modality lacking an auditory component, where materials are lip-read. Moreover, by comparing memory performance of young poor readers with that of adult ones, one might get a picture of the possible improvement of memory skills over time and its relation to persistent reading impairments.

Memory Deficits in Poor Readers: Cause, Consequence, or Neither?

With a taste for simple questions in the face of complex issues, one might be tempted to ask whether the memory difficulties of poor readers are a cause or a consequence of their reading difficulties. But it is unlikely that a simple answer to this question will be forthcoming. One critical factor for understanding the role of memory for reading concerns the involvement of immediate memory in reading acquisition. Proposals in this area have greatly benefited from interaction with models of the reading process (Bertelson, 1986; Seidenberg & McClelland, 1989; Seymour, 1986). But what is needed even more critically is a theory of reading *acquisition* that is different from a theory of the reading process. Presently, partial insight in this critical issue must be sampled from what amounts so far to research traditions with a somewhat different focus. One research tradition considers reading acquisition as a process that builds on what is made available to fluent speakers as a consequence of their speech competence. Learning to read requires making use of already unconsciously available speech representations by making these available in the course of acquiring grapheme-to-phoneme correspondences (Bertelson & de Gelder, 1989; Bertelson and de Gelder, 1990; Shankweiler et al., 1979; Liberman, Chapter 1). This perspective, popular as it was in the 1970s, may not stand up to critical scrutiny, as the notion of becoming aware or "phonological awareness" taken as an autonomous and sufficient explanatory factor might well be somewhat misleading (de Gelder, 1990). Still, accepting this perspective it is easy to imagine how reading and memory are linked because learning to read and reading require phonological storage and recoding of the written words (Liberman et al., 1977).

On the face of it, emphasis on the role of memory combines well with evidence from studies on memory performance, investigations of phonological similarity effects, and word-length effects in beginning, poor, and good readers. In turn, one sees how these data might converge with a notion developed in a different context, namely that phonological recoding is the representation format best suited to immediate memory (e.g. Baddeley, 1966; Conrad, 1964; see Baddeley, 1990, for an overview). This does not mean that nonphonetic recoding is ruled out, but it seems to be the more exceptional route, taken only by some populations in some circumstances, for example, to some extent by congenitally deaf readers (Frumkin & Anisfeld, 1977; Campbell, 1989) who were also poorer readers. Against this background there was reason to suspect that poor readers might be impaired in their phonological recoding skills. Developments in memory research brought the notion of specialised subsystems and dissociated impairments to the foreground. Data from poor memory performance of impaired readers fitted this picture well as the poor performance was specific for verbal material (e.g. Shankweiler et al., 1979). Moreover, research on immediate memory showed that, depending on whether the materials to be remembered are spoken or not, the memory performance does show a specific pattern, as confirmed again in Crowder and Surprenant (Chapter 3).

Taken together, these developments underscore the notion that reading acquisition might be related to specific phonological aspects of immediate memory. More recent evidence has prompted a still more precise focus. Whereas the original study by Shankweiler et al. (1979) showed that poor readers suffered comparatively less from acoustically confusable materials, later research has challenged that simple picture of poor readers not having a phonological recoding strategy available. A recent study by Brady, Mann, and Schmidt (1987) concludes that it is not so much phonological recoding as such, i.e. the reliance upon a phonological code in memory tasks, as the efficiency with which a phonological coding strategy is used by poor readers. More recently, a more specific picture of the involvement of phonological memory has been proposed, implying not so much recoding, but a hypothetical subsystem in the form of a phonological store which might possibly be impaired in poor readers (Gathercole & Baddeley, 1990). According to this view, specific impairments in immediate phonological memory are the bedrock of the explanation of reading impairments, to the exclusion of, for example, perceptual or representational problems.

Baddeley and Hitch (1974) and Baddeley (1986) have addressed these structural aspects of working memory and have also dealt with successive discoveries of phenomena pointing to the phonological specificity of the articulatory loop: the acoustic similarity effect and the word-length effect. Before raising the issue of impairments, we note some facts that led to a refinement of this approach by proposing a distinction within the articulatory loop, between phonological store and a rehearsal process. Although the word-length and the acoustic similarity effect are two clear signatures of speech coding in short-term memory, they may correspond to two different dimensions of immediate memory. The former suggests an active process (either of rehearsal when the input is speech or of encoding and rehearsal in the case of written input) weighted down by longer words, whereas the latter is presented as a passive store where similarity between neighbours generates confusion leading to impaired recall (Baddeley, 1986). These various aspects of phonological memory have generated many attempts at finding a locus of memory impairments in poor readers. To summarise the available evidence we mention a couple of highlights. No difference has been found to exist between length of the articulatory loop as such and age or developmental language impairment (Hulme & Mackenzie, 1992). Contrary to initial suspicions, it is now clear that poor readers do encode verbal input phonologically. Their serial recall performance is affected by phonetic similarity of the list items and they do show a word-length effect (Gathercole & Baddeley, 1990). One intriguing recent finding that partly explains earlier contradictory findings with the phonological similarity effect in poor readers is that the negative effect of phonological similarity increases with age (Hulme, 1984).

This newer version of the phonological memory model has been applied to understanding memory problems in language-impaired children. Against this background, Gathercole and Baddeley (1990) argue that the locus of the memory impairment must be the passive phonological input store, a proposal compatible with the repeated observation that no other structural part of working memory seems to be radically impaired in poor readers. However, Hulme challenges the need to appeal to a separate input store, arguing that the specific data requiring it can be dealt with by the single notion of an articulatory loop. Confusability would thus be a matter of relative difference in articulatory features as is the case with acoustically similar items (Hulme & Mackenzie, 1992). As a matter of fact, the notion of acoustic similarity is somewhat inappropriate here as we are talking about phonological memory processes and consequently, what must be at stake is phonetic similarity, and thereby independent of input modality whether acoustic or visual. Whether phonetic underdetermination and its consequence, phonetic confusability, has its locus in memory, whether in the phonological input store, or in articulatory rehearsal is a matter for later concern. No doubt it will be hard to separate, conceptually as well as empirically, issues of phonological memory and issues of speech representation per se. Looking at memory for linguistic material in two modalities might be of some help.

Similarities Between Visual and Auditory Input Modalities for Speech in Immediate Memory

Auditory input is not the only source of speech information. As a matter of fact, for normal subjects, whether in normal or in poor auditory input conditions, as well as for subjects with sensorial deficits, lip-reading contributes significantly to speech understanding (Summerfield, 1987; Massaro, 1987; Campbell, 1989). An opening for the notion of development in visual speech processing was made by data from Massaro and his colleagues (Massaro, Thompson, Barron, & Laren, 1986) showing clearly that visual speech perception develops over time. Summerfield (1991) has shown that large individual variations notwithstanding, lip-reading skill is not related to general intellectual abilities but seems to be modular, together with linguistic competence in general. Although we are presently still unclear about the visual speech processor, just as we are about the auditory speech processor or about the mechanism whereby visual and auditory input combine, there is general agreement that both input modalities share computational resources such as might be provided by a common abstract speech representations of a speech module. Against this background we conjectured that when a memory deficit would be observed with auditorily presented verbal material, a similar deficit would also show up in visual speech processing (e.g. de Gelder & Vroomen, 1988). Besides, the fact of the multimodality of speech input raises the issue whether populations suffering from perceptual or representational problems would gain an advantage from concurrent presentation in two modalities. For example, one might imagine that the extra visual information in audio-visual speech would boost performance compared with auditory only presentation.

The immediate serial recall paradigm offers a chance for an in-depth exploration of memory impairments. Recent evidence suggests clearly that immediate serial recall has two characteristics—recency and suffix effects—that might very well be speech-specific in the sense that they are only observed when the incoming information is coded as speech (see Crowder & Surprenant, Chapter 3). Results of an earlier study with normal subjects showed that processing of heard and of lip-read speech exhibit clear similarities. Recency occurs for lip-read input as it is long known to occur for heard input. This fact underscores the similarities between heard and lip-read speech and it thereby makes a study of memory for speech presented in another modality than the more standard auditory one a worthwhile tool. Moreover, it is generally agreed that this symmetry between the heard and lip-read input modalities reflects a common underlying linguistic interpretation of these immediate memory phenomena. From this perspective the finding of a symmetrical impairment in memory for heard and lip-read speech would surely be understandable.

The Why's of Poor Memory and its Persistence over Time

To summarise so far, immediate memory as examined by the serial recall paradigm for heard as well as lip-read material exhibits a couple of characteristic aspects like good recall of the earliest items (primacy), good recall of the last item (recency), and in between poorer recall of the intermediate terms. Absence of recency would reflect poor phonological storage in working memory. The few studies with adult dyslexics, most of them presenting neuropsychological case studies, have not yielded a clear picture. Campbell and Butterworth (1985) reported a case (RE) of developmental dyslexia. RE showed good speech perception together with impaired phonological memory as manifested in the absence of a word-length effect and a phonetic similarity effect, as well as absence of recency, which is of particular interest for the present study. In the domain of acquired disorders this possibility of a dissociation between speech perception and verbal memory has been debated since the patient first presented by Warrington and Shallice (1969). A recent study by Martin and Breedin (1992) of patients with short-term memory deficits presents clear evidence in favour of such a dissociation between memory and speech perception. Of course, whether any symmetry should be expected between developmental and acquired disorders as concerns the relation between speech perception and phonological processing disorders is very much an open issue. And before dealing with it, a clear picture is needed on the memory abilities in adults who suffered from developmental reading disorders.

EXPERIMENT 1

The first experiment was undertaken in order to obtain a systematic picture of serial recall for digits that were heard, lip-read, or heard-plus-lip-read in poor readers and normal children matched on chronological age. Experiment 2 investigated serial recall of normal adults with adults who had suffered from reading backwardness since childhood.

Method and Results

Subjects. Two groups were tested: a group of 12 poor readers (10 male, 2 female) and a control group of 12 subjects individually matched on chronological age with the poor readers (7 male, 5 female). All subjects were given two reading tests that required reading aloud Dutch real words (the Brus 1-minute test) or pseudowords in 1 minute. The results on these tests are presented in Table 7.1. On the standardised word-reading test, poor readers were lagging more than two years behind their age matches.

Design and Stimuli. A video of a speaker reciting digit lists was recorded and previously used in de Gelder and Vroomen (1992). In the heard-plus-lip-read presentation, one could hear the speaker as well as watch her lips move. For the lip-read presentation, the sound track was deleted and subjects had to rely entirely on lip-reading. For the heard-only presentation, a soundtrack of the digits was recorded and inserted into the video tape showing the speaker's face while she was sitting quietly. Lists consisted of five monosyllabic digits. The end of the lists could be followed by a speech suffix (the word "stop") or a pure tone. The speech suffix was presented in either the heard-only, lip-read, or heard-plus-lip-read mode. Standard serial-recall instructions were given to the subjects.

Figure 7.1 displays the mean proportion correct recall as a function of presentation mode and serial position for the two groups. Poor readers performed worse than controls, but given this overall difference, their performance showed all the typical characteristics of normal subjects. Lip-read lists were more difficult to recall than lists presented in the other modalities, and suffixes interfered with recall, particularly at the final serial positions.

An ANOVA on the proportion of correct responses indicated that recall of poor readers was worse than that of controls [$F(1,22) = 27.79$, $P < 0.001$]. There were main effects of the presentation mode of the list [$F(2,44) = 69.67$, $P < 0.001$], of the suffix [$F(3,66) = 15.61$, $P < .001$], and serial position [$F(4,88) = 47.36$, $P < 0.001$]. The interactions between presentation mode of the list and suffix [$F(6,132) = 2.40$, $P < 0.05$], and list and serial position [$F(8, 176) = 2.80$, $P < 0.01$] were significant, as were the interactions between group and serial position

TABLE 7.1
Details of the Poor Readers and the Chronological Age (CA) Control Group

		Age (Year; month)		*Reading Words*		*Reading Pseudowords*	
Group	*N*	Mean	Range	Mean	Range	Mean	Range
Poor readers	12	10;2	9;4–11;4	24.4	5–39	11.3	3–16
CA	12	10;2	9;4–11;4	73.6	50–101	45.1	31–62

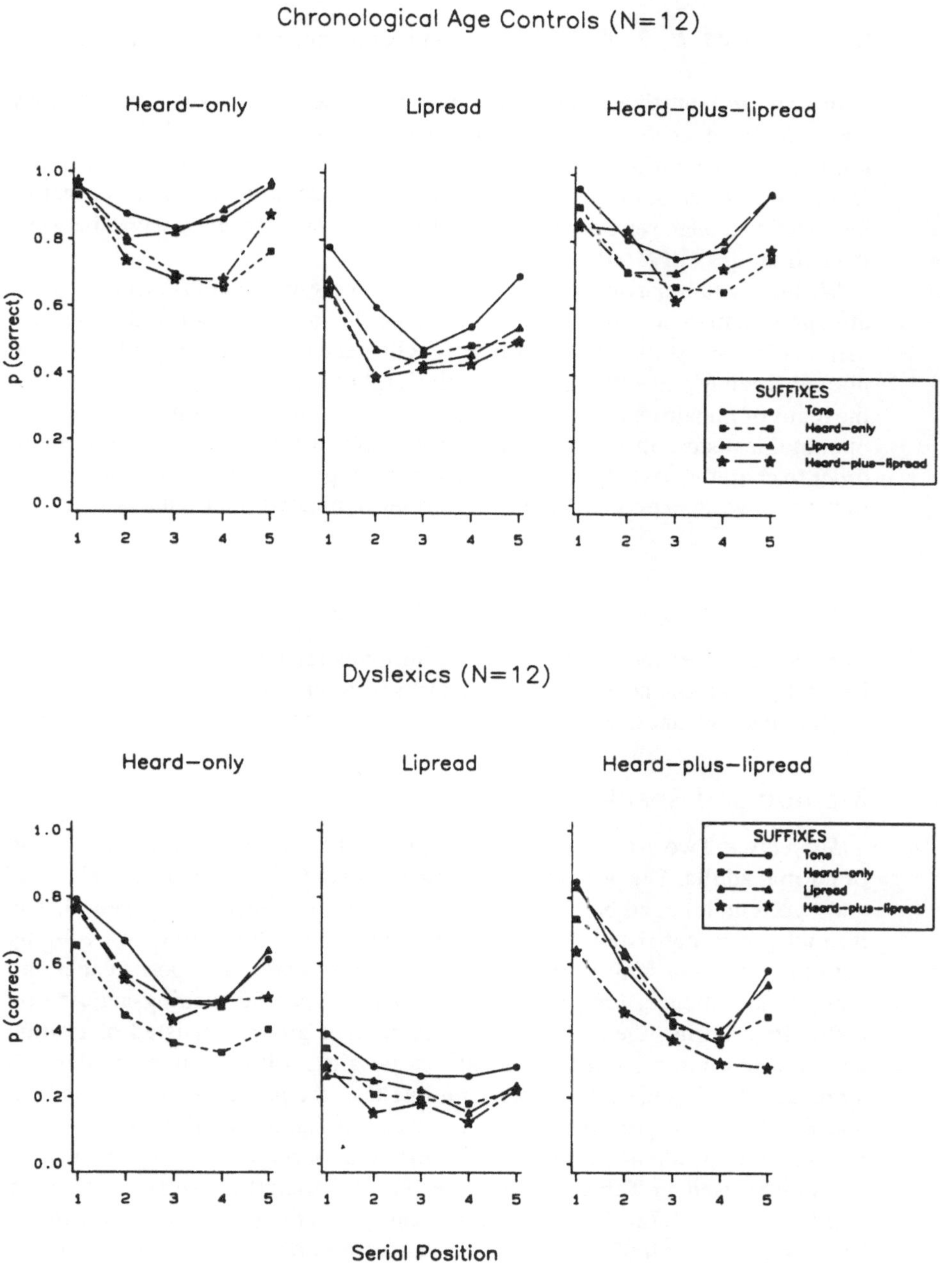

FIG 7.1 Mean proportion of correct recall of the poor readers and the control group for heard, lip-read and heard-plus-lip-read lists.

[$F(4,88) = 4.47$, $P < 0.002$], and between group, modality of the list, and serial position [$F(8,176 = 4.81$, $P < 0.001$].

In order to investigate the recency part of the serial position curve, recency was calculated as the difference in proportion of correct recall between the ultimate and penultimate item. An ANOVA with groups as between-subjects factor and presentation mode of the list and suffix as within-subjects factors indicated that there were no significant differences in the recency scores between the two groups (all $P > 0.10$)

We briefly summarise the main findings, delaying an in-depth discussion until after presentation of Experiment 2. Experiment 1 shows that poor readers do have memory impairments with heard as well as lip-read presentation, while showing normal recency and suffix effects. At first sight then, these results suggest that the locus of impairment is not in the mechanisms or structural dimensions of the phonological store itself, as normal recency and suffix effects are observed. In order to chart the development of the memory impairment over time, we looked in the following experiment at the performance of adult poor readers.

EXPERIMENT 2

The second experiment was conducted to investigate short-term memory for heard, lip-read, and heard-plus-lip-read lists in adult subjects who suffered from reading backwardness during childhood and to compare it with normal adults.

Method and Results

Subjects. Two groups were tested: a group of adult poor readers and a group of normal adults. The poor readers group consisted of eight subjects (six male and two female) aged between 18;0 and 36;6 years (mean = 24;1 years). The normal group consisted of ten adults (seven male, three female), ranging between 25;3 and 46;0 years (mean age = 34;8 years). The poor readers all complained about a long and clear history of specific reading-acquisition difficulties during their childhood. The control group consisted of normal adults who were matched as closely as possible with the poor readers on attained school grades. The Brus 1-minute test, the pseudoword reading test, and RAVEN's progressive matrices were administered to all subjects of the normal adult group and to five subject of the poor readers group. The results are summarised in Table 7.2: Poor readers were slightly worse in reading words [($t(13) = 1.72$, $P = 0.10$], significantly worse in reading pseudowords [$t(13) = 5.54$, $P < 0.001$], whereas there was no difference in the raw scores on the RAVEN [($t(13) < 1$, n.s.].

Design and Stimuli. The same as in Experiment 1, except that the list length was seven instead of five items.

TABLE 7.2
Details of the Adult Poor Readers and the Adult Control Group

		Age (Year; month)		*Reading Words*		*Reading Nonsense Words*		*RAVEN*	
Group	*N*	Mean	Range	Mean	Range	Mean	Range	Mean	Range
Poor readers	8	24;1	18;0–36;6	79.4	58–103	36.8	26–54	52.2	49–58
Control	10	34;8	25;3–46;0	95.7	68–114	70.2	52–86	50.4	41–56

Figure 7.2 displays the mean proportion correct recall as a function of presentation mode and serial position for the two groups. As can be seen, recall of the poor readers was worse than that of the controls, particularly at the middle serial positions. Recency effects were present in both groups, and suffixes interfered with recency.

Poor readers had poorer overall recall than controls [$F(1,16) = 8.61, P < 0.01$]. There were main effects of presentation mode of the list [$F(2,32) = 18.67, P<0.001$], suffix [$F(3,48) = 15.05, P < 0.001$], and serial position [$F(6,96) = 34.27, P < 0.001$]. Of interest was an interaction between group and serial position [$F(6,96) = 4.28, P < 0.001$]. Inspection of Fig. 7.2 suggests that, compared with normal readers, poor readers performed particularly worse at middle serial positions, but not on the initial or final ones. There was a significant interaction between suffix and serial position [$F(18,288) = 4.16, P < 0.001$], and a significant second-order interaction between group, suffix, and serial position [$F(18,288) = 1.83, P < 0.03$]. The interaction between presentation mode of the list, suffix, and serial [$F(36,567) = 1.85, P < 0.002$] was also significant.

The amount of recency was calculated as in Experiment 1 by subtracting the proportion of correct recall of the penultimate item from the final one. An ANOVA on the recency scores showed that suffixes interfered with recency [$F(3,48) = 6.37, P < 0.001$], and that the effect of a suffix depended on the modality of the list [$F(6, 96) = 2.37, P < 0.05$]. There was also a significant interaction between group and suffix [$F(3,48) = 4.92, P < 0.01$]. As can be seen in Fig. 7.2, poor readers had larger recency effects in the no-suffix condition, but this may be caused by the fact that recall of the final item in control subjects is at ceiling in the no-suffix conditions.

GENERAL DISCUSSION

The major question that motivated this study was whether the memory impairments of poor readers already documented for heard speech would also be observed for lip-read speech, and whether this would be a permanent feature

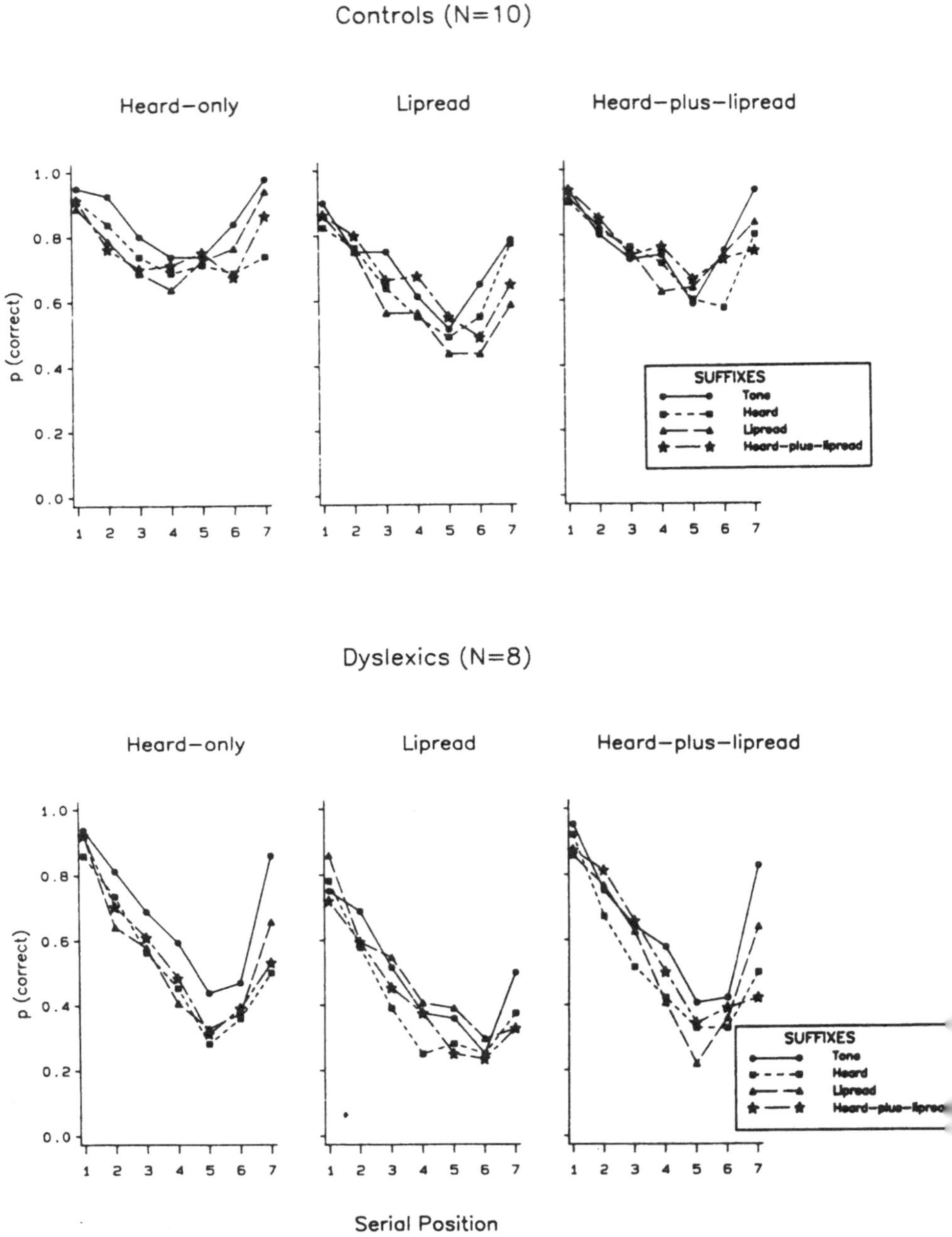

FIG 7.2 Mean proportion of correct recall of the adult poor readers and the control group for heard, lip-read, and heard-plus-lip-read lists.

of poor readers' memory into adult age. If so, the symmetry across two physically very different input modalities would clearly support the notion of a phonological deficit. Of course, our interest was not just establishing the symmetry of the memory impairment. We expected that the comparison between heard and lip-read speech, the pattern of recency effects, and the strength of suffix effects within and across modalities would throw new light on the possible concommitants of the memory deficit. The present results, taken together, are compatible with the idea that reading deficits are associated with a critical impairment in phonological memory but, at same time, they establish clearly that the impairment apparently leaves unaffected the classic signature of immediate memory for spoken material, i.e. the recency effect. The obvious question raised again by these data, as by all the previous results on immediate memory impairments, is what might explain this impaired memory of poor readers. Some specific aspects of this study throw light on that issue.

We first turn to the critical difference between normal and poor readers. A major finding of the present study is that overall recall performance is worse in the poor readers, whether young or adult, compared to controls. This result does not come as a surprise, but no ready explanation is available. To introduce the discussion on the more critical aspects, we submit that poor readers are not qualitatively different from normal readers in recall of lists, whether heard, lip-read, or heard-plus-lip-read, that is if one discounts for the poorer level of performance in the middle positions. Specifically, we see that the shape of the recall curves is the same, that primacy and recency effects are of comparable size, and that a suffix does have the same effect on recency as in normal readers. This comes out very clearly in the data from the adult populations. We submit then that some aspects of the poor readers' performance, which one might call "structural" for the time being, are present as clearly in poor readers as they are in normal ones. The recall curves of the latter do show clear primacy and recency effects, and in lists with a suffix we note suffix effects. Speaking at a descriptive level, the only critical difference between the groups is thus one of overall digit span. Our systematic finding contrasts with what previous little there is known about adult developmental dyslexics. Campbell and Butterworth (1985) did find a span reduction of two digits with heard lists and hardly any recency, in contrast with what is observed here both for the young and the adult group. Campbell and Butterworth suggest that their subject might have a deficit in input phonology, but confess to being unable to specify whether this is a matter of representations that are poorly specified, poorly represented, or poorly accessed. Which of these possibilities is favoured by the present results?

The present results do not directly contribute, one way or the other, to the notion that poor readers' memory is a function of poor representations. Thus, there is no reason to suspect that serial recall in poor readers is less efficient because the processes involved in the phonetic analysis of speech are more noisy, so that the phonological representations are less discriminable from each other during storage, rehearsal, or retrieval. Poor input representations or imperfect extraction of phonological information are thus not at stake in dyslexics' poor memory performance. We first note that there was no advantage of bi-modal over auditory-only presentation in the poor reader groups. Thus, providing extra visual information did not improve poor readers' memory performance. Moreover, the hypothetical condition of less discriminability among input representations might actually be realised when subjects have to remember phonetically similar memory items, like for instance in the case of rhyme. It is well known that phonological similarity leads to poorer recall in normals, and, indeed, the phonological similarity effect has also been observed in children with reading disorders (Gathercole & Baddeley, 1990), which might suggest that poor phonological representations are not the major cause of reduced span in poor readers. Even more convincing is the fact that the phonological similarity effect is mostly confined to the final serial positions: Recency is almost absent in phonologically similar items, whether heard or lip-read, but primacy is unaffected (de Gelder & Vroomen, 1994; see also Watkins, Watkins, & Crowder, 1974). One would therefore expect that if reduced discriminability were the cause of the reduced span, it would show up in the recency part of the serial position curve. It is, however, clear from the present data that the span reduction of the poor readers is not in the recency part of the serial position curve, but that it is much more confined to the middle items.

The basic question on the possible causes of poor memory becomes thus much more focused if we admit that poor performance occurs against a background of memory processes that seem structurally very normal in the sense that they exhibit all the properties that are presently taken to be the signature of immediate memory for spoken language. The present study establishes this finding very clearly. Let us examine two further issues it raises. First, the present data on the similarity of performance in the lip-read and the auditory modality may be integrated in the more general context of modality effects in immediate serial recall. Second, these modality effects must be related to current explanations of poor phonological memory. Data from this study together with other results from experiments on modality effects might suggest an explanation for the reduced digit span of poor readers. A candidate here is the notion of efficiency of rehearsal and, what is by some perceived as its cause, speech articulation rate. We now examine those two issues.

The comparison between heard and lip-read speech belongs to a larger framework of studies examining the effect of modality of presentation on recall. The classical notion of the modality effect refers to the robust observation of a recall advantage of the terminal item of a memory list as is observed in the auditory, but not in written presentation. The original explanation of this effect invoked an echoic memory facilitation exclusively for the last-presented auditory item. The most elaborate approach came from the theory of pre-acoustic storage defended by Crowder and Morton

(1969) in the late 1960s. This approach elaborates on the notion that the last-item advantage derives from sensorial properties present in one modality, but not in the other. It is worth recalling this discussion in the present context because the very facts that challenged this notion of sensory-based advantage, i.e. strong recency effects with lip-read material, make the paradigm interesting for the study of memory of impaired readers. Indeed, there is no reason to believe that these subjects have an auditory impairment. As a matter of fact, presentation of lip-read lists can be used to investigate the linguistic as opposed to the sensory locus of the deficit in patients (Howard & Franklin, 1990). The issue of a phonological impairment is, in contrast, still a definite possibility. The similarity observed here between lip-read and auditory presentation fits in well with a theoretical approach that emphasises the abstract linguistic nature of the mechanisms responsible for recency effects. As far as this storage of the last item is based on an abstract phonological code, no impairment seems to exist in the poor reader population. It is thus not surprising that we observed in another study that poor readers do fully show the classical modality effect (de Gelder, Vroomen, & Popelier, 1994).

Digit span is related to rehearsal and more specifically seems to be a function of the speed of articulation that increases with age in normal subjects, but not with the same ratio in language-disordered children. One question is then whether the concept of speed of articulation can serve as an explanation for memory impairments in poor readers. The similarity between lip-read and auditory presentation must be based on phonological storage in both cases. With this approach we can also analyse the similarities in overall recall across formats. Rehearsal, for example as pictured in a theory of the phonological loop, explains well the typical pre-recency shape of recall curves. Such rehearsal engages phonological representation processes. The notion advanced recently is that rehearsal speed increases with age but might increase at a slower pace in poor readers and remain at a lower platform in adult poor readers. So far we have conducted an indirect investigation of this effect in the adult readers. We indeed observed that when normal subjects were given a concurrent articulation task, performance dropped by an overall 15% correct and their recall curves were now virtually identical with those of adult poor readers who were not engaged in a concurrent articulation task (de Gelder & Vroomen, submitted). It indicates that poor rehearsal processes might play a major role in the impoverished memory performance of poor readers.

ACKNOWLEDGEMENTS

Preparation of this chapter was partly supported by the Ministry of Education and Scientific Research of the Belgian French Community (Concerted Research Action "Language Processing in Different Modalities").

REFERENCES

Baddeley, A.D. (1966). Short-term memory for word sequences as a function of acoustic, semantic and formal similarity. *Quarterly Journal of Experimental Psychology, 18*, 362–365.

Baddeley, A.D. (1986). *Working memory*. Oxford University Press.

Baddeley. A.D. (1990). *Human memory: Theory and practice*. Hillsdale, NJ: Lawrence Erlbaum Associates Inc.

Baddeley, A.D., & Hitch, G. (1974). Working memory. In G.A. Bower (Ed.), *Recent advances in learning and motivation* (Vol. 8). New York: Academic Press.

Bertelson, P. (1986). The onset of literacy: Liminal remarks. *Cognition, 24*, 1–30.

Bertelson, P., & de Gelder, B. (1989). Learning about reading from illiterates. In A.M. Galaburda (Ed.), *From reading to neurons*. Cambridge, MA: MIT Press.

Bertelson, P., & de Gelder, B. (1990). The emergence of phonological awareness. In I. Mattingly & M. Studdert-Kennedy (Eds.), *The motor theory of speech perception*. Hillsdale, NJ: Lawrence Erlbaum Associates Inc.

Brady, S., Mann, V., & Schmidt, R. (1987). Errors in short-term memory for good and poor readers. *Memory and Cognition, 15*, 444–453.

Campbell, R. (1989). Lipreading. In A.W. Young & H.D. Ellis (Eds.), *Handbook of research on face processing*. Amsterdam: North-Holland.

Campbell, R., & Butterworth, B. (1985). Phonological dyslexia and dysgraphia in a highly literate subject: A developmental case with associated deficits of phonemic processing and awareness. *Quarterly Journal of Experimental Psychology, 37A*, 435–475.

Conrad, R. (1964). Acoustic confusion in immediate memory. *British Journal of Psychology, 55*, 75–84.

Crowder, R.G., & Morton, J. (1969). Precategorical acoustic storage (PAS). *Perception and Psychophysics*, 5, 363–373.

Crowder, R.G., & Surprenant, A.M. (this volume). On the linguistic module in auditory memory. In B. de Gelder & J. Morais (Eds.), *Speech and reading* (pp. 49–64). Hove, UK: Lawrence Erlbaum Associates Ltd.

de Gelder, B. (1990). Phonological awareness, misidentification, and multiple identities. In J.A. Edmondson, C. Feagin, & P. Mülhauser (Eds.), *Development and diversity: Linguistic variation across time and space*. Arlington: Texas Publications.

de Gelder, B., & Vroomen, J. (1988, August). *Bimodal speech perception in young dyslexics*. 6th Australian Language and Speech Conference, Sydney.

de Gelder, B., & Vroomen, J. (1991). Phonological deficits: Beneath the surface of reading-acquisition problems. *Psychological Research, 53*, 88–97.

de Gelder, B., & Vroomen, J. (1992). Abstract versus modality-specific memory representations in processing auditory and visual speech. *Memory and Cognition, 20*, 533–538.

de Gelder, B., & Vroomen, J. (in press). Memory for consonants versus vowels in heard and lipread speech. *Journal of Memory and Language*.

de Gelder, B., & Vroomen, J. (submitted). Serial recall of poor and normal readers with concurrent articulatory suppression.

de Gelder, B., Vroomen, J., & Popelier, T. (1994). *Serial recall of adult dyslexics as a function of input modality*. Paper presented at the 12th European Workshop on Cognitive Neuropsychology, Bressanone, Italy, 23rd–28th January 1994.

Frumkin, B., & Anisfeld, M. (1977). Semantic and surface codes in the memory of deaf children. *Cognitive Psychology, 9*, 475–493.

Gathercole, S.E., & Baddeley, A.D. (1990). Phonological memory deficits in language disordered children: Is there a causal connection? *Journal of Memory and Language, 29*, 336–360.

Howard, D., & Franklin, S. (1990). Dissociations between component mechanisms in short-term memory: Evidence from brain-damaged patients. In D.E. Meyer & S. Kornblum (Eds.), *Attention and performance, Vol. XIV*. Cambridge, MA: MIT Press.

Hulme, C. (1984). Development differences in the effects of acoustic similarity on memory span. *Developmental Psychology, 20*, 650–652.
Hulme, C., & Mackenzie, S. (1992). *Working memory and severe learning difficulties*. Hillsdale, NJ: Lawrence Erlbaum Associates Inc.
Liberman, A.M. (this volume). The relation of speech to reading and writing. In B. de Gelder & J. Morais (Eds.), *Speech and reading* (pp.17–31). Hove, UK: Lawrence Erlbaum Associates Ltd.
Liberman, I.Y., Shankweiler, D., Liberman, A.M., Fowler, C., & Fischer, F.W. (1977). Phonetic segmentation and recoding in the beginning reader. In A.S. Reber & D. Scarborough (Eds.), *Towards a psychology of reading: The proceedings of the CUNY conference*. Hillsdale, NJ: Lawrence Erlbaum Associates Inc.
Martin, R.C., & Breedin, S.D. (1992). Dissociations between speech perception and phonological short-term memory deficits. *Cognitive Neuropsychology, 9*, 509–534.
Massaro, D.W. (1987). *Speech perception by ear and eye: A paradigm for psychological inquiry*. Hillsdale, NJ: Lawrence Erlbaum Associates Inc.
Massaro, D.W., Thompson, L.A., Barron, B., & Laren, E. (1986). Developmental changes in visual and auditory contributions to speech perception. *Journal of Experimental Child Psychology, 41*, 93–113.
Seidenberg, M.S., & McClelland, J.L. (1989). A distributed developmental model of word recognition and naming. *Psychological Review, 96*, 523–568.
Seymour, P.H.K. (1986). *Cognitive analysis of dyslexia*. London: Routledge & Kegan Paul.
Shankweiler, D., Liberman, I.Y., Mark, L.S., Fowler, C.A., & Fischer, F.W. (1979). The speech code and learning to read. *Journal of Experimental Psychology: Human Learning and Memory, 5*, 531–545.
Summerfield, A.Q. (1987). Some preliminaries to a comprehensive account of audio-visual speech perception. In B. Dodd & R. Campbell (Eds.), *Hearing by eye: The psychology of lipreading*. Hillsdale, NJ: Lawrence Erlbaum Associates Inc.
Summerfield, A.Q. (1991). Visual perception of phonetic gestures. In I.G. Mattingley & M. Studdert-Kennedy (Eds.), *Modularity and the motor theory of speech perception*. Hillsdale, NJ: Lawrence Erlbaum Associates Inc.
Wagner, R.K., & Torgesen, J.K. (1987). The nature of phonological processing and its causal role in the acquisition of reading skills. *Psychological Bulletin, 101*, 192–212.
Warrington, E.K., & Shallice, T. (1969). The selective impairment of auditory verbal short-term memory. *Brain, 92*, 885–896.
Watkins, M.J., Watkins, O.C., & Crowder, R.G. (1974). The modality effect in free and serial recall as a function of phonological similarity. *Journal of Verbal Learning and Verbal Behavior, 13*, 430–447.

III READING IN DIFFERENT ORTHOGRAPHIES

8 Cognitive Processes in Writing Chinese Characters: Basic Issues and Some Preliminary Data

Sam-Po Law
Institute of History and Philology, Academia Sinica, Taiwan

Alfonso Caramazza
The Johns Hopkins University, Baltimore, MD, USA

INTRODUCTION

The characteristics of the Chinese writing system, in contrast with alphabetic writing systems such as English, have attracted much attention from researchers who are interested in reading and writing. The main question is whether the cognitive processes underlying reading and writing in a logographic system such as Chinese differ from those in an alphabetic system. If the answer is positive, what is the nature of the differences, in the whole organisation of the cognitive system and in the types of representations computed within each component of the system?

The purpose of this chapter is three-fold. In the first section, a discussion of the basic features of the orthographic system in Chinese is presented. We will focus only on those characteristics that we consider relevant to cognitive functioning; their theoretical significance will be outlined along the way. The second section of the chapter describes a research project designed to address questions about the organisation and structure of the cognitive system that underlies the ability to write Chinese; in particular, we describe a test battery containing various lists constructed to examine writing performance in brain-damaged subjects. In the third section, we will present some preliminary data of the project. The data will be discussed from the perspective of the issues raised in the first section.

Bold numbers in square brackets in text refer to Chinese characters in the table on p.145 Numbers in parentheses refer to numbered examples in text.

CHARACTERISTICS OF CHINESE SCRIPT AND THEIR ROLES IN PROCESSING

Internal Structure of Chinese Characters

All Chinese logographs are monosyllabic. Although Chinese is a lexical tone language,[1] in which variations in pitch signify differences in lexical meaning, tones are not marked orthographically. In addition, the great majority of characters are morphemes. With the shift from monosyllabic to bisyllabic words in the language, most characters in current usage are bound morphemes.[2]

Chinese characters are made up of spatial arrangements of strokes. There are eight major types of strokes (Hoosain, 1991), as shown in (1) together with their names.

(1) Major types of strokes composing Chinese characters

a. 點 ㇔
"dot"

b. 橫 一
"horizontal stroke"

c. 直 丨
"vertical stroke"

d. 曲 ㄑ
"bent stroke"

e. 撇 丿
"stroke made in the lower left direction"

f. 捺 ㇏
"downstroke slanting toward the right"

g. 挑 ㇂
"downstroke slanting toward the right ending with a hook"

h. 鉤 亅
"hook"

Finer distinctions produce approximately 20 strokes (Wang, 1973). In general, a stroke is a line which is completed every time the pen leaves the paper. These strokes combine to form radicals, which may further combine to form more

---

[1] There are six distinct tones in Cantonese Chinese, including four level tones (high, mid, mid-low, and low) and two rising tones (high and low). They can be represented numerically as "55" for high level tone, "33" for mid level tone, "22" for mid-low level tone, "11" for low level tone, "35" for high rising tone, and "13" for low rising tone. Mandarin Chinese has four distinct tones, level, rising, dipping and falling.

[2] However, the most frequently occurring words are monosyllabic. This phenomenon has been referred to as the "Monosyllabic myth" (De Francis, 1950).

1	力	30	壁	59	移動	88	尼古丁
2	金	31	氵	60	討論	89	卡路里
3	虫	32	糹	61	貧窮	90	士多啤梨
4	艹	33	木	62	高低	91	盤尼西林
5	氵	34	扌	63	上落	92	涼
6	扌	35	艹	64	出入	93	良
7	寸	36	檯燈	65	父母	94	梁
8	牙	37	牙膏	66	兄弟	95	量
9	止	38	油船	67	檯燈	96	涼 in 涼快
10	土	39	皮鞋	68	盞	97	躉
11	王	40	肝病	69	張	98	跌
12	米	41	飛機	70	毛筆	99	失
13	湖	42	炒飯	71	枝	100	僕
14	氵	43	跑鞋	72	條	101	菐
15	胡	44	笑聲	73	飛機	102	日
16	古	45	藍天	74	架	103	口
17	月	46	喜劇	75	葡萄	104	⺮
18	木	47	飛跑	76	蘿蔔	105	艹
19	杉	48	焦黃	77	蝴蝶	106	又
20	松	49	拋上	78	螞蟻	107	阝
21	桃	50	放下	79	蜥蜴	108	爪
22	梨	51	做完	80	蜘蛛	109	瓜
23	檯	52	猜中	81	蟋蟀	110	才
24	椅	53	放大	82	玻璃	111	寸
25	土	54	扯爛	83	玫瑰	112	𠂉
26	坡	55	性急	84	鸚鵡	113	婆
27	地	56	頭痛	85	咖啡	114	氵
28	塔	57	彈琴	86	結他	115	女
29	堡	58	唱歌	87	巴士	116	街音

complex characters. In most dictionaries, one may find around 200 radicals.[3] They are used to organise lexical entries. Each character in a dictionary is decomposed into a radical (normally the part that is written first in producing a character, hence, usually the left or the top part of a logograph) and a remainder. Many of these radicals are also characters on their own. About 90% of characters are phonetic compounds. They are composed of a signific,[4] which indicates some meaning aspect of the character containing it, and a phonetic, which provides a clue to the pronunciation of the whole character. The diagram in (2) shows that radicals can be functionally categorised into four groups.

(2)

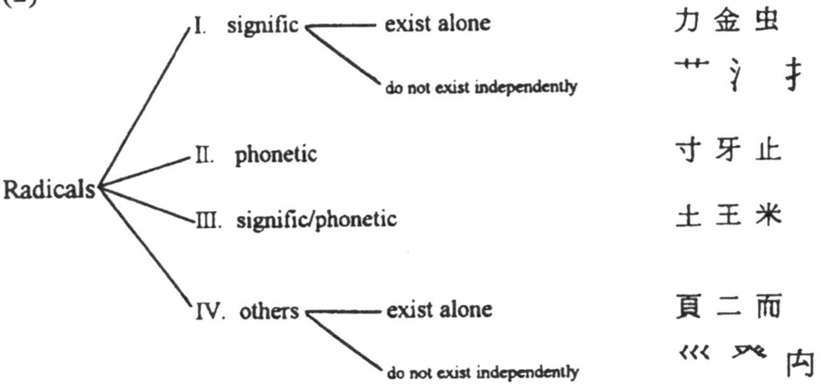

Among these radicals, there are those that function unambiguously as significs: (the orthographic forms in group I, i.e. [**1**] "energy", [**2**] "gold", [**3**] "worm", [**4**] (a signific related to "plants"), [**5**] (a signific related to "liquid"), and [**6**] (a signific related to "hand"); those that are unambiguously phonetics: the forms in group II, i.e. [**7**] "inch", [**8**] "tooth", and [**9**] "stop"; and those that appear as phonetics in some characters and significs in others: the forms in group III, i.e. [**10**] "earth", [**11**] "a last name", and [**12**] "rice".[5] It should be noted that the radicals that act as phonetics constitute only a subset of the phonetics in the language because

---

[3] We are not prepared to make the assumption that these radicals correspond to basic units of writing; however, due to their prevalence in discussions of Chinese orthography, and the fact that they function as the entry points in most dictionaries, we find it convenient, at this point, to use the term "radical" in describing the structure of Chinese characters.

[4] In the literature on the Chinese writing system, one may encounter discussions in which "radical" and "signific" are used interchangeably. In this paper, the term "radical" is used to refer to the set of constituents that can be found at the beginning of most dictionaries, and the term "signific" to those radicals that are associated with some meaning.

[5] Lian (1985) examined 280 phonetic components and found that only six phonetics do not have independent existence. This means that the great majority of radicals that can function as the phonetic of a character — groups II and III in (2) — are existing characters.

many phonetics are composed of two or more radicals. For example, the character **[13]** [wu] meaning "lake" is composed of a signific **[14]** related to the concept of "liquid" and a character **[15]** [wu]; the latter character itself consists of a phonetic **[16]** [gu] and a signific **[17]** related to the meaning "period". On the other hand, all significs are radicals. Finally, the "others" category (group IV) includes radicals that never appear as either phonetics or significs in characters. This category, like the "signific" category (group I), contains forms that are existing characters and ones that do not have independent existence. In the following, we will first consider some facts about the phonetic and its significance in processing. This will be followed by a discussion of the signific and its possible role in the processing of single characters.

Phonetic Component

Characteristics. There are approximately 800 phonetics in Chinese (Hoosain, 1991). In modern-day usage, about 26%[6] of phonetic compounds have the same pronunciation as their phonetics (Zhu, 1987). A survey of the activation regions[7] of 201 phonetics by Fang, Horng, and Tzeng (1986) found that in 18% of these regions the pronunciation of the phonetic is identical to the pronunciation of all the phonetic compounds containing it. In addition, for regions that are associated with two or more phonological forms, 67% of the time the sound of the phonetic belongs to the dominant phonological group, hence the potential use of the phonetic as a phonological cue. Furthermore, in situations where a phonetic compound does not share the same sound with its phonetic, they often differ only by the aspiration of their first consonant, or the first consonant as a whole, in addition to tonal difference. In sum, phonetics vary in the degree to which they dominate the pronunciation of the characters containing them; the phonological relationship between a phonetic compound and its phonetic can be one of identity, similarity, or unrelatedness.

With respect to position of occurrence, the majority of phonetic compounds have their phonetic component on the right,[8] but a phonetic can also appear on the left, the top, or the bottom of a character. In addition, most phonetics may

[6] Although the statistics provided here come from studies on Mandarin Chinese, based on one of the authors' intuition as a native speaker of Cantonese Chinese (S.-P. Law), the use of phonetics as cues to the pronunciation of a unfamiliar phonetic compound is also significant to the Cantonese reader.

[7] An activation region contains all characters sharing the same phonetic component.

appear in different locations within characters, as illustrated in (3) a, b, and c; a small number of them occupy a fixed position, as shown in (4) a and b. The latter also tend to occur on the right side of a character.

Role in Processing. The properties of the phonetic as just described naturally raise the question of whether it has a role in reading Chinese. Fang, Horng, and Tzeng (1986) found that the pronunciation latencies of characters

(3)	Phonetic	Phonetic compound		
a.	合 hap 22[9] "to join"	盒 hap 22 "box"	給 kap 55 "to give"	鴿 gap 33 "pigeon"
b.	方 fong 55 "square"	芳 fong 55 "aromatic"	仿 fong 35 "to imitate"	放 fong 13 "to release"
c.	亡 mong 11 "to die"	忘 mong 11 "to forget"	芒 mong 55 "mango"	忙 mong 11 "busy"

[8] This is true of radicals that function only as phonetics, as well as those that may appear as significs in some characters and phonetics in others. Some Cantonese examples of signific/phonetic radicals are given in (i).

i)	Radical	As Signific		As Phonetic	
	土 tou 35 "earth"	坑 ha:ng 55 "ditch"	壁 bik 55 "wall"	吐 tou 33 "to spit"	杜 dou 22 "a last name"
	馬 ma 13 "horse"	騾 lϕy 11 "mule"	駕 ga: 33 "to drive"	媽 ma: 55 "mother"	碼 ma: 13 "yard"
	米 mai 13 "rice"	糊 wu 11 "paste"	粉 fan 35 "powder"	迷 mai 11 "to bewitch"	咪 mei 55 "a meow"

(4)

	Phonetic	Phonetic compound		
a.	少 siu 35 "few"	秒 miu 13 "second (time)"	眇 miu 13 "tiny"	妙 miu 22 "amusing"
b.	童 tung 11 "child"	膧 dzung 35 "swollen"	鐘 dzung 55 "clock"	瞳 tung 11 "pupil (of an eye)"

containing a phonetic with high consistency values[9] were significantly shorter than those with low consistency values. In naming characters that serve as phonetics in phonetic compounds, the consistency effect was again observed. High-consistency simple characters were named faster than low-consistency simple characters. Finally, naming latencies for pseudocharacters composed of a commonly occurring signific and a phonetic were shorter for those containing a high-consistency phonetic than for those with a low-consistency phonetic. These results provide strong evidence for the important function of the phonetic in reading.[10]

However, one may make an even stronger case for the use of the phonetic. It has been noted that there are many radicals, which are characters themselves and therefore have a pronunciation, that never appear as a phonetic in any complex character. If phonetic components are distinguished from other nonphonetic radicals, it should be possible to demonstrate that pseudocharacters containing a nonphonetic radical and a signific are responded to differently from phonetic compounds (be they real lexical items or pseudocharacters). For instance, the former might produce long naming latency, as compared to the time taken in naming phonetic compounds, or the subjects might simply be reluctant to provide a pronunciation for such nonphonetic pseudocharacters. If this were the case, it would suggest that orthographic forms that function as phonetics are

---

[9] Consistency value indicates the extent to which an activation region, which includes all phonetic compounds sharing the same phonetic component *and* the phonetic component itself as a character, is dominated by a phonological form. A high consistency value means that most of the characters in a region have the same pronunciation.

[10] Fang, Horng and Tzeng account for the findings using the activation-sythesis model proposed by Glushko (1979); the findings are used as evidence against a dual-mechanism theory of reading. However, it does not seem to be the case that the activation-synthesis model exclusively explains the consistency phenomenon. The very notion of an activation region containing characters having the same phonetic testifies to the special role that the phonetic plays in reading. The findings are not inconsistent with a model in which the phonetics are elements underlying a nonlexical mechanism (or a grapheme-syllable conversion mechanism), which supports the reading of pseudo-phonetic compounds.

marked as such in the lexicon. There are some findings which may lend support to this view. Lian (1985) compared the naming latencies of three types of simple characters—(I) characters that function as the phonetic component in other characters and have a high consistency value, (II) characters that can occur as the phonetic in other characters but with a low consistency value, and (III) "nonphonetic" characters, which are graphs that do *not* serve as the phonetic component in other characters. The results were consistent with those in Fang, Horng, and Tzeng's study, in that characters of type (II) were named significantly more slowly than type (I); in addition, "nonphonetic" orthographs had longer response times than those in type (I), but shorter than characters in type (II), although the difference in reaction time between types (I) and (III), and that between types (II) and (III) did not reach significance.

Given the important function of the phonetic in reading, one may wonder about its significance in writing. To investigate its role in written production, the characteristics discussed so far need to be taken into consideration, i.e. the possible existence of an inventory of phonetic components in the language, the degree of similarity in pronunciation between a phonetic compound and its phonetic, the position in which a phonetic occurs, and its consistency value.

If only a subset of simple characters (which may consist of a single radical or a combination of radicals) is explored for the purpose of providing phonetic cues to the sound of more complex characters, one may raise the question of whether a distinction is made in the lexicon that separates these forms from nonphonetic pronounceable simple characters. Furthermore, one may wonder if these phonetics are marked for some special features, one being the position of occurrence. As mentioned earlier, within the set of orthographic forms that are used as phonetics, the majority of phonetic compounds have their phonetic on the right, which can be considered the "default" position for the phonetics. If phonetic components are spatially coded, then in cases where a subject has difficulty in producing a phonetic compound (as a result of impaired representation of the lexical entry in question, or unsuccessful accessing of the target character), several kinds of output are possible. It is possible that the identity of the phonetic is preserved but its position is not, resulting in phonetic component transposition. It is also possible that the identity of the phonetic is unavailable, and a lexical or a phonetic substitute is used. In the former situation, the substituting character may be similar in pronunciation to the target—the output is then a phonologically plausible error. In the latter situation, the element replacing the target phonetic may also be a phonetic, occurring in a position where it normally does.

The similarity in phonological form between a phonetic compound and its phonetic, and the consistency value of a phonetic component, may also play a role in written production. Again if a subject experiences difficulty in retrieving a phonetic compound, given two phonetics that are candidates for filling in the phonetic slot of the output character, it is plausible that the one with a higher consistency value has a higher probability of being selected.[11] In situations where the performances on phonetic compounds differing in degree of phonological similarity to their phonetic component are compared (assuming that the compounds to be produced are balanced for character frequency), it is plausible that the ones that are identical in sound with their phonetic are more likely to be produced correctly, as compared to the ones that are only similar in pronunciation to the phonetic, which in turn may result in better performance than for those phonetic compounds that bear no phonological resemblance with their phonetic.

In summary, factors such as the form in which phonetics are represented in the lexicon (whether they are distinguished from other pronounceable parts, and whether their position of occurrence is marked), the phonological similarity between phonetic components and compounds containing them, and the degree to which characters sharing a phonetic is associated with a single phonological form, may be involved in the processing of writing Chinese orthographs.

Signific Component

Characteristics. Before we begin to discuss the properties of the signific and its function in writing, it is important to note that the relationship between a signific and its associated conceptual content can be very general and vague. For example, the signific for wood with the form [**18**] appears in characters denoting different kinds of trees, such as [**19**] "fir" and [**20**] "pine", fruits, such as [**21**] "peach" and [**22**] "pear", and furniture that is normally made of wood, such as [**23**] "table" and [**24**] "chair"; the signific [**25**] meaning "earth" occurs in graphs related to natural formation, such as [**26**] "slope" and [**27**] "ground", a building or part of a building, e.g. [**28**] "tower", [**29**] "castle", and [**30**] "wall". It is important to keep the foregoing in mind so as to put into perspective the usefulness of the signific as a semantic cue to the meaning of a character.

Another point that needs to be clarified is that the context in which significs can occur is not limited to phonetic compounds, because there are characters which contain a signific and a remainder with no pronunciation. Some examples are given in (5).

(5)a. signific on the left

僕	抛	派	杉
buk 22	**pau 55**	**pai 33**	**tsa:m 33**
"servant"	**"to throw"**	**"to distribute"**	**"pine"**

[11] This would be the case if all factors involved are equal. In the scenario described in the text, one such factor is that characters containing one of these two competing phonetics have comparable frequencies of occurrence.

b. signific at the bottom

棄	桑
hei 33	song 55
"to give up"	"a kind of tree"

Although generally speaking, all significs have some associated meaning, they vary greatly in the degree to which a Chinese reader associates certain semantic properties with them. More specifically, for some significs native speakers do not hesitate to provide conceptual content to them, such as the ones in the left column in (6); whereas for others, a meaning may be given after taking into consideration the meanings of characters containing the particular signific in question, such as those in the right column in (6). The ability to arrive at a connected semantic notion may depend on the level of education of individual speakers. The former type of significs will henceforth be referred to as "strong" significs, and the latter type as "weak" significs. A strong signific usually appears in a large number of commonly occurring characters that are semantically related; by contrast, a weak signific occurs in a comparatively small number of characters that often do not occur frequently in the language.

(6)

Strong significs		Weak significs	
氵	liquid	彡	beauty
糸	silk/clothing/weaving	月	period
木	wood/plant	缶	container
扌	hand	戈	weapon/fighting
𧾷	foot	貝	money
艹	plant	阝	district/area

It is important to bear in mind that even for a strong signific, it is still possible to find characters whose meaning is not compatible with that of the signific in question. This is illustrated in (7) in which each row consists of six characters having the same signific. The three on the left have meanings consistent with their signific, while the ones on the right do not. The signific [**31**] in the first row has the meaning "water/liquid" [**32**] in the second row is connected to "silk/weaving"; [**33**] in the third row indicates "plant/wood"; [**34**] in the fourth row is associated with "hand"; finally, [**35**] in the last row means "plant/flower".

(7)

Compatible			Incompatible		
湖 wu 11 "lake"	河 ho 11 "river"	浮 fau 11 "to float"	演 jin 35 "to act"	添 tim 55 "to add"	派 pai 33 "to distribute"
線 sin 33 "thread"	絹 gyn 33 "stiff silk"	織 dzik 55 "to weave"	細 sai 33 "small"	緣 jyn 11 "fate"	絕 dzyt 22 "extreme"
桑 song 55 "a kind of tree"	杏 hang 22 "almond"	椅 ji 35 "chair"	檢 gim 35 "to examine"	棄 hei 33 "to discard"	權 kyn 11 "power"
打 da: 35 "to hit"	推 tui 55 "to push"	拋 pau 55 "to throw"	拒 kɸy 13 "to refuse"	據 gɸy 33 "to base on proof"	技 gei 22 "skill"
菜 tsoi 33 "vegetables"	蘭 la:n 11 "orchid"	葵 kwai 11 "sunflower"	萬 ma:n 22 "ten thousand"	薪 san 55 "salary"	若 joek 22 "if"

In addition to the strength of association between a signific and some meaning, and the semantic compatibility between a character and its signific, it is also found that there can be a many-to-one mapping between significs and conceptual properties, that is, more than one signific may be linked to a semantic notion. In almost all these cases, it is observed that one of the significs exists as a character and others have no independent existence. Some examples are given in (8), in which each row contains a set of significs associated with the specified meaning. The signific that can exist independently is listed at the beginning of the row.

Hoosain (1991) considers the significs without independent existence derivatives of the signific that can occur alone. In other words, a hierarchical relationship is imposed on significs connected to a notion. An alternative view is that the set of significs involved are simply various forms expressing a certain meaning, and no hierarchy is implied.

In terms of position of occurrence, Hoosain (1991) surveyed 67 significs that individually appear in at least 20 characters. The general tendency is that significs occupy the left side in characters with left/right configuration, and the top part

(8)

Character	Meaning	Position of occurrence			
		Left	Right	Top	Bottom
水	water	氵			氺 水
火	fire	火			火 灬
心	heart (emotion)	忄			⺗ 心
人	human	亻		人	
手	hand	扌			手
衣	clothes	衤			衣
刀	knife		刀	刂	刀
犬	dog	犭	犬		
絲	silk	糹			糸
肉	flesh	月			月 肉

in characters having top/bottom arrangement. The distribution of these significs in terms of their location is shown in (9) taken from Hoosain (1991, p. 11, Table 2.2).

While many significs occur in different places in a character, a significant number of significs appear in fixed locations. Some examples are given in (10).

In short, significs vary greatly in how strongly they are linked to some meaning aspect. Moreover, characters containing a strong signific may not all be

(9) Frequency of location of significs within a character

Top	11
Bottom	3
Left	41
Right	10
Peripheral	2

(10)a Significs with different positions of occurrence

Signific	Examples: left	right	top	bottom
火	爐		螢	煲
山	岐		嶺	巒
木	杉		杏	桑
食	餓			餐
隹		雞	隻	雀
鬼	魁	魄		魔
鳥	鴕	鴨		鷹

b Significs with fixed positions

Position of signific	Significs				
Left	亻	忄	扌	彳	
Right	刂				
Top	艹	入	宀	穴	⺮
Bottom	灬	⺗	皿	示	

semantically compatible with their signific. More than one signific may be connected to a particular meaning. In such cases, some of the significs have independent existence, whereas others cannot occur alone. With respect to location of occurrence, most significs occupy the left half or the top part of a character. Although many significs can appear in more than one position, a number of them have fixed locations.

Given that few significs are *reliably* related to semantic features, it is not clear what can be expected in terms of the error patterns involving the signific part of a character. However, in light of the perception most Chinese have about the signific being a functionally "well-defined" orthographic form (e.g. significs are entry points in a dictionary, and they can provide a clue to the meaning of an unfamiliar graph), it is plausible that significs are independently represented in the lexicon, along with information about their position of occurrence. If this is correct, specific types of writing errors can be expected. In particular, error types such as substitution, deletion, transposition, and addition that have been found to involve letters in English and Italian (Caramazza & Miceli, 1989, 1990; Caramazza, Miceli, Villa, & Romani, 1987; McCloskey, Goodman-Schulmann, & Aliminosa, 1990), may refer to the signific component. In other words, the signific may be substituted, deleted, transposed, or added as a whole. Furthermore, if spatial information of the signific is coded, in substitution and addition errors, the introduced signific should occupy a position it normally would when it appears in other characters. These errors were indeed found in our preliminary data to be reported in the third section of the chapter.

Although the phonetic and the signific components have been considered independently, we recognise that the two are not independent; in fact, they must interact in complicated ways. Given the fact that phonetic compounds (which constitute 90% of Chinese characters) are composed of a signific and a phonetic, the location where a signific occurs, to a large extent, constrains the shape and the position in which a phonetic may appear, and vice versa. In discussing the two components separately, it is hoped that we have at least singled out those features that are most likely to be involved in processing. Finally, it should be noted that only phonetic compounds and characters with a part that is identifiable as a signific have been examined, and we have said little about the representation and processing of simple characters.

The Internal Structure of Multicharacter Words

Although the 50 to 60 most frequently occurring lexical items are monosyllabic, Chinese words are overwhelmingly multisyllabic (mainly bisyllabic). The shift from monosyllabic to multisyllabic starting 70 to 80 years ago was partly instigated by the effort to make the written language reflect speech and to avoid homophony. Multisyllabic words can be categorised into compounds and loan-words; the latter include monomorphermic multisyllabic words and those that are phonetic transcriptions of foreign terms. We will begin with compounds because they constitute the largest class of multicharacter words.

Compounds

Chinese has very little in the way of inflection; nevertheless, compounding is extremely productive. Compounds are a type of word made up of two or more existing words. There has been much discussion about the proper definition of a compound in Chinese, as a result of the difficulty in distinguishing bound and free morphemes. In this chapter, we will adopt the definition in Chao (1968), which says that a compound is made up of two or more morphemes (free or bound,[12] and excluding affixes) combined to form a new word. Compounds may be categorised according to the transparency in meaning and the structural and semantic relationship that exist among component morphemes: (1) compositional compounds, whose meaning can be derived straightforwardly from their constituents; (2) co-ordinate compounds; and (3) idiomatic compounds, whose meaning is at best metaphorically related to their elements. The table in (11) summarises the different compound types we will discuss.

(11) Compound types

Category	*Form class*	*Internal structure*	*Meaning transparency*
Compositional	Nominal	N-N, V-N	Transparent
	Verbal	V-V resultative, V-N V-V subordinative, N-V	
Co-ordinate	Nominal	N-N, V-V	Transparent
	Verbal	V-V	
Idiomatic	Nominal	N-N, V-N	Metaphorical or opaque
	Verbal	V-V, V-N, N-V	

Compositional Compound. We will focus on those compound types that are most common and have larger memberships.[13] In nominal compositional compounds, N-N and V-N types, the first element functions like a modifier. Some examples of the N-N type are **[36]** "table-lamp", **[37]** "tooth-paste", **[38]** "oil-ship", **[39]** "leather-shoe", and **[40]** "liver-disease (hepatitis). Examples of the V-N type include **[41]** "fly-machine" (aircraft), **[42]** "fry-rice" (fried rice), **[43]**

[12] The inclusion of multimorphemic words containing bound morphemes to the category compound is somewhat justified, considering the fact that many morphemes that were once free forms in classical Chinese are now bound morphemes.

[13] A few other types discussed in Chao (1968) and not included here are; (1) $[CL\ CL]_N$, nominal compounds made up of classifiers; for example, 行列 "column-row" (format, formation). (2) $[N\ CL]_n$, composed of a noun followed by the classifier of that noun; these compounds are used to refer to the object depicted as a general class, e.g. 馬匹 "horse-CL" (horses), 房間 "room-CL" (rooms). (3) $[N\ locative]_{loc}$, e.g. 屋內 "house-in" (the inside of the house), 城外 "city-outside" (the outside of the city). (4) $[V\ N]_{Adv}$, e.g. 用心, "use-heart" (careful(ly)).

"run-shoe" (running shoes), **[44]** "laugh-sound" (laughter), **[45]** "blue-sky",[14] and **[46]** "happy-play" (comedy). A detailed discussion of the semantic relations between the two constituents in the N-N type and that of the V-N type can be found in Li and Thompson (1981) and Chao (1968), respectively. Their discussions clearly demonstrate the versatility and productivity of normal compositional compound.

Verbal compositional compounds include V-V subordinative, V-V resultative, N-V, and V-N compounds. In V_1-V_2 subordinative compounds, V_1 always has the function of modifying what is denoted by V_2, be it some sort of an action or a state. For instance, the compound **[47]** "fly-run" means that someone runs so fast as if he or she is flying; the word **[48]** "burnt-yellow" has the meaning "scorched-yellow". In contrast, the first verbal element in V_1-V_2 resultative compounds depicts some action and V_2 either describes some aspect of the consequence of the action or the extent to which the action is accomplished, for example, **[49]** (throw (something) upward), **[50]** (put down), **[51]** (to finish doing something), **[52]** (to guess right), **[53]** (to enlarge), **[54]** (to tear apart), etc. Generally speaking, in resultative compounds, V_1 can be either transitive or intransitive and V_2 tends to be intransitive; whereas in subordinate compounds, items occupying V_1 position are almost always intransitive, and V_2 may be either. In N-V compounds, the N satisfies the external argument of the V[15] (i.e. the argument that is projected onto the subject NP of the V), for example, **[55]** "personality-hurry" (impatient) and **[56]** "head-ache" (to have a headache), and in V-N compounds, the two components have the relation of predicate–internal argument; hence the latter are also referred to as V-object compounds, e.g. **[57]** "play-piano" and **[58]** "sing-song".

Co-ordinate Compound. Like the compositional compound, the meaning of a co-ordinate compound can be easily derived from that of its constituents. The relationship between components in this type of compound may be synonymous (V-V verbal compounds), e.g. **[59]** (move-move), **[60]** (discuss-discuss), **[61]** (poor-poor); antonymous (V-V nominal compounds), e.g. **[62]** "high-low" (height), **[63]** "ascend-descend" (fluctuation), **[64]** "exit-enter" (difference); or they can be members of the same class of objects (N-N nominal compounds), e.g. **[65]** "father-mother" (parents), **[66]** "older brother-younger brother" (sibling).

Co-ordinate and compositional compounds differ in several respects. First, the constituents in co-ordinate V-V compounds are not separable, whereas those in

---

[14] In this chapter, we treat the so-called adjectives as stative verbs, based on the arguments that "adjectives" show many verb-like behaviours. For example, they appear in predicate position of a sentence without a copula; they can form A-not-A questions; they may be directly negated by the negative particle *m*; and they can take aspectual markers.

[15] Occasionally, an N-V compound can function as a noun; for example, 軍變 "soldier-change" can mean either *to mutiny* or *mutiny*, or 地震 "earth-shake" can mean *to have an earth-quake* or *earthquake*.

resultative compounds can be separated by the "potential" infix *dak* (similar to -able in English) or the negative particle *m*. Second, co-ordinate verbal compounds can undergo reduplication (V_1-$V_2 \rightarrow V_1\ V_2\ V_1\ V_2$) to mean "try doing V a little"; on the other hand, neither kind of verbal compositional V-V compounds can be reduplicated. Third, in co-ordinate compounds, the two components are always of the same verb type, e.g. action verb-action verb, stative verb-stative verb, etc. Such restrictions do not apply to compositional V-V compounds—the elements within a compound may belong to different verb classes. Finally, unlike compositional compounds, co-ordinate compounds are not productive. In other words, they are lexical items that must be learned individually.

The same difference in productivity is also found between co-ordinate N-N compounds and compositional N-N compounds. The former are not productive and must be learned as separate lexical items, whereas the latter are the most productive of all compound types. Furthermore, co-ordinate N-N compounds are not conjoined nouns in that the ordering of components within the compound is fixed.

Idiomatic Compound. Idiomatic compounds have meanings that do not relate straightforwardly to their components. The connection is often metaphorical or inferential, and in many cases there does not seem to be any apparent semantic relation between the word as a whole and its constituents. Some examples of each sub-type of idiomatic compound are given below.

	N-N	銀河"silver-river" (the milky way)
		魚雷"fish-thunder" (torpedo)
Nominal	V-N	紅娘"red-mother" (matchmaker)
		熱門"hot-door" (popular item)
	V-N	開刀"open-knife"(to operate)
		傷心"hurt-heart" (to hurt someone)
	N-V	年青"year-green" (young)
Verbal		天眞"sky-real" (naive)
	V-V	私奔"private-run" (to elope)
		貪污"crave-dirty" (corrupt)

Just like co-ordinate compounds, idiomatic compounds are not productive and must be learned individually.

Headedness. The three categories of compounds we have discussed differ not only in the degree of transparency in meaning, but also in their internal structure, in particular, in the relationship among their constituents. The central issue concerns the notion of a head—whether a compound is headed and the directionality of its head—initial versus final.[16] Analogous to the head of a phrase, the head of a compound word is the constituent that shares with the whole compound syntactic and semantic characteristics. In other words, the head belongs to the same form class as that of the compound containing it, and it carries the essential meaning of the compound as a whole.

Given this criterion of the head, nominal compositional compounds can be said to be head-final, based on the fact that it is the second component of such compounds that determines the selection of a classifier. For example, [**67**] "table-lamp" takes the classifier [**68**] appropriate for lamp, and not [**69**] for table; [**70**] "feather-pen" (ink brush) selects [**71**] as its classifier, agreeing with pen rather than [**72**] with feather. Compounds of the V-N type also require a classifier appropriate for the N constituent, e.g. [**73**] "fly-machine" (aircraft) takes [**74**]. Thus, for both N-N and V-N compounds, the first element functions like a modifier; it describes some property of the object denoted by the second component.

On the other hand, the directionality of the head in verbal compositional compounds is not as uniform. Applying the criterion of the head just mentioned, N-V compounds are head-final because the compound is of the same grammatical category as its second element, and that the meaning of the compound is related more closely to the verbal constituent than its nominal component. The greater semantic contribution of V_2 in V_1-V_2 subordinative compounds suggests that they are head-final, as V_1 always modifies what is denoted by V_2. Examples of the two compound types can be found in the section on "Compositional Compound", and are not repeated here.

In contrast, the first component in V_1-V_2 resultative compounds depicts some action and V_2 either describes some aspects of the consequence of the action or the extent to which the action is accomplished. Li (1990) suggested that these compounds are head-initial. By assuming that V_1 is the head of V_1-V_2 resultative compounds, Li claimed that the behaviours concerning the theta-role assignment of such compounds can be accounted for; more specifically, Li observed that it is the theta-role prominency of V_1, but not V_2 that is maintained in the theta-grid

[16] We are interested in the headedness of compounds because Packard (1990) reported the grammar of a Chinese agrammatic patient, and made the observation that the patient tended to omit halves of compound words. In all instances except one, it is the head that is retained.

of the compound. Finally, verbal V-N compounds, using the criterion stated at the beginning of this section, are said to be head-initial.[17]

As for the other two compound categories, co-ordinate and idiomatic compounds, they are generally accepted to be exocentric (headless). Hence, to summarise our discussion of the internal structure of different compounds with respect to the head, only compositional compounds are endocentric. Nominal compositional compounds, V-V subordinative and verbal N-V compounds are head-final; while V-V resultative and verbal V-N compounds are head-initial.[18]

Monomorphemic Multisyllabic Word

The great majority of morphemes in Chinese are monosyllabic; nevertheless, there is a small number of multisyllabic morphemes. Some examples include [**75**] "grapes", [**76**] "carrot", [**77**] "butterfly," [**78**] "ant", [**79**] "lizard", [**80**] "spider", [**81**] "cricket", [**82**] "glass", and [**83**] "rose", [**84**] "parrot" etc. According to Li and Thompson (1981), these multisyllabic morphemes are borrowed from other languages. Several interesting characteristics can be found in monomorphemic multisyllabic words. With relatively few exceptions, the component characters in these words are "good" phonetic compounds in the sense that the pronunciations of these characters are often identical to their phonetic; in addition, the significs contained in these characters are always semantically consistent with the whole word. For example, the signific denoting worm/insect appears in "butterfly", "ant", "cricket", "lizard"; the one for "plant/vegetables" can be found in "grapes", "carrot". Third, the characters in these words rarely occur in any other lexical contexts; in other words, they seldom combine with characters to form other two-character words, unlike the majority

[17] The claim that verbal V-N compounds are headed is much weaker than that about other types of compositional compounds, as their constituents can often be separated by a quantifier or a possessive. For instance, 跳舞 "jump-dance" (to dance), one can say 跳三隻舞 "jump-three-CL-dance" to mean to dance three dances; or 接班 "receive-shift" (to take one's turn on duty), one may say 接他班 "receive-his-shift" to mean to take his shift. Hence, such compounds are very much phrase-like. In fact, distinguishing V-N compounds from real V-O construction has been discussed by many without finding any satisfying solution.

[18] One may question the usefulness of the notion of a head in describing the internal structure of compounds, since only some compounds are headed and within endocentric compounds of the same form class, the position of the head is not uniform. Our view can be summarised by the conclusions in Anderson (1992) regarding compounding. "In the case of compounds, the traditional notion of an internal head may have a role to play; but there is no reason to believe that all words of this sort have a head, or that when they do, there is a single uniformity of structure that allows us to identify its position within a word." Furthermore, "it may well be the case that the 'setting' of [the] parameter generally obeys substantial regularities within a particular language, although such regularities do not appear to be absolute in nature." (p. 311)

of logographs in the language. One may say that the associability of these characters is very low.[19]

Phonetic Transcription of Foreign Words[20]

These words resemble the phonological forms of the borrowed items (albeit with some modifications due to differences between the phonology of the language from which the borrowed word comes and that of Chinese, and the nature of character-syllable mapping in the orthographic system in Chinese). There are about 670 loans, excluding geographic names and personal names, according to Novotna (1967). These loan-words differ from the previous word type in several respects. Monomorphemic multisyllabic words are overwhelmingly bisyllabic; whereas phonetic loan-words are often more than two syllables in length. The average length of these loans is 3.27 syllables (Novotna, 1967). Some examples of phonetic loans include: **[85]** [ga-*fɛ*] "coffee", **[86]** [git-ta]: "guitar", **[87]** [ba-si] "bus", **[88]** [nei-gu-ding] "nicotine", **[89]** [ka-lou-lei] "calorie", **[90]** [si-do-bɛ-lei] "strawberry", and **[91]** [pun-lei-sai-lam] "penicillin". The choice of a character to represent a certain syllable is more a matter of convention than of their semantic properties.[21] As a result, many of the component characters do not contain a signific that is related to the meaning of the whole word. In fact, many characters found in phonetic loans are simple characters. While logographs in monomorphemic multisyllabic words appear in very limited contexts, characters in phonetic loan-words are by themselves single morphemes, and therefore can be found in other multisyllabic words.

In summary, multicharacter words can be distinguished into compounds, monomorphemic multisyllabic words, and phonetic loan-words. Compounds can be further classified, on the basis of internal structure and the semantic relation between the compound as a whole and its constituents, into compositional, co-ordinate, and idiomatic compounds. In terms of headedness, only compositional compounds are headed; the other compounded types and loan words do not have a head. Moreover, in compositional compounds, the

---

[19] As the name has already suggested, the meaning of monomorphemic multisyllabic words, in general, cannot be gathered from their components; however, in some of these words, one element seems to carry the essential meaning, as seen in its ability to appear in phrases with idiomatic meaning, for example, the second character of "spider" 蛛 in the phrase 蛛絲馬跡 "clues", and the second element of "butterfly" 蝶 in the phrase 狂風浪蝶 "lascivious men". These characters seem to have established some degree of independence.

[20] For a detailed discussion of phonetic loan-words, refer to Novotna (1967). Here we focus only on those aspects that are distinct from other multicharacter words discussed so far.

[21] It can be seen that attempts are made, in some cases, to select logographs that are semantically related to the meaning of loan-words. For instance, the characters 維他命 denoting "vitamin" can be interpreted as "to uphold other's life". However, such examples are very few, and the semantic relation between such a phonetic loan-word and its components is often remote and inaccurate.

directionality of the head is uniform for nominal but not so for verbal compounds. The former is head-final, and for the latter, N-V and V-V subordinative compounds are head-final, whereas V-N and V-V resultative compounds are head-initial.

Issues in Processing Multicharacter Words

The dominance of multisyllabic words in the lexicon naturally raises the question of whether these words are stored as single units along with their constituents, or only the latter are listed. Furthermore, given the differences in the structure and the relationship among the constituents in various types of multisyllabic words, is it possible that these word types are represented differently in the lexicon? Some findings from a preliminary study on the processing of compositional and idiomatic compounds using a lexical decision task suggest that the two word types may be distinct at some level (Tzeng, personal communication). Compositional and idiomatic compound words were chosen on the basis of word frequency and the frequency of their constituent characters. Hence, there were four sub-types of stimuli in each compound type: high word frequency-high character frequency (HW-HC), high word frequency-low character frequency (HW-LC), low word frequency-high character frequency (LW-HC) and low word frequency-low character frequency (LW-LC). On the whole, for both compound types, items with high word frequency were responded to faster than those with low word frequency. For idiomatic compounds, character frequency does not seem to have any effect on lexical decision time. On the other hand, an interaction between word frequency and character frequency was found among compositional compounds. Whereas word frequency had little influence on lexical decision time for LC items, it had an important effect for HC stimuli, with HW-HC compositional compounds showing the shortest reaction time (as compared with all other HW items), and LW-HC words the longest (as contrasted with other LW words). These data suggest that the two compound types are distinct at some level of processing.

The structural and semantic characteristics of different compound types as presented in (11) provide a valuable opportunity to address the issue of how multicharacter words are processed. Recall that in each of the three compound categories, there exist subtypes of one form class composed of elements of another grammatical class, for example, verbal compositional V-N and N-V compounds, nominal co-ordinate V-V compounds, and nominal idiomatic V-N compounds. It has been proposed (Bates, Chen, Tzeng, Li, & Opie, 1991) that if a patient were to present with a form class effect for single-character words (e.g. a noun/verb dissociation), and if the same dissociation were to be observed in multicharacter words of the types just mentioned, then one might be inclined to conclude that compounds are represented in whole word units. Notice also that in each compound category, there are words of the same internal structure but which belong to different form classes, i.e. nominal V-N versus verbal V-N in compositional compounds, nominal V-V versus verbal V-V in co-ordinate compounds, and nominal V-N versus verbal V-N in idiomatic compounds. The hypothetical patient who shows a noun/verb dissociation at the level of single-character word may also have differential performances on the whole compound word types.

With respect to the role of the head of a word in processing, Packard (1990) suggests that the head may have a special status, such that it tends to be better preserved. Given that compositional compounds are considered endocentric, and co-ordinate and idiomatic compounds are exocentric, one may expect comparable levels of performance across components in co-ordinate and idiomatic compounds, but higher rates of errors on the nonhead component, as compared to that of the head, in compositional compounds. As for loan-words, including both monomorphemic multisyllabic words and phonetic loans, we suggested earlier that they are not headed, like co-ordinate and idiomatic compounds. Thus, errors are not expected to cluster in one specific position.

Summary

The characteristics of the Chinese orthographic system raise many questions about their role in writing. With respect to the phonetic component, it was noted that only a subset of pronounceable parts are used as phonetics, that they may vary in consistency value, and that a phonetic may be identical, similar, or unrelated in sound to the phonetic compound containing it. In addition, the majority of phonetics occupy the right half of a character, but they may also appear on the left, at the top or at the bottom. How does the consistency value and the degree of phonological similarity influence the retrieval of phonetic compounds? How would the loss of spatial information of the phonetic (especially ones that occupy a position other than the right) affect the forms of the written output in brain-damaged subjects?

Significs constitute only a subset of the radicals in the language. Although significs have associated meanings, they vary in their strength of association. Even characters with a strong signific are not necessarily all related to the meaning of their signific. Furthermore, more than one signific may be linked to the same general meaning. This many-to-one relationship for significs may be considered as indicating that there are various surface forms of the same concept, or that one of the significs in such a set is the underlying form and the others are derivatives. Although the signific component as a useful cue to the meaning of characters may be overestimated, there is no doubt that significs are treated as functionally well-defined orthographic forms by Chinese readers/writers. Hence, it seems reasonable to assume that they are represented in the lexicon as single units, such that they are processed as wholes. Finally, analogous to the phonetic component, significs may be marked for their position of occurrence in the lexicon. In cases where this information is lost, signific transposition errors may occur.

We have also seen that multicharacter words are categorised into compounds and loan-words. The former can be distinguished on the basis of the degree of semantic transparency, the internal structure, and the relationship among constituents. The latter include both monomorphemic multisyllabic words and phonetic loan-words. One important issue concerns the nature of storage of multisyllabic words in the lexicon. Additionally, it is recognised that the head of a word is an important notion in discussing word internal structure; it will be interesting to see if it also has a role to play in the processing of compounds.

The ways in which the lexical system can break down as revealed by patterns of writing errors of aphasic patients will give us insights into the functional architecture of the system, the nature of representations at different levels of processing, and the cognitive processes underlying different processing components.

A DYSGRAPHIA AND DYSLEXIA BATTERY IN CANTONESE CHINESE

A battery for Chinese aphasic patients focusing on their performance in reading and writing of single words has recently been developed. It consists of eight lists, four of which are designed to examine many of the issues outlined in the previous section. This section described the characteristics of these lists[22]

Phonetic Component List

To investigate the role of the phonetic in terms of its position of occurrence within a character, and the degree of phonological similarity between it and the containing character, a Phonetic Component List was constructed. It contains a total of 160 characters. Forty items that do not have any pronounceable parts are used as fillers. All the other items have at least one pronounceable constituent; they are equally divided into four groups according to the location of the phonetic—*Right*, *Left*, *Top*, and *Bottom*. Within each group, 10 items have identical pronunciation as their phonetic (the *Same* condition). Ten are similar in sound to their phonetic (the *Similar* condition), which means that a character and its phonetic differ by tone and/or the aspiration of the onset. The other 10 items do not bear any phonological resemblance with their phonetic (the *Unrelated* condition). Notice that many of the stimuli in each group carry a signific which itself is a character, they are items considered to have more than one

[22] The lists are designed to study both reading and writing processes. Given the focus of this chapter is on writing, one may find that some of the characteristics of the lists to be described are not directly related to writing, but more to reading.

pronounceable component. Some examples from each condition are given in (12); the pronunciations of each example and its phonetic component are given, with the latter in parentheses.

(12)

Condition	Examples	
Right/Same	胞 bau 55 (bau 55)	恢 fui 55 (fui 55)
Right/Similar	控 hung 33 (hung 55)	誤 ng 22 (ng 11)
Right/Unrelated	飲 jam 35 (him 33)	填 tin 11 (dzan 55)
Left/Same	碩 sɛk 22 (sɛk 22)	郊 gau 55 (gau 55)
Left/Similar	剩 sing 22 (sing 11)	判 pun 33 (bun 33)
Left/Unrelated	堆 dui 55 (tou 35)	耐 løy 22 (ji 11)
Bottom/Same	皇 wong 11 (wong 11)	蒼 tsong 55 (tsong 55)
Bottom/Similar	崩 bang 55 (pang 11)	箭 dzin 33 (tsin 11)
Bottom/Unrelated	罪 dzøy 33 (fei 55)	登 dang 55 (dau 35)
Top/Same	型 jing 11 (jing 11)	烈 lit 22 (lit 22)
Top/Similar	盛 sing 22 (sing 11)	紫 dzi 35 (tsi 35)
Top/Unrelated	皆 gai 55 (bei 35)	雪 syt 33 (jy 13)
Filler	烏 wu 55	鬼 gui 35

The average number of strokes, mean character frequency[23] and the frequency range in each condition are shown in (13).

[23] Character and word frequency values in this chapter are based on Wu and Liu (1987).

(13) Character Complexity and Frequency of Items in each Condition (Phonetic component list)

Condition	*Mean number of strokes*	*Mean frequency*	*Frequency range*
Right/Same	11.9	13.8	1–32
Right/Similar	12.3	16.2	2–57
Right/Unrelated	12.0	18.0	3–32
Left/Same	11.8	19.6	3–88
Left/Similar	12.5	14.4	1–63
Left/Unrelated	12.1	15.5	4–47
Bottom/Same	12.0	22.0	1–52
Bottom/Similar	13.0	20.0	2–70
Bottom/Unrelated	10.8	18.0	2–35
Top/Same	11.7	15.1	1–36
Top/Similar	12.7	16.3	2–48
Top/Unrelated	11.5	18.7	1–50
Filler	11.23	14.5	1–52

The effect of consistency value on written production is not studied here because this information is not yet available for Cantonese.

Signific Component List and Semantic Category List

The effects of the strength of association between a signific and some meaning, and the semantic compatibility between a character and its signific, on writing performances are evaluated by two lists—Signific Component List and Semantic Category List.[24] The Signific Component List includes 833 characters containing a total of 90 significs.[25] The items are coded along two parameters—example versus nonexample and ambiguous versus unambiguous form. If the meaning

[24] No quantitative study evaluating the strength of semantic association of individual significs has been conducted. For the time being, judgements concerning this and the semantic consistency between a character and its signific are made based on the intuition of a few native speakers.

[25] Note that among these 90 significs, there are groups of semantically related significs.

of an item is consistent with the meaning associated with its signific, it is considered as an *Example* of that signific; on the other hand, if the meaning of the character is unrelated to that of its signific, it is treated as a *Nonexample*. Furthermore, a character containing more than one constituent that looks like a signific is referred to as an ambiguous form. Depending on the positions of the signific-like components in question, such a character can be analysed as a *Legitimate ambiguous form* or *illegitimate ambiguous form*. More specifically, an item is called a legitimate ambiguous form if all the constituents being considered occupy positions in which they would occur if they functioned as significs; otherwise, it is considered an illegitimate ambiguous form. Items containing semantically related significs are also marked in order to detect the occurrence of subsitution errors among them.

The average character frequency is 43.6; the frequency range is < 1 to 2536. The mean number of strokes is 12.4, with a range from 3 to 28. As for the distribution of Examples and Nonexamples, there are 482 Examples (57.8%) and 351 Nonexamples (42.2%). With respect to ambiguous forms, we have 128 Legitimate ambiguous items and 290 Illegitimate ambiguous characters. The distribution of ambiguous forms as a function of Example versus Nonexample is shown in (14).

(14) Distribution of Ambiguous Items in Terms of Semantic Consistency

	Legitimate	*Illegitimate*
Example	75	162
Nonexample	53	128

As mentioned earlier, the semantic association between a signific and some semantic property can sometimes be vague and obscure, and often does not correspond very well to contemporary categorisation of objects and events (some examples were given earlier). The Semantic Category List is constructed to examine the function of the signific from a different view to the previous list. More specifically, characters are selected on the basis of semantic categories. As one may expect, the same signific can be found in items in more than one category, and a semantic category may contain characters representing several significs, not counting significs that are considered as alternative expressions of the same notion. The two lists together can be used to study how category-specific impairment may be manifested in Chinese—is it along the line of significs or semantic categories?

The Semantic Category List contains 49 different categories—many of which are the same as those in Battig and Montague (1969)—totalling 761 items. The category size varies from as few as 6 to as many as 44 items;[26] the average is 15.5 items/category. Sixteen semantic categories consist of verbs, e.g. "psych verb", "perception", "movement", "language/speech", etc.; the rest contain nouns. The categories in this list also differ greatly in terms of the variety of significs represented. For example, no more than two significs are found in "sea animals", "birds", "flowers" and "fruits", whereas categories like "colour", "crime/misdeed", and "psych verb" have more than half a dozen significs each.

Multicharacter Words

To understand the nature of representation of multisyllabic words in the lexicon, and to examine the status of the head of a word in processing multicharacter lexical items, a Compound List was constructed. It contains 170 two-character compounds, covering all the compound types listed in (11). The number of items in each word type and its frequency range are shown in (15).

(15) Frequency Range and Number of Items in each Compound Subtype (Compound List)

Category	*Form class*	*Internal structure*	*No. of items*	*Frequency range*
Compositional	Nominal	N-N	15	1–16
		V-N	15	1–55
	Verbal	V-V resultative	10	1–28
		V-N	10	1–49
		V-V subordinative	10	1–8
		N-V	10	1–11
Co-ordinate	Nominal	N-N	10	1–226
		V-V	10	2–207
	Verbal	V-V	20	1–210
Idiomatic	Nominal	N-N	15	1–21
		V-N	15	1–31
	Verbal	V-V	10	1–35
		V-N	10	1–37
		N-V	10	1–12

[26] The small number of items in some categories is due to the fact that the Semantic Category List consists of single characters, and that most Chinese words are compositional compounds. For example, the word for "snake" (as a general category) is the character 蛇, whose signific 虫 is associated with "worm/insect". This character appears in the final position of many compounds (the head position) denoting specific kinds of snakes, such as 響尾蛇 "rattle snake" or 眼鏡蛇 "cobra". The nonhead elements in these compound words indicate some characteristics of the objects, and seldom contain a signific semantically related to the whole compound.

The list is currently being refined in order to make the items comparable in terms of character complexity and frequency across compound types. It is for this reason that loan-words are not yet included, as monomorphemic multisyllabic words tend to have high numbers of strokes (hence, they are orthographically quite complex), and phonetic loan-words tend to be more than two syllables in length. Ideally, the final version of the list will include compounds containing the same characters appearing in the head and nonhead positions, so that one can examine the claim about the special status of the head in endocentric compounds.

Other Lists

The battery also contains four other lists designed to study the effects of form class, word frequency, and imageability.

Monosyllabic Form Class List

This list consists of 20 unambiguous function words, 20 unambiguous nouns and 20 unambiguous verbs. All items have unambiguous pronunciations. The frequency range, mean frequency, and the mean number of strokes in each form class are summarised in (16).

(16) Character Frequency and Complexity of Items in each Form Class (Monosyllabic Form Class List)

	Frequency range	*Mean frequency*	*Mean no. of strokes*
Functor	11–2921	794.75	8.40
Noun	3–662	128.60	8.65
Verb	16–716	208.95	8.75

All six tones in Cantonese are represented by items in each form class. On the whole, the items cover 15 of the 19 onsets in the language, 14 out of 17 different rhymes without a coda, 8 out of 17 different nonchecked rhymes (rhymes with a coda other than /p/, /t/, /k/), and 6 out of 17 different checked rhymes (rhymes ending on /p/, /t/, /k/). The distribution of open versus closed syllables in each form class is shown in (17).

(17) Distribution of Open/Closed Syllable over Form Class (Monosyllabic Form Class List)

	Open syllable	*Closed syllable*
Functor	12	8
Noun	11	9
Verb	10	10

Bisyllabic Form Class List

This list contains 20 unambiguous functors, 20 unambiguous nouns, and 20 unambiguous verbs. The frequency range, mean frequency, and the mean number of strokes of each character in the items are given in (18).

(18) Word Frequency and Mean Number of Strokes of each Component Character (Bisyllabic Form Class List)

	Word frequency	*Mean frequency*	*1st character*	*2nd character*
Functor	40–1903	403.65	7.90	9.30
Noun	1–335	108.70	8.95	8.35
Verb	9–363	115.70	9.20	8.00

Like the monosyllabic form class list, all six tones are represented by items in each grammatical class. On the whole, the items in the list cover all 19 different onsets; in addition, 15 out of 17 coda-less rhymes, 13 out of 17 nonchecked rhymes, and 9 out of 17 checked rhymes are found. The distribution of open versus closed syllables in each position within items in each form class is shown in (19).

(19) Distribution of Open/Closed Syllables over Form Class (Bisyllabic Form Class List)

	Functor		*Noun*		*Verb*	
	1st char.	*2nd char.*	*1st char.*	*2nd char.*	*1st char.*	*2nd char.*
Open syllable	12	12	6	10	7	12
Closed syllable	8	8	14	10	13	8

Frequency List

This list consists of 90 monosyllabic stimuli that have unambiguous pronunciations. Half are of high frequency, and the other half of low frequency. The high-frequency items are equally divided into three grammatical classes—noun, verb, and function word. This is also true of the low-frequency items. The mean frequency and mean number of strokes of items in each condition are shown in (20).

(20) Character Frequency and Complexity of Items in each Condition (Frequency List)

Condition	*Mean frequency*	*Mean no. of strokes*
High-frequency functor	969.60	7.33

(cont'd)

Low-frequency functor	23.87	8.06
High-frequency noun	142.60	8.00
Low-frequency noun	11.50	7.86
High-frequency verb	131.00	8.30
Low-frequency verb	12.20	8.26

All six distinct tones in Cantonese are found in high- as well as low-frequency items. Eighteen out of 19 different onsets, 15 out of 17 coda-less rhymes, 11 out of 17 nonchecked rhymes, and 11 out of 17 checked rhymes appear in the items. The distribution of open versus closed syllables is shown in (21).

(21) Distribution of Open/Closed Syllables in each Condition (Frequency List)

	High functor	*Low functor*	*High noun*	*Low noun*	*High verb*	*Low verb*
Open syllable	11	7	7	7	9	10
Closed syllable	4	8	8	8	6	5

Imageability List

This list contains 60 bisyllabic unambiguous nouns, including all 20 nouns in the Bisyllabic Form Class List. Half of the items are of high imageability and the other half are of low imageability. Nine bisyllabic nouns from the Form Class List are found in the low imageability condition, and the other 11 nouns appear in the high imageability condition. The frequency range, frequency average, mean imageability value, and the average number of strokes of the first and second character within items of the two conditions are shown in (22).

(22) Word Frequency, Imageability Value, and Complexity of Component Character in each Condition (Imageability List)

	Frequency range	*Mean frequency*	*Imageability*	*1st char.*	*2nd char.*
High imageability	1–398	78.27	5.48	8.63	8.76
Low imageability	1–390	83.93	2.36	8.93	9.36

All tones are represented by the items. Eighteen of 19 onsets appear in the list; in addition, the items contain 15 out of 17 coda-less rhymes, 15 out of 17 nonchecked rhymes and 9 out of 17 checked rhymes. The frequency of occurrence of open and closed syllables in the stimuli is shown in (23).

(23) Distribution of Open/Closed Syllables over Components in High and Low Imageability Conditions

	High imageability		*Low imageability*	
	1st char.	*2nd char.*	*1st char.*	*2nd char.*
Open syllable	13	16	14	14
Closed syllable	17	14	16	16

PRELIMINARY DATA

This section presents writing errors in the preliminary data of our project investigating reading and writing processes of single words in Chinese aphasic patients. Data from six Cantonese Chinese aphasic patients were collected during the period between July and August 1992 in Hong Kong. We will focus on errors from three patients because they have at least secondary school education, they write with their preferred hand, and none of them suffers from apraxia. Information about these patients is summarised in (24).

(24) Patient information

	D.G.	Y.K.	C.L.
Age	38	49	41
Gender	F	M	M
Handedness	Right	Right	Right
Post-onset (in months)	10	9	13
Former occupation	Policewoman	Journalist	Head of a department of a major airline
Education level	High school	University	High school
Etiology	Subarachnoid haemorrhage caused by aneurism at the left carotid artery	Subarachnoid haemorrhage with hydrocephalus caused by aneurism at the right antero-communicatory artery	Left lateral cerebral haemorrhage, craniotomy done

The results on a reading/writing screener developed for Cantonese patients showed that the three subjects performed perfectly on repetition of monosyllabic and multisyllabic words, direct and delayed copying of single characters of various degree of complexity, auditory comprehension, reading comprehension, and reading aloud of single-character and two-character words of different form classes and frequencies of occurrence. With respect to oral naming of line drawings of common objects ($N = 25$), D.G. and Y.K. were 100% correct on this task, and C.L. was able to produce the correct names for 16 of the 25 pictures. On those occasions where he failed to provide the correct names for the presented objects, he could nevertheless name some action associated with the object, or describe physical attributes and functions of the object. All these patients made errors in the written picture-naming task and the writing-to-dictation task. They were subsequently asked to participate in a more extensive naming task and a writing-to-dictation task.

The organisation of this section parallels that of the first section. Errors are divided into those at the character level and those concerning multisyllabic words. The former is further divided into whole-character and subcharacter errors. Whole-character errors are basically character substitutions. We will only consider an error as a character substitution if the target stimulus and the response do not share any orthographic resemblance. In the analysis of subcharacter errors we will focus on those involving the signific or the phonetic component.

Errors Related to Single Characters

Character Substitution

Due to the great number of homophonous heterographs in the language, single-character targets were always presented in disambiguatory contexts. For example, the character [**92**] [loeng 11] which is phonetically identical to [**93**], [**94**], and [**95**], just to name a few homophones, was presented as [96] in ("cool"). Of all the errors that are existing characters and do not share any orthographic components with their target, the majority of errors are phonologically similar to the target response. They are usually identical in sound to the target, or the two differ only by tone. On a few occasions, the two differ by the initial consonant. Some examples are given in (25); the characters on the left are stimuli, and those on the right are the responses.

(25)a Output identical in sound to the target

	Target	Response
i	皆 gai 55 also	佳 gai 55 nice
ii	愁 sau 11 sad	仇 sau 11 enemy
iii	越 jyt 22 overtake	月 jyt 22 month

iv	栗 lφt 22 chestnut	律 lφt 22 regulation
v	麥 mak 22 wheat	墨 mak 22 ink

b Output differing by tone to the target[27]

	Target	Response
i	陣 dzan 22 formation	震 dzan 33 shake
ii	問 man 22 ask	文 man 11 article
iii	僅 gan 35 barely	近 gan 22 near
iv	田 tin 11 farmland	天 tin 55 sky
v	枝 dzi 55 branch	字 dzi 22 word

c Output differing by a consonant

	Target	Response
i	東 dung 55 east	通 tung 55 pass through
ii	售 sau 22 sell	後 hau 22 behind

[27] These patients scored 100% correct on repetition of single characters and phrases; we thus have reason to believe that the errors do not arise from the input level.

The examples are selected from errors in the writing-to-dictation task. As the gloss indicates, the stimuli and the characters produced do not have any semantic relation; in fact, the two do not belong to the same form class in many cases. One may question what is phonological similarity between two forms to a speaker of a language whose mapping between sounds and orthographic forms is syllabic. Keung and Hoosain (1979) conducted a study on perceptual salience of Chinese syllables and found that tone is perceptually less salient than consonants and vowels. This may explain why there were many errors which differ from their target by only a tone feature.

In addition to phonologically plausible errors, there are a number of semantic errors in the corpus. The examples are given in (26).[28]

(26)	Target	Response
i	回 wui 11 return	歸 gui 55 return
ii	刀 dou 55 knife	叉 tsa: 55 fork
iii	襪 mat 22 sock	腳 goek 33 foot
iv	伯 ba:k 33 uncle	爸 ba: 55 father
v	也 ja 13 also	這 dzɛ 35 this

[28] If we relax the criterion of character substitution to include those that have a phonetic or a signific in common with the target, but the component in question is in different positions of occurrence, then we have two more semantic errors, as shown below:

	Target	Response
a	肺 fai 33 lungs	胃 wai 22 stomach
b	樹 sy 22 tree	葉 jip 22 leaf

vi	較 gau 13 comp. marker	使 si 35 causative marker

Example (26)iii comes from the written picture-naming task, the others from the writing-to-dictation task. Except for (26)iv, the output characters do not resemble their target in sound. Examples (26)v and vi are within form class substitutions; both the stimuli and the responses are functors.

Finally, we had one error where the target and the response bear no phonological, visual, or semantic relationship with each other, as illustrated in (27).

(27)	棒 pa:ng 13 stick	叠 dip 22 pile up

Subcharacter Errors

The errors to be discussed include responses from both single-character and multicharacter stimuli. A response that shares with its target a signific or a phonetic component, regardless of whether the output itself is an existent character or not, is considered an error at the subcharacter level.[29] We will begin

[29] There were errors in our corpus involving orthographic "parts" that are larger than a stroke but do not have the function of a signific or a phonetic. Some examples are:

(i)a	掌 dzoeng 35 "palm"	 (pseudo-character) (substitution of 宀 for 龸)
b	魂 wan 11 "soul"	 (pseudo-character) (substitution of 丶 for 厶)
c	檸 ling 11 1st character in "lemon"	 (pseudo-character) (substitution of  for 宀)
d	鬼 guai 35 "ghost"	 (pseudo-character) (deletion of 厶)

We will discuss errors of this sort in a future paper devoted to investigating the basic orthographic constituents of the writing system in Chinese.

discussing errors involving the signific, followed by those related to the phonetic. Pseudocharacter examples are used wherever they are available, because outputs that are existing characters are always open to the interpretation that they may in fact be character substitutions.

Signific Component Errors. We have considered the possibility that radicals that are used as semantic cues to the meaning of characters are distinguished from other radicals in the lexicon, and that their position of occurrence is also coded. This means that if the identity of the signific in a target character is lost, the result is either a substitution or a deletion error, and in the former case, the substituting element is also a signific.

An examination of the data shows that the majority of errors involving the signific are substitutions. Examples are given in (28); the phonetic transcriptions in parentheses correspond to the sounds of the phonetic component in individual target characters. The semantic properties associated with the signific of the stimuli and the substitutions are given in square brackets.

(28) Signific substitution errors

	Target	Response
i	貓 mau 55 (miu 11) [beast] cat	 [worm/insect]
ii	跌 dit 33 (sat 55) [foot] to fall	蛈 [worm/insect]
iii	鈕 lau 35 (tsau 35) [metal] button	杻 [wood/plant]
iv	筆 bat 55 [bamboo] pen	 [plant]
v	螺 lo 35 (lɵy 22) [worm/insect] conch	[30] [field]
vi	踢 tɛk 33 (ji 22) [foot] to kick	揚 [hand]

[30] This may be an anticipatory error as the substituting signific and the first constituent in the remainder are identical in form.

All these examples come from the writing-to-dictation task, and in all cases, the responses are pseudocharacters. Three points are worth considering: (1) the element substituting for the target is also a signific; (2) the substitute occupies the same position as the target signific,[31] except for the last error [**97**] (foot of a hill); and (3) the substitute appears in a position where it normally would be when it functions as a signific in other characters. These three characteristics suggest that a distinction between significs and nonsignific radicals is made in the lexicon, that the signific component corresponds to a constituent in the orthographic representations at some level of processing for it to be replaced as wholes, and that the signific component (both the target and the substitute) is spatially coded so as to explain the observations that the substitute appears in the same position as the target signific, and that it occupies its usual position when it is a signific in other characters. However, we also acknowledge that observations (2) and (3) may simply be an artifact of the tendency that most significs appear on the left or at the top of a character. When a signific is randomly chosen to substitute for the target, the one that is selected probably appears in one of the two positions as well. The fact that all stimuli in (28) have their signific either on the left or at the top provides some ground for this reasoning. In short, more data are needed to shed light on the issue regarding the presence of spatial coding of the signific component.

Besides substitutions, one may also expect deletion errors to occur when the identity of the signific is underspecified. Deletion errors from the writing-to-dictation task are presented in (29).

(29) Signific deletion errors

	Target	Response
i	茄 kɛ 35 squash	加 ga: 55 to add
ii	菠 bo 55 spinach	波 bo 55 wave

[31] In only two of the signific substitution errors in our corpus (including those with real character ouputs) where the substitute is in a different position from the target signific, as shown in (i).

(i)a	籃 la:m 11 basket	艦 la:m 22 warship
b	茄 kɛ 35 squash	架 ga: 33 frame or CL for vehicles

However, as the output is an existing character in both cases, they may be whole character substitutions.

iii	菇 gu 55 fungus	姑 gu 55 aunt
iv	蝴 wu 11 1st character in butterfly	胡 wu 11 a last name
v	芽 nga: 11 bean sprout	牙 nga: 11 tooth

All the output graphs are real characters. Except for (29)i, the stimulus and the response in each example are phonetically identical. Hence, they may be interpreted as phonologically plausible errors. This is not an unreasonable interpretation given that none of the target characters in (28) is identical in sound to its phonetic component. Less ambiguous signific deletion errors would involve either phonetic compounds whose pronunciation differs from that of their phonetic (e.g. [**98**] dit 33 "to fall" → [**99**] sat 55 "to lose"), or phonetic compounds whose phonetic does not exist alone (e.g. [**100**] buk 22 "servant" → [**101**]).

Another possible type of errors involving the signific is addition errors. Examples from our corpus are shown in (30).

(30) Signific additions

	Target	Response
i	摩 mo 55 to touch	 (pseudo-character)
ii	蜢 ma:ng 35 grasshopper	 (pseudo-character)
iii	奉 fung 22 to offer	俸 fung 35 salary (an archaic term)
iv	羊 joeng 11 sheep	洋 joeng 11 ocean

These errors are taken from the writing-to-dictation task, except for (30)iv, which is from the written picture-naming task. In example (30)i, a signific associated with the meaning "plant/wood" is added to the target; in (30)ii, the response seems to be a combination of two errors, a signific substitution and a signific addition. The former replaces the original signific linked to "worm/insect" with one related to "beast"; the latter adds a signific associated with "plants" to the target. The responses in (30)iii and iv are real characters; (30) iii is phonologically similar to the stimulus, and (30) iv is identical in sound to its target. Unlike substitution and deletion errors, it is not clear how signific addition errors arise.

Phonetic Component Errors. Analogous to errors involving the signific component, in cases where the identity of the phonetic component of a target character is not adequately specified, phonetic substitutions or deletions may also occur. The examples in (31) and (32) illustrate phonetic substitution errors.

(31) **Phonetic component substitutions (non-existent character response)**

	Target	Response
i	煮 dzy 35 (dzɛ 35) to cook	 (sy 35) (pseudo-character)
ii	盅 dzung 55 (dzung 55) container	 (tsyn 33) (pseudo-character)
iii	塔 ta:p 33 (da:p)[32] tower	 (da:p 33) (pseudo-character)
iv	抓 dzau 35 (dzau 35) to scratch	 (gua: 55) (pseudo-character)
v	財 tsoi 11 (tsoi 11) fortune	 (tsyn 33) (pseudo-character)

[32] Although the phonetic component is listed in the dictionary as an independent character, it is a very low-frequency character. The first author has consulted a few native speakers who have college education in Taiwan; most of them do not recognise it.

vi 菇 
gu 55 (gu 55) (wu 11)
fungus (pseudo-character)

vii 爺 
jɛ 11 (jɛ 11) (tsɸy 35)
grandfather (pseudo-character)

viii 霉 
mui 11 (mui 13) (mou 13)
moldy (pseudo-character)

(32) Phonetic component substitutions (real character response)

i 盅 盔
dzung 55 (dzung 55) kwai 55 (fui 55)
container helmet

ii 盅 盃
dzung 55 (dzung 55) bui 55 (bat 55)
container cup (as an award)

iii 蟬 蟾
sim 11 (da:n 55) sim 11 (dzim 55)
cicada 1st syllable of "toad"

iv 胸 腔
hung 55 (hung 55) hong 55 (hung 55)
chest cavity

The ones listed in (31) have pseudocharacter responses, and those in (32) have real character output. As the responses in (32) are existing orthographs, they may be considered lexical substitutions.

The phonological forms in parentheses represent the sound of the phonetic component in individual graphs. A comparison between the phonetic component of each of the output graphs in (31) and its corresponding target characters in terms of phonological shape does not seem to show that the two forms are necessarily related. In addition, unlike the situation in signific substitutions, not all substituting elements in (31) function as a phonetic component in real characters, i.e. (31)i, iii, and vi. This may have something to do with the rather extensive use of existing characters (whether they are simple characters or phonetic compounds) as the phonetic component of new characters, as seen in the creation of logographs representing Cantonese lexical items that had no corresponding written forms. One may also notice that the stimuli and the responses in (31) are visually similar, except for (31)vi. It is thus arguable that the errors are in fact the results of substitution, deletion, or addition of some part not corresponding to the phonetic component. More specifically, it is plausible that (31)i and ii may, in fact, involve the addition of [**102**] and [**103**] respectively; (31)iii and vii involve the substitution of [**104**] for [**105**], and [**106**] for [**107**] respectively; (31)iv and v are the results of stroke substitutions, such that [**108**] becomes [**109**], and [**110**] becomes [**111**], respectively; finally, (31)viii is the product of the deletion of [**112**]. Although such possibilities cannot be ruled out, the fact that in all these errors, the resultant forms contain a signific and a remainder that is an existing character suggests that the responses were more likely to be the products of phonetic substitution.

As in the case of significs, the lack of information concerning the content of the phonetic in a stimulus may result in phonetic deletions. Errors of this type are shown in (33).

(33) Phonetic deletions

	Target	Response
i	蜢 ma:ng 35 grasshopper	虫
ii	趾 dzi 35 toe	𧾷
iii	猴 hau 11 monkey	犭
iv	賬 dzoeng 33 bill	貝
v	煙 jin 55 cigarette	火
vi	浮 fau 11 to float	氵

Errors in (31) and (33) show that the phonetic component can be substituted or deleted as a whole. This implies that the phonetic may correspond to a constituent at some level of processing.

It is worth noting that there were no phonetic addition errors in our preliminary data corpus. This may be due to the fact that the insertion of a phonetic component into a graph that already has a phonetic would result in a grossly ill-formed graph. If this reasoning is correct, its significance would be that, given a damaged system, not only are the possible forms of writing errors constrained (i.e. errors are not generated randomly), but the output may be subject to the filtering of orthographic well-formedness conditions, in this case, the condition that a character cannot have more than one phonetic component.

Before we end the discussion of errors involving the signific or the phonetic component, we would like to note that there were no transposition errors in our corpus. In fact, examining the data reported in previous studies (Huang, 1984; Li, Hu, Zhu, & Sun, 1984; Lyman, Kwan, & Chao, 1938; Naeser & Chan, 1980; Tzeng, Hung, Chen, Wu, & Hsi, 1986), we were able to find only one transposition error, as shown in (34). One plausible reason for the rarity of this type of errors is that a transposition error occurs when only the spatial information of the elements involved is lost, but their content is still retained. In the case of a phonetic compound, so long as the spatial code of either the phonetic or the signific is preserved, the possible position of occurrence of the other element is greatly restricted. This means that correct production of a phonetic compound is possible despite incomplete spatial information of the constituents.

(34) A transposition error from Lyman, Kwan, & Chao (1938)

期(a period of time) ----> 月其

Summary

We began this section with a discussion of whole character substitutions, where the response does not resemble its target in orthographic shape. It was observed that the majority of errors of this sort are phonologically plausible errors. The target and the response are highly similar in their phonetic form. A few semantic errors were also found. At the subcharacter level, it was noted that substitution and deletion errors may involve the signific or the phonetic. These errors can be considered the results of underspecification of the identity of the components in question. The signific component was always substituted or deleted as a whole. In substitution errors, the replacement is also a signific, and the target and the substituting signific do not necessarily have any semantic relation. In the great majority of cases, the substitute occupies the same position as the target signific. The signific component can also be added to a character already having a signific. In both substitution and addition errors, the signific in question always appears in a position where it normally would be when it functions as a signific in other characters. As for errors involving the phonetic, it was found that the phonetic component can be substituted or deleted as a unit. However, unlike the situation with the signific, the substituting phonetic may sometimes be one that does not function as a phonetic in other characters, although it is an existing character itself. The target phonetic and the replacement are not necessarily similar phonologically. Contrary to what was observed for the signific, we did not find any phonetic insertion errors. The latter observation may have something to do with the fact that whereas there are complex characters containing two signific-like elements (e.g. [**113**] "grandmother" contains [**114**] and [**115**]), no character has more than one phonetic component. Hence, adding a phonetic to a character already having a phonetic will result in an ill-formed orthograph. Finally, there were no transposition errors in our preliminary data. The observations made about the errors associated with the phonetic and the signific suggest that these components correspond to constituents at some level of processing, and that information regarding their position of occurrence is coded.

Errors on Multicharacter Words

We will discuss in this section incorrect responses to multisyllabic stimuli in which the erroneous characters do not visually resemble their corresponding target (those errors where the output characters and their target have some components in common have been discussed in the previous section). Due to the limited amount of data available, this discussion will be relatively brief. Basically, the errors can be categorised into phonologically plausible and partial responses. Errors of the former kind are listed in (35); they are organised by word type. All the substituting elements are existing characters, but the resultant character combinations, except for (35)iv, do not amount to any meaningful units, as expressed by the gloss. Although by treating the character combination in (35)iv [**116**] as a compositional compound, one may possibly derive some meaning out of it, the combination is not an existing lexical item. In terms of phonological similarity, except for (35)ii, the target and the output character either have identical pronunciation or differ only by tone.

The other type of errors is partial responses; they are listed in (36). Responses of this sort can again be found in various word types. In all the errors listed, except for (36) vi and xvi, the constituent character that is more frequent in occurrence

(35) **Phonologically plausible errors**

Compositional compound

	Target	Response
i	蛋 糕 da:n 22 gou 55 cake	蛋 高 da:n 22 gou 55 egg tall (non-word)

ii	蛋 糕 da:n 22 gou 55 cake	胆 糕 da:m 35 gou 55 gall bladder / pastry (non-word)

Co-ordinate compound

iii	喜 愛 hei 35 ngoi 33 to adore	起 外 hei 35 ngoi 22 rise / outside (non-word)

Idiomatic compound

iv	佳 音 gai 55 jam 55 carol/good tidings	街 音 gai 55 jam 55 street / sound (sound from the street)

Monomorphemic multi-syllabic word

v	狐 狸 wu 11 lei 35 fox	胡 李 wu 11 lei 13 a last name / a last name (non-word)

and has fewer strokes is the one produced. The character may be the first component, i.e. (36)i to v, xi to xiii, and xvi, or the second component, i.e. (36)vi to x, xiv, xv, and xvii.

(36) Partial responses

	Target	Response
	Compositional compound	
i	小 麥 siu 35 mak 22 wheat	小 siu 35 little
ii	白 兔 ba:k 22 tou 33 rabbit	白 ba:k 22 white
iii	工 廠 gung 55 tsong 35 factory	工 gung 55 labor
iv	牙 刷 nga: 11 tsa:t 33 toothbrush	牙 nga: 11 tooth

v	花 fa: 55 vase	樽 tsɸn 55	花 fa: 55 flower
vi	白 bak 22 rabbit	兔 tou 33	兔 tou 33 rabbit
vii	蕃 fa:n 55 tomato	茄 kɛ 35	茄 kɛ 35 squash
viii	斑 ba:n 55 zebra	馬 ma 13	馬 ma 13 horse
ix	酒 dzau 35 wine glass	杯 bui 55	杯 bui 55 cup
	Idiomatic compound		
x	蝸 wo 55 snail	牛 ngau 11	牛 ngau 11 cow
xi	小 siu 35 clown	丑 tsau 35	小 siu 35 little
	Co-ordinate compound		
xii	分 fan 55 to separate	散 sa:n 33	分 fan 55 to separate
xiii	告 gou 33 to tell	訴 sou 33	告 gou 33 to indict/to inform
xiv	滿 mun 13 to satisfy	足 dzuk 55	足 dzuk 55 enough/foot
xv	站 dza:m 22 to stand	立 lap 22	立 lap 22 to stand/to erect

xvi	蘿	蔔	蘿
	lo 11 carrot	bak 22	lo 11
	Phonetic loan-word		
xvii	結	他	他
	git 33 guitar	ta: 55	ta: 55 he

Based on an observation of the oral production of an agrammatic patient in Packard (1990), we raised a question earlier about the possible special status of the head of a compound in written production. Our preliminary data are not sufficient to shed much light on the issue. Nevertheless, one may conjecture what sorts of writing errors would occur if the head of a word were better preserved. Two kinds of errors may be found—partial responses and those resulting from erring in a constituent character. Partial responses may take the form that the character occupying the head position is more likely to be produced, whether the head is in the initial or in the final position. Substitution errors might be characterised by a pattern where characters occurring in nonhead positions have higher error rates than those functioning as the head. Future observation of written production of multisyllabic words will, it is hoped, be able to address the issue.

CONCLUSION

The differences between the Chinese writing system and alphabetic systems range from the general visual shape and the composition of orthographs, to the sound-orthographic form relationship. In addition, a notable difference between the two kinds of system is the presence of a signific component providing a semantic cue to the meaning of many Chinese characters. Contrary to the view still held by many that the mapping between sound-character is very opaque in Chinese, the great majority of characters contain a phonetic component supplying a phonetic cue to their pronounciation. We suggested in this chapter that these components provide important means to investigate the cognitive processes underlying writing in Chinese. Hence, many questions concerning the computation of characters are raised particularly in respect to the position of occurrence of these components within characters and the degree of reliability to which they perform their respective function. The abundance of compounds in the language further raises issues regarding their nature of storage in the lexicon and the role of their head (in the case of endocentric compounds) in processing. Many of these questions in fact have counterparts in alphabetic writing systems. Neuropsychological studies on the writing processes in English and Italian have found that the loss of information about the content and/or the ordering of letters composing a word may result in letter substitution, deletion, addition, shift, and transposition errors. Questions about the nature of storage of morphologically complex words in these languages have long been a focus of attention. In particular, are morphologically complex words represented as wholes or in terms of their constituent morphemes in the lexicon?

Preliminary data from our study investigating the reading and writing performances of Chinese brain-damaged patients show that the identity and the spatial code of the signific and the phonetic can be subject to selective impairment, such that the signific component can be substituted, deleted, or added in its entirety, and the phonetic component can be replaced or omitted as a whole, indicating that they correspond to constituents in the orthographic representations of phonetic compounds at some level of processing. The paucity of transposition errors and the lack of phonetic additions were explained in terms of constraints on possible output imposed by the compositional properties of characters. Additionally, a good proportion of our data consists of real word responses that phonologically resemble their target. These errors are analogous to phonologically plausible errors often found in patients of alphabetic writing systems. As these responses may also be interpreted as lexical substitutions, future studies should pay attention to the occurrence of pseudocharacter responses containing a phonetic component close in sound to their target. Our limited data on multicharacter words unfortunately do not provide much insight into the questions raised about their representation and processing in the cognitive system, but we are hopeful that further investigation can shed light on the issues.

ACKNOWLEDGEMENTS

This work was suported in part by a grant from the Human Frontier Science Program and by NIH grant NS22201 to Alfonso Caramazza. The authors are grateful to Mr Samuel Leung, Mr Man-Tak Leung, and Ms Lena Mak for help in referring patients to us.

REFERENCES

Anderson, S. R. (1992). *Amorphous morphology*. Cambridge University Press.

Bates, E., Chen, S., Tzeng, O., Li, P., & Opie, M. (1991). The noun-verb problem in Chinese aphasia. *Brain and Language*, *41*, 203–233.

Battig, W. F., & Montague, W. E. (1969). Category norms for verbal items in 56 categories: A replication and extension of the Connecticut norms. *Journal of Experimental Psychology*, 80, Part 2, 1–46.

Caramazza, A., & Miceli, G. (1989). Orthographic structure, the graphemic buffer and the spelling process. In C. von Euler, I. Lundberg, & G. Lennerstrand (Eds.), *Brain and Reading*, Macmillan/Wenner-Gren International Symposium Series.

Caramazza, A., & Miceli, G. (1990). The structure of graphemic representations. *Cognition*, *37*, 243–297.

Caramazza, A., Miceli, G., Villa, G., & Romani, C. (1987). The role of graphemic buffer in spelling: Evidence from a case of acquired dysgraphia. *Cognition*, *26*, 59–85.

Chao, Y. R. (1968). *A grammar of spoken Chinese*. Berkeley, CA: University of California Press.

De Francis, J. F. (1950). *Nationalism and language reform in China*. Princeton University Press.

Fang, S.-P., Horng, R.-Y., & Tzeng, O. (1986). Consistency effects in the Chinese characters and pseudo-character naming tasks. In H. S. R. Kao & R. Hoosain (Eds.), *Linguistics, psychology, and the Chinese language*. Centre of Asian Studies, University of Hong Kong.

Glushko, R. J. (1979). The organization and activation of orthographic knowledge in reading aloud. *Journal of Experimental Psychology: Human Perception and Performance*, *5*, 674–691.

Hoosain, R. (1991). *Psycholinguistic implications for linguistic relativity: A case study of Chinese*. Hillsdale, NJ: Lawrence Erlbaum Associates Inc.

Huang, C.-Y. (1984). Reading and writing disorders in Chinese—some theoretical issues. *Psychological studies of the Chinese language*. Hong Kong: The Chinese Language Society of Hong Kong.

Keung, T., & Hoosain, R. (1979). Segmental phonemes and tonal phonemes in comprehension of Cantonese. *Psychologia: An International Journal of Psychology in the Orient*, *22*, 4, 222–224.

Li, C. N., & Thompson S. A. (1981). *Mandarin Chinese: A functional reference grammar*. Berkeley, CA: University of California Press.

Li, X.-T., Hu, C.-Q., Zhu, U.-L., & Sun, B. (1984). Neurolinguistic analysis of Chinese alexia and agraphia. *Psychological studies of the Chinese language*. Hong Kong: The Chinese Language Society of Hong Kong.

Li, Y.-F. (1990). On V-V compounds in Chinese. *Natural Language and Linguistic Theory*, *8*, 178–201.

Lian, Y.-W. (連韻文) (1985). 中文唸字歷程的探討:聲旁的語音觸發作用 [An investigation of the processes in character naming in Chinese: The influence of the phonetic omponent]. Unpublished master's thesis, National University of Taiwan, Taipei, Taiwan.

Lyman, R. S., Kwan, S. T., & Chao, W. H. (1938). Left occipito-parietal brain tumour with observation on alexia and agraphia in Chinese and English. *Chinese Medical Journal*, *54*, 491–516.

McCloskey, M., Goodman-Schulmann, R. A., & Aliminosa, D. (1990). *The structure of output orthographic representations: Evidence from an acquired dysgraphic patient*. Paper presented at the meetings of Academy of Aphasia, Baltimore, MD.

Naeser, M. A., & Chan, S. W.-C. (1980) Case study of a Chinese aphasic with the Boston Diagnostic Aphasia Exam. *Neuropsychologia*, *18*, 389–410.

Novotna, Z. (1967). Linguistic factors of the low adaptability of loan-words to the lexical system of modern Chinese. *Monumenta Serica*, *26*, 103–118.

Packard, J. L. (1990). Agrammatism in Chinese: A case study. In L. Menn & L. K. Obler (Eds.), *Agrammatic aphasia: a cross-language narrative sourcebook*. Philadelphia, PA: John Benjamins Publishing.

Tzeng, O. J.-L., Hung, D. L., Chen, S., Wu, J., & Hsi, M.-S. (1986). Processing Chinese logographs by Chinese brain-damaged patients. *Graphonomics: contemporary research in handwriting*. Amsterdam: Elsevier Science Publishers B.V.

Wang, W. S.-Y. (1973). The Chinese language. *Scientific American*, *228*, 50–60.

Wu, R.-T. & Liu, I.-M. (吳瑞屯 及 劉英茂) (1987). 中文字詞語音,語意屬性的研究 [A study of the phonological and semantic properties of Chinese lexical items]. National University of Taiwan, Taipei, Taiwan.

Zhu, Y. P. (1987). *Analysis of cueing functions of the phonetic in modern Chinese*. Unpublished paper, East China Normal University.

9 Phonological Processes in Serbo-Croatian and English

Georgije Lukatela
University of Belgrade, Serbia

M.T. Turvey
University of Connecticut, Storrs, CT, USA
and Haskins Laboratories, New Haven, CT, USA

INTRODUCTION

Dual-process theory (Coltheart, 1978) has motivated most of the laboratory research on recognising and pronouncing words. According to this theory, two independent processes—a direct, visual process and a mediated, phonological process—govern the accessing of the internal lexicon, a mental dictionary containing relatively permanent information about the identity of individual words. The uses of the two independent processes are not equal. The primary access route is the direct process which entails a mapping between orthographic features of individual printed/written words and lexical representations. The secondary access route is provided by the mediated process, which involves a set of grapheme-phoneme correspondence rules turning spellings into phonological representations, and a subsequent mapping from those phonological representations onto lexical entries. According to the theory, whereas the mediated route might dominate word identification in early stages of reading, it is the direct route that characterises reading fluency. And whereas phonological mediation is needed for reading new words and nonwords, the direct visual route is mandatory for exceptional spellings and is preferred for familiar words.

A recent criticism of the dual process theory is that the appeal to a rule-governed phonological process to access the lexicon is superfluous: For all word forms, lexical access is achieved in a word-specific manner, by the direct visual route (Humphreys & Evett, 1985). In this chapter we will consider evidence from studies with Serbo-Croatian-language materials and from studies with English-language materials that suggest a different criticism of the dual process theory: The primary constraint on lexical access is phonological, not visual, and this constraint arises not through explicit rules but through continuous statistical regularity (Van Orden, Pennington, & Stone, 1990).

Empirical support for phonological mediation has not been bountiful. Rubenstein, Lewis, and Rubenstein's (1971) demonstration that lexical decisions are slower for homophones (e.g. "yolk") and pseudohomophones, that is, nonwords homophonous with real words (e.g. "trate"), was originally taken as evidence for speech-related processes in word identification. Subsequent research, however, found that the homophony effect on "yes" responses could be eliminated by including many pseudohomophones as foils (Davelaar, Coltheart, Besner, & Jonasson, 1978), suggesting that the phonological route was optional, and probably used only for the processing of nonwords. The pre-lexical phonological processing of a nonword such as "trate" produces a representation which activates the lexical entry for the word "trait", making the rejection of TRATE difficult. Because this evidence for pre-lexical phonology was provided by the slower rejection latencies, it gave rise to doubts about phonology's role in actual word identification. It was argued that even if phonological coding does occur, it occurs too slowly to be of use in lexical access (e.g. Henderson, 1982; McCusker, Hillinger, & Bias, 1981). As Coltheart, Davelaar, Jonasson, and Besner (1977, p. 551) remarked: "Unequivocal evidence for this view would be obtained by demonstrating that the phonological code for a word is sometimes used in making the 'yes' response to that word in a lexical decision or categorization task; such a demonstration remains to be achieved."

Research in the past few years on rapid semantic categorisation has provided such a demonstration in English (Van Orden, 1987; Van Orden, Johnston, & Hale, 1988). The basic observation is that subjects produce larger false positive error rates when they respond to foils that are homophonic to category exemplars (e.g. "rows" for the category "a flower") than when they respond to spelling control foils (e.g. "Robs"). Further, false positive errors to nonword homophone foils (e.g. "sute" for "an article of clothing") exceed false positive errors to nonhomophonic nonword spelling controls; the phonological characteristics of the nonword foils are critical. In our opening section we report a number of similar demonstrations of phonological influences on positive lexical decision responses and naming times that are found in studies with Serbo-Croatian materials. In the subsequent sections we present data obtained in a variety of different contexts that amplify the claim that phonology plays a central role in word recognition in both Serbo-Croatian and English.

THE PHONOLOGICAL AMBIGUITY EFFECT IN SERBO-CROATIAN

Because of the use of two, partially overlapping alphabets, and because of the one letter–one phoneme principle for both alphabets, it is possible to construct letter strings in Serbo-Croatian that can be read legally in more than one way. Take "BETAP" as an example. Read strictly through the letter-to-sound correspondences of the Cyrillic alphabet, this letter string is pronounced /vetar/ and is a high-frequency word meaning "wind". Read strictly through the letter-to-sound correspondences of the Roman alphabet, "BETAP" is pronounced /betap/, a nonword. Reading with a mixture of the two sets of correspondences, Cyrillic and Roman, leads to the pronunciations /vetap/ and /betar/, which are also nonwords. The word meaning "wind" is transcribed in the Roman alphabet as "Vetar." This letter string supports only a single reading, /vetar/. No other readings are possible. "VETAR", unlike its Cyrillic mate "BETAP", is phonologically unambiguous. In the lexical decision and naming tasks, the latencies for "BETAP", and for letter strings like it, are considerably longer than the latencies for "VETAR", and for letter strings like it, even though the two letter strings are equal in frequency, syllabic structure, number of letters, and meaning. This contrast has been called the phonological ambiguity effect.

The effect of phonological ambiguity on "yes" responses in lexical decision and naming implies that phonology mediates word identification. The same conclusion holds for nonwords. Rejection latencies are slowed for the phonologically ambiguous nonword "BEMAP" relative to its phonologically unambiguous nonword mate "VEMAR". (Arguably, "BEMAP" is coded into more phonological forms than "VEMAR" and, because of this, rejection latencies for "BEMAP" are slowed relative to those for "VEMAR".) The fact that the phonological ambiguity effect occurs for both words and nonwords suggests that phonological mediation must be routine. Significantly, the phonological ambiguity effect is generally larger for words than nonwords (e.g. Feldman & Turvey, 1983; Lukatela, Popadic, Ognjenovic, & Turvey, 1980; Lukatela et al., 1989a). As already noted, experiments showing that homophony influences nonword processing more so than word processing have been interpreted to mean that phonological coding must be rare in ordinary word recognition (Coltheart et al., 1977; Henderson, 1982; McCusker et al., 1981). Applying this logic to the Serbo-Croatian results, phonological coding must be routine in ordinary word recognition because phonological ambiguity influences the processing of words more than the processing of nonwords.

It has often been suggested that phonological mediation should reveal effects dependent on the number of letters or syllables in a word (Forster & Chambers, 1973; Fredriksen & Kroll, 1976; Green & Shallice, 1976). Letter-length effects have been observed regularly in naming but hardly ever in lexical decision experiments using English-language materials (Henderson, 1982). The lack of such effects in lexical decision is used to argue that, contrary to dual process theory, there is no phonological route to the lexicon. Results from research with Serbo-Croatian materials demonstrate "number-of-constituents effects" and lead, thereby, to the contrary conclusion. "KOTBA" has one ambiguous letter (b), "BETAP" has two ambiguous letters (B and P), and "CABAHA" has three (c, b, and h). In each example the remaining unambiguous letters are shared letters. In the lexical decision task with such stimuli, the phonological ambiguity effect is larger the greater the number of ambiguous letters (Feldman & Turvey, 1983; Feldman, Kostic, Lukatela, & Turvey, 1983). The implication is that there is a pre-lexical process that is phonologically analytic (Turvey, Feldman, & Lukatela, 1984).

Other evidence points in the same direction. We would expect a phonological route to the lexicon to be largely indifferent to variables related to words, such as grammatical role and familiarity. The inflected nouns of Serbo-Croatian are most frequent and most prominent grammatically in the nominative singular form. A common finding is that nominative singulars are responded to faster than oblique forms (e.g. Lukatela, Carello, & Turvey, 1987). For example, "VENA" ("vein" in nominative singular) is responded to much faster than "VENI" (same word in dative or locative singular). However, if "VENA" and "VENI" are written in Cyrillic, that is, "BEHA" and "BEHИ," respectively, then the less frequent and less grammatically prominent dative/locative form BEHИ is responded to faster. The latency difference between "BEHA" and "VENA" is large (the phonological ambiguity effect); in contrast, the latencies to "BEHИ" and "VENI" do not differ (Feldman et al., 1983). The process underlying the phonological ambiguity effect is not affected by the grammatical significance of word stimuli. Furthermore, the effect has been shown to be indifferent to frequency; it is of the same magnitude for both frequent and infrequent words (Lukatela & Turvey, 1987).

There are two kinds of error patterns that enforce the notion of phonological mediation. Rejection of "BETAP"-type word as a word occurs on a high proportion of the times such a word is presented, for example, 20% (Lukatela, et al., 1978, experiment 1), 19% (Lukatela et al., 1978, experiment 2), 26% (Lukatela et al., 1980), 22% (Lukatela et al., 1989a, experiment 1), and 21% (Lukatela et al., 1989a, experiment 2). In these examples, average false negatives on phonologically unambiguous words were in the range of 1–4%. False negatives of the order of 20–25% suggest a process in which the representation activating the lexicon frequently does not correspond to a word. This is understandable if (a) "BETAP" can give rise to a number of phonological representations that do not correspond to a word, and (b) the lexicon is accessed through phonological representations. The same conclusion follows from a consideration of false positive responses.

There are two significant types of phonologically ambiguous nonwords in Serbo-Croatian. One type comprises letter strings that are (a) composed of shared letters, one or more of which are ambiguous; (b) unreadable as a word in either Roman or Cyrillic; and (c) unreadable as a word in a mixture of both alphabets. The other type satisfies (a) and (b) but not (c). Consider the nonword "HAPEB" as an example of the second type. If the letter-phoneme correspondences of both alphabets are applied to "HAPEB," then one of the resulting six phonological descriptions corresponds to a word, namely, /napev/ meaning "tune". It comes about by assigning the phoneme /n/ to H by the Cyrillic alphabet, the phoneme /p/ to P by the Roman alphabet, and the phoneme /v/ to B by the Cyrillic alphabet. Compare "HAPEB" to a nonword of the first type, such as "BEMAP". "BEMAP" has all but one letter in common with a real word ("BETAP"), and all but one phoneme in common with this real word. "HAPEB" similarly has all but one letter in common with a real word (")(AJTEB"). However, "HAPEB" has all phonemes in common with a real word, if both alphabets apply. If lexical access is visual, then false positives to "BEMAP" and "HAPEB" should be few and equal. In contrast, if lexical access is based on phonemic descriptions computed pre-lexically, and if the computation is analytic, assigning as many phonemes per letter as permitted, then false positives should be greater for "HAPEB". Experimentation shows that "BEMAP" and its unambiguous nonword control "VEMAR" generate the same small number of false positives (about 2–3%). When preceded by a neutral context word, "HAPEB" generated 31% false positives; when preceded by an associate of /napev/, namely, "MELODIJA" ("melody"), "HAPEB" generated 55% false positives (Lukatela et al., 1989b). The latencies of the false positives in the neutral and associative contexts were 890msec and 779msec, respectively. Furthermore, the false positive "yes" response times to "HAPEB"-type nonwords and correct "yes" response times to their corresponding control words (e.g. "NAPEV") were closely similar, 824msec to 795msec. The same pattern of results in respect to "BETAP" and "VETAR", and "HAPEB" and "NAPEV", held for naming (Lukatela et al., 1989a; Lukatela et al., 1989b). These results are understandable if (a) a phonologically ambiguous nonword can give rise automatically to all of the phonological representations that its letter structure permits; (b) for some phonologically ambiguous nonwords one of the automatically generated phonological representations corresponds to a word; and (c) the lexicon is accessed through phonological representations.

PSEUDOHOMOPHONIC ASSOCIATIVE PRIMING IN ENGLISH

Associative priming is the improvement in word identification that follows from preceding the target word by an "associate", for example, "table"–"chair", where the control is provided by the same target word following a nonassociate, for example, "novel"–"chair". This effect is said to arise from the connections within the internal lexicon.

Consider the task of naming the pseudohomophone "chare" following the associate "table". If the phonology of "table" is computed pre-lexically, and this representation is used to access the lexicon, then TABLE would activate fully its lexical representation /table/ and activate partially, through lexical interconnections, the associated representation /chair/. The preactivation of /chair/ could benefit the naming of "chare" in two ways. The first way is based on the reasonable assumption that the pre-lexically computed phonology is incomplete, for example, it would not specify stress. Consequently, to name a word, the full phonology must be retrieved from the lexicon. If "chare" is coded phonologically prior to lexical access, then it will contact /chair/ in the lexicon and, because of the associative priming of /chair/, retrieve the full phonology faster following TABLE than following a nonassociate. The second way "chare" could benefit from the priming of /chair/ is based on the assumption that the pre-lexical computation of phonology and the accessing of lexical phonology ordinarily interact in the determination of a letter string's name. If so, then "chare" will benefit from the prior presentation of "table" through the feedback from the preactivated lexical item /chair/ to the process by which the phonology of "chare" is assembled. (The notions of assembled phonology and lexical phonology are not mutually exclusive, and in interpretations of Serbo-Croatian word-naming the need for both sources of phonological information has been repeatedly underscored [Carello, Lukatela, & Turvey, 1988; Lukatela & Turvey, 1987; Lukatela et al, 1989b; Lukatela & Turvey, 1990a]). Arguments of a similar kind apply to the even more interesting case in which the pseudohomophone is in the role of the prime, for example, "tayble"–"chair". According to the phonological mediation hypothesis, the context stimulus "tayble" will activate the lexical entry /table/ and, by lexical interconnections, the associate /chair/. As a result, naming "chair" will benefit from the prior processing of "tayble".

In sum, the phonological mediation hypothesis of dual process theory makes the following predictions: (a) A target pseudohomophone will be named faster in the context of an associate of the pseudohomophone's source word than in an unrelated context; and (b) a target word will be named faster in the context of a pseudohomophone whose source word is an associate of the target word than in the context of a pseudohomophone whose source word is unrelated to the target word. Four experiments were conducted with pseudohomophones in a primed naming task. In two experiments, target pseudowords that sounded like real words, for example, "chare", were preceded either by context words that related associatively to the word with which the target was homophonic, "table"–"chare", or by context words that were not associatively related, "novel"–"chare". Control pairs were "table"–"thare" and "novel"–"thare" (in the first experiment) and "table"–"chark" and "novel"–"chark" (in the second experiment). The prior presentation of "table" relative to the prior presentation of "novel" benefited the naming of "chare" but not the naming of "thare" or "chark". The third experiment placed pseudohomophones in the role of primes, that is, "tayble"–"chair", with such pairs comprising only 8% of all pairs seen by a subject in order to counter guessing strategies. If the prime "tayble" activated /table/, then /chair/ would be activated associatively and the target "chair" would be named faster than if "tarble" was the prime. This result was obtained. The fourth experiment extended the design of the third to include "table"–"chair" pairs and a comparison of a short (280msec) and a long (500msec) delay between context and target onsets. The results of this experiment are presented in Table 9.1. The priming due to associated pseudohomophones was unaffected by onset asynchrony and equal in magnitude to that due to associated words.

TABLE 9.1
Mean Naming Latencies L (in msec) and Error Rate ER (in %) for "Table"–"Chair", "Tayble"–"Chair", and "Tarble"–"Chair" Pairs and their Unrelated Controls

	Context–Target Relation			
	Related		*Unrelated*	
Context	*L*	*ER*	*l*	*ER*
SOA = 500msec				
Word	527	2.29	545	1.25
Pseudohomophone	537	0.21	552	1.04
Pseudohomograph	549	1.25	544	0.83
SOA = 280msec				
Word	543	0.83	556	1.46
Pseudohomophone	555	1.46	573	1.67
Pseudohomograph	572	0.42	571	0.83

Source: Lukatela and Turvey (1991).

The general consensus is that associative priming—whether the mechanism be spreading activation, expectancy set, or resonant matching (Stone & Van Orden, 1989)—is a lexical process. In order for the observed associative effects to have occurred, there must have been lexical access. Because of the homophony conditions under which these effects occurred, it must have been the case that the lexical representations accessed were phonological, and that the access was through phonology. It seems unlikely that an account of the data can be given in terms of a model that does not grant a central role to phonology in lexical access. Consider analogy models (e.g. Glushko, 1979), for example. "Tayble" would be assigned a phonology by analogy with its orthographic neighbours. To enhance the naming of "Chair," this assembled phonological representation /table/ would have to affect the lexical representation of "Chair." The minimal implication of that /table/ must function as a lexical access code, triggering lexical processes beneficial to the eventual naming of "Chair."

SIMILAR PROCESSING OF ENGLISH WORDS AND THEIR PSEUDOHOMOPHONIC COUNTERPARTS

According to models that draw the distinction between assembled phonology and accessed phonology, "Tayble" should be affected by concurrent demands on processing capacity more so than "Table." A phonological code for "Tayble" cannot be found by the direct route and must be assembled; in contrast, a phonological code for "Table" can be found directly rendering the assembled phonology unnecessary. If assembling phonology demands more processing capacity then the more demanding the concurrent activity the larger the difference in naming times between "Tayble" and "Table." In contrast, if "Tayble" and "Table" are named in the same way (for example, both rely on assembled phonology), as suggested by the experiments of Lukatela and Turvey (1991), then increasing the difficulty of concurrent activity should affect the naming latencies of each in equal degrees.

Experiments show that processing low-frequency (LF) words demands more capacity than processing high-frequency (HF) words (Becker, 1976; Herdman & Dobbs, 1989; Paap & Noel, 1991). Experiments also show, however, that LF (regular) words are typically named as fast as HF (regular) words (Seidenberg, Waters, Barnes, & Tannenhaus, 1984; Taraban & McClelland, 1987). One interpretation is that the process of assembling the phonology of LF words must often occur at a pace that is faster than direct lexical access and commensurate with the pace of direct lexical access for HF words. Consequently, reducing available capacity should enhance the naming latency difference beween LF and HF regular words; with less capacity, naming LF words should be more dependent on the direct route, which is slower than the direct route for HF words (Paap & Noel, 1991).

Consider the LF word "Foal" and the HF word "Door" and their pseudohomophones "Fole" and "Dore", respectively. Consider the task of naming these letter strings in the context of concurrently holding in memory either five digits (high load) or one digit (low load). According to the dual-process theory we should see the following outcomes: (a) "Fole" and "Dore" should be named more slowly under the high load than under the low load; (b) the difference in naming times between "Foal" and "Door" should be greater under the high load than under the low load; and, therefore, (c) the dependency of "Fole" and "Dore" on load should be different from the dependency of "Foal" and "Door" on load. The implications of Lukatela and Turvey's (1991) experiments do not lead to such detailed predictions but they do point to a very different major expectation: Words and nonwords homophonic to them should be affected similarly by load variation.

To adjudicate between these contrasting expectations, the following paradigm was used (Lukatela & Turvey, 1993): Between the presentation and recall of a number, subjects in two experiments named a visually presented letter string—either a pseudohomophone (e.g. "Fole," "Dore") or its real word counterpart ("Foal," "Door"). Relative to a one-digit memory load, a five-digit load speeded up the naming of LF words (e.g. "Foal" and their pseudohomophones ("Fole") and slowed down the naming of HF words (e.g. "Door") and their pseudohomophones ("Dore"). This feature is unexpected from a model of oral reading in which nonwords are named by a slow process that assembles the letter string's phonology and words are named by a fast process that accesses a phonology already assembled in the lexicon. Pseudohomophones should be uniformly slowed by increased concurrent demands on attention, as should LF words, given that they rely heavily on the more attention-consuming process of assembled phonology. In sum, "Fole" and "Dore" should have been affected similarly by load, with poorer performance under the higher load, and "Foal" and "Door" should have been affected dissimilarly by load, with the higher load more detrimental to "Foal" than to "Door". Clearly, these predictions of dual process theory were not confirmed. The main feature of the data is consistent, however, with the results of Lukatela and Turvey (1991): A nonword homophonic with a word is processed like that word.

Nonwords homophonic with HF words behaved like HF words, and nonwords homophonic with LF words behaved like LF words. Why should this be so? In processing terms, what makes "Foal" more like "Fole" than like "Door," and what makes "Door" more like "Dore" than like "Foal?" If lexical representations are phonological, and are characterised by thresholds (Morton, 1969) or file positions (Foster & Bednall, 1976) that reflect their respective frequencies of occurrence, then the equivalencies of "Foal" and "Fole," on the one hand, and "Door" and "Dore", on the other hand, would be potentially understandable. The latter is insufficient, however, to account for the slower naming of pseudohomophones and the direction of the load effect as a function of frequency. To capture both the sameness and the difference in processing "Door" and "Dore" (or "Foal" and "Fole") a notion such as pattern covariance seems to be required. The orthographic structures of "Door" and "Dore" will both specify the same pattern of phonologic subsymbols. Denoting orthographic subsymbols by *o* and phonologic sybsymbols by *p*, the two functional relations between *o* and *p* involving "Door" and "Dore" are alike in *p* and in aspects of *o* but different in other aspects of *o* and in the connection weights between *o* and *p*. If connections are weaker for the mapping "Dore" → /door/ than for the mapping "Door" → /door/, then naming "Dore" will be slower than naming "Door." However, give the overlap in subsymbols and connections, any process that affects the one mapping (and/or its output) is likely to affect the other mapping (and/or its output) similarly. Behind the preceding analyses is the theme that assembled phonology is not based on explicit rules, as traditionally argued in dual-process theory (e.g. Coltheart, 1978), but on processes constrained implicitly by the continuous statistical regularity of orthographic-phonologic pairings (Van Orden et al., 1990).

Armed with the foregoing perspective on the commonalities and differences between a word and its homophonic nonword partner, we can turn to the more perplexing question of why the five-digit load should enhance "Foal" and "Fole" and impede "Door" and "Dore." A number of accounts of word identification assume a verification stage in which the results of stimulus encoding—candidate representations of the input—are compared to the representation of the input in the sensory store (e.g. Paap, Newsome, McDonald, & Schvaneveldt, 1982). Verification results in a match or a mismatch. If the degree of fit between the visual sensory evidence and a candidate representation exceeds a decision criterion, then the item is recognised and the appropriate articulatory units are activated. (The inclination to ascribe a verification process to naming is not altogether common. Some argue that in evaluating the nature of lexical access, naming has an advantage over lexical decision in that it does not necessitate post-lexical processes. In signal detection terminology, whereas lexical decision involves sensitivity and bias, naming involves only sensitivity; it does not entail a decision that requires a criterion [Seidenberg, Waters, Sanders, & Langer, 1984].)

We can entertain the possibility that the effects of load were localised at the post-lexical verification step. That a verification step may have to be appealed to is suggested by the lexicality by frequency interaction. Whereas "Fole" was named almost as quickly as "Foal," "Dore" was named much more slowly than "Door." Intuitively, for the average reader, criteria for (expectations about) the visual form befitting /door/ are more explicit and stringent than those about the visual form befitting /foal/. In consequence, the phonological representation /foal/ is accepted as befitting "Foal" and "Fole" with near equal speed but the phonological representation /door/ is accepted as befitting DORE relatively slowly compared to the acceptance that it befits "Door." Clearly, a key idea with respect to verification is "criterion level". Is criterion level affected by load? A lowering of criterion commensurate with the demands of concurrent activity would explain the faster naming of "Foal" and "Fole" when five-digits were being remembered but it would not explain the slower naming of "Door" and "Dore" under the same conditions. That the effects of variations in cognitive load and of other task features such as context (e.g. proportion of exception foils, proportion of nonwords, and so on) can be traced to adjustments in a single parameter, such as criterion level, is an attractive idea (see Stone & Van Orden, 1993). What is needed to make it work in the present context is an understanding of how a single direction of change in criterion level can interact with frequency to produce an increase in naming time when frequency is high and a decrease in naming time when frequency is low. A consideration of processes below the verification stage might be required. Let us suppose that concurrent cognitive activity induces a reduction in (a) the criterion level and (b) the weights on the connections between orthographic and phonologic subsymbols proportional to their magnitudes, with both reductions scaled to the difficulty of the concurrent activity. A possible outcome of (b) is that a high cognitive load will reduce the efficacy of networks subserving HF words to a more significant degree than it will reduce the efficacy of networks subserving LF words. If the advantage of (a) outweighs the disadvantage of (b) for LF words, and if the advantage of (a) does not outweigh the disadvantage of (b) for HF words, then the observed interaction of load and frequency would result.

BACKWARD AND FORWARD PRIMING BY PHONOLOGY IN ENGLISH AND SERBO-CROATIAN

The results discussed in the preceding sections were in respect to experimental procedures that could be applied in one or the other language but not both. In this section we consider experimental results from paradigms that are equally applicable in both languages. As we shall see, comparable results are obtained with one of these paradigms and contrary results are obtained with the other paradigm.

Backward-priming experiments entail the identification of briefly exposed target words under backward-masking conditions with the following key features: The masks are nonwords, phonologically related or unrelated to the targets, and themselves followed by patterned stimuli to reduce their identification and, thereby, guessing strategies about target/mask relationships. The figural structure of the masks, and comparable intensities of the targets and masks, confine the masking effects on the targets to primarily central processes (Michaels & Turvey, 1979; Turvey, 1973). Perfetti, Bell, and Delaney (1988) argued that if phonology is computed automatically, then phonological similarity between the mask and target will reduce the interruption of central processing normally induced by the mask. They reasoned that a phonologically similar mask will reinforce the phonological information activated partially by the target. In contrast, a phonologically dissimilar mask will activate partially other phonological information. If it is the case that lexical activation follows from phonological information, then a target preceding a phonologically similar mask will be identified better than a target preceding a phonologically dissimilar mask. The idea is that lexical entries partially activated by a target will be activated further by a subsequent mask with common phonological properties. The outcomes of experiments by Naish (1980) and by Perfetti et al. (1988), both using native speakers/readers of English and English-language materials, were in agreement with this prediction, as were the experiments of Lukatela and Turvey (1990b) using native speakers/readers of Serbo-Croatian and Serbo-Croatian materials. All of these experiments showed significantly higher levels of target identification for homophonous masking than for nonhomophonous masking. Put differently, none showed graphemic backward-priming effects over and above phonological priming effects.

A large number of experiments demonstrate unequivocally that with Serbo-Croatian materials there is *no orthographic priming in lexical decision or naming over and above phonological priming* (Lukatela & Turvey, 1990a; Lukatela, Carello, & Turvey, 1990a). In these experiments, the primes and targets consist of phonologically unique letter strings written either in different alphabets (e.g. prime is in Cyrillic, target is in Roman) and different cases, or in the same alphabet (both are in Cyrillic) and the same case. When they are in the same case the graphemically dissimilar/phonologically similar pairs never share more than one letter in common, and often they share none; the graphemically similar/phonologically similar pairs share all but one letter in common. In different cases and alphabets, there are no visually identical letter forms.

Lukatela and Turvey (1990a) made five main observations: (1) Phonological similarity effects in both lexical decision and naming are independent of graphemic similarity; (2) phonological similarity need not enhance lexical decision—the direction of its effect depends on lexicality, target familarity, and the form of the similarity (specifically, the position of the phoneme that distinguishes prime and target) (see also Lukatela et al. 1990a, 1990b); (3) phonological similarity speeds up the naming of words and nonwords by the same amount (see also Lukatela et al., 1990a); (4) the effect of phonological similarity is nullified in naming but not in lexical decision by a difference in the stress patterns of the prime and target; and (5) effects of phonological similarity are manifest even when the prime is a masked nonword.

In respect to English, the status of forward phonological *and* orthographic priming is unclear. Although Hillinger (1980) provided evidence for strictly phonological priming in the lexical decision task, the observation has not been replicated in further experiments with lexical decision (Martin & Jensen, 1988) and in experiments using naming latency (Peter, Turvey, & Lukatela, 1990). These same experiments, however, also failed to demonstrate any benefits to processing of a graphemically similar preceding stimulus.

In sum, whereas forward-priming effects of phonology are easy to demonstrate in Serbo-Croatian they are very hard to demonstrate in English. Why this difference should exist, given the sameness of the two languages to the backward effects of phonological similarity, is unclear at this stage. Further research will be needed to identify the source of this task by language interaction.

SUMMARY

In the different lines of research summarised here, we have sought to underscore the central role of phonology in word identification in both English and Serbo-Croatian. The focus of our concluding remarks is why research in English may, on occasion, be less successful in demonstrating phonology's role than research in Serbo-Croatian or, conversely, why phonology's role may be more transparent in research with Serbo-Croatian than in research with English.

In several papers (e.g. Feldman & Turvey, 1983; Lukatela et al., 1990a; Lukatela et al., 1980; Lukatela & Turvey, 1987, 1990b) we have suggested that the differences between English word processing and Serbo-Croatian word processing lies in the relative prominence of a level of processing units representing the phonemes of the language. The extreme view is that whereas such a layer exists for Serbo-Croatian, intermediary between letter units and word units, it does not exist for English. Many models of English word processing conform to this view in making little, if any, use of phonological information in word identification. The moderate view is that a level of phoneme units does exist and does participate in English word processing, but that its contribution is less distinct than in Serbo-Croatian. Recent experiments with English may be taken as consistent with this moderate position (Perfetti et al., 1988; Rosson, 1985; Van Orden, 1987; Van Orden, Johnston, & Hale, 1988). An appreciation of why a phoneme level may differ in the distinctiveness of its role across languages is provided through the notion of covariant learning (Lewicki, 1986; Van Orden, 1987). The basic hypothesis is that any linguistic features that frequently covary with orthographic features will become associated. As a consequence of covariant learning, a word's spelling will activate most strongly those linguistic features that covary to the highest degree with its orthographic features. Thus, the process of identifying a particular word will be dominated by the subset of linguistic features that are most likely to be functional for the multiple occurrences of that word. In Serbo-Croatian, the consistency of letter–phoneme correspondences in the written language will bias the word processing mechanism, through covariant learning, to a marked dependency on letter units–phoneme units connections. Because the consistencies in written English may range across several linguistic levels (Rozin & Gleitman, 1977), the involvement of a phonemic level of processing will be less distinguished, and the dependency on letter–phoneme connections less pronounced.

The foregoing ideas converge on a possible understanding of the different status of phonological priming in the two languages. Suppose that phonological priming reflects pre-lexical activity defined over letter–phoneme connections. In English, the number of these connections would be very large. There would be many connections representing the many relations at the grain size of individual letters, and probably at coarser grains involving multiple letters. In Serbo-Croatian, by contrast, the number of these connections would be very small. Besides a contrast of number, these connections in English and Serbo-Croatian would contrast in mean strength, specifically, the mean level of activation of a letter unit required to active a phoneme unit. The connections would be stronger on the average in Serbo-Croatian than in English, with greater uniformity of strengths across the letter-to-phoneme connections in Serbo-Croatian than in English. In sum, because the pre-lexical connections of Serbo-Croatian are few and strong, phonological priming is reliable; because the pre-lexical connections of English are many and weak, phonological priming is unreliable. Experiments and simulations of the respective cognitive microstructures will be needed to clarify the contrasting opportunities that each language provides for phonological processes to influence measures of word recognition.

ACKNOWLEDGEMENTS

This research was supported in part by National Institute of Child Health and Human Development Grants HD–08945 and HD–01994 to the first author and Haskins Laboratories respectively. Correspondence should be addressed to G. Lukatela or M.T. Turvey, Haskins Laboratories, 270 Crown Street, New Haven, CT 06510, USA.

REFERENCES

Becker, C.A. (1976). Allocation of attention during visual word recognition. *Journal of Experimental Psychology: Human Perception and Performance, 2*, 556–566.

Coltheart, M. (1978). Lexical access in simple reading task. In G. Underwood (Ed.), *Strategies of information processing*. London: Academic Press.

Coltheart, M., Davelaar, E., Jonasson, J.T., & Besner, D. (1977). Access to internal lexicon. In S. Dornic (Ed.), *Attention and performance Vol. VI*, pp. 535–555). New York: Academic Press.

Carello, C., Lukatela, G., & Turvey, M.T. (1987). Rapid naming is affected by association but not by syntax. *Memory and Cognition, 16*, 187–195.

Davelaar, E., Coltheart, M., Besner, D., & Jonasson, J.T. (1978) Phonological recoding and lexical access. *Memory and Cognition, 6*, 391–402.

Feldman, L.B., Kostic, A., Lukatela, G., & Turvey, M.T. (1983). An evaluation of the "Basic orthographic syllabic structure" in a phonologically shallow orthography. *Psychological Research, 45*, 55–72.

Feldman, L.B., Lukatela, G., & Turvey, M.T. (1985). Effects of phonological ambiguity on beginning readers of Serbo-Croatian. *Journal of Experimental Child Psychology, 39*, 492–510.

Feldman, L.B., & Turvey, M.T. (1983). Word recognition in Serbo-Croatian is phonologically analytic. *Journal of Experimental Pychology: Human Perception and Performance, 9*, 288–298.

Foster, K.I., & Bednall, E.S. (1976). Terminating and exhaustive search in lexical access. *Memory and Cognition, 4*, 53–61.

Forster, K.I., & Chambers, S.M. (1973). Lexical access and naming time. *Journal of Verbal Learning and Verbal Behavior, 12*, 627–635.

Fredriksen, J.R., & Kroll, J.F. (1976). Spelling and sound: Approaches to the internal lexicon. *Journal of Experimental Psychology: Human Perception and Performance, 2*, 361–379.

Glushko, R. (1979). The organisation and activation of orthographic knowledge in reading aloud. *Journal of Experimental Psychology: Human Perception and Performance, 5*, 674–691.

Green, D.W., & Shallice, T. (1976). Direct visual access in reading for meaning. *Memory and Cognition, 4*, 753–758.

Henderson, L. (1982). *Orthography and word recognition in reading*. New York: Academic Press.

Herdman, C.M., & Dobbs, A.R. (1989). Attentional demands of visual word recognition. *Journal of Experimental Psychology: Human Perception and Performance, 15*, 124–132.

Hillinger, M.L. (1980). Priming effects with phonemically similar words: the encoding-bias hypothesis reconsidered. *Memory and Cognition, 8*, 115–123.

Humphreys, G.W., & Evett, L.J. (1985). Are there independent lexical and nonlexical routes in word processing? An evaluation of the dual-route theory of reading. *The Behavioral and Brain Sciences, 8*, 689–740.

Lewicki, P. (1986). Processing information about covariations that cannot be articulated. *Journal of Experimental Psychology: Learning, Memory and Cognition, 12*, 135–146.

Lukatela, G., Carello, C., & Turvey, M.T. (1987). Lexical representation of regular and irregular inflected nouns. *Language and Cognitive Processes, 2*, 1–17.

Lukatela, G., Carello, C., & Turvey, M.T. (1990a). Phonemic priming by words and pseudowords. *European Journal of Cognitive Psychology, 2*, 375–394.

Lukatela, G., Carello, C., & Turvey, M.T. (1990b). Phonemic, associative, and grammatical context effects with identified and unidentified primes. *Language and Speech, 33*, 1–18.

Lukatela, G., Feldman, L.B., Turvey, M.T., Carello, C., & Katz, L. (1989a). Context effects in bi-alphabetical word perception. *Journal of Memory and Language, 28*, 214–236.

Lukatela, G., Popadic, D., Ognjenovic, P., & Turvey, M.T. (1980). Lexical decision in a phonologically shallow orthography. *Memory and Cognition, 8*, 124–132.

Lukatela, G., Savic, M., Gligorijevic, B., Ognjenovic, P., & Turvey, M.T. (1978). Bi-alphabetical lexical decision. *Language and Speech, 21*, 142–163.

Lukatela, G., & Turvey, M.T. (1987). Loci of phonological effects in recognising words written in a shallow orthography. *Psychological Research, 49*, 139–146.

Lukatela, G., & Turvey, M.T. (1990a). Phonemic similarity effects and prelexical phonology. *Memory and Cognition, 18*, 128–152.

Lukatela, G., & Turvey, M.T. (1990b). Automatic and prelexical computation of phonology in visual word identification. *European Journal of Cognitive Psychology, 2*, 325–343.

Lukatela, G., & Turvey, M.T. (1991). Phonological access to the lexicon: Evidence from associative priming with pseudohomophones. *Journal of Experimental Psychology: Human Perception and Performance.*

Lukatela, G., & Turvey, M.T. (1993). Similar attentional, frequency, and associative effects for pseudohomophones and words. *Journal of Experimental Psychology: Human Perception and Performance, 19*, 166–178.

Lukatela, G., Turvey, M.T., Feldman, L.B., Carello, C., & Katz, L. (1989b). Alphabet priming in bi-alphabetical word perception. *Journal of Memory and Language, 28*, 237–254.

Martin, R.C., & Jensen, C.R. (1988). Phonological priming in the lexical decision task: A failure to replicate. *Memory and Cognition, 16*, 505–521.

McCusker, L.X., Hillinger, M.L., & Bias, R.G. (1981). Phonological recoding and reading. *Psychological Bulletin, 89*, 217–245.

Michaels, C.F., & Turvey, M.T. (1979). Central sources of visual masking: Indexing the structures supporting seeing at a single brief glance. *Psychological Research, 41*, 1–61.

Morton, J. (1969). Interaction of information in word recognition. *Psychological Review, 76*, 165–178.

Naish, P. (1980). The effects of graphemic and phonemic similarity between targets and masks in a backward visual masking paradigm. *Quarterly Journal of Experimental Psychology, 32*, 57–68.

Paap, K.R., Newsome, S.L., McDonald, J.E., & Schvaneveldt, R.W. (1982). An activation–verification model for letter and word recognition: The word superiority effect. *Psychological Review, 89*, 573–594.

Paap, K.R., & Noel, R.W. (1991). Dual-route models of print to sound: Still a good horse race. *Psychological Research, 53*, 13–24.

Perfetti, C.A., Bell, L.C., & Delaney, S. (1988). Automatic (prelexical) phonetic activation in silent word reading: Evidence from backward masking. *Journal of Memory and Language, 27*, 59–70.

Peter, M., Turvey, M.T., & Lukatela, G. (1990). Phonological priming: Failure to replicate in the rapid naming task. *Bulletin of the Psychonomic Society, 28*, 389–392.

Rosson, M.B. (1985). The interaction of pronunciation rules and lexical representations in reading aloud. *Memory and Cognition, 13*, 90–98.

Rozin, P., & Gleitman, L.R. (1977). The structure and acquisition of reading, II. The reading process and the acquisition of the alphabetic principle. In A. Reber & D. Scarborough (Eds.), *Towards a psychology of reading*. Hillsdale, NJ: Lawrence Erlbaum Associates Inc.

Rubenstein, H., Lewis, S.S., & Rubenstein, M.A. (1971). An evidence for phonemic reading in visual word recognition. *Journal of Verbal Learning and Verbal Behavior, 10*, 645–654.

Seidenberg, M.S., Waters, G.S., Barnes, M.A., & Tannenhaus, M.K. (1984). When does irregular spelling or pronunciation influence word recognition? *Journal of Verbal Learning and Verbal Behavior, 23*, 383–404.

Seidenberg, M.S., Waters, G.S., Sanders, M., & Langer, P. (1984). Pre- and postlexical loci of contextual effects on word recognition. *Memory and Cognition, 17*, 315–328.

Stone, G.O., & Van Orden, G.C. (1989). Are words represented by nodes? *Memory and Cognition, 17*, 511–524.

Stone, G., & Van Orden, G.C. (1993). Strategic control of processing in word recognition. *Journal of Experimental Psychology: Human Perception and Performance, 19*, 744–774.

Taraban, R. & McClelland, J.L. (1987). Conspiracy effects in word pronunciation. *Journal of Memory and Language, 26*, 608–631.

Turvey, M.T. (1973). On peripheral and central processes in vision: Inferences from masking with patterned stimuli. *Psychological Review, 80*, 1–52.

Turvey, M.T., Feldman, L., & Lukatela, G. (1984). The Serbo-Croatian orthography constrains the reader to a phonologically analytic strategy. In L. Henderson (Ed.), *Orthographies and reading* (pp. 81–89). Hillsdale, NJ: Lawrence Erlbaum Associates Inc.

Van Orden, G.C. (1987). A ROWS is a ROSE: Spelling, sound and reading. *Memory and Cognition, 15*, 181–198.

Van Orden, G.C. (1991). Phonologic mediation is fundamental to reading. In D. Besner & G. Humphreys (Eds.), *Basic processes in reading: Visual word recognition*. Hillsdale, NJ: Lawrence Erlbaum Associates Inc.

Van Orden, G.C., Johnston, J.C., & Hale, B.L. (1988). Word identification in reading proceeds from spelling to sound to meaning. *Journal of Experimental Psychology: Learning, Memory, and Cognition, 14*, 371–385.

Van Orden, G.C., Pennington, B.F., & Stone, G.O. (1990). Word identification in reading and the promise of subsymbolic psycholinguistics. *Psychological Review, 97*, 488–522.

10 Non-semantic Reading in Kanji and English: Universal and Language-specific Features

Sumiko Sasanuma
International University of Health and Welfare, Otawara City, Japan

Karalyn Patterson
MRC Applied Psychology Unit, Cambridge, UK

INTRODUCTION

The ways in which different orthographies (e.g. Japanese kanji, Japanese kana, and the English alphabet) encode the pronunciations and meanings of the words in the spoken languages are quite dissimilar. This dissimilarity might be expected to constitute an important variable exerting differential effects on the processing procedures used, that is: (1) in computation of a phonological representation corresponding to the pronunciation of the written word; and (2) in computation of a semantic representation corresponding to the meaning of the written word.

In this chapter, we will focus on the first type of computation used in transcoding from orthography to phonology, and examine how these different ways of encoding in different orthographies are reflected in the reading behaviour of neurological patients with different orthographic backgrounds. Specifically, we will use our reported data on a particular pattern of reading impairment, sometimes called "nonsemantic reading" (Shallice, 1988), manifested by Japanese- and English-speaking neurological patients (Patterson & Hodges, 1992; Sasanuma, Sakuma, & Kitano, 1992), in such a way that comparisons can be made between their performance patterns, and discuss universal and script-specific features of reading.

BACKGROUND

Characteristic Features of Nonsemantic Reading in English

In the early 1980s (1980–86), there was a series of case studies of neurological patients who exhibited various degrees of correct reading of exception words in

English without comprehending their meaning. Among these patients were WLP with pre-senile dementia (Schwartz, Saffran, & Marin, 1980), HTR with a progressive illness of unknown origin (Shallice, Warrington, & McCarthy, 1983), MP with head trauma due to a motor accident (Bub, Cancelliere, & Kertesz, 1985), and another pre-senile dementia patient KT (McCarthy & Warrington, 1986). As "exception" words (e.g. PINT and FLOOD, where the correspondence between letter clusters and phonemes is not regular or predictable) are unlikely to be processed correctly by means of subword orthography-to-phonology correspondence rules, the patients who can pronounce these words correctly but not comprehend them have led these authors to conclude that it must be possible to access word-specific phonology independently from semantic information. However, investigators of these cases also report that the patients' performance on exception words was considerably worse than on regular words and the majority of errors on exception words were regularisations (pronouncing PINT as [pɪnt], which is very close to a pattern of impairment known as surface alexia (Patterson, Marshall, & Coltheart, 1985). Thus, the hypothesis of nonsemantic lexical procedures in reading words in English remains unsettled. Our comparative study of two groups of patients with different orthographic backgrounds may add some new perspectives on this issue.

Brief Introduction to Japanese Kanji and Kana

In written Japanese, two orthographies, kanji and kana, are used in combination. They are distinct from each other as well as from alphabetic orthographies, such as English, in the way each encodes spoken language or phonological information. In kana characters, which correspond directly to syllables or the moraic segments of spoken Japanese, this relationship is highly regular and rule-governed, with one-to-one correspondences between individual characters and their pronunciations. In contrast, kanji, morphographic or logographic characters of Chinese origin, represent the other extreme, where the same character can have several completely different pronunciations or readings, depending on different lexical and morphological contexts. For instance, a single kanji word 月 meaning "moon" is pronounced as [tsuki] (which is a kun-reading corresponding to the native Japanese pronunciation of the word) and so pronounced when it is a part of a compound 月見 [tsukimi] meaning "moon viewing", but the same kanji has to be pronounced as [getsu] when it is a part of another compound 月曜 [getsuyoo] meaning "Monday". That is to say, the orthography-to-phonology relationship for kanji words is highly dependent on intraword context, each kanji whole word providing necessary information about the pronunciation of its component characters. Furthermore, a kanji character cannot be phonologically decomposed: In the character 月 [tsuki], there are no identifiable components corresponding to the phonemes [t] and [u], etc., nor even to the syllables [tsu] and [ki]. These features of the relationship between orthography and phonology in kanji may have the following implication for kanji processing: the pronunication of a kanji word can be computed *only* by whole-word, lexical procedures. Therefore, convincing documentation of correct pronunciation of kanji in the absence of comprehension in Japanese neurological patients would constitute compelling evidence for a word-specific procedure from orthography to phonology independent of lexical semantics.

NONSEMANTIC READING IN KANJI

The Japanese data used for the present comparison were extracted from a longitudinal study of three demented patients (Sasanuma et al., 1992) as part of the Tokyo Metropolitan Institute of Gerontology Research Project on Dementia.

Characteristics of the Patients

The subjects were three patients with a clinical diagnosis of probable dementia, consecutively referred to the Psychological Section of Matsudo Hospital for neuropsychological assessment. Table 10.1 summarises the demographic information on these patients, including age, gender, years of education, and clinical diagnosis. All of them were right-handed. The initial interview with each patient and his/her family disclosed that some episodes of memory failure or behavioural characteristics indicative of early signs of the disease were present about 12 to 18 months prior to their first visit to the hospital. Neurological examination at the time of initial interview of each patient was essentially negative with respect to focal abnormalities, and instead a mild to moderate degree of bilateral generalised cortical atrophy was disclosed on computed tomography (CT) and/or magnetic resonance imaging (MRI) scanning.

Cognitive Abilities. At the initial examination, all three patients showed only mild impairment on one or two subtests in one or two of the four major cognitive domains (orientation, memory, language, and visuo-spatial abilities) in the Higher Brain Function Test (Sasanuma et al., 1985). The general pattern and the rate of decline on various subtests in the following months were more

TABLE 10.1
Demographic Information on 3 Japanese Patients

Patient	*Age at 1st Exam.*	*Sex*	*Educ. (yrs)*	*Diagnosis*
KS	54	M	11	DAT
MS	67	F	12	DAT
NO	74	M	14	DAT

DAT: Dementia of the Alzheimer Type

or less similar among the three patients: faster and greater decline on subtests that tap recent memory (delayed *story recall*), semantic aspects of linguistic processing (*confrontation naming*, *word fluency*, and *reading comprehension* of 10 words both in kanji and kana), and visuo-spatial and constructive abilities, in contrast to much slower and smaller amount of decline on those subtests that tap immediate memory (*sentence repetition*, *digit span forward*), and phonological aspects of language (*pronunciation* of the same set of 10 words used for *reading comprehension*). In fact, in each of the three patients, pronunciation of the 10 written kanji and kana words continued to be flawless until the very end of the three-year study.

Tests

The major test used was a 50-item Kanji Pronunciation-Comprehension Test (KPCT). Two other tests, the Higher Brain Function Test (HBFT) for evaluation of the patients' overall cognitive abilities and a semantic categorisation test, were also given to each patient in parallel with the KPCT.

50-item Kanji Pronunciation-Comprehension Test (KPCT). This test comprises a total of 50 target kanji words (all nouns) selected in such a way that the distribution of frequency of usage of these words is a representative sample of kanji words occurring in daily newspapers and magazines. Eight of these 50 words represented the frequency range of greater than 400 per million, nine words of less than 15 per million, and the remaining words the intermediate range (National Language Research Institute, 1970). Twenty-eight of the 50 words consisted of two kanji characters, and the other 22 were single-character words. Each word was printed in bold type, 2.5cm in size, at the centre of a white card. For the reading task, each patient was asked to read the word on each card aloud. For the comprehension task, the word-to-picture matching paradigm was used, where each patient was asked to point to the picture that matched the stimulus word among a display of four pictures consisting of the target, a semantically related distractor, a phonologically related distractor, and an irrelevant drawing.

The Interval of Test Sessions and the Length of the Follow-up. As a general rule, the tests were given every six months in the early stage of the disease process when the patients demonstrated mild cognitive deficits, and every three months at the later stages when the speed of decline became more rapid. The study was continued as long as the patient was able to respond reliably to the tests. The length of the follow-up using HBFT for each patient was 36, 28, and 36 months, respectively. However, we had to stop administering the KPCT a few months earlier in each case (29, 26, and 33 months, respectively) because the patients in advanced stages of dementia became too fatigued to complete this rather lengthy test.

Results

Table 10.2 summarises the three patients' performance on repeated administration of the KPCT. It is clear that pronunciation of the 50 written kanji words in each patient was retained at a very high level during the whole period of the three-year study, which is in sharp contrast to a steady decline in their ability to match the same set of words to pictures.

Pronunciation Performance. The pronunciation of most of the 50 words by the three patients was virtually flawless in both accuracy and speed throughout the three-year study. Particularly striking was the ease or automaticity with which they pronounced each word, even at the advanced stages when comprehension performance had dropped to chance level in each patient. The patient's response times (RTs) for the individual test words were not measured at the time of testing, but according to the subjective impression of the two experienced examiners, they were clearly within the normal range across the whole span of the longitudinal study.

Table 10.3 summarises the types of errors made by the three patients over the last three to four testing sessions. They were: (1) "visual" (e.g. 文学 [bungaku] → 文字 [modʒi]; (2) "phonological" (e.g. [kakoo] → [gakoo]); (3) "no response"

TABLE 10.2
Performance (% Correct Responses) for KS, MS, NO on the KPCT during the 3-year Study

				MPIE			
Patient		18	24	27	29		
KS	Pronunciation	100	92	94	90		
	Comprehension	88	36	18	—		
				MPIE			
		9	16	22	26		
MS	Pronunciation	100	98	92	78		
	Comprehension	72	56	42	20		
				MPIE			
		0	12	18	24	30	33
NO	Pronunciation	100	100	100	96	98	96
	Comprehension	92	86	40	50	42	22

Note: MPIE, the number of Months Post Initial Examination.

TABLE 10.3
Types of 33 Pronunciation Errors made by KS, MS, and NO Across the Whole Series of Testing Sessions during the 3-year Study

Error	*KS*	*MS*	*NO*	*Total*
(1) Visual	2	1	1	4
(2) Phonological	4	2	0	6
(3) No response	6	6	2	14
(4) Compound formation	–	4	2	6
(5) Subcharacter reading	–	3	–	3
Totals	12	16	5	33

(ignoring or skipping the target word and going to the next one); (4) "compound formation", or reading aloud a single-character word as if it were a compound or multicharacter word containing the target kanji as a component character (e.g. 富 [tomi] "wealth" → 富士山 [fudʒ isan] "Mount Fuji"); and (5) "subcharacter reading", or reading only one component of the target kanji character (e.g. 朝 [asa] "morning" → 十日 [tooka] "10 days" or "10th day"). The last type of error was exhibited only by MS and appears to reflect a perceptual disorder observed in demented patients at moderate to advanced stages of disease.

Comprehension Performance. As shown in Table 10.2, the speed of decline in comprehension performance was somewhat variable among the three patients: KS showed the most rapid decline, followed by MS and NO. Analyses of comprehension errors revealed that semantic errors (pointing to the semantic distractor instead of the target) constituted the majority (83–71%) of errors in the early stage of the disease process in all three patients. In the subsequent stages, however, "irrelevant responses" or "no responses" became more prevalent in all patients, with no discernible patterns in their errors towards the end of the three-year study. The dimension of word frequency was loosely related to accuracy of responses: Mean correct responses for the 15 high- and 15 low-frequency words were 58% and 36%, respectively.

Additional tests that showed a close parallel to the KPCT comprehension task in terms of both the rate and magnitude of performance decline were: three subtests of the HBFT (*naming*, *category-based word fluency*, and *follow commands*) and the Semantic Categorisation of Kanji Words (a classification task to assess knowledge of the category membership of 26 names of animals and another 26 names of foods presented in kanji). Taken together, these findings appear to suggest a common underlying dysfunction of semantic memory.

NONSEMANTIC READING IN ENGLISH

The English data to be considered in this chapter come from a recent study of "semantic dementia" (Hodges, Patterson, Oxbury, & Funnell, 1992; Patterson & Hodges, 1992), a form of dementing disease in which both the locus of brain abnormality and the cognitive consequences are different from, and more circumscribed than, those typical of DAT. This means that the cross-orthography comparision that this chapter discusses is based on a comparison of patients with somewhat differing aetiologies and general patterns of cognitive deficit. None the less, some provocative points emerge from this imperfect comparison. In the final discussion, we will attempt to extend the comparison with a brief review of pertinent findings from English speakers/readers with DAT and from Japanese speakers/readers with a deficit similar to semantic dementia.

"Semantic dementia" derives its name (originally bestowed by Snowden, Goulding, & Neary, 1989) from the fact that the prominent cognitive deficit in this condition is a disruption of semantic memory—that is, knowledge of facts and of the meanings of words and objects. As this is a recently identified condition, neuropathological data are scarce. However, structural and functional brain imaging have demonstrated marked focal atrophy/hypometabolism in the temporal neocortex, often primarily in the left hemisphere (see Hodges et al., 1992, for further details). This contrasts with the bilateral posterior occipito-parietal abnormalities characteristic of DAT (e.g. Neary et al., 1987). An hypothesis suggested by Hodges (1993; Hodges et al., 1992) is that semantic dementia may reflect Pick's disease with predominantly temporal lobe involvement.[1]

Deterioration of semantic memory has devastating consequences for both receptive and expressive vocabulary: Patients with semantic dementia gradually lose the ability both to comprehend and to produce words that were once well within their vocabularies (see Hodges et al. 1992, for detailed investigations in five cases). Both speech comprehension and production are language abilities that obviously rely on knowledge of the meanings of words, whereas reading aloud is not necessarily such a task; therefore it is of considerable theoretical interest whether oral reading performance is disrupted by, or remains immune to, the loss of semantic memory. This question was addressed for the alphabetic but phonologically "deep" orthography of English in a study by Patterson and Hodges (1992) of six patients with progressive loss of word meaning. Although the patients have progressive deteriorating conditions, the data presented for them (unlike the longitudinal data from the Japanese patients) are cross-sectional. There are two reasons for this: (1) although a subset of the English patients are in fact being studied longitudinally, good long-term data for these cases are not yet available; and (2) several of the patients were already too severely affected on initial presentation to permit long-term testing.

[1] Two of the patients in the Hodges et al. (1992) study have subsequently died and had confirmed Pick's disease at post mortem.

Five of the six patients had a clinical diagnosis of progressive focal dementia or primary progressive aphasia. None of the patients had any of the marked deficits in perceptual processing, spatial skills, or episodic memory that are so characteristic of DAT; and, with the possible exception of one case (KT; McCarthy & Warrington, 1986), none showed generalised dementia. With regard to the quality of their language output, these patients resembled the fluent anomic progressive aphasic cases of Poeck and Luzzatti (1988) rather than the agrammatic nonfluent progressive aphasic cases described by Mesulam (1982).

The six patients were described by Patterson and Hodges (1992) as representing two approximate levels of severity of impaired vocabulary and word comprehension: profound and more moderate. This was a somewhat subjective judgement, based on a composite of performance over many different tests, and also a relative judgement, in the sense that *all* of the patients were impaired at any language task requiring referential meaning: object naming, category-based word fluency (e.g. "Name all of the animals that you can think of"), word definitions (e.g. "Explain to me what a guitar is"), semantic feature questions (e.g. "Does a tiger have stripes?"), etc. The rough division according to level of severity will, however, be maintained here, because it imposes some meaningful order on the reading data.

Relevant features of the six cases are listed in Table 10.4. Detailed individual case histories will not be given here.[2]

Whilst the patients of Sasanuma et al. (1992) were assessed for comprehension (word-picture matching) on the words that constituted the oral reading test, this was not done for the English cases. Obviously, the best procedure is to use identical materials for assessment of these two potentially dissociable aspects of reading. The "excuse" for violating this procedure is that the Patterson and Hodges study was designed primarily to assess the effects of word frequency and regularity of spelling-to-sound correspondences on oral reading performance. As it happens, picturable object names are biased towards lower-frequency words; also, many object names in English are multisyllabic and it is easier to categorise monosyllabic words as regular or exceptional in spelling-to-sound correspondences. Therefore, in order to examine oral reading performance on a large set of monosyllabic items with exceptional spelling-sound correspondences and covering a substantial range of word frequencies, the Patterson and Hodges reading list included many words (e.g. abstract nouns, verbs, function words, etc.) that are not easily tested for comprehension via word-picture matching.

---

[2] This is due to the large number of cases and the fact that each patient has already been described in the literature: All six are summarised in Patterson and Hodges (1992); FM, JL, and PP are presented in greater detail in Hodges et al. (1992); KT was studied and the data published by McCarthy and Warrington (1986) and TOB, the most published case of the six, by McCarthy and Warrington (1988, 1990), Parkin (1993), and Tyrrell, Warrington, Frackowiak, and Rossor (1990).

TABLE 10.4
Nonsemantic Reading in English: Features of "Semantic Dementia"

Feature	*FM*	*JL*	*TOB*	*PB*	*KT*	*PP*
Gender/Handedness	F/L	M/R	M/R	M/R	M/R	F/R
Age at testing	55	60	64	72	54	69
Locus of atrophy/ Hypometabolism	L. temp.	Bilat. temp. (R>L)	L. fronto-temp.	L. parieto-temp.	Bilat. fronto-temp.	L. fronto-temp.
Pre-morbid occupation	Care assist.	Co. owner/dir.	Civil serv.	Divis. co. manager	Businessman, banker	Secretary
VIQ	76	76	95	?	?	74
PIQ	98	85	116	107	?	97

Note: F/L denotes 'female, left-handed'; M/R, 'male, right-handed', etc.
L. temp., left temporal; Bilat. temp., bilateral temporal; VIQ, Verbal IQ; PIQ, Performance IQ.

The list of words used to assess oral reading contained 252 monosyllabic English words; more to the point, these 252 words comprised 126 pairs of regular and exception words matched for length in letters, written word frequency (Kucera & Francis, 1967), and initial phoneme. The words were taken from three frequency bands, which, when crossed with the regular/exception variable, yields a total of six word conditions. The mean frequencies and examples of each of these six word sets are displayed in Table 10.5.

Three of the six patients (FM, TOB, and PB) were presented with the 252 words in randomised order on a computer screen, and asked to read them aloud; one patient (JL) read the 252 words, which were each printed on a card and presented over the desk. KT was not, in fact, tested as part of this study; however, from a large corpus of his word reading responses (McCarthy, personal communication), KT could be "tested" *post hoc* on about two-thirds of the current word list. Finally, PP was tested as part of the Patterson and Hodges (1992) study, but in a rather different manner from the other patients, because she had a severe letter identification deficit and could not read. If asked to read printed words, PP replied that she could not; if strongly encouraged to do so, she attempted to read letter-by-letter, but with little success. Like many patients with this sort of problem in letter recognition, however, PP could perform the task of word identification from oral spelling (e.g. "What does M, I, N, T spell?"), and it is this task which forms the basis of the data reported from her.

TABLE 10.5
Mean Word Frequencies (roughly per million, from Kucera & Francis, 1967) and Examples of Words for Each of the 6 Conditions

Word Frequency	*Regular*	*Exception*
High Frequency		
Mean frequency	798.8	784.0
Examples	black	blood
	board	broad
	nine	none
Medium Frequency		
Mean frequency	41.4	41.6
Examples	guess	gross
	bulk	bull
	pine	pint
Low Frequency		
Mean frequency	5.0	5.7
Examples	broach	brooch
	carve	caste
	sag	sew

The proportions of words in each set read aloud correctly by each of the six patients are shown in Table 10.6, where the patients are grouped according to the approximate levels of comprehension loss, with the four less severely affected patients (FM, JL, TOB, and PB) at the top, and the most severely affected patients (KT and PP) at the bottom. The results are easy to summarise because, despite very different levels of overall performance, all patients showed the same effects: (1) a substantial superiority in reading regular as compared to exception words; (2) a substantial effect of word frequency; and (3) a marked frequency-by-regularity interaction, such that declining word frequency harmed performance on exception words much more than on regular words. Only PP, the most severely affected patient, showed any notable impact of frequency on regular word naming, and this was very likely an effect of word length rather than frequency: Although the regular and exception words were matched pairwise for length, there was a minor increase in word length as word frequency declined. This small confound between frequency and length had, as expected, no detectable consequences on accuracy for the five patients engaged in a "normal" reading task; but PP performed worse on longer items, perhaps because of the working-memory load involved in identifying words from oral spelling. The data in Table 10.6 demonstrate, however, that regularity of spelling-sound correspondences was the primary determinant of performance even for PP: On the highest-frequency words (and also the shortest: mean length for the high-frequency words = 4.1 letters), PP correctly identified 86% and 36%, respectively, of the regular and exception words.

There is one remaining point of interest in these accuracy results, although it must remain somewhat speculative until longitudinal data become available. Disregarding PP (whose "reading" task was not a normal one), it appears that severity of semantic loss has little or no bearing on the ability to assign correct

TABLE 10.6
Percentage of Correct Reading Responses

	Regular			*Exception*		
Comp. Loss	*High Frequency*	*Medium Frequency*	*Low Frequency*	*High Frequency*	*Medium Frequency*	*Low Frequency*
"Moderate"						
FM	98	100	95	95	81	62
JL	100	93	93	90	86	74
TOB	100	100	90	93	67	50
PB	98	90	93	86	71	48
"Severe"						
KT	100	93	92	50	31	8
PP	86	82	62	36	18	8

pronunciations to regular words: Compare, for example, the accuracy scores on regular words for FM and KT, who differed very substantially in their performance on various comprehension tests. In contrast, there may be a predictable relationship between extent of comprehension loss and success in exception-word reading.

With regard to reading errors, most of these were so-called "pure" regularisation errors, where the patient's pronunciation of the word corresponded exactly to the regular (or most typical) pronunciation for the spelling pattern in question (e.g. SHOE read aloud as if it rhymed with "toe", PINT with "mint", HAVE with "save", and so on). For case JL, only 50% of his errors were such pure regularisations, but the corresponding figures for the remaining patients were between 74% (PP) and 93% (KT). Nonregularisation errors were either real-word (e.g. SUITE → "suit") or nonword (e.g. DOUGH → "daug") responses that resembled the target string.

In conclusion, with markedly impaired reading of exception, relative to regular, words and a preponderance of regularisation errors, these six patients have an acquired disorder of reading known as surface dyslexia (Marshall & Newcombe, 1973; Patterson, Marshall, & Coltheart, 1985).

DISCUSSION

The major findings can be summarised as follows. The three Japanese DAT patients retained excellent ability to read aloud kanji words of a wide frequency range throughout the three-year longitudinal study; this stands in marked contrast to the progressive deterioration of their ability to comprehend the same set of words. The six English patients with focal "semantic dementia", although not studied longitudinally, were also suffering from progressive deterioration in comprehension. Although they retained good ability to read aloud words with predictable spelling-to-sound correspondences, they were markedly impaired in reading words which deviate from typical correspondences, especially lower-frequency words; and the degree of this surface dyslexia roughly matched the degree of comprehension loss. How is this major discrepancy between the Japanese and the English results to be explained?

The first factor that must be considered is the difference between the two groups of patients. The three Japanese patients had a diagnosis of probable DAT, with bilateral and diffuse cortical involvement as indicated by CT and MRI scanning. The pattern of their cognitive impairment was consistent with this diagnosis, with progressive deterioration of a wide range of cognitive abilities, including episodic memory and visuo-spatial abilities as well as semantic memory. The six English patients, on the other hand, had a diagnosis of probable progressive focal dementia, with a predominantly left temporal lobe locus as indicated by MRI or single photon emission computed tomography (SPECT) scanning. According to the hypothesis of Hodges et al. (1992), the patients' only primary impairment is in semantic memory, and all of their observed cognitive impairments (e.g. in expressive and receptive language, object recognition, etc.) are secondary to this semantic memory deficit.

Are the different aetiologies of the two patient groups sufficient to explain the observed differences in pattern of reading performance? An answer to this question obviously requires evidence about exception-word reading in English patients with DAT and about kanji word reading in Japanese patients with focal "semantic" dementia.

With regard to the former, there are surprisingly few studies of English-speaking DAT patients that include a detailed assessment of reading and an explicit comparison of performance on regular and exception words. Furthermore, where relevant data do exist, they fail to give an unequivocal answer to the question of interest here. Among group studies that are not designed to specify the precise relationship between a given patient's semantic memory loss and his/her reading performance, some suggest that exception-word reading can be intact in DAT (Friedman, Ferguson, Robinson, & Sunderland, 1992), whereas others suggest that exception-word reading is typically impaired relative to controls, at least at later stages of the disease (Fromm, Holland, Nebes, & Oakley, 1991; Patterson, Graham, & Hodges, 1994). The most detailed and sophisticated single-case study of an English patient (Schwartz et al., 1979; 1980) was a longitudinal study of patient WLP with a diagnosis of pre-senile dementia and "bilateral diffuse involvement of the cerebral hemispheres" (Schwartz et al., 1980, p. 286). WLP, at one stage, showed essentially no oral reading deficit on exception words relative to regular words despite her substantial word comprehension deficit, but this was followed about 10 months later by the emergence of mild surface dyslexia. We cannot directly compare the severity of dementia in general, nor the severity of word comprehension deficit in particular, between WLP when she started to show errors on exception words and the three Japanese patients at their advanced stages of dementia. In terms of the performance level of oral reading, however, the second Japanese patient, MS, had a 22% error rate on the 50 kanji words at the last testing session; this is roughly similar to WLP's 28% error rate in reading exception words. The nature of the reading errors was, however, entirely different: Whereas the majority of WLP's errors were regularisations of exception words, none of MS's errors were indicative of subword orthography-to-phonology transcoding, as will be discussed shortly.

The other side of the coin is more informative. There have been several case studies in recent years of Japanese patients with a diagnosis of "slowly progressive aphasia without generalised dementia" (SPA) (Mesulam, 1982; Poeck & Luzzatti, 1988). Of 10 such patients, 7 had focal brain involvement predominantly of the left temporal lobe, confirmed by CT/MRI, SPECT, and/or positron emission tomography (PET) scanning (Hamanaka & Yamaguchi, 1987; Kato et al., 1991; Sakurai et al., 1991). Types of aphasia manifested by these seven patients include transcortical sensory aphasia (three patients), atypical Wernicke's aphasia (one) and amnesic aphasia (three). Common to all these types of aphasia were comprehension deficits, naming difficulties, and greater impairment of kanji than kana processing coupled with fluent oral output. Two of the three patients with transcortical sensory aphasia demonstrated some features of Gogi (word-meaning) aphasia.

Gogi aphasia, first described by Imura (1943), is a variant of transcortical sensory aphasia with a core impairment of word meaning that is reflected in moderate to severe impairment in word comprehension and production, plus selective deficits of reading (and writing) kanji words with preserved oral reading and writing to dictation of kana words without comprehension. The peculiar type of paralexic error for kanji words associated with Gogi aphasia is so called "*on-kun* confusion". It consists of the assignment of a more typical *on* or *kun* pronunciation to the component character of a multicharacter kanji word, disregarding the word-specific kanji reading (see Table 10.7 for some examples of these errors). One could not exactly call this type of error "nonlexical" reading, because—unlike alphabetic characters—most single kanji characters are themselves lexical items. However, given that the correct pronunciation of a given kanji in a multicharacter word is determined by intraword context, *on-kun* confusions do seem to reflect a kind of "subword" processing of the component kanji characters, and may even be thought of as the kanji equivalent of regularisation errors in English. *On-kun* confusions are particularly likely to occur in response to a special class of low-frequency words known as "jukujikun", in which the pronunciation of the word is arbitrary and independent of any standard pronunciation of the component characters.[3]

Of the seven Japanese SPA patients described earlier, with a cognitive impairment as well as neurological data resembling the English "semantic dementia" syndrome, only the two with Gogi aphasic characteristics exhibited a few errors of this type in oral reading of kanji words (the quantitative data are not presented in the report). Other types of reading errors were diverse, including "visual", "phonological", and "no response".

In addition to the seven reported cases of progressive aphasia, four cases of temporal-type Pick's disease (with bilateral but asymmetrical left > right temporal lobe atrophy confirmed by brain imaging or pathologic examination at autopsy) are reported by Kurachi and Matsubara (1991). In all four cases, transcortical sensory aphasia with some features of Gogi aphasia constituted the sole clinical manifestation in the early stages of the disease process. In a detailed neuropsychological study of one case, MO, who exhibited rather typical features of Gogi aphasia, Matsubara et al. (1984) reported a few clear-cut instances of *on-kun* confusion errors in reading aloud kani words (Table 10.7).

---

[3] As the correct pronunciation of the character in some jukujikun words is not any standard (*on* or *kun*) reading, pronunciation errors on these words may not actually be *on-kun* confusions. The term "*on-kun* confusion", therefore, may not be quite accurate when used with jukujikun words, but we are using it due to the lack of a better term.

TABLE 10.7
Examples of *on-kun* Confusion Errors by Patients with Gogi Aphasia

相手 [aite] "opponent" → [sooʃu]	(a)
大抵 [taitee] "almost" → [ootee]	(a)
田舎 [inaka] "countryside" → [denʃa]	(b)
煙草 [tabako] "cigarette" → [kemurikusa]	(b)
中風 [tʃuuhuu] "stroke' → [nakakaze]	(c)
皮肉 [hiniku] "sarcasm" → [kawaniku]	(c)
梅雨 [baiu] "rainy season" → [umeame]	(c,e)
真面目 [madʒime] "serious" → [ʃinmenboku]	(d)
人形 [ningjoo] "doll" → [dʒinkei]	(d)
時雨 [ʃigure] "shower in late fall" → [tokiame]	(e)

Note: The correct reading and its meaning is shown on the left of the arrow and the incorrect reading (which makes little sense) is shown on the right.

Errors reported by: (a) Imura (1943); (b) Fujii and Morokuma (1959); (c) Koshika, Asano, Imamichi, & Miyazaki (1969); (d) Matsubara et al. (1984); and Kato et al. (1991).

To summarise, recent case studies of Japanese patients with brain atrophy in the left temporal region (seven cases) as well as with temporal-type Pick's disease (four cases) have shown a selective impairment in the oral reading of kanji relative to kana;[4] this pattern of kanji/kana dissociation in Japanese might be considered an approximate parallel of a selective impairment on exception words relative to regular words in English. Furthermore, at least one study of English-speaking patients with probable DAT failed to detect any significant impairment in exception-word reading (Friedman et al., 1992), although there is some inconsistency between this and other studies on the topic. Taken together, these two parallel phenomena may imply that, in the present study, the discrepancy in oral reading performance between the Japanese DAT cases and the English focal dementia cases is primarily attributable to the difference in aetiology. If this is true, then the major question of interest is: Why is reading of kanji in Japanese and of exception words in English apparently so much more vulnerable to focal dementia than to DAT? We cannot offer more than a tentative answer, but existing knowledge about localisation of functions in the brain would predict that impairment of word meaning (or more generally of semantic

[4] The reader should perhaps be reminded that, in contrast to these "focal" patients, the three DAT patients showed no dissociation between kanji and kana in either oral reading or reading comprehension. The dissociation that they showed was between comprehension and pronunciation, for both kanji and kana words.

memory) may tend to emerge in more profound form as a consequence of focal dementing disease with major involvement of the left temporal lobe rather than as a consequence of DAT with diffuse cortical damage. Patterson and Hodges (1992) argue that one of the consequences of the loss of word meaning is that the translation from orthography to phonology is forced to rely more on subword segments, resulting in a selective deficit for exception words relative to regular words in English.

We would, of course, be delighted if our comparative research made some small contribution to an understanding of the cognitive sequelae of different varieties of progressive brain disease. However, our goal in comparing "nonsemantic" reading across the very different orthographies of English and Japanese kanji was, in fact, to learn something about universal and script-specific features of reading. We are convinced that, even if the different patient types represent a major component of the explanation for the observed reading behaviour, this is not the whole story. Another important component is almost certainly the different nature of the two writing systems (i.e. morphographic kanji vs. alphabetic English). There are many dimensions where these writing systems differ, but the one of particular relevance here is the nature of the mapping between orthography and phonology, and specifically the level at which the reader can extract useful generalisations about this mapping.

English, despite its notorious irregularities, is an alphabetic system in which there are powerful statistical regularities of letter-sound mappings. Even in *extremely* exceptional words, it is almost invariably the case that only part of the word (e.g. the AU in GAUGE, the OLO in COLONEL, etc.), has a pronunciation unsupported by generalisations from the rest of the vocabulary. The reading system is sensitive to such statistical regularities, which reveal themselves in "neighbourhood" effects. Data from normal readers (e.g. Jared, McRae, & Seidenberg, 1990) suggest that even for skilled English readers, a target word's neighbourhood of friends and enemies (i.e. orthographically similar words that, respectively, support or contradict the subword spelling-sound relationships embodied in the target word) continues to play a major role in the computation of the word's phonological representation. These neighbourhood effects are especially apparent for low-frequency words that have not had much influence on setting parameters of the reading "network" (Seidenberg & McClelland, 1989). In our view, the reading behaviour of the English patients with semantic dementia demonstrates the strength of these subword statistical regularities, which are revealed when other factors that operate mainly or exclusively at the whole-word level (in particular, familiarity with a word's meaning and pronunciation) are disrupted by brain malfunction (see Patterson & Hodges, 1992, for discussion).

In kanji, by contrast, it appears that there is no dependable subword level over which the reader can learn to generalise. Although most kanji characters have only two or three common pronunciations (one *kun*-reading and one or two *on-*

readings), none of these could be described as the most regular or typical pronunciation. It is said that the *kun* pronunciation is usually appropriate when the character forms a word on its own, and an *on* pronunciation when it is part of a multicharacter word; however, there are many exceptions to both of these "generalisations". Exceptions to the first arise from the fact that many characters have no *kun*-reading (according to Paradis, Hagiwara, & Hildebrandt, 1985, this is true for 38.1% of the 2000 most common kanji characters). Exceptions to the second arise from the fact that a character in a multicharacter word may take one of several *on*-readings or indeed its *kun*-reading (if there is one). Furthermore, even the approximate statistical regularity of *kun* for single and *on* for multicharacter words may be less important than it seems due to the fact that Japanese text is written without spaces between words. A text is usefully parsed by the visual differences between kanji (used for nouns and for the roots of many verbs and adjectives) and the two kinds of kana (hiragana, used for inflections and function words and some substantive words as well; katakana, used for the many 'loan' words in present-day Japanese); but due to the lack of spaces between words, it will not be obvious on a purely visual basis whether several successive kanji characters form one or two words. Therefore, in normal reading of text, the predictive value of this "clue" to pronunciation may be more apparent than real.

A study of recognition (rather than speeded pronunciation) for kanji words (Morton, Sasanuma, Patterson, & Sakuma, 1992) demonstrated significant identity priming (that is, identification of a word was facilitated if that same word had been encountered earlier), but failed to show significant priming either from component characters to words containing these or from multicharacter words to their component characters. This suggests that, in some sense, the most powerful unit in kanji is the word rather than the character. What we are proposing here is that the same may be true for the units involved in computing a pronunciation for a written kanji word. We assume that a Japanese reader's procedures for this computation would discover a subword (presumably character) level at which to generalise about the mapping between orthography and phonology if such a level were useful. Various lines of evidence, including the data presented here on successful oral reading of kanji by severely demented patients, suggest that a subword level may play no prominent role in computing pronunciations of kanji words. In this regard, kanji would be uniquely different from alphabetic and syllabic writing systems, and indeed from Chinese.

ACKNOWLEDGEMENTS

We are grateful to our colleagues Ms Naoko Sakuma, Dr Kunitaka Kitano, and Dr John R. Hodges for allowing us to use some of the data published in co-authored papers (i.e. Sasanuma, Sakuma, & Kitano, 1992; and Patterson & Hodges, 1992).

REFERENCES

Bub, D., Cancelliere, A., & Kertesz, A. (1985). Whole-word and analytic translation of spelling to sound in a non-semantic reader. In K.E. Patterson, J.C. Marshall, & M. Coltheart (Eds.), *Surface dyslexia: Neuropsychological and cognitive studies of phonological reading*, (pp. 15–34). London: Lawrence Erlbaum Associates Ltd.

Friedman, R.B., Ferguson, S., Robinson, S., & Sunderland, T. (1992). Dissociation of mechanisms of reading in Alzheimer's Disease. *Brain and Language*.

Fromm, D., Holland, A.L., Nebes, R.D., & Oakley, M.A. (1991). A longitudinal study of word-reading ability in Alzheimer's Disease: Evidence from the National Adult Reading Test. *Cortex, 27*, 367–376.

Fujii, I. & Morokuma, O. (1959). A case of *gogi* (word-meaning) aphasia. *Clinical Psychiatry, 1*, 431–435 (in Japanese).

Hamanaka, T. & Yamaguchi, H. (1987) Slowly progress aphasia in the praesenium with much later onset of generalized dementia–report of two cases. *Proceedings of the Joint Japan–China Stroke Conference*, Hirosaki/Tokyo, 1986 (ed. by Reimeikyo Rehabilitation Hospital, Aomori).

Hodges, J.R. (1993). Pick's disease. In A. Burns & R. Levy (Eds.), *Dementia*. London: Chapman and Hall.

Hodges, J.R., Patterson, K., Oxbury, S., & Funnell, E. (1992). Semantic dementia: Progressive fluent aphasia with temporal lobe atrophy. *Brain, 115*, 1783–1806.

Imura, T. (1943). Aphasia: Characteristic symptoms in Japanese. *Psychiatria et Neurologia Japonica, 47*, 196–218. (in Japanese)

Jared, D., McRae, K. & Seidenberg, S. (1990). The basis of consistency effects in word naming. *Journal of Memory and Language, 29*, 687–715.

Kato, T., Tuji, M., Ogasawara, Y., Hamanaka, T., & Nakanishi, M. (1991). Primary degenerative dementia presenting as slowly progressive aphasia: Report of 6 cases. *Japanese Journal of Neuropsychology, 7*, 164–169. (in Japanese)

Koshika, K., Asano, N., Imamichi, H., & Miyazaki, S. (1969). A case of gogi (word-meaning) aphasia. *Clinical Psychiatry, 11*, 212–216 (in Japanese).

Kucera, H. & Francis, W.N. (1967). *Computational analysis of present-day American English*. Providence, RI: Brown University Press.

Kurachi, M. & Matsubara, S. (1991) . Clinicopathology and brain imaging of Pick's disease. *Japanese Journal of Neuropsychology, 7*, 10–18 (in Japanese).

Marshall, J.C. & Newcombe, F. (1973). Patterns of paralexia: A psycholinguistic approach. *Journal of Psycholinguistic Research, 2*, 175–199.

Matsubara, S., Enokido, H., Torii, H., Hiraguchi, M., & Ainoda, N. (1984). A case of presenile dementia with Gogi (word-meaning) aphasia. *Brain Function Research, 4*, 59–69 (in Japanese).

McCarthy, R. & Warrington, E.K. (1986). Phonological reading: Phenomena and paradoxes. *Cortex, 22*, 359–380.

McCarthy, R. & Warrington, E.K. (1988). Evidence for modality-specific meaning systems in the brain. *Nature, 334*, 428–430.

McCarthy, R. & Warrington, E.K. (1990). The dissolution of semantics. *Nature, 348*, 599.

Mesulam, M.M. (1982). Slowly progressive aphasia without generalized dementia. *Annals of Neurology, 11*, 592–598.

Morton, J., Sasanuma, S., Patterson, K., & Sakuma, N. (1992). The organisation of the lexicon in Japanese: single and compound kanji. *British Journal of Psychology, 83*, 517–531.

National Language Research Institute (1970). *Studies on the vocabulary of modern newspapers: Vol. 1. General description and vocabulary frequency tables*, Tokyo: National Language Research Institute.

Neary, D., Snowden, J.S., Shields, R.A., Burjan, A.W.I., Northen, B., MacDermott, N., Prescott, M.C., & Testa, H.J. (1987). Single photon emission tomography using 99-m Tc-HM-PAO in the investigation of dementia. *Journal of Neurology, Neurosurgery and Psychiatry, 50*, 1101–1109.

Paradis, M., Hagiwara, H., & Hildebrandt, N. (1985). *Neurolinguistic aspects of the Japanese writing system*. Orlando, FL: Academic Press.

Parkin, A.J. (1993). Progressive aphasia without dementia due to focal left temporo-frontal hypometabolism—a clinical and cognitive neuropsychological analysis. *Brain and Language, 44*, 201–220.

Patterson, K.E. & Hodges, J.R. (1992). Deterioration of word-meaning: Implications for reading. *Neuropsychologia, 30*, 1025–1040.

Patterson, K., Graham, N., & Hodges, J.R. (1994). Reading in dementia of the Alzheimer type: A preserved ability? *Neuropsychology, 8*, 395–407.

Patterson, K.E., Marshall, J.C., & Coltheart, M. (Eds.), (1985). *Surface dyslexia: Neuropsychological and cognitive studies of phonological reading*. Hove, UK: Lawrence Erlbaum Associates Ltd.

Poeck, K. & Luzzatti, C. (1988). Slowly progressive aphasia in three patients: The problem of accompanying neuropsychological deficit. *Brain, 111*, 151–168.

Sakurai, Y., Takeda, K., Bandoh, M., Ishikawa, T., & Iwata, M. (1991). Neuropsychological studies on slowly progressive fluent aphasia. *Japanese Journal of Neuropsychology, 7*, 170–177 (in Japanese).

Sasanuma, S., Itoh, M., Watamori, T., Fukuzawa, K., Fukusako, Y., & Monoi, H. (1985). Linguistic and nonlinguistic abilities of the Japanese elderly and patients with dementia. In H.K. Ulatowska (Ed.), *The aging brain*, (pp.175–200). San Diego, FL: College Hill Press.

Sasanuma, S., Sakuma, N., & Kitano, K. (1992). Reading kanji without semantics: Evidence from longitudinal study of patients with dementia. *Cognitive Neuropsychology, 9*, 465–468.

Schwartz, M.F., Marin, O.M., & Saffran, E.M. (1979) Dissociations of language function in dementia: A case study. *Brain and Language, 7*, 277–306.

Schwartz, M.F., Saffran, E.M., & Marin, O.S.M. (1980). Fractionating the reading process in dementia: Evidence for word-specific print-to-sound associations. In M. Coltheart, K. Patterson, & J.C. Marshall (Eds.), *Deep dyslexia*, (pp.259–269). London: Routledge & Kegan Paul.

Seidenberg, M.S. & McClelland, J.L. (1989). A distributed, developmental model of word recognition and naming. *Psychological Review, 96*, 523–568.

Shallice, T. (1988). *From neuropsychology to mental structure*. Cambridge University Press.

Shallice, T., Warrington, E.K., & McCarthy, R. (1983). Reading without semantics. *Quarterly Journal of Experimental Psychology, 35A*, 111–138.

Snowden, J.S., Goulding, P.J., & Neary, D. (1989). Semantic dementia: A form of circumscribed cerebral atrophy. *Behavioural Neurology, 2*, 167–182.

Tyrrell, P.J., Warrington, E.K., Frackowiak, R.S.J., & Rossor, M.N. (1990). Heterogeneity in progressive aphasia due to focal cortical atrophy. *Brain, 113*, 1321–1336.

11 Learning to Be a Conspirator: A Tale of Becoming a Good Chinese Reader

Ovid J.L. Tzeng
National Chung Cheng University, Chia Yi, Taiwan
University of California, Riverside, CA
The Salk Institute for Biological Studies, San Diego, CA

Zhong Hui Lin
National Tsing Hua University, Taiwan

Daisy L. Hung
National Chung Cheng University, Chia Yi, Taiwan
University of California, Riverside, CA
The Salk Institute for Biological Studies, San Diego, CA

Wei Ling Lee
Tan Tock Seng Memorial Hospital

INTRODUCTION

To become literate in a language, such as English, children must grasp the principles of the alphabet, so that they can learn new words by using these principles rather than by sole memorising. However, not all children can master the mappings between spellings and sounds. Rozin, Poritsky, and Sotsky (1971) taught a group of Philadelphia 2nd-grade schoolchildren with serious reading problems to read English written with Chinese characters. As a consequence, these children made rapid progress in reading, suggesting that their difficulty in reading lies in the mapping between graphemes and phonemes and in the blending of the phonetic elements of words. As Chinese orthography maps directly on to speech at the level of words and syllables rather than of phonemes, these children are able to read characters directly without going through the mapping and blending processes. This research appears to uphold the traditional view of Chinese orthography, that Chinese is an ideographic or logographic writing system and does not convey any phonological information.

If one carefully observes the evolution of writing, one would discover that the relation between script and meaning has become more and more abstract, whereas the relation between script and speech has become increasingly clear. DeFrancis, on the basis of detailed analyses of various writing systems from the perspective of their historical development, claimed that any fully developed writing system is speech-based, even though the way speech is represented in the script varies from one system to another (DeFrancis, 1989). He especially emphasised that Chinese orthography is also a speech-based script as 85% or more characters are phonograms, in which one part of the character carries clues about its pronunciation.

Most Chinese characters consist of two components, a semantic component, suggesting the character's meaning, and a phonetic component, hinting at the character's pronunciation. For example, the character 媽 is written with a phonetic element 馬 /ma/ to represent the sound of the compound character and a semantic component 女 to indicate the meaning related to "female". However, possibly because of historical sound change and the influence of dialects, many phonetic components in compound characters have gradually lost the function of providing exact phonological information. Among the modern Chinese characters used in mainland China, only 39% of simple characters can validly serve as phonetic components in compound characters, and only 48% of compound characters are pronounced as their phonetic compounds (Zhou, 1978). Therefore, even researchers who are aware that most Chinese characters contain phonetic as well as semantic components tend to ignore the former and to overemphasise the latter (Kolers, 1969). As not all phonetic components can efficiently provide clues for character pronunciation, people used to take the view that Chinese characters can only be read in their entirety and that no orthography-phonology correspondence (OPC) *rule* is involved in reading.

THE NATURE OF CHINESE ORTHOGRAPHY

Chinese writing was possibly pictographic in origin (Hung & Tzeng, 1981). Then there came ideograms, which were frequently formed by putting several pictograms together to suggest an idea. For instance, putting two trees together side by side could mean "wood" 林. Subsequently, owing to difficulties with such a way of forming characters to represent abstract concepts, phonograms were invented. Typically, a phonogram consists of two components. One is a semantic component which gives the reader a hint as to the character's meaning. The other is a phonetic component that indicates the character's pronunciation. In addition, Chinese characters map on to speech at the syllabic level.

One way to investigate whether readers use knowledge of orthography-phonology correspondences (OPC) in reading is to examine whether the written units with a regular and straightforward encoding of phonology are easier to process than the ones for which the mapping between the written units and the phonological codes is irregular. An advantage for regular English words over exceptional ones has been demonstrated by many western researchers (Baron &

Strawson, 1976; Glushko, 1979, Gough & Cosky, 1977; Stanovich & Bauer, 1978). Interestingly, recent experimental studies on Chinese character recognition also observed a similar pattern (Fang, Horng, & Tzeng, 1986; Lien, 1985; Seidenberg, 1985), suggesting that Chinese characters are not read via a direct character-specific route as previously thought and that OPC knowledge is used in reading.

Despite the fact that recent studies have revised the stereotyped impression of Chinese orthography and have helped us to understand the process of Chinese character recognition better, we know little about Chinese children's character recognition. The main purpose of the present study is to examine Chinese children's use of orthographic knowledge in reading characters.

In 1838, Chinese writing was designated "logographic" by the Franco-American scholar Peter S. DuPonceau. The term was revived in the 1930s by Boodergand and has been taken up by many scholars. However, that designation is wrong. A logograph is usually defined as a graphic symbol that represents a word. For example, "&" represents the word "and". And logographic writing is widely characterised by a complete absence of any phonetic component. Chinese writing violates the principles of logographic writing because, as mentioned earlier, most Chinese characters can be divided into two components, one which provides some semantic information and the other a phonological hint. Therefore, it is misleading to claim that Chinese writing is logographic.

Careful analysis shows that some compound characters are pronounced exactly as their phonetic component. For example, 油 and its phonetic component 由 are both read as /you/. Other compound characters however, do not sound the same as their phonetic component. For example, 迪 is read as /di/ whereas its phonetic component 由 is read as /you/. Compound characters sharing the same phonetic component are sometimes all read in the same way. For example, compound characters 拒, 炬, 苣, and 矩, which share the phonetic component 巨, are all read as [ju]. But in other cases, characters (e.g. 油 /you/, 迪 /di/, and 袖 /xiou/) sharing the same phonetic component are read in different ways.

THE ROLE OF CHINESE ORTHOGRAPHY IN CHARACTER NAMING

Results from several recent studies strongly suggest that the nature of Chinese orthography influences Chinese adults' character-naming performance (Fang et al., 1986; Lien, 1985; Seidenberg, 1985). Following Glushko's (1979) classification, Fang et al. (1986) divided Chinese compound characters into two types. The first type is the consistent type, defined as a compound character whose pronunciation is consistent with other compound characters having the same phonetic compound, regardless of possible tonal discrepancy. For example, 距 /ju/ is a consistent character because its pronunciation is consistent with other compound characters (e.g. 拒, 炬, 苣, and 矩), whose phonetic component is 巨. The second type is the inconsistent type, defined as a compound character whose pronunciation is not consistent with other compound characters having the same phonetic component. For example, 抽 /chou/ is an inconsistent character because its pronunciation is not consistent with other compound characters (e.g. 油 /you/, 迪 /di/, and 袖 /xiou/) whose phonetic component is 由. The inconsistent characters were themselves subdivided into regular and irregular ones. A regular character can be defined as a character that is read the same way as its phonetic component. For example, 油, /you/ is a regular character because it is read the same as its phonetic component 由 /you/. An irregular character is one which is not read the same way as its phonetic component. For example, 抽 /cho/ is an irregular character because it is not read the same way as its phonetic component 由 /you/. All in all, three types of characters were generated. The first type was Regular/Consistent, defined as characters (e.g. 距) that sound the same not only as their phonetic components but also as other characters that contain the same phonetic components. The second type was Regular/Inconsistent, defined as characters (e.g. 油) that sound the same as their phonetic component, but differently from other characters that contain that phonetic component. The third type was Irregular/Inconsistent, defined as characters (e.g. 抽) that sound neither as their phonetic component nor as other characters having that phonetic component.

Subjects were asked to name these characters. The result showed that Regular/Consistent characters were pronounced faster than Regular/Inconsistent and Irregular/Inconsistent characters, whereas the latter two types did not differ significantly. A similar trend was also observed by Lien (1985). In addition, character consistency also influenced subjects' naming of simple characters, defined as the ones (e.g. 巨) that usually serve as phonetic components in compound characters (Fang et al., 1986). Consistency in pronunciation is measured by the relative size of a phonological group within a given activation region. For example, if the activation region of the phonetic component 由 contain 12 items, namely, 由, 油, 柚, 鈾, 釉, 迪, 笛, 軸, 宙, 抽, 袖, 岫, the consistency value for 由 is 0.42 (i.e. 5/12 because only the first five items are read as /you/. The investigators found that the simple characters (e.g. 亭) with high consistency were read more quickly than the ones (e.g. 白) with low consistency. On the other hand, they constructed pseudocharacters by combining simple characters (serving as phonetic component) with radicals. The pronunciations of the simple characters were taken as models for the pronunciation of the pseudocharacters. These pseudocharacters varied in consistency value. Interestingly, the pattern of pseudocharacter naming highly resembled that of real character naming. That is, high-consistency pseudocharacters (e.g. 泟) were read faster than low-consistency ones (e.g. 彳少). These results indicate that Chinese readers also use knowledge of OPC in naming real characters and pseudocharacters.

Seidenberg (1985) looked at Chinese subjects' performance in naming phonograms and nonphonograms. Phonograms (e.g. 病 or 挺) refer to the compound characters whose phonetic components provide clues relevant to pronunciations. Nonphonograms (e.g. 高 or 桑) refer to those characters that do not provide clues to pronunciations, although some of them might function as phonetic components in other compound characters. He found that when the items were of high frequency, there was no difference between naming phonograms (e.g. 病) and naming nonphonograms (e.g. 高). However, when the items were of low frequency, phonograms (e.g. 挺) were read faster than nonphonograms (e.g. 桑), suggesting that, similarly to what happens in English word pronunciation, orthographic knowledge has greater influence on the pronunciation of low-frequency characters than on that of high-frequency ones.

Like beginning readers of English, Chinese children have to learn to recognise characters whose pronunciation is irregular. Lien (1985) found that children had a higher error rate for naming irregular than regular (consistent or not) characters. But studies on Chinese children's character processing have been so scarce that we cannot further understand the influence of Chinese orthography on their character recognition. Children's use of orthographic knowledge to deal with characters thus becomes the main concern in this chapter.

THE EXPERIMENT

The present experiment used a pseudocharacter-naming task to explore children's use of OPC knowledge in phonological processing. Because the pronunciations of pseudocharacters are not stored in memory, the possibility of direct memory retrieval is excluded. The subjects' task was, in Session 1, to name the pseudocharacters as quickly as possible and, in Session 2, to name the simple characters that construct the pseudocharacters. A comparison was made between real character and pseudocharacter naming.

Three factors were manipulated. First, grade (3rd vs. 6th grade) was manipulated to examine the developmental trend of phonological decoding skill. Second, as phonological decoding skill is positively correlated with reading ability (Perfetti & Hogaboam, 1975), reading ability (good vs. poor) was taken into consideration.

The third factor was stimulus type. Studies on English word-naming suggest that the pronunciation of a word may be influenced by its lexical neighbours (Glushko, 1979). Furthermore, the influence of a word's neighbours is related to properties such as the number of its "friends" and the relative frequencies of its "friends" and its "enemies" (Coltheart & Leahy, 1992; Laxon, Coltheart, & Keating, 1988; Treiman, Goswami, & Bruck, 1990). Therefore, in order to further understand children's use of OPC knowledge in phonological processing, the following properties of pseudocharacters' neighbourhood were taken into consideration: the consistency and regularity of the neighbours; the number of regular and of irregular neighbours; and the frequencies of regular and of irregular neighbours.

In Session 1, there were three major types of pseudocharacters, each representing one level of consistency. The first category included pseudocharacters with only regular neighbours (the Regular Only condition, abbreviated as RO). For example, [illegible] has only regular neighbours such as, 健, 毽 and 腱. The second category included pseudocharacters with both regular and irregular neighbours (the Mixed condition). For example, 衱 has regular neighbours such as 级 /ji/ and irregular ones such as 吸 /xi/. The third category included pseudocharacters with irregular neighbours only (the Irregular Only condition, abbreviated as IO). For example, [illegible] has only irregular neighbours such as 跌 /die/, 秩 /zhi/, and 轶 /yi/. The Mixed condition was subdivided into three categories. The first category included pseudocharacters with many regular neighbours but few irregular ones (the Regular Dominant In Number condition, abbreviated as RDIN). For example, 朎 has many regular neighbours such as 零, 铃, 领, 龄, 聆, 伶, 羚, 鸰, and 玲 (all read as /ling/), but only one irregular neighbour, 冷 /leng/. The second category included pseudocharacters with few regular neighbours, but one of which is relatively high in frequency compared with the irregular neighbours (the Regular Dominant In Frequency condition, abbreviated as RDIF). For example, 衱 has only two regular neighbours, 级 and 汲 (both read as /ji/), but 级 is higher in frequency than the irregular neighbours, 吸 /xi/ and 圾 /se/. The third category included pseudocharacters with few regular neighbours, which are lower in frequency than all (or most) of the irregular neighbours (the Irregular Dominant In Frequency condition, abbreviated as IDIF). For example, [illegible] has one lower-frequency regular neighbour, 咚 /dong/, and two higher-frequency irregular neighbours, 终 /zhong/ and 疼 /teng/.

When encountering an unknown compound character, most Chinese children and adults tend to regularise it. That is, they read its phonetic component. If children simply adopt the read-the-phonetic strategy to deal with novel characters, the above five types of pseudocharacters should not differ in naming latencies nor in numbers of regular responses, because the simple characters used to construct these pseudocharacters were matched in terms of frequency as closely as possible. However, according to the lexical analogy models (e.g. Glushko, 1979; Taraban & McClelland, 1987), the pronunciation of a novel character is influenced by its neighbours. And Fang et al. (1986) found that low-consistency pseudocharacters were read slower than high-consistency ones. If the same is the case for children, the RO condition should yield faster and more regularised responses than the Mixed condition, which in turn should yield faster and more regularised responses than the IO condition. Following Fang et al.'s (1986) counting, the mean consistency values of these three types of pseudocharacters are 1, 0.61, and 0.25, respectively.

If the regularised pronunciations of novel characters depend on the number of their regular neighbours, subjects should be more likely to regularise the pseudocharacters in the RDIN condition than in the RDIF and the IDIF conditions because regular neighbours are fewer in the latter two conditions than in the former one. Furthermore, the latter two conditions should yield no difference in occurrence of regular responses because both types of pseudocharacters have similar numbers of regular and irregular neighbours. However, if regularisation of pseudocharacters depends on the relative frequencies of their regular and irregular neighbours, subjects should be more likely to regularise pseudocharacters in the RDIF condition than in the IDIF condition.

As for naming of simple characters, Fang et al. (1986) found that a consistency effect also took place in naming simple characters, suggesting that OPC knowledge is used in naming such items. If the same holds for children, they should take less time to name high-consistency simple characters than low-consistency ones. In other words, the pattern of reaction times for naming simple characters should be similar to that for naming pseudocharacters.

METHOD

Subjects

Forty 3rd graders (mean age 9) and 40 6th graders (mean age 11.8) were selected from several classes on the basis of reading ability. Each grade level included 20 good and 20 poor readers. Their reading ability was assessed by their grades in Chinese class in the last semester. Their mean grades in Chinese class in the last semester are presented in Table 11.1.

Material

All stimulus items were printed vertically on 254 × 127cm cards with 10 items on each card. Each experimental card contained 10 items of the same type, whereas each practice card contained 10 items of various types. The size of each

TABLE 11.1
Subjects' Mean Grades in Chinese Class

	good	*poor*
3rd grade	97.8	68.85
6rd grade	96.85	42.9

Most of these subjects are the students of Chu-Nan elementary school except three 3rd graders with poor reading ability, who were recruited from another school, Ilo-Chun elementary school, because the number of subjects was not large enough.

item was 1.5 × 1.5cm and the distance between two items was 1cm. In Session 1, subjects received 4 practice cards and 10 experimental cards. In Session 2, subjects received 5 experimental cards.

Each pseudocharacter was made up of one radical and one simple character, the latter serving as phonetic component. The radical and the phonetic component of each pseudocharacter were arranged in a left-right formation, with the radical on the left and the phonetic component on the right side. The pairings of radicals and simple characters were under the restriction that the outcome did not resemble any real character. The items used for the experiment were constructed by 50 simple characters, each of which constructed 2 pseudocharacters. Therefore, 100 pseudocharacters were constructed. As for the pseudocharacters used for practice, some of them were rare characters, which are not known by children, and the other ones were constructed by other simple characters. In Session 2, the exerimental material included the 50 simple characters used to construct the pseudocharacters in Session 1.

In principle, a neighbour of a pseudocharacter consists of one radical and one phonetic component which is the same as in the pseudocharacter. However, readers easily mistake the radicals of characters for their phonetic components when the latter look like certain high-frequency radicals. Take the character 視 as an example. 見 is easily mistaken for the phonetic component and 礻 for the radical, whereas in fact it goes the other way round. Characters such as 視 are taken as the pseudocharacters' neighbour constructed by the simple characters such as 見, whereas the simple character such as 見 serves as the radicals in the characters such as 視. The numbers and the frequencies of the pseudocharacters' neighbours were based on NICT (1967). As the subjects were children, the rare characters such as 郜 (their frequency is usually 1) were not taken into consideration.

Based on the properties of the pseudocharacters' neighbours, five types of pseudocharacters were created. All stimulus items used in the experiment are presented in the Appendix. As mentioned already, the five following types of pseudocharacters were used: Regular Only (RO), Regular Dominant In Number (RDIN). Regular Dominant in Frequency (RDIF), Irregular Dominant In Frequency (IDIF), and Irregular Only (IO).

The five types of pseudocharacters were matched as closely as possible in terms of frequency of the constituent simple characters, numbers of alternative pronunciations, and numbers of neighbours. In addition, mean numbers and mean summed frequencies of regular and irregular neighbours were calculated. Take the RDIF pseudocharacter 礻及 as an example. The frequency of the constituent simple character 及 is 573. 礻及 has three possible pronunciations: /ji/, /xi/, and /se/. And it has four neighbours: 級 /hi/, 汲 /ji/, 吸 /xi/, and 圾 /se/. Two of them are regular, 級 and 汲. The summed frequency of the two regular neighbours is 538 (i.e. 525 級 + 3 汲). The other two are irregular, 吸 and 圾. The summed frequency of the two irregular neighbours is 199 (i.e. 182 吸 + 17 圾). The statistics concerning the properties of the pseudocharacters are presented in Table 11.2.

TABLE 11.2
The Properties of the Pseudocharacters

	RO	*Mixed*			*IO*
		RDIN	*RDIF*	*IDIF*	
mean freq. of simple characters	439.4	444.7	445.7	450.0	437.1
mean number of alternative pro.	1	3.5	2.9	3.3	3.2
number of neighbours	3.7	10.3	4.0	4.2	3.8
mean number of regular neighbours	3.7	7.1	1.5	1.5	0
mean summed freq. of regular neighbours	382.3	959.6	364.2	23.7	0
mean number of irregular neighbours	0	3.1	2.5	2.7	3.8
mean summed freq. of irregular neighbours	0	388.4	100.5	496.3	443.2

Note. freq = frequency
pro. = pronunciations
RO = Regular Only
RDIN = Regular Dominant In Number
RDIF = Regular Dominant In Frequency
IDIF = Irregular Dominant in Frequency
IO = Irregular Only

Design

A 2 (grade) × 2 (reading ability) × 5 (stimulus type) mixed design was employed in Session 1. Grade and reading ability were treated as between-group variables. There were two levels of grade: grade 3 and grade 6. There were two levels of reading ability: good and poor. Stimulus type was a within-subject variable. There were five levels of stimulus type: RO, RDIF, RDIN, IDIF, and IO. Two trials were run for each stimulus type condition. Each subject received 4 practice trials and 10 experimental trials, and each experimental trial used one of the 10 experimental cards. Block randomisation was employed. Each block contained five trials corresponding to five stimulus type conditions, respectively.

The design of Session 2 was basically the same as that of Session 1 except that the stimulus items were real and simple characters. Each subject received five experimental trials corresponding to the five types of simple characters, respectively. The order of the five stimulus trials was counter-balanced across subjects by a Latin Square procedure.

Procedure

The subjects were tested individually. They sat in front of a table with one stack of four practice cards, two stacks of five experimental cards for Session 1, and one stack of experimental cards for Session 2. Each stack of stimulus cards was covered with a heavy blank card. One card was displayed for each trial. Instructions were given before each task. In Task 1, the instructions were as follows:

> In this session, you will see ten characters printed vertically on each card. None of the characters has been learned by you previously. Please use your imagination to guess the pronunciations of these characters as quickly as possible, one by one, from top to bottom. You can neither skip nor point at any of them while reading them. Furthermore, each character can be read only once. If you have any question, you can ask me now. If not, let's do some practice.

In Session 2, the instruction was the same as the one in Session 1 except for the fact that subjects were informed of the type of the task (i.e. naming real characters) to be performed.

The time for naming all 10 items on one card was measured with a stop watch. Responses were recorded on a tape recorder. The time between trials was short, representing only the delay required to record the naming time and to display a new stimulus card.

RESULTS

Pseudocharacter Naming

Reading Times. The mean reading times for each card are shown in Table 11.3. The effect of stimulus type was significant [$F(4,304) = 18.0, P < 0.05$], whereas those of grade and reading ability were not. Only the IO pseudocharacters differed from the others (by Scheffe's tests at $P < 0.05$). No interaction was significant.

Number of Regular Responses. The pronunciation of a pseudocharacter was considered regular if it was read like its phonetic component, regardless of possible tonal discrepancy. The mean numbers of regular responses for each type of item are shown in Table 11.4.

TABLE 11.3
The Mean Reading Times (Sec.) in Session 1

	Type of Pseudocharacters				
	RO		*Mixed*		*IO*
Reading Ability		*RDIN*	*RDIF*	*IDIF*	
Grade 3					
good	11.15	11.80	12.25	11.58	13.95
poor	12.46	12.35	12.35	13.36	14.42
Grade 6					
good	10.74	11.63	11.92	11.69	13.60
poor	11.37	11.06	11.22	12.24	13.69

TABLE 11.4
The Mean Numbers of Regular Responses in Session 1

	Type of Pseudocharacters				
	RO	*Mixed*			*IO*
Reading Ability		*RDIN*	*RDIF*	*IDIF*	
Grade 3					
good	9.80	8.43	8.75	6.85	4.45
poor	8.30	8.25	8.65	6.70	5.83
Grade 6					
good	9.78	8.50	7.70	6.53	4.20
poor	8.25	8.15	8.03	6.33	5.10

The stimulus type effect was again significant [$F(4, 304) = 194.9$]. So was the interaction reading ability × stimulus type [$F(4, 304) = 15.62$, $P < 0.05$]. Compared to poor readers, good readers made more regular responses in the RO condition but fewer in the IO condition. All differences between pairs of stimulus type conditions were significant except the one between RDIF and RDIN. These differences were more evident for the good readers than for the poor readers.

Types of Irregular Responses. The pronunciation of a pseudocharacter was considered irregular if it was read differently from its phonetic component. Generally, the irregular responses could be divided into five types.

1. Neighbour: The pseudocharacter was pronounced like one of its irregular neighbours. For example, [illegible] was read as 細 /xi/.
2. Radical: The subject read the item as if its radical was the phonetic component. For example, [illegible] was read as 車 /che/.
3. Graphic Association: The subject read the pseudocharacters on the basis of some graphic association. For example, [illegible] was read as 軌 /guei/.
4. Semantic Association: The subject read the pseudocharacters on the basis of some semantic association. For example, [illegible] was read as 歡 /huan}.
5. Miscellanea: The pronunciation could not be categorised into one of the above four types. For example, [illegible] was read as /neng/.

Among these five types of irregular responses, Neighbour responses occurred most frequently. The distribution of the irregular Neighbour responses in different conditions was the main concern of the present study, hence it will be the focus of our analysis. The mean numbers of irregular Neighbour responses in the four conditions are shown in Table 11.5

TABLE 11.5
The Mean Number of Irregular Neighbour Responses in Session 1

	Type of Pseudocharacters			
	Mixed			*IO*
Reading Ability	*RDIN*	*RDIF*	*IDIF*	
Grade 3				
good	1.05	0.68	2.88	4.38
poor	0.98	0.23	1.78	2.10
Grade 6				
good	1.30	1.93	3.28	4.35
poor	0.68	0.48	2.03	1.93

The effects of reading ability and stimulus type were significant [F(1, 76) = 14.9, and $F(3, 228) = 112.3$, respectively $P < 0.05$]. All differences between pairs of conditions were significant except for RDIF and RDIN. Stimulus type interacted with both grade [$F(3, 228) = 3.21$] and reading ability [$F(3, 228) = 14.9$]. The effect of grade was significant only for the RDIF condition, where the 6th graders made more irregular Neighbour responses than the 3rd graders. The good readers made more of these responses than the poor readers in all but the RDIN condition.

Simple Character Naming

Reading Times. The mean reading times for each card are shown in Table 11.6. The effects of reading ability and stimulus type were significant [$F(1, 76) = 11.1$, and $F(4, 304) = 3.37$, respectively $P < 0.05$]. There were, however, no significant differences between pairs of stimulus conditions.

Mispronunciations. The mispronunciations of the simple characters could be divided into five types:

1. Derivative: The simple character was mistaken for one of those compound characters in which it serves as a phonetic component. For example, 斗 /dou/ was read as one of its derivatives, 科 /ke/. The compound characters were considered as derivatives of the simple character regardless of their historical origin. This type of error also included the tonal errors affected by the derivatives of the simple characters. For example, 令 was read as the second tone, which was possibly influenced by its derivative 玲.

TABLE 11.6
The Mean Reading Times (sec.) in Session 2

	Type of Pseudocharacters				
	RO	*Mixed*			*IO*
Reading Ability		*RDIN*	*RDIF*	*IDIF*	
Grade 3					
good	6.78	6.69	6.64	6.95	6.67
poor	8.89	8.44	8.49	9.88	9.11
Grade 6					
good	7.02	6.76	6.61	6.93	6.62
poor	8.70	7.76	7.97	8.31	8.80

2. Tonal confusion: This type included tonal errors which could not be accounted for by the character's derivatives. For example, 景, which should have been read as the second tone, was read as the first tone.
3. Graphic confusion: Simple characters were pronounced like graphically similar characters. For example, 司 was read as 可.
4. Semantic confusion: Simple characters were pronounced like other semantically related characters. For example, 丙 was read as 乙 or 甲. The three characters, 甲, 乙, and 丙 represent the first, the second and the third of the 10 Heavenly Stems, respectively.
5. Miscellanea: The mispronunciation could not be categorised into any of the above four types. For example, 化 was read as /nong/.

The mean numbers of the different error types are shown in Table 11.7.

TABLE 11.7
The Mean Numbers of Various Errors in Session 2

	Error types				
Reading Ability	*Derivative*	*Tonal Confusion*	*Graphic Confusion*	*Semantic Confusion*	*Miscellanea*
Grade 3					
good	0.90	0.05	0.20	0.05	0.10
poor	5	0.35	1.40	0.35	2.80
Grade 6					
good	0.10	0.05	0.10	0.00	0.15
poor	2.80	1.35	1.15	0.40	2.95

Mean numbers of Derivative errors for the five stimulus type conditions are shown in Table 11.8.

The effects of grade, reading ability and stimulus type were all significant [$F(1, 76) = 11.8$, $F(1, 76) = 60.8$, $F(4, 304) = 21.9$, respectively]. Stimulus type interacted with both grade [$F(4, 304) = 3.74$] and reading ability [$F(4, 304) = 14$]. Grade was significant only for IDIF and IO, where the 3rd-graders made more Derivative errors than the 6th-graders. Reading ability had an effect for all the stimulus conditions except RO.

DISCUSSION

The results suggest that by grade 3, children know which part of a character can provide phonological information. Moreover, the properties of the pseudocharacters' neighbours influenced their pronunciation, suggesting that the children did not choose pronunciations for novel characters casually or randomly. Their naming of novel characters was plausible and systematic, especially for the good readers. It is evident that children use their acquired OPC knowledge to deal with novel characters. In addition, the results from the analysis of mispronunciations of simple characters show that simple character naming was also influenced by their derivatives, suggesting that OPC knowledge is used to decode both real characters and pseudocharacters.

Despite the fact that the overall statistical analysis did not support the prediction that among the five types of pseudocharacters the RO pseudocharacters would be named fastest, the direction of differences in naming latency exhibited the expected pattern in good readers. In addition, the IO pseudocharacters were named slowest of all stimulus types, suggesting again an influence of phonological consistency on pseudocharacter naming.

TABLE 11.8
Mean Numbers of Derivative Errors in Session 2

	Type of Pseudocharacters				
	RO	*Mixed*			*IO*
Reading Ability		*RDIN*	*RDIF*	*IDIF*	
Grade 3					
good	0.00	0.25	0.05	0.30	0.30
poor	0.20	1.70	0.45	1.50	1.15
Grade 6					
good	0.00	0.05	0.00	0.05	0.00
poor	0.10	1.55	0.30	0.55	0.30

According to the hypothesis considered in the Introduction, if children regularise novel characters solely on the basis of their phonetic component, the different stimulus type conditions should not yield different numbers of regular responses. If, on the other hand, the regularisation of novel characters is influenced by their neighbours, following lexical analogy models (i.e. Glushko, 1979; Taraban & McClelland, 1987), the RO pseudocharacters should be regularised more than the Mixed ones, and the IO pseudocharacters should be least likely to be regularised. The results supported exactly these predictions. Furthermore, the results of the analysis of irregular Neighbours responses showed that such responses were the most frequent ones among the various types of irregular responses and the IO condition yielded more irregular Neighbours responses than the Mixed conditions, providing additional convincing evidence that children used their acquired OPC knowledge in phonological processing.

Additionally, the IDIF condition yielded fewer regular responses than both the RDIN and the RDIF conditions, whereas the latter two conditions did not differ significantly, suggesting that the regularised pronunciations of novel characters depend on the relative frequencies of their regular and irregular neighbours rather than on the numbers of regular neighbours. It seems that the influence of neighbours on novel character processing is related to their frequency but not to their number. However, the earlier analysis suggests that the number of pseudocharacters' neighhours may influence naming performance because the comparison of consistency values is based on the number of neighbours of the pseudocharacters. Therefore, additional research is needed to examine the role of the number of neighbours in character reading.

Basically, there is no radical difference between the strategies used to read novel characters by respectively younger and older children, nor by poor and good readers. Slight but statistically significant differences between good and poor readers were found in this experiment. First, a significant difference was observed in the numbers of regular responses produced by respectively the good and the poor readers in the RO and the IO conditions: The poor readers gave fewer regular responses than the good readers in the RO condition but more than the good readers in the IO condition. Furthermore, for the poor readers, the number of regular responses observed in the RO condition was almost the same as in conditions RDIN and RDIF, whereas for the good readers there were significantly more regular responses in the RO condition than in conditions RDIN and RDIF. Also, the poor readers gave fewer irregular Neighbour responses in the Mixed and IO conditions than the good readers. It seems that the good readers master OPC knowledge better than the poor readers.

Fang et al. (1986) found a consistency effect in simple character naming. Thus, the RO simple characters in this experiment should be named fastest and the IO simple characters should be named slowest. Despite the fact that children's simple character-naming latencies did not suggest children's use of the OPC knowledge in simple character-naming, mispronunciation errors on simple characters did. Many of the mispronunciation errors on the simple characters in this experiment were related to orthography-phonology correspondences. For example, 足 /zu/ was read at 捉 /zho/. A similar trend was observed by Lien (1985), who found that children made many Derivative errors in naming compond characters. In the present experiment, 3rd graders made more Derivative errors than 6th graders and the poor readers more than good readers, which suggests that unskilled readers are more influenced than skilled readers by OPCs when naming real characters.

Thus, the major findings of the present study are as follows. First, children's pseudocharacter naming shows a consistency effect. Second, the frequency of neighbours influences their pronunciation of pseudocharacters. Third, there is no radical difference between younger and older readers, nor between poor and good readers in the strategy used to read novel characters, although good readers appear to master OPC knowledge better than poor readers. Fourth, the influence of OPC knowledge on character-naming is greater in unskilled than in skilled readers.

For beginning readers of English, the essential task is to grasp the principle of alphabetic representation. They have to learn about the relationship between spellings and sounds. Otherwise, novel words can only be memorised by rote, which is a very inefficient strategy. For Chinese children, orthography-phonology correspondences are not explicitly taught. Characters are usually learned via intensive and labourious writing practice. Nevertheless, the children are still able to grasp the principles of Chinese orthography and to acquire the knowledge of the orthography-phonology correspondences, which is used in naming both real and novel characters, suggesting that when learning characters, children not only learn how to name characters but also acquire the orthographic knowledge underlying the mapping between print and sound.

Like naming English words, naming Chinese characters is influenced by the pronunciation of other orthographically similar characters, which cannot be accounted for by traditional dual-route models, for which Chinese characters are read through a direct character-specific route. The fact that consistency effects are found in naming real and novel characters can be predicted by lexical analogy models (e.g. Glushko, 1979; Taraban & McClelland, 1987).

Lexical analogy models are established on the basis of the consistency effect in word recognition and pronunciation. Recent studies suggest that the speed with which a given word is read depends not only on the frequency of that word, but also on the properties of its neighbours, specifically the respective frequencies of its "friends" and "enemies" (Jared, McRae, & Seidenberg, 1990). In the present study, the type of response (i.e. a regular or an irregular one) a pseudocharacter gets is determined by the relative frequencies of its regular and irregular neighbours. To understand Chinese people's reading behaviour, one needs a model of character recognition that takes account of the detailed properties of each character's neighbours.

The present study provides not only experimental data to show how Chinese children use their orthographic knowledge in naming novel characters, but also additional convincing evidence of the psychological reality of the phonological aspects of Chinese orthography. However, so far, the previous and the present studies only show that Chinese orthography may influence character pronunciation. Waters, Seidenberg, and Bruck (1984) have investigated children's and adults' use of spelling-sound information in lexical naming, lexical decision, and sentence acceptability tasks. In the lexical naming task, subjects were required to name words. In the lexical decision task, they were required to decide about the lexicality of letter sequences (i.e. lexical or nonlexical). In the sentence acceptability task, they had to decide if sentences containing the words used in the former two tasks made sense. Three types of words were used: regular spelling-sound words (e.g. MUST), irregular spelling-sound words (e.g. HAVE), and irregular spelling words (e.g. ACHE). Waters et al. found that for adults, the effect of spelling and spelling-sound regularity was, in all three tasks, limited to the lower-frequency words, whereas for younger and poorer readers, these effects were found also on the higher-frequency ones. The fact that spelling-sound regularity affected readers' performance on sentence acceptability indicates that access to phonological information is not an artifact of having to pronounce a word. Therefore, additional research is needed to investigate the influence of Chinese orthography on higher-level reading behaviour in order to further understand the relationship between orthography and reading.

ACKNOWLEDGEMENTS

The research reported here was supported by a grant from the National Science Council of the Republic of China (NSC82–0301–H–194–018–Y) to the first author.

REFERENCES

Baron, J., & Strawson, C. (1976). Use of orthographic and word-specific knowledge in reading words aloud. *Journal of Experimental Psychology: Human Perception and Performance, 2*, 386–293.

Coltheart, V., & Leahy, J. (1992). Children's and adults' reading of nonwords: Effects of regularity and consistency. *Journal of Experimental Psychology: Learning, Memory, and Cognition, 18*, 718–729.

DeFrancis, J. (1989). *Visible Language: The diverse oneness of writing systems.* Honolulu: University of Hawaii Press.

Edfelt, A.W. (1960). *Silent speech and silent reading.* Chicago: University of Chicago Press.

Fang, S.P., Horng, R.Y., & Tzeng, O.J.L. (1986). Consistency effects in the Chinese character and pseudo-character naming tasks. In H.S.R. Kao & R. Hoosain (Eds.), *Linguistics, psychology and the Chinese language* (pp. 11-21). Hong Kong: University of Hong Kong.

Glushko, R.J. (1979). The organization and activation of orthographic knowledge in reading aloud. *Journal of Experimental Psychology: Human Perception and Performance, 5*, 674–691.

Gough, P., & Cosky, M. (1977). One second of reading again. In N.J. Castellan, D.B. Pisoni, & G.R. Potts (Eds.), *Cognitive theory* (Vol. 2). Hillsdale, NJ: Lawrence Erlbaum Associates Inc.

Hung, D.L., & Tzeng, O.J.L. (1981). Orthographic variation and visual information processing. *Psychological Bulletin, 90*, 377–414.

Jared, D., McRae, K., & Seidenberg, M.S. (1990). The basis of consistency effects in word naming. *Journal of Memory and Language, 29*, 687–715.

Kolers, P.A. (1969). Some formal characteristics of pictograms. *American Scientist, 57*, 348–363.

Laxon, V.J., Coltheart, B., & Keating, C. (1988). Children find friendly words friendly too: Words with many orthographic neighbours are easier to read and spell. *British Journal of Educational Psychology, 58*, 103–119.

Lien, Y.W. (1985). *Consistency of the phonetic clues in the Chinese phonograms and their naming latencies*. Master's thesis submitted to National Taiwan University.

National Institute for Compilation and Translation. (1967). *A study on the high-frequency words used in Chinese elementary school reading material*. Taipei, Taiwan: Chung Hwa Book Co., Ltd.

Perfetti, C.A., & Hogaboam, T. (1975). The relationship between single word decoding and reading comprehension skill. *Journal of Educational Psychology, 67*, 461–469.

Rozin, P., Poritsky, S., & Sotsky, (1971). American children with reading problems can easily learn to read English represented by Chinese characters. *Science, 171*, 1264–1267.

Seidenberg, H.S. (1985). The time course of phonological code activation in two writing systems. *Cognition, 19*, 1–30.

Seidenberg, H.S., & McClelland, J.-L. (1989). A distributed, developmental model of word recognition and naming. *Psychological Review, 96*, 523–568.

Stanovich, K.E., & Bauer, D.W. (1978). Experiments on the spelling-to-sound regularity effect in word recognition. *Memory and Cognition, 6*, 410–415.

Stroop, J.R. (1935). Studies of interference in serial verbal reactions *Journal of Experimental Psychology, 18*, 643–662.

Taraban, R., & McClelland, J.L. (1987). Conspiracy effects in word pronunciation. *Journal of Memory and Language, 26*, 608–631.

Treiman, R., Goswami, U., & Bruck, M. (1990). Not all nonwords are alike: Implications for reading development and theory. *Memory and Cognition, 18*, 559–567.

Waters, G.S., Seidenberg, M.S., & Bruck, M. (1984). Children's and adults' use of spelling-sound information in three reading tasks. *Memory and Cognition, 12*, 293–305.

Zhou, Y.G. (1978). To what degree are the "phonetics" of present-day Chinese characters still phonetic? *Zhongguo Yuwen, 146*, 172–177.

APPENDIX: THE STIMULI

Session 1: Pseudocharacters

RO *RDIN* *RDIF* *IDIF* *IO*

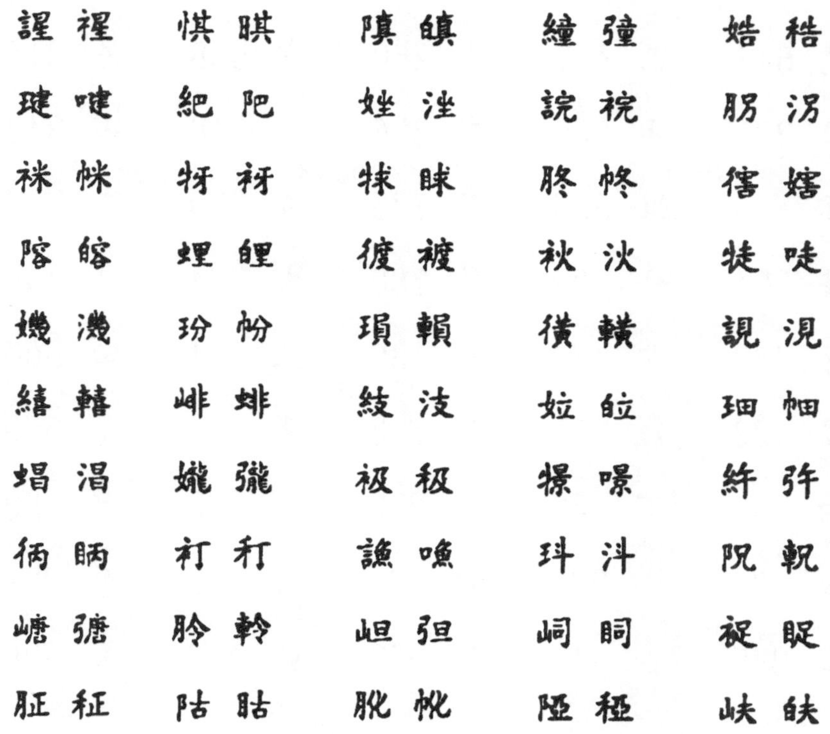

Session 2: Simple Characters And Their Frequencies

RO		*RDIN*		*RDIF*		*IDIF*		*IO*	
星	744	其	693	眞	709	童	436	告	441
建	613	巴	437	坐	260	完	538	另	215
米	281	牙	65	求	336	冬	148	害	342
容	418	里	396	度	775	黄	650	走	758
幾	854	分	1303	員	780	火	724	見	758
喜	382	非	474	支	139	立	1021	田	300
昌	122	龍	271	及	573	景	174	午	570
丙	40	丁	66	魚	253	斗	43	兄	95
唐	95	令	231	旦	30	司	280	足	228
正	845	古	411	化	602	亞	486	失	626

IV READING ACQUISITION AND ITS IMPACT ON LANGUAGE PROCESSES

12 Phonological and Grammatical Skills in Learning to Read

Peter Bryant
University of Oxford, UK

TWO POSSIBLE FACTORS IN LEARNING TO READ

In the dispute about the effectiveness of the "real books" approach, or of the "whole language" approach as it is often called in America (Liberman & Liberman, 1992), the real disagreement is about what it is that children have to learn in order to be able to read. The case for real books is founded on the idea that learning to read is a natural development. The idea has been championed for many years by Kenneth Goodman (1967; 1982) who argued that learning to read is not all that different in kind from learning to speak. Children learn to read by being exposed to written language in much the same way as they learn to speak by being exposed to spoken language. The only difference is that they can use their knowledge of spoken language and its constraints to help them to decipher written text. They can use their understanding of the meaning of the rest of the sentence to help them to reach a reasonable conclusion about any written word whose meaning at first escapes them.

Goodman called this the "psycholinguistic guessing game" and he claimed that it not only helps the child to read unknown words; it also helps him or her learn to recognise the word next time without having to rely on the contextual prop of the rest of the sentence. He argued that the main force in learning to read is the children's use of context to help them to learn new words.

The contrary position is that children should be taught "phonics" first of all: They have to be thoroughly at home with letter–sound relationships before they can make any real progress in reading or writing. Those who hold this view believe that in order to understand the alphabet children have to learn to do something which in a sense goes against the psychological grain. They have to begin to analyse the sounds in words: they have to break up words into phonological segments—usually phonemes—because these are the sounds that alphabetic letters represent.

CHILDREN'S PHONOLOGICAL AWARENESS

It is often quite difficult for people to see why phonology should be a genuine barrier to reading. Children string phonemes together into real words with no difficulty and distinguish words like "cat" and "hat" on the basis of single phonemes. Why should there be any problem? The answer is to be found in a series of experiments that began in the 1960s on children's ability to make explicit phonological judgements. The younger children's performance in these tasks seemed to show that by and large they are quite incapable of making distinctions that are transparently clear to any literate adult. Bruce (1964), for example, gave children between the ages of 5 and 9 years a "subtraction" task, in which they had to work out what a word like "sand" would sound like if a particular sound—"n" in this example—were removed from it. This was very difficult for children under the age of 10 years and impossible for 5-year-old children (their mean score was actually zero).

Children's difficulty in making explicit judgements about phonemes was also demonstrated in the well-known tapping task devised by Liberman, Shankweiler, Fischer, and Carter (1974). Four-, five- and six-year-old children had to learn to tap out either the number of syllables or the number of phonemes in a word spoken to them by the experimenter. The phoneme task was a great deal easier than the syllable task at all age levels, and (again) was impossible for the youngest children.

There is a possible connection to be made between the difficulty that young children have with explicit judgements about phonemes and learning to read. Whether one makes this connection depends on one's views of the importance of the alphabet and of learning grapheme–phoneme correspondences in reading. Children should be quite unable to learn about the alphabetic code if they are unable to break words down into their component phonemes.

In fact, the evidence definitely does suggest a connection between children's skills in phoneme tasks and the progress that they make in learning to read. First, there are strong correlations between children's reading levels and their success in phoneme detection tasks even after stringent controls for differences in IQ (Stanovich, Cunningham, & Cramer, 1984; Stanovich, Cunningham, & Freeman, 1984; Tunmer, Herriman, & Nesdale, 1988; Lundberg, Oloffson, & Wall, 1980).

Secondly, many of the children who are particularly backward in reading are also particularly unsuccessful in tasks in which they have to manipulate grapheme–phoneme correspondences. It has been found that dyslexic children read a series of real words with as much success as other (younger) children who have achieved the same level of reading but are much worse than the other children when it comes to reading pseudowords (e.g. "wef" and "slosbon")

(Frith & Snowling, 1983; Baddeley, Ellis, Miles, & Lewis, 1982). Because it is likely that the main way to read these pseudowords is by grapheme–phoneme correspondence, these studies may show that children who are behind in reading are also less able than most to break words up into their constituent phonemes.

Thirdly, intevention seems to work. Lundberg, Frost, and Petersen (1988) gave a group of kindergarten children prolonged extra phonological experience, much of which involved breaking words into phonemes and constructing words from phonemes. These children eventually learned to read more successfully than others who had received as much extra attention, but of a non-phonological kind.

These studies seem to show that children face a formidable phonological barrier when learning to read, and that their success in surmounting it will play a part in the progress that they make in learning to read. The studies also suggest that children become explicitly aware of phonemes because they are taught about them when they are learning how to read. This is certainly the view of Morais and colleagues (Morais, Cary, Alegria, & Bertelson, 1979; Morais, Bertelson, Cary, & Alegria, 1986). In two studies this research team made comparisons between adults in Portugal who were illiterate and others who had been illiterate most of their lives but had recently taken literacy courses and could read. In the first study these people had either to work out what a word would sound like if the first sound were removed ("purso"–"urso") or if a particular initial sound were added to it ("alacho"–"palacho"). The illiterate group was a great deal worse at these tasks than the "ex-illiterates".

In the next study illiterates and people who had recently become literate were given the same kind of phoneme task but were also given other tasks: in one of these they had to judge whether words rhymed or not and in another they had to make musical discriminations. Again, the illiterates were at a particular disadvantage in the phoneme task, and their scores were lower than those of the literate people in the rhyme task as well.

Thus, adults who have not learned to read had much the same difficulties as young children in tasks involving explicit judgements about phonemes. Morais and his colleagues concluded that explicit awareness of phonemes is a product of being taught about the alphabet.

If this claim is correct, there should also be differences between children learning an alphabetic orthography and those learning an orthography which is not alphabetic. The Japanese orthography is a mixture of two kinds of script: one logographic, the other syllabic. The syllabic scripts (there are in fact two Japanese syllabaries) work at a grosser level than the phoneme because most Japanese syllables involve more than one phoneme. According to Morais' hypothesis, Japanese children should be comparatively insensitive to phonemes. Mann (1986) tested this idea in a comparative study of 6-year-old Japanese and American children. She gave them the phoneme and syllable tapping task, and also two subtraction tasks, in one of which they had to work out what a word would sound like without its initial phoneme and in another what it would sound like without its initial syllable. The American 6-year-olds were considerably better than the Japanese in the phoneme tasks but not in the syllable tasks. This result supports the claim that people in the West first become aware of phonemes as a result of learning to read.

Thus, there is empirical support for the idea that children who have just come to school at the age of 5 or 6 years and are learning an alphabetic orthography must be taught how to disentangle phonemes. However, the importance of this teaching must depend on the nature of the phonological task in learning to read. Morais and his colleagues assume that the grapheme–phoneme correspondence lies at the heart of learning to read. They claim that children have to master the connection between alphabetic letters and individual phonemes in order to be able to learn to read. If grapheme–phoneme units are so important their case is indeed a convincing one.

There is, however, a counter-argument, and it is based on a certain scepticism about the overriding importance of the grapheme–phoneme connection. Of course children have to understand the connection between sounds and letters at this level, but this connection can be made at other levels too. Strings of letters like "ight" and "and" quite reliably represent sounds, and these are sounds which contain more than one phoneme each. Are there phonological sensitivities that are relevant to phonological segments of this sort?

We have seen that young children do not have much difficulty in disentangling syllables. They are also reasonably proficient with another kind of phonological unit that lies somewhere between the phoneme and the syllable. I refer to rhyme and alliteration. There is a great deal of empirical evidence (Dowker, 1989; Lenel & Cantor, 1981; MacLean, Bryant, & Bradley, 1987; Bryant, Bradley, MacLean, & Crossland, 1989) to show that children enjoy and are sensitive to rhyme. Pre-school children do quite well, and consistently above chance level, in rhyme detection tasks and they are quite good at producing rhyming and alliterative poems.

If one assumes that the only important phonological requirement in learning to read is to master grapheme–phoneme correspondences, then one would not connect these early phonological skills and success in reading. Rhyming sounds usually comprise more than one phoneme: the rhyming sound in "sand" and "hand", for example, is "-and" and it consists of three phonemes.

However, something must be wrong with this assumption. We now have evidence for a strong link between children's ability to detect rhyme and alliteration in the pre-school period and their success years later on in reading. Several longitudinal studies have shown this. One was by Bradley and Bryant (1983). We gave 400 4- and 5-year-old children rhyme and alliteration tests before they had begun to learn to read, and then followed their progress in reading and also in mathematics over the next three to four years. There was a very strong relation between the rhyme and alliteration measure taken at the beginning of the project and the children's reading scores at its end when they were 8–9 years old. This relation was stronger even than the relation between IQ and reading and it remained significant after stringent controls for differences among the children in intelligence and in vocabulary.

This study also involved intervention. A small group of children was given extra practice with rhyme and alliteration over a two-year period, while they were 6 and 7 years old, and this experience had an effect—albeit a modest one—on their reading. When reading was tested later, these children fared better than a comparable control group who had been given as much extra attention but none of it involving rhyme and alliteration.

A later study (Bryant, Bradley, MacLean, & Crossland, 1989) confirmed the strong longitudinal connection between children's early rhyming skills and their eventual progress in reading. In this study the first measures of rhyme and alliteration were taken when the children were 3¼ years old, and yet proved to be extremely powerful predictors of reading (but not of their mathematical success), even after controls for differences in IQ, in vocabulary, and in social background. There is no doubt now about the connection. The more sensitive children are to rhyme and alliteration before they begin to learn to read, the better on the whole their progress in reading will be. There is a definite link here between a pre-school and presumably untaught phonological skill and learning to read.

So here is a dispute. On the one hand there is the impressive claim that it is quite hard for children to learn about grapheme–phoneme correspondence and that they only become aware of the way in which words can be broken up into phonemes as a result of being taught to do so at school. On the other hand we have found a definite connection between a phonological skill that they acquire without the help of formal teaching long before they go to school and their success in reading.

Fortunately, this is a conflict which can be resolved, but the solution depends on a fairly broad idea about the role of phonological skills in learning to read. One must recognise first that there is no reason why phonological codes in reading should operate just at the level of the phoneme. There are, as we have seen, other regular correspondences between sound and script. Because children have a lively sense of rhyme before they learn to read, let us turn to rhyming sounds. "Hand" and "stand" rhyme and the rhyming sound—"and"—is spelled in the same way in both words. This sort of relation is not an entirely regular one, for the rhyming sounds in many pairs of words, such as "fight" and "white", are spelled differently. But there is less variation in the way that rhyming sounds are spelled than in the way that the same phoneme is represented in different words.

Rhyming sounds in one-syllable words usually represent a speech unit that lies somewhere between the phoneme and the syllable. "Sand" and "hand" are monosyllables and the rhyming sound is only part of each syllable. Halle and Vergnaud (1980) claim that within syllables there is a natural distinction between the "onset" and the "rime". The onset is the opening consonant or consonant cluster if the syllable does begin in such a way and the rime consists of the vowel sound and any following consonants.

We can turn now to young children. There is, as we have seen, a connection between their rhyming skills and their awareness of rimes at any rate. There is also evidence that after they start school they progress from being able to divide words into intrasyllabic units (onset and rime) to being able to analyse them in terms of their constituent phonemes. The results of a study by Kirtley, Bryant, MacLean, and Bradley (1989) suggest this development strongly. The study was based on the fact that intrasyllabic units sometimes consist of one phoneme only. Therefore children, who can distinguish onset from rime, should be able to identify phonemes when these represent an intrasyllabic unit. In this study a large group of 5-year-old children was given an oddity task in which they heard, in a series of trials, four words, three of which contained the same particular phoneme, but the fourth did not. In some trials this shared sound was the words' onset ("peg", "land", "pin", "pot"), whereas in others it was the last sound ("sit", "dot", "pet", "car") and therefore was only part of the rime.

Children who can manage the onset/rime distinction but cannot make finer phonological distinctions should do well in the first condition and badly in the second, because in the first they only have to analyse onset, whereas in the second they have to take apart the rimes in each word. One can make another prediction: if children begin to be able to detect phonemes as a result of being taught to read, then those who have made no progress in reading should be quite unable to do the end-sound task, whereas those who have made progress should do reasonably well in this task.

Both predictions were correct. The beginning-sound task (onset) was a great deal easier than the end-sound task (part of the rime). Furthermore, when the children were divided into those who could read no words at all in a reading test and those who could read some words, the first group produced scores above chance level in the beginning-sound task only and chose randomly in the end-sound task. The second group, on the other hand, performed above chance level in the end-sound task, and therefore was able to some extent at least to divide the rime into its constituent phonemes.

This last result is further evidence for the Morais hypothesis that children begin to be able to break words up into constituent phonemes as a result of learning to read. But does that leave any role for the awareness of onset and rime, which clearly precedes by quite a long time the experience of learning to read?

We (Goswami & Bryant, 1990) have come to the view that this form of awareness also plays an important part in learning to read. We start with the observation, already described, that children's rhyming skills predict their success in reading, but we now have much more specific information about how this connection actually works.

Usha Goswami (1986, 1988a, b) has shown that even beginning readers realise that particular letter sequences symbolise sounds that often contain more than one phoneme. She worked with relatively difficult words like "beak", and "peak"—words which on the whole 6- and 7-year-old children do not read successfully. In a series of trials she told them the meaning of one of the words like "peak" and then asked them to read other words, some of which contained the same spelling sequence such as "beak". She found that children were more likely to read new words with the same spelling sequence than they were other words such as "lake" with different letter sequences and different sounds. Further work by Goswami also established that they do so when reading stories and also when they are writing. Finally (Goswami, 1991), she established a direct connection between these analogies and intrasyllabic units by showing that young children make analogies about letter sequences that represent intrasyllabic units far more easily than they do about other letter sequences. For example, they can see the analogy between the written words "trim" and "trot" more readily than between "wink" and "tank" (in the former pair the common spelling sequence represents the onset and in the latter it represents only part of the rime).

The developmental and the causal sequence seem clear. Before they learn to read children can make explicit judgements about the intrasyllabic units, onset, and rime. These speech units are spelled in a reasonably regular manner, and young children seem to become aware of this regularity early on in learning to read. Their sensitivity to onset and rime has an effect on their progress in reading and writing. When they have learned something about reading and writing, their experience with alphabetic letters makes it possible for them to begin to break words up into their constituent phonemes. At one level—that of onset and rime—phonological skills are a cause of reading, and at another level—that of the phoneme—its result.

GRAMMATICAL SKILLS AND READING

Children's Dependence on Context

The now undoubted connection between children's phonological skills and their progress in reading is one of the most interesting discoveries in recent empirical work on reading, but no one, I think, is making the claim that this is all that there is to learning to read. It certainly is not all there is to reading itself, because it is obvious to anyone who has seen children wrestling with a passage of writing that they use the context as much as they can to help them decipher what is on the page. There is, not surprisingly, a great deal of empirical evidence that context is a help to them (West & Stanovich, 1978; Perfetti, Goldman, & Hogaboam, 1979). Children are more likely to decipher the word "mouse" if it follows the statement "The cat chased the . . ." than if it is presented on its own.

However, there is a great difference between demonstrating that children use context to help them to read on the one hand and establishing that their use of context helps them to learn to read on the other. A child's experience of deciphering the word "mouse" through a helpful context may not make it any more likely that he or she will be able to work out what that written word means the next time.

Two kinds of evidence at least are needed to show that children's use of context helps them learn to read. One needs to show first that the experience of reading particular words in context does make it more likely that they will read those words in the future. Secondly, one has to demonstrate a connection between the syntactic and semantic skills on which children depend in order to take advantage of the context and these children's success in reading.

It so happens that there is a great deal less of the first than of the second kind of evidence, and what there is is not at all striking. Some studies (e.g. Schatz & Baldwin, 1986) led to negative results. Others (e.g. Nagy, Herman, & Anderson, 1985) produced tiny effects. The most impressive study to date of the effect of reading words in context on the likelihood that children will read these words better in the future is a comparatively recent one by Nagy, Anderson, and Herman (1987). They gave 8-, 10- and 12-year-old children passages of prose to read in one session (different children were given different passages). In a second session a week later they gave the same children a written multiple-choice test in which they had to choose the correct definition for several target words, some of which were taken from passages that they had read and others from passages given to other children.

There was an effect of reading words in context, but a very small one. The variable—whether the children were dealing with words that they had read in context or not—accounted for less than 1% of the variance between the children. Even this small effect should be treated cautiously. First, there was no control for familiarity. The children might have done better with the words that they had read before simply because they had come across them, and not because they had come across them in a meaningful passage. There was no control for this possibility, although a control would have been easy to find. Another difficulty is that it is not at all clear what the children had learned. They might have known the words in question in their spoken form and thus have learned to read them as a result of coming across them in context; or they could have learned the meaning of the word both in spoken and in written form for the first time by reading it in context. The authors do make an estimate of the words whose meaning the children might have known in their spoken form at the beginning of the study, but it is just a guess. It would have been possible to find out which of the words the children knew in their spoken form before the study started.

The second line of research—the study of the relationship between children's ability to make explicit semantic and syntactic judgements and their success in reading—is better represented in research on children's reading. A good example of this sort of study is a large scale experiment by Willows and Ryan (1986) with 6-, 7- and 8-year-old children.

They gave the children three types of test of "grammatical" sensitivity, and it is worth noting that here and in most other studies of this question the tests tapped semantic and syntactic skills at the same time. In one test children heard some incorrect sentences and were asked to locate the error and to correct it. In another they heard a set of quite complex sentences and were asked to repeat them: The experimenters wanted to know if they would relay the grammatical construction properly. The third test was a spoken cloze test: the children had to complete an incomplete sentence by filling in a missing word. At the same time Willows and Ryan gave these children various reading tests, some of which involved reading prose passages and others just a series of single words, and they also tested the children's vocabulary and their nonverbal intelligence.

There was a clear relationship between the measures of grammatical sensitivity and the children's success in reading, and this connection held even after controls for the effects of differences in vocabulary and nonverbal intelligence. Willows and Ryan favour a causal explanation (1986, p. 263): "Our data raise the possibility that in contrast to what may occur at later stages, reading skill in the early stages may in part be a function of greater reliance on linguistic information." However, there is a clear alternative, which is that the direction of cause and effect may go the other way: it is not at all a far-fetched suggestion that the experience of reading successfully may make children more sensitive to grammatical distinctions. The authors acknowledge this problem, but offer no solution to it.

Other studies have produced much the same results and share exactly the same ambiguity. Fowler (1988), Bowey (1986a, b), and Bowey and Patel (1988) have also reported strong relationships between children's grammatical skills and their success in reading, but have given us no way of deciding the direction of cause and effect in this relation. We need a solution to this problem: there is no point in establishing a strong connection between two variables if one cannot also find out how one affects the other.

The most significant step in that direction was the adoption of a reading-age-match design, first by Guthrie (1973) and then by Tunmer, Nesdale, and Wright (1987). In reading-age-match studies children who have been relatively unsuccessful at learning to read are compared with children who have had a reasonable amount of success, but care is taken to make sure that the two groups—successful and unsuccessful—are actually at the same absolute reading level. This means, of course, that the successful group will consist of children who are younger than those in the unsuccessful group. The point of having two groups with the same reading level is that any difference between them cannot be attributed to one group having advanced further with reading than the other, because both are at the same level. Therefore differences between them should have more to do with the causes than with the effects of success in reading (Bryant & Goswami, 1986).

Guthrie's (1973) study was one of the first examples of this kind of study. His chief concern was the effects of children's sensitivity to grammar on their progress in reading. His study showed that children who are successful in reading also make fewer semantic and syntactic errors and are more successful in a multiple choice version of a cloze task (which he called a "maze" test) than other children who are less successful in reading, even when the actual reading level of the different groups is the same. However, not much store can be put on this intriguing result because the maze test was given in written form, and therefore taxed children's reading skills as well. We need results from a spoken test of grammatical sensitivity.

Tunmer et al. (1987) compared a group of 8-year-old poor readers with a group of 6-year-old good readers: the mean reading age of these two groups was the same. They were given a spoken cloze task, and also a sentence correction task in which they had to either correct an ungrammatical sentence ("Tom has two kitten") or put a wrongly ordered one into the right order ("Clapped his hand Mark"). (Again these tests made no distinction between semantic and syntactic factors.) The poor readers, despite being older and generally more advanced, were less successful than the good readers at these grammatical tasks.

This is a result of some importance: it is the first and still the strongest piece of evidence that children's grammatical skills might have a potent effect on their progress in reading. There is a definite effect here, but nevertheless we need to be cautious. We can conclude that children's grammatical sensitivities play an important role in learning to read, but we still cannot be sure that this is because children use these sensitivities to help them take advantage of the context. That is not necessarily the path between grammatical skills and reading. As we shall see later, there is at least one other convincing reason why grammatical skills may have an effect on learning to read.

Reading-age matches are only one solution to the problem of determining cause and effect. Another is the longitudinal study. If a factor such as children's grammatical sensitivity affects their reading, then measures of this factor which are taken *before* they begin to read should be related to their eventual success in reading. Of course, the timing here is all important: Predictive studies in which the first measure of grammatical sensitivity is taken after children begin to learn to read will be unconvincing—at any rate as far as conclusions about cause and effect are concerned.

Yet most of the longitudinal work on this question, has suffered from bad timing. In longitudinal studies by Bohannon III, Warren-Leubecker and Helper (1984) and by Tunmer et al. (1988), most of the children were given their first grammatical tests some time after they had begun to learn to read.

To my knowledge, the only study which reports relationships between measures of grammatical judgements taken before children began to read and their eventual success in reading was done by Rego (1991). Her measures of the children's grammatical judgements once again involved judgements about incorrect sentences. In her study, however, these tasks were given to children relatively early on—at the age of 4 years 6 months and 5 years 6 months—before the children had made any progress in reading. Yet their performance in these tasks was related to their reading levels at the age of 6 years 11 months, even after stringent controls for differences in IQ, vocabulary, and memory skills. In the tests of reading that Rego gave at the end of her project the children had to read passages of prose and also lists of single words. There was a significant relationship between children's early grammatical skill and both kinds of reading test: if there is an effect of grammatical sensitivity on children's reading it is not confined to reading passages of prose in which the children can make use of context. It works when context is no longer available.

There is more to be said about this study. Rego was not content with the implicit and usually untested assumption that grammatical sensitivity affects reading through the use of context. She decided to test this idea directly. In the later stages of the project she gave each child words which he or she had not been able to read in a single-word reading test (different words for different children) embedded in a meaningful sentence. Her measure of the child's use of context was the extent to which he or she could take advantage of the context and read these hitherto inaccessible words. Rego found a strong relationship between the earlier grammatical sensitivity scores and the extent to which children did take advantage of context in this way.

Another positive point about the Rego study was that she did not just look at the predictive power of measures of grammatical sensitivity. She administered phonological tests as well, which included judgements about rhyme and about phonemes. Furthermore, her outcome measures included a comprehensive "invented spelling" task, which, briefly, was a measure of the children's ability to use grapheme–phoneme rules when writing words.

She found that the phonological measures were good predictors of the children's success in reading just as the grammatical measures were. In fact, of the two kinds of measure, the phonological ones were easily the more powerful predictors. But, more interestingly, she also found a striking specificity in the predictive relationships. The grammatical measures predicted the children's use of context to help them read words that they could read in isolation, but the phonological tests did not. The phonological tests predicted the children's performance in the invented spelling task, but the grammatical measures did not. So, for the first time we have evidence of two separate sensitivities, grammatical and phonological, both contributing to children's progress in reading but doing so in quite different ways. Phonological skills help children to come to grips with the alphabetic code; grammatical skills make it possible for them to use context to decipher unfamiliar words. Both connections contribute to their success in reading.

This conclusion seems a heartening one. If it is right, it means that we do not have to worry about which of these skills to encourage. We have to encourage both, and we need to be concerned if children are weak on either.

Grammatical Skills and Orthography

One other possible influence of grammar on reading is that children's sensitivity to syntax might help them to learn orthographic rules. This is a point that has until now been almost completely ignored by research workers. In order to make it clear I first need to define what I mean by "orthographic" rules.

The definition of what is orthographic varies from author to author, although there is general agreement that from the age of roughly 7 to 8 years children's main task in reading and spelling is to learn orthographic rules that transcend simple letter–sound relationships. The idea of a relatively late development of orthographic knowledge plays a central role both in Marsh and Desberg's (1983) and in Frith's (1985) theories of the course of reading and spelling. However, very little research has been done on the acquisition of this knowledge.

There are two possible definitions of what an orthographic rule is. One is that learning about any spelling sequence that cannot be decoded on the basis of single letter–sound associations is orthographic learning. Under this definition the sequence "ight", for example, is an orthographic sequence. But this definition seems too broad to me, and it certainly does not come late in the process of learning to read. We have already seen from Goswami's work that this kind of knowledge comes at an early stage: Children soon understand that letter sequences often represent particular phonological segments.

The second definition of orthographic rules states that these are conditional rules: the child has to learn that a sound is usually represented in one way if one condition holds but that it is (again, usually) spelled differently under another condition. The most obvious example is the way in which the grammatical status of a word often determines its spelling. For instance, we represent the "w" sound with a "wh" in interrogatives but with a "w" in many other words, and we usually represent the final morpheme in past verbs with "ed" even in words such as "mixed" or "waited", which end with a "t" or with an "id" sound in their spoken form. Also we end plural words, such as "socks", with an "s", whereas the ending in singular nouns with the same end sounds (e.g. "box") is often not spelled this way. These are conditional rules (although there are exceptions to them).

Conditional rules are, prima facie, more complex than straightforward associations between letters or letter sequences and sounds. So, children may only manage to learn such rules some time after they have mastered the alphabetic code.

However, there is little evidence on this point. Sterling's (1983) work on 12-year-old English children's spelling errors shows that by that age they have on the whole grasped the need for "-ed" in past verbs. There is also an extremely interesting study by T. Carraher (now T. Nunes) (1985) that concerns the Portuguese language. In Portuguese the same end sound is spelled "-isse" in a verb and "-ice" at the end of an abstract noun. Carraher gave Brazilian children aged 13 years and more real verbs and abstract nouns with this ending to write, and also some made-up abstract nouns, which therefore they could not have encountered before; the Portuguese equivalent of "Chineseness" was one of these. She found that the children often made errors with these endings, but that those who did manage to assign the appropriate endings for this sound to verbs and abstract nouns had clearly formed a rule, for these children invariably also gave the correct abstact-noun endings to the made-up abstract nouns.

Hoewever, we know very little about the earlier acquisition of this knowledge. We also do not know whether children of any age realise, for example, that the morpheme applies only to past verbs and not to other parts of speech that end in similar ways (e.g. "next").

Recently, we have done some preliminary longitudinal work with 7- and 8-year-old children (Bryant, Nunes, & Bryant, unpublished study). This study lasted for a year and during that time we repeatedly tested the same children's ability to spell three kinds of word. The examples given of the three types of words all concern the conditional, orthographic rule that the ending of past verbs is written as "ed" even when the actual sound is a "t" or an "id". The first set of words were *regularly spelled verbs*, such as "stopped": Their spelling pattern was determined by the word's grammatical status because the end "t" sound was represented as "ed", the word being a past verb. The second set of words were *exception verbs*, such as "kept" and "slept": Their spelling sequences were actually exceptions to these same rules because the end "t" sound was spelled as a "t" despite the word being a past verb. The third set of words were *nonverbs*, such as "next" and "past", that contained the same sounds in the same position, but these words were not past verbs and naturally the end sound was spelled with a "t".

Our results demonstrate that it takes children some time to master such conditional orthographic rules, and they also suggest a clear developmental progression:

1. *Alphabetic.* At first children concentrate on literal phonetic transcription, based on grapheme–phoneme correspondences. They tend to write "shopped" as "shopt" and "kept" as "kept", which means that they often spell the regular words incorrectly and the exceptions correctly.

2. *Variations without rules.* Later on the children show clear signs of realising that sounds such as the final "t" are sometimes spelled differently, but they have not learned how this depends on the lexical properties of the words that they are writing. So they may write "helped" correctly, but at the same time overgeneralise by writing "slept" as "sleped" and "next" as "nexed", even though, when younger, they had spelled "slept" and "next" correctly. Thus they

overgeneralise to other verbs and to nonverbs as well. There is actually a strong increase with age in the number of overgeneralisations that children make with these two kinds of words.

There is also a striking correlation among the children between the number of one kind of overgeneralisation (to other verbs) and the number of the other kind (to nonverbs). So, children appear not to be using grammatical rules when deciding how to spell the final "t" sound.

These confusions are particularly common in the case of homophonic words that have a different grammatical status—for example, "passed" and "past".

3. *Rules without exceptions.* The next step is to learn about the importance of the words' grammatical status. Children begin, for example, to confine the "ed" sequence to the endings of past verbs. However, they have continuing difficulties with exceptions to these orthographic rules. They still make the "sleped" for "slept" error quite frequently, and there is a strong correlation between the number of times that each child spells words like "shopped" correctly and the number of times that he or she incorrectly assigns the "ed" ending to exception words like "slept": This is a striking result, for one rarely finds a positive correlation between a correct and an incorrect pattern of responses. However, the number of overgeneralisations to nonverbs declines and is no longer correlated to the number of the overgeneralisations to verbs.

4. *Rules with exceptions.* Finally, children seem to learn the rules and the exceptions, although their mastery of the exceptions is rarely complete.

The study shows that children at this age (7 to 9 years) are beginning to come to grips with the relationship between the grammatical status of the words that they have to write and their spelling patterns. The extraordinarily interesting mistakes that they make show that we cannot take the learning of these conditional orthographic rules for granted. They do not come easily to young children.

There seem to be two possible accounts of the ways in which they learn to spell words of the sort that we have been considering. One is that they are not applying rules at all when they learn about these words, and that they simply learn to spell them on a rote basis. But this seems unlikely, given our finding that even at an early stage children are apparently looking for rules. The correlation at the beginning between overgeneralisations to exception verbs and to nonverbs suggests this, and so does the later correlation between correct use of the "ed" morpheme and its incorrect use in exception verbs. Also, the demonstration by Carraher, which we described earlier on, that children form abstract rules about the spelling of words in different grammatical categories is very strong evidence that children do learn rules that are conditional on grammatical differences.

If this is the case, then children's sensitivity must play a part, because these rules are conditional on the words' syntactical status. However, this brings us to the same kind of question about cause and effect that we encountered with the phonological problem.

One hypothesis is that the acquisition of these conditional spelling rules depends on the development of explicit syntactic awareness. Children who are explicitly aware of the grammatical status of a word will as a result be more likely to learn conditional orthographic rules by which the grammatical status of a word determines its spelling pattern.

The alternative hypothesis is that the causal link is in the opposite direction. Children become increasingly aware of the grammatical status of words as a direct result of learning characteristic spelling patterns. At the moment we do not know which of the two hypotheses is the right one. My own view is that either of these hypotheses is as plausible as the other. But there should be no difficulty in finding an answer to this question. Research on phonological skills and reading has shown us how to achieve this.

CONCLUSION

Research on the links between children's grammatical sensitivities, their use of context, and their success in learning to read is not as far advanced as is research on the importance of children's phonological skills. However, it is now clear that there is a link between children's grammatical acumen and their reading. There is also some evidence that, as many people have suggested, this pathway is from (1) grammatical sensitivity through (2) the use of context to (3) learning to read.

The existence of this pathway provides us with a powerful argument for making sure that children are given at an early age the experience of reading meaningful passages of prose with contexts that interest them and that they can understand.

However, we still need more research, particularly in the form of intervention studies, to establish the significance of this route to reading. It would also be quite wrong to think of it as the only possible route from grammar to reading. Perhaps the reason why people have concentrated so much on the child's use of context is that it is so obvious: children plainly show that they are guessing and making inferences about difficult words. The other possible way in which children's grammatical knowledge could influence their progress in reading—their use of syntactical knowledge to help them to learn orthographic rules—is not so obvious, but it is as interesting and could be as important.

This last point is a reminder that there are many routes to reading. Reading is a complicated business and it involves language at many different levels. It certainly makes many demands on children's phonological and syntactical knowledge, and it seems very likely that these forms of knowledge are not adequate in young children, as far as reading is concerned, at the time that they begin to read.

REFERENCES

Baddeley, A.D., Ellis, N.C., Miles, T.R., & Lewis, V.J . (1982). Developmental and acquired dyslexia: A comparison. *Cognition, 11*, 185–199.

Bohannon III, J.N., Warren-Leubecker, A., & Helper, N. (1984). Word order awareness and early reading. *Child Development, 55*, 1541–1548.

Bowey, J. (1986a). Syntactic awareness and verbal performance from pre-school to fifth grade. *Journal of Psycholinguistics Research, 15*, 285–308.

Bowey, J. (1986b). Syntactic awareness in relation to reading skill and ongoing comprehension monitoring. *Journal of Experimental Child Psychology, 41*, 282–299.

Bowey, J.A., & Patel, R.K. (1988). Metalinguistic ability and early reading achievement. *Applied Psycholinguistics, 9*, 367–383.

Bradley, L., & Bryant, P.E. (1983). Categorising sounds and learning to read—a causal connection. *Nature, 301*, 419–521.

Bruce, D.J. (1964). The analysis of word sounds. *British Journal of Educational Psychology, 34*, 158–170.

Bryant, P.E., Bradley, L., MacLean, M., & Crossland, J. (1989). Nursery rhymes, phonological skills and reading. *Journal of Child Language, 16*, 407–428.

Bryant, P.E., & Goswami, U. (1986). The strengths and weaknesses of the reading level design—comment on Backman, Mamen and Ferguson. *Psychological Bulletin, 100*, 101–103.

Bryant, P.E., MacLean, M., Bradley, L.L., & Crossland, J. (1990). Rhyme, alliteration, phoneme detection and learning to read. *Developmental Psychology, 26*, 429–438.

Carraher, T.N. (1985). Exporaçoes sobre o desenvolvimento da competencia em ortografia em Portuguès. *Psicologia: Teoria e Pesquisa, 1*, 269–285.

Dowker, A. (1989). Rhymes and alliteration in poems elicited from young children. *Journal of Child Language, 16*, 181–202.

Fowler, A.E. (1988). Grammaticality judgements and reading skill in grade 2. *Annals of Dyslexia, 38*, 73–93.

Frith, U. (1985). Beneath the surface of developmental dyslexia. In K. Patterson, M. Coltheart, & J. Marshall, *Surface Dyslexia* (pp. 301–330). Hove, UK: Lawrence Erlbaum Associates.

Frith, U., & Snowling, M. (1983). Reading for meaning and reading for sound in autistic and dyslexic children. *British Journal of Developmental Psychology, 1*, 329–342.

Goodman, K. (1967). Reading: A psycholinguistic guessing game. *Journal of the Reading Specialist*, 126–137.

Goodman, K. (1982). Miscue analysis: Theory and reality in reading. In F.K. Gollasch (Ed.), *Language and literacy: The selected writings of Kenneth S. Goodman*. Boston: Routledge & Kegan Paul.

Goswami, U. (1986). Children's use of analogy in learning to read: A developmental study. *Journal of Experimental Child Psychology, 42*, 73–83.

Goswami, U. (1988a). Children's use of analogy in learning to spell. *British Journal of Developmental Psychology, 6*, 21–33.

Goswami, U. (1988b). Orthographic analogies and reading development. *Quarterly Journal of Experimental Psychology, 40A*, 239–268.

Goswami, U. (1991). Learning about spelling sequences: The role of onsets and rimes in analogies in reading. *Child Development, 62*, 1110–1123.

Goswami, U., & Bryant, P. (1990). *Phonological skills and learning to read*. Hove, UK: Lawrence Erlbaum Associates Ltd.

Gough, P.B., & Hillinger, M.L. (1980). Learning to read: An unnatural act. *Bulletin of the Orton Society, 30*, 179–196.

Guthrie, J.T. (1973). Reading comprehension and syntactic responses in good and poor readers. *Journal of Educational Psychology, 65*, 294–299.

Halle, M., & Vergnaud, J. (1980). Three dimensional phonology. *Journal of Linguistic Research, 1*, 83–105.

Kirtley, C., Bryant, P., MacLean, M., & Bradley, L. (1989). Rhyme, rime and the onset of reading. *Journal of Experimental Child Psychology, 48*, 224–245.

Lenel, J.C. & Cantor, J.H. (1981). Rhyme recognition and phonemic perception in young children. *Journal of Psycholinguistic Research, 10*, 57–68.

Liberman, I.Y., & Liberman, A. (1992). Whole language versus code emphasis: Underlying assumptions and their implications for reading instruction. In P. Gough, L.C. Ehri, & R. Treiman (Eds.), *Reading acquisition* (pp. 343–366). Hillsdale, NJ: Lawrence Erlbaum Associates Inc.

Liberman, I.Y., Shankweiler, D., Fischer, F.W., & Carter, B. (1974). Explicit syllable and phoneme segmentation in the young child. *Journal of Experimental Child Psychology, 18*, 201–212.

Lundberg, I., Frost, J., & Petersen, O. (1988). Effects of an extensive program for stimulating phonological awareness in preschool children. *Reading Research Quarterly, 23*, 263–284.

Lundberg, I., Olofsson, A., & Wall, S. (1980). Reading and spelling skills in the first school years predicted from phonemic awareness skills in kindergarten. *Scandinavian Journal of Psychology, 21*, 159–173.

MacLean, M., Bryant, P.E., & Bradley, L. (1987). Rhymes, nursery rhymes and reading in early childhood. *Merrill-Palmer Quarterly, 33*, 255–282.

Mann, V.A. (1986). Phonological awareness: The role of reading experience. *Cognition, 24*, 65–92.

Marsh, G., & Desberg, P. (1983). The development of strategies in the acquisition of symbolic skills. In D.R. Rogers & J.A. Sloboda, *The acquisition of symbolic skills* (pp. 149–154). New York: Plenum Press.

Morais, J., Bertelson, P., Cary, L., & Alegria, J. (1986). Literacy training and speech segmentation. *Cognition, 24*, 45–64.

Morais, J., Cary, L., Alegria, J., & Bertelson, P. (1979). Does awareness of speech as a sequence of phones arise spontaneously? *Cognition, 7*, 323–331.

Nagy, W., Herman, P., & Anderson, R. (1985). Learning words from context. *Reading Research Quarterly, 20*, 233–253.

Nagy, W.E., Anderson, R.C., & Herman, P.A. (1987). Learning word meanings from context during normal reading. *American Educational Research Journal, 24*, 237–270.

Perfetti, C., Goldman, S., & Hogaboam, T. (1979). Reading skill and the identification of words in discourse context. *Memory and Cognition, 7*, 273–282.

Piaget, J. (1952). *The child's conception of number*. London: Routledge & Kegan Paul.

Rego, L. (1991). *The role of linguistic awareness in children's reading and spelling*. D.Phil. thesis, Oxford University.

Schatz, E., & Baldwin, R.S. (1986). Context clues are unreliable predictors of word meanings. *Reading Research Quarterly, 21*, 439–453.

Stanovich, K.E., Cunningham, A.E., & Cramer, B.R. (1984). Assessing phonological awareness in kindergarten children: Issues of task comparability. *Journal of Experimental Child Psychology, 38*, 175–190.

Stanovich, K.E., Cunningham, A.E., & Freeman, (1984). Intelligence, cognitive skills and early reading progress. *Reading Research Quarterly, 19*, 278–303.

Sterling, C.M. (1983). Spelling errors in context. *British Journal of Psychology, 74*, 353–364.

Treiman, R. (1983). The structure of spoken syllables: Evidence from novel word games. *Cognition, 15*, 49–74.

Tunmer, W.E., Herriman, M.L., & Nesdale, A.R. (1988). Metalinguistic abilities and beginning reading. *Reading Research Quarterly, 23*, 134–158.

Tunmer, W.E., Nesdale, A.R., & Wright, A.D. (1987). Syntactic awareness and reading acquisition. *British Journal of Developmental Psychology, 5*, 25–34.

West, R.F., & Stanovich, K.E. (1978). Automatic contextual facilitation in readers of three ages. *Child Development, 49*, 717–727.

Willows, D., & Ryan, E.B. (1986). The development of grammatical sensitivity and its relationship to early reading achievement. *Reading Research Quarterly, 21*, 253–265.

13 The Impact of Learning to Read on the Functional Anatomy of Language Processing

Thomas H. Carr
Michigan State University, East Lansing, MI, USA

Michael I. Posner
University of Oregon, Eugene, OR, USA

INTRODUCTION

Word recognition has been called "the foundation of the reading process" (Gough, 1984; Stanovich, 1991). Support for this view is easy to find. A large body of cognitive evidence indicates that words are functional units of perceptual and linguistic analysis during reading (Carr, 1986; Rayner & Pollatsek, 1989). Skill at word recognition is a major contributor to individual differences in first-language reading comprehension among children and remains an important contributor among adults (Adams, 1990; Carr & Levy, 1990; Perfetti, 1985; Stanovich, 1986; Stanovich, 1991). Skill at word recognition, including accurate visual-orthographic encoding in particular, is an important predictor of both reading comprehension and acquisition of new vocabulary from context during second-language reading development (Brown & Haynes, 1985; Haynes & Carr, 1990).

In this chapter we use recent discoveries about the neural basis of cognitive processing to help understand word recognition and its place in reading development. Our goal is to explore possible changes in the functional organisation of language-processing structures in the brain that might accompany the initial emergence of literacy and support its exercise. After a general discussion of language mechanisms, their operation, and their regulation as illuminated by the classic forms of evidence from neuropsychology, we focus on the perceptual encoding mechanisms that participate in reading, with particular emphasis on two anatomically localised encoding mechanisms recently identified by a functional imaging technique called positron emission tomography (PET). One of these two mechanisms, which we call the prestriate visual word form system (Prestriate VWFS), is specialised to support only reading. It appears to be an orthographic processor whose primary component resides in the left-medial prestriate visual cortex of literate adults—or at least, those whose major language is English. The second, which we will call the frontal lexical semantics area (FLSA), is located in the left inferior prefrontal cortex. The FLSA participates more widely in language processing, serving semantic functions for listening and perhaps for signed language as well as for reading. We consider the operation of these mechanisms, their development, and in the case of the Prestriate VWFS, how it comes to be integrated into the spoken language system to create a reading system.

METHODS OF BRAIN IMAGING

The past decade has seen considerable progress in developing tools to map the functional anatomy of human cognition. Five major sources of evidence are now available concerning the loci of brain activities involved in particular task performances.

PET. Metabolic activity and changes in cerebral blood flow, both correlated with neuronal activity, can be measured via a number of *in vivo* neuroimaging methodologies (Potchen & Potchen, 1991; Raichle, 1987). For studies of word recognition the primary method has been positron emission tomography (PET), in which a low-level radioactive tracer is introduced into the brain's blood supply in order to track either blood flow patterns or metabolic activity, depending on the tracer. PET can identify sources of processing activity over the entire brain and localise separate sources when they are a few millimetres apart. A minimum time average of about 40 seconds is necessary to obtain a blood flow image (Fox, Mintun, Reiman & Raichle, 1988; Raichle, 1987; Posner, Petersen, Fox, & Raichle, 1988). Much longer averaging times are necessary for metabolic images, making blood flow the presently preferred method for cognitive studies. PET blood flow imaging provides relatively high spatial resolution for locating sources of increased neural activity during relatively sustained bouts of task performance.

ERP. Electrical activity, recorded from arrays of scalp electrodes via electroencephalography, and magnetic activity, recorded from detectors near the skull via magnetoencephalography, can be averaged over trials to measure event-related potentials (ERPs) time-locked to the occurrence of particular stimuli during reading performance. ERP recordings provide a continuous record with good temporal resolution, but spatial resolution and localisation remain a problem. Efforts to solve these problems involve the use of dense electrode arrays and newly developed mathematical methods of locating generators from the distribution of ERP activity across the electrodes (Dale & Sereno, 1993; Gevins, 1990; Rohrbaugh, Parasuraman, & Johnson, 1990; Scherg, Vajsar, & Picton, 1989). Magnetic recordings may prove particularly helpful in solving the generator localisation problem, because the magnetic field undergoes less distortion due to brain mass than does the electric field and hence its measurement may be inherently more spatially precise than electrical measurements. However, magnetic recordings require specific information on where to place the limited number of detectors currently available in most magnetic systems.

FMRI. Blood flow imaging by PET and electrical imaging by ERPs possess complementary strengths and weaknesses, one providing good spatial localisation but no real-time temporal resolution at all, the other providing good temporal information but imprecise and often ambiguous spatial information. A second, newer method of blood flow imaging, using Functional Magnetic Resonance Imaging (FMRI) rather than PET, provides spatial localisation as good as PET or better and allows an image to be constructed in less than 100ms, with successive images taken once every 2.5 to 3 seconds (Belliveau et al., 1990; McCarthy et al., 1993; Potchen & Potchen, 1991). Current theory has it that FMRI estimates changes in the blood flow by measuring changes in the relative amounts of oxygenated versus deoxygenated haemoglobin present in brain regions that are metabolically active during task performances. This technique is just beginning to be applied to studies of language processing and word recognition, but it seems likely to replace PET as the method of choice for such studies.

Lesions. A fourth source of data on functional anatomy involves observation of task performance by patients suffering from localised lesions to specific brain regions. This is the oldest of the neural methods, but it is still developing. Increased sophistication both in the choice of task performances and in the identification of lesion locations via structural-anatomical MRI or X-ray-based computerised tomography (CT) is improving the utility of this long-standing cognitive neuropsychological approach (Damasio & Damasio, 1989; Knight, 1990; Shallice, 1988).

Single-cell Recording. A fifth class of methods provides converging evidence of a type that is rarely obtainable from normal humans, but may be recorded from some surgery patients and can also be recorded via depth electrode from intact monkey brain. This is the electrical activity of individual cells during particular task performances (Wise & Desimone, 1988). While animal models may not be very useful for language tasks, they are well developed for studies of attention (LaBerge, 1990; Posner & Peterson, 1990).

Complementarity and Convergence Among Methods

None of these methods is an ideal tool. There are problems of invasiveness, resolution, and interpretation of what is being measured that must be considered in selecting among them. However, one aspect that is still poorly understood by many observers of cognitive neuroscience is the degree to which the methods complement each other when they can be combined. For example, the advent of *in vivo* structural-anatomical imaging techniques such as MRI and CT have tremendously increased our ability to be accurate about the location and development of lesions (Damasio & Damasio, 1989). The influence of the lesion can be traced over time as its size and impact on surrounding tissue change, and sets of patients whose lesions overlap quite precisely can be selected for group studies. In the presence of these anatomical imaging techniques the human lesion method has become a far more useful tool. Similarly, the relatively poor spatial accuracy of ERP recording can be offset by PET or FMRI imaging and the temporal imprecision of PET can be compensated for by ERP. Thus a combination of electrical (or magnetic) imaging with blood flow imaging can yield far more information about brain activity during real-time task performance than any one of the techniques alone.

Such multimethod studies of brain activity can be closely integrated with cognitive evidence obtained from chronometric analysis of task performance by subjects in the same or very similar experimental paradigms (Besson et al., 1994; Chertkow et al., 1990; Petersen et al., 1989; Posner et al., 1988). Chronometric analysis exposes the logical organisation and time course of the information processing operations the brain is carrying out (see e.g. Bower & Clapper, 1989; McClelland, 1979; Meyer, Irwin, Osman, & Kounios, 1988; Posner, 1978; Posner & McLeod, 1982; Sperling & Dosher, 1986; Sternberg, 1969). To date, mental chronometry has supplied most of the evidence used by cognitive theorists in building computational models of the representation of linguistic knowledge and the skills of language processing, including word recognition. However, information on the spatial and temporal distribution of brain activity can increase the power of the cognitive modelling enterprise while simultaneously increasing the biological fidelity of the models being constructed. Elsewhere we have tried to illustrate the application of neural evidence to fundamental issues concerning separability, localisation, and modularity of function in the computational modelling of word recognition as done by literate adults (Posner & Carr, 1992), and to the question of whether word recognition should be regarded as "automatic" (Carr, 1992; Compton, Grossenbacher, Posner, & Tucker, 1991; Posner, Sandson, Dhawan, & Shulman, 1989). Here we consider its application to the study of reading development.

THE "STANDARD VIEW" OF THE FUNCTIONAL ANATOMY OF LANGUAGE PROCESSING

Figure 13.1 depicts the broad outline of what might be called the "standard view" of language processing structures in the human brain. Beginning with the work of Broca on stroke patients, neuropsychological analysis of the effects of traumatic brain lesion—supplemented by the commissurotomy or "split-brain" work of

Sperry, Gazzaniga, and others along with neuropsychologically motivated studies of normal adults and children—has resulted in wide adoption of several propositions about neural language processing (see e.g. Baynes, 1990; Coltheart, 1985; Coltheart, Sartori, & Job, 1990; Galiburda, 1990; Kolb & Whishaw, 1990; McCarthy & Warrington, 1990; Shallice, 1988). These propositions include the following:

1. In the large majority of people, the left hemisphere of the cerebral cortex plays a more important role in language processing than does the right hemisphere.

2. Left lateralisation for language-related functions does not appear to be as strong in infants as in adults; hence lateralisation of language processing has a developmental component. This claim applies in a relatively weak form to normal development and in a much stronger form to the structural plasticity that allows recovery of function following brain lesion. In the normally developing brain, lateralisation of language-related information processing is present early on and increases somewhat with development. Much larger developmental changes occur in the ability to reorganise language structures if a crucial component is damaged. Plasticity is considerable during infancy and early childhood but declines dramatically during adolescence.

3. The major linguistically defined domains of language processing are phonology (or dynamic visual pattern, if one is examining signed language rather than spoken language), lexical semantics, propositional semantics, syntax, and articulation (vocal for spoken language, manual for signed language). To characterise literate language users, another domain must be added—orthography, or the visual organisation of the writing system. Left lateralisation is greater in some of these domains than in others. For example, phonology and syntax appear to be strongly left lateralised in the adult language user, whereas lexical semantics may be less so according to lesion and split-brain studies. Furthermore, evidence favouring a genetically specified sensitive or critical period during development is much more compelling for phonology and syntax than for lexical semantics or for orthography (Johnson & Newport, 1989; Meier & Newport, 1990).

4. Within the left hemisphere itself, there is additional localisation of specific linguistic functions. Perceptual and receptive semantic operations for spoken language have traditionally been viewed as posterior functions, with critical processing components and fibres of passage located in temporal and temporoparietal cortex near the sylvan fissure, posterior and superior to primary auditory cortex. This region includes Wernicke's Area. Syntactic and articulatory operations have been viewed as anterior functions, localised in frontal cortex just across the sylvan fissure from the receptive-semantic structures, in proximity to primary motor areas. This region includes Broca's Area.

5. Although not nearly as well studied, subcortical structures are also involved in language functioning (e.g., Cappa et al., 1983; Crosson, 1985; Damasio &

Damasio, 1989; Demonet, Puel, Celsis, & Cardebat, 1990; Kennedy & Murdoch, 1989). These include sites in thalamus, basal ganglia, and cerebellum. The particular sites and their computational roles are under considerable debate. Speculative proposals go well beyond the perceptual input regulation or motor control functions one might initially think to associate with these structures. They include higher-level cognitive operations such as monitoring of semantic content (e.g. Crosson, 1985). There is still relatively little agreement on the exact role of subcortical structures at this time.

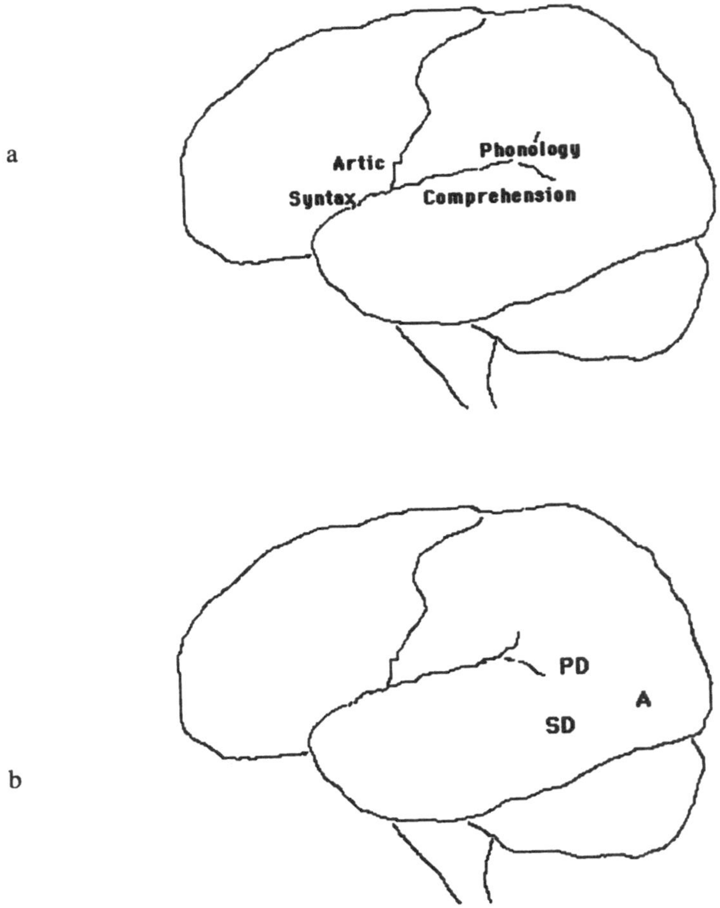

FIG 13.1a & b. Fig 13.1a: Side view of the left hemisphere of the brain, showing major regions thought from neuropsychological evidence to be critically involved in the comprehension and production of spoken language. Artic stands for articulation. Fig 13.1b: Brain regions thought from neuropsychological evidence to be specifically involved in reading without much contribution to spoken language processing. Damage to the region A produces pure alexia, damage to the region SD produces surface dyslexia, and damage to the region marked PD produces phonological dyslexia (adapted from McCarthy & Warrington, 1990).

6. Gaining the ability to read depends on recruiting additional structures that support visual encoding of written words and transmit visual information to the higher-level phonological, semantic, syntactic, and articulatory structures of the spoken (or signed) language system. The latter structures are thought to be largely shared across language skills, serving the same functions for reading written text as for listening to speech or watching sign. Studies of trauma-induced reading disorder indicate that the two reading-specific input functions of visual encoding and transmission to other language structures can be damaged relatively independently of one another. This suggests that the two functions are supported by anatomically separable processing structures.

Brain regions clearly implicated in these functions are identified in Fig. 13.1b, which is adapted from McCarthy and Warrington (1990, chapter 10). Damage to the area labelled A in Fig. 13.1b is associated with pure alexia, in which all fluent reading activities are degraded (although speech processing remains intact). This suggests that visual encoding depends in some crucial way on structures located in this vicinity or projecting through it. Damage to the area labelled SD is associated with a syndrome called surface dyslexia, in which familiar words no longer enjoy special status relative to orthographically regular but unfamiliar pseudowords. High-frequency words are recognised no more rapidly or accurately than low-frequency words, and words with exceptional correspondences between spelling and pronunciation, such as "blood" or "pint", are pronounced as if they followed the common or rule-governed patterns. Damage to the more superior area labelled PD is associated with an essentially opposite syndrome, called phonological dyslexia, in which familiar words are recognised relatively normally but the ability to deal with pseudowords and low-frequency words is compromised. This pattern suggests that the transmission function is supported by two major pathways from visual encoding to higher lexical processing. One is a so-called "direct" route based on associations to particular familiar visual forms. The direct route passes through A and SD. The other is a route mediated by pre-lexical assembled phonology that passes through A and PD.

The claims about reading we have made so far have become quite well established in neuropsychological literature. Additional possibilities are more speculative. Beyond the obvious requirement for specialised visual encoding, a degree of modality specificity may eventually characterise phonological and semantic encoding, with different (but perhaps spatially proximate or even partially overlapping) structures devoted to listening and reading. This possibility is a matter of debate (e.g. Hillis, Rapp, Roman, & Caramazza, 1990). Finally, it has been suggested that early damage to left basal ganglia impairs reading development even though equally early left cortical damage might not (Aram, Gillespie, & Yamashita, 1990). If so, then reading-relevant plasticity declines more rapidly in subcortical language structures than in cortical ones.

NEW INSIGHTS INTO THE FUNCTIONAL ANATOMY OF READING

Recent findings from PET imaging studies have confirmed the general cognitive-anatomical picture of the recognition of written words derived from the lesion work and extended it in several areas. We will consider three of them: orthographic, phonological/articulatory, and semantic encoding.

Orthographic, Phonological/Articulatory, and Semantic Encoding

PET images that illuminate orthographic, phonological/articulatory, and semantic encoding have been constructed in a number of studies, using a subtraction technique whose logic is rather like Donders'. During one imaging period subjects perform a task that ought to emphasise a particular targeted component operation or sequence of operations involved in word recognition. Call this the target task. During another imaging period, subjects perform a baseline task that ought to involve all the operations of the target task except the targeted operations. The PET image constructed during the baseline task is then subtracted from the image constructed during the target task. The resulting "targeted operations image" consists of the brain regions whose blood flow rate during the target task is significantly different from the rate observed during the baseline task. This image is taken to localise the neural activity specific to the targeted operations. The locations of these regions can then be plotted on a schematic map of the brain.

Orthographic Encoding and the Prestriate Visual Word Form System. Figure 13.2a shows a subtraction-based map from PET work by Petersen et al., (1989) at Washington University. The targeted operations were those of passive silent reading. The subjects were adults literate in English. Each subject read silently as a series of concrete nouns was presented one by one at a central fixation position. The baseline task required fixation at the central position, marked by a cross, in an attempt to engage the general visual information acquisition operations of the target task without engaging the content-specific operations particular to reading.

Relative to the baseline task, silent reading increased activity in a number of prestriate visual areas distributed both laterally and medially in both the left and right hemispheres, relatively early in the ventral pathways thought to mediate object recognition (see Livingstone & Hubel, 1988; Rueckl, Cave, & Kosslyn,

1989). Some of these prestriate sites, especially those in the right hemisphere, respond to many different types of complex visual patterns and hence are not specific to reading. For example, a right occipito-temporal area active in PET studies using both words and consonant strings appears to be related to the detection of visual features (Corbetta, et al., 1990). Studies using dense electrode arrays to record event-related potentials suggest that this area is activated by visual patterns within about 100msec after stimulus presentation (Compton et al., 1991). Subsequent PET work by Petersen, Fox, Snyder, and Raichle (1990) found that one of the prestriate sites, in the medial left hemisphere, is specialised for reading. This site is identified in Fig. 13.2a. It responds to words and to orthographically regular pseudowords but not to random letter strings. This left-medial prestriate site is only active during reading, producing no response to auditorily presented words or pseudowords. Therefore it appears to constitute a specifically *orthographic* encoding mechanism—it is the structure we call the prestriate visual word form system (Prestriate VWFS). Corroborative evidence comes from Compton et al. (1991). Their dense-array ERP recordings showed activity in electrodes placed over the left posterior cortex that differentiated between words and consonant strings within about 200msec following input. The timing of this activation, which has been replicated by Besson et al. (1994), is consistent with a orthographic encoding mechanism that takes visual features or shape information as its input.

Our name for this mechanism is an elaboration of the name used by Petersen et al. (1989; 1990). This was simply the visual word form system (VWFS), a term that has gained common usage in both the neuropsychological and cognitive literatures (e.g. Coltheart, 1985; Humphreys, Evett, & Quinlan, 1990). The reason for complicating the terminology arises from additional evidence from PET imaging work by Chertkow et al. (1990) at McGill University. In this study, several different kinds of judgement tasks performed on visually but not auditorily presented words produced activation in the same left-medial prestriate region that Petersen et al. (1989) called the VWFS. Chertkow et al., however, reached a different conclusion about the nature of this prestriate region. One of the tasks used by Chertkow and colleagues was a version of the passive silent reading task used by Petersen et al. (1989). Unlike Petersen et al., Chertkow et al. observed activation in inferior temporal cortex and the amygdala in addition to activation in left-medial prestriate cortex. The inferior temporal region is identified in Fig. 13.2b. The temporal activation led Chertkow et al. to propose that lexical representations are actually located in the object recognition structures of inferior temporal cortex, specifically in area IT, with the prestriate region providing pre-lexical preparatory processing rather than instantiating the visual word forms themselves.

Whether Chertkow and colleagues' view is right or not remains to be seen. They presented each word for one second followed by a one-second blank interval, whereas Petersen et al. (1989) presented words at a rate of one per second with no intervening delays. This methodological difference may have introduced short-term memory processes into Chertkow et al.'s task that did not occur in Petersen et al.'s, and activation in temporal cortex and amygdala would be expected with short-term memory involvement. In addition, the same temporal regions were active in another task, which required Chertkow et al.'s subjects to decide whether the referent of each of a series of written animal names had horns, antlers, long ears, or other protuberances on its head. Thus the temporal activation in Chertkow et al.'s study could also be associated with imagery-like manipulations of the referents' representations rather than with lexical processing per se. The difference between the conclusions of Petersen et al. (1989; 1990) and Chertkow et al. (1990) remains to be resolved. Until it is, we have at least two possible interpretations of the VWFS—one in which it consists of a single structure localised in left-medial prestriate cortex, and another in which it is distributed, with an early component in prestriate cortex and a later component in temporal cortex. Hence we refer to the prestriate structure as the Prestriate VWFS in light of the possibility that it may turn out not to be the entire VWFS but only an early component of it. This

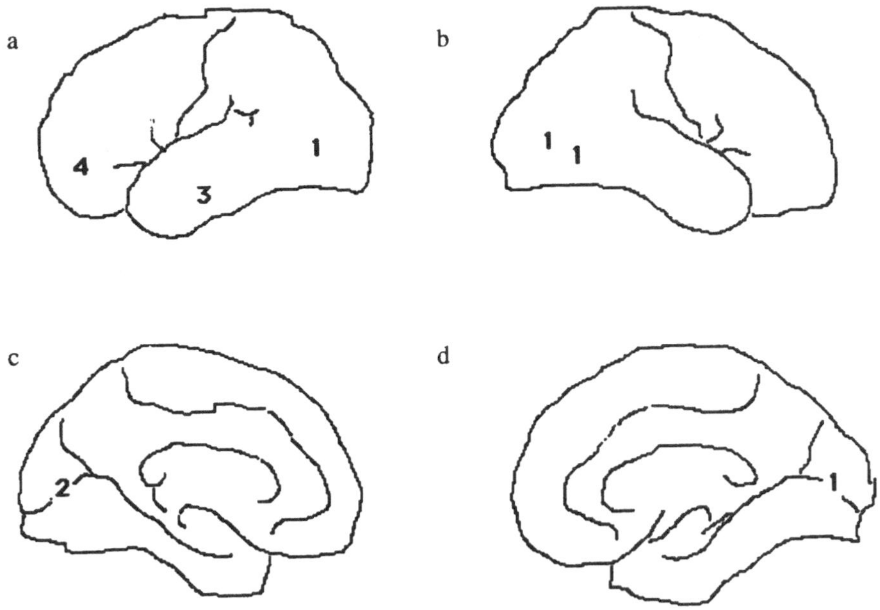

FIG 13.2a–d. Fig. 13.2a: a lateral view of the left hemisphere; Fig 13.2b: a lateral view of the right hemisphere; Fig 13.2c: a medial view of the left hemisphere; Fig 13.2d: a medial view of the right hemisphere. Regions 1 are active in PET blood flow studies during visual processing of a variety of complex patterns, including letter strings of all kinds. Region 2 is the left-medial prestriate site we are calling the Prestriate VWFS. Region 3 is the inferotemporal (IT) site found to be active during passive reading by Chertkow et al. (1990). Region 4 is the left inferior prefrontal site we call the FLSA (adapted from Peterson et al., 1989).

discussion shows the importance of methods such as PET that can expose the organisation and participation of these anatomically defined areas in different reading tasks.

The "Primary Gateway" Hypothesis. Can anything definitive be said at this time about what the Prestriate VWFS does for the reading system? Petersen et al. (1989), Petersen et al. (1990), and Chertkow et al. (1990) all found that the left-medial prestriate area was the earliest structure in the visual processing pathway to distinguish orthographicallly well-formed letter strings from other stimuli. This finding suggests that the Prestriate VWFS occupies a central place in the visual encoding processes of reading, regardless of which interpretation of the role of temporal cortex turns out to be correct.

Our hypothesis is that the Prestriate VWFS acts as the "primary gateway" to the reading system, activating shape-based codes for all orthographically well-formed letter strings that are then transmitted forward in the system for further linguistic analysis. We believe that the prestriate structure should be viewed as critical to the gateway's operation even if the VWFS does turn out to have another component localised in temporal cortex. The "standard view" of neural language processing derived mainly from the lesion literature is consistent with the primary gateway hypothesis, because damage to left prestriate visual areas is the usual source of pure alexia and is often involved, along with parietal or temporoparietal damage, in a closely related syndrome called letter-by-letter reading. The primary gateway hypothesis is also consistent with several current computational models of word recognition (regardless of other features of the models that make them quite different from one another). These include the first formulation of the interactive activation model by McClelland and Rumelhart (1981), the parallel-distributed processing version of the interactive activation model by Seidenberg and McClelland (1989), the connectionist obligatory phonological recoding model of Van Orden, Pennington, and Stone (1990), and the multiple route architecture that Carr and Pollatsek (1985) call the parallel coding systems model. In McClelland and Rumelhart's model, the Prestriate VWFS would correspond to the lexical level of processing if Petersen et al.'s interpretation is correct, and to an intermediate level not included in the model if Chertkow et al.'s is correct. In both Seidenberg and McClelland's model and Van Orden et al.'s, it would correspond to orthographic processing, and in Carr and Pollatsek's model it would correspond to orthographic elaboration of the visual code. Although different names are used, these mechanisms perform roughly the same functions in these various models (with the possible exception of McClelland and Rumelhart's, as noted above).

An Alternative to the Primary Gateway? Although the standard literature on neuropsychological research is consistent with the primary gateway hypothesis, complications arise on further inspection of that literature. Daniel Bub (personal communication) describes a patient with left prestriate damage who shows very restricted oral word reading, often displays painfully dysfluent letter-by-letter reading, and shows no improvements in reading from semantic priming. Nevertheless, this patient performs speeded lexical decision in a perfectly normal fashion, even with relatively long words and orthographically well-formed distractors. Normal proficiency at lexical decision is quite unusual among pure alexics, but above-average performance is not uncommon. For example, Coslett and Saffran (1989) describe four letter-by-letter readers with left prestriate damage who were significantly above chance at lexical decisions about briefly presented letter strings, and who could categorise printed words acccording to basic semantic dichotomies such as whether the referent of the word was animate or inanimate.

These patients' reading activities constitute evidence for an alternative route to some source of lexical knowledge that does not require the orthographic analysis we attribute to the Prestriate VWFS. The existence of such a route is generally consistent with computational models that include holistic lexical representations activated directly from visual feature information in addition to analytic representations that require orthographic codes as their input. An example is Allen's PISA model (Allen & Emerson, 1991; Allen & Madden, 1990; Allen, McNeal, & Kvak, in press). Thus an issue in the interpretation of the functional role of the Prestriate VWFS is whether it serves as the primary gateway to the reading system, or as one of two gateways operating in parallel, one feeding an analytic word recognition system and the other feeding a nonanalytic, holistic one.

In addition to its importance for deciding the architecture of mature word recognition, this distinction carries implications for reading development. If the Prestriate VWFS is a single gateway to the reading system and there are systematic individual differences in its development and operation, then these individual differences will work to set limits on reading development. If, instead, the Prestriate VWFS and another access route operate in parallel, then the relative efficiency of the two routes, their relative integration into the pre-existing language system, and their respective strengths and weaknesses at representing linguistically relevant properties of the letter string and transmitting those properties to phonological, semantic, and articulatory encoding mechanisms will set limits in a more complex way.

What can be said about the properties of the alternative route that would allow us to evaluate these possibilities? First, the alexic patients of Bub and colleagues and Coslett and Saffran clearly have access to lexical knowledge, probably semantic in content. However, it is important to note that although these patients can often tell whether a letter string is a word, they cannot tell which word it is, and most importantly, they cannot read very well. Therefore, this alternative route provides relatively nonspecific information, and it does not appear to be a primary reading pathway that can stand alone in driving the language processing system. Secondly, in the PET studies of normal word processing by adult readers of English, the left-medial prestriate area always becomes active, whereas no right-hemisphere sites have yet been found that distinguish words and pseudowords from random letter strings. From these facts, we tentatively conclude that the Prestriate VWFS is a structure whose input is necessary for the word recognition system to operate accurately and efficiently. The alternative route available to pure alexics who have lost the Prestriate VWFS is at most supplementary and is sufficient only for certain loosely constrained semantic judgements. How this route is supported neurally remains a mystery. The important point for present purposes, however, is that the known properties of the alternative route reinforce the view that the Prestriate VWFS is critical to accurate and efficient word recognition.[1]

Development of the Prestriate VWFS. If the Prestriate VWFS serves a primary gateway function for the mature reading system, then its development matters to reading acquisition. Neural evidence from young children is needed to trace the emergence of the Prestriate VWFS, but little is currently available. This is an issue we will consider later. For the moment, we use cognitive evidence to construct hypotheses, taking the occurrence of efficient orthographic encoding in word-processing tasks as a behavioural marker of the functionality of the visual orthographic encoding mechanism.

Beginning with work by Eleanor Gibson and her colleagues (reviewed in chapter 7 of Gibson & Levin, 1975), comparison of performance on three kinds of letter strings has been used to diagnose early perceptual learning in the encoding mechanisms of reading: words, pseudowords, and random letter strings. Sensitivity to lexical familiarity has been inferred from an advantage in processing words relative to random letter strings. Note, however, that lexical familiarity combines three logically separable word properties: familiarity per se, the possession of lexically specific representations corresponding to the word's meaning and pronunciation, and the possession of orthographic structure. Sensitivity to orthographic structure in the absence of familarity or pre-existing lexically specific representations has been inferred from an advantage in processing pseudowords relative to random letter strings. Finally, differences between words and pseudowords have been used to determine whether familiarity or the possession of lexically specific representations confers a processing advantage over and above the advantage due to orthography.

Seminal results using this logic came from Gibson, Osser, and Pick (1963). In tachistoscopic full report, first-graders showed an advantage for three-letter and five-letter words over random letter strings of similar length, a smaller advantage for three-letter pseudowords over random letter strings, but no advantage for five-letter pseudowords, which were reported no more accurately

---

[1]It is conceivable that the alternative route arises from Hebbian learning processes that relate early feature analysis activity perhaps in right hemisphere prestriate cortex to subsequent semantic activity, perhaps in the frontal structures that will be discussed later in this chapter.

than random strings. Third-graders were very good on all three types of three-letter stimuli, indicating an overall improvement in visual analysis and comparison processes relative to first-graders. In addition, they showed an advantage for five-letter pseudowords over random strings, which had not been shown by first-graders. This advantage for five-letter pseudowords, however, was not as large as the one for five-letter words.

Thus, in the work of Gibson et al. (1963), a word advantage appeared quite early, whereas a pseudoword advantage emerged more gradually. It is well documented that literate adults show advantages for both words and pseudowords in tachistoscopic tasks and the advantage for pseudowords is sometimes as large as that for words (e.g. Baron & Thurston, 1973; Carr, Davidson, & Hawkins, 1978; Gibson, Pick, Osser, & Hammond, 1962; Johnston & McClelland, 1980; Manelis, 1974; McClelland & Rumelhart, 1981; Miller, Bruner, & Postman, 1954; Paap, Newsome, McDonald, & Schvaneveldt, 1982; Reicher, 1969). It appears, then, that the adult pattern of performance is acquired incrementally during the first few years of formal reading instruction and attendant reading experience, first appearing for particular familiar stimuli and then generalising to unfamiliar stimuli constructed in similar ways.

Gibson and colleagues suggested that early in reading acquisition perceptual learning consists of storing representations for individual words encountered in various reading activities. As reading experience grows and the number of stored word-specific representations increases, the perceptual apparatus abstracts across the lexical representations to identify features or patterns that characterise words in general. These general patterns, representing orthographic structure, gradually become the basis for processing letter strings, allowing the perceptual advantage that was originally restricted to familiar words to generalise to any letter string whose spelling conforms to the patterns. Gibson considered such perceptual learning both to underlie and to be critical to normal reading development with alphabetic writing systems. Support for this view is not hard to find in the cognitive and cognitive-developmental literature (see e.g. Baron, 1979; Brooks, 1977; Brown & Carr, 1993; Feustel, Shiffrin, & Salasoo, 1983; Frith, 1985; Marsh, Friedman, Welch, & Desberg, 1981; Salasoo, Feustel, & Shiffrin, 1985; Seymour & MacGregor, 1984).

The developmental trend reported by Gibson and colleagues has been confirmed by many subsequent investigations using tachistoscopic recognition as well as other tasks, including searching for a pre-specified target letter in the three kinds of letter strings and same–different matching of simultaneously presented pairs of letter strings (see e.g. Barron, 1986; Carr, 1981; Doehring, 1976; Downing & Leong, 1982; Frith, 1985; Gough, Juel, & Griffith, 1991; Manis, Szeszulski, Holt, & Graves, 1990; Marsh et al., 1981; Massaro & Taylor, 1979; Perfetti, 1985; Rozin & Gleitman, 1977; Seymour & MacGregor, 1984). Furthermore, the effectiveness of orthographic processing is a predictor of reading success. Manis et al. (1990) found that speed and accuracy on several lexical discrimination tasks that depended on orthographic rather than phonological analysis distinguished dyslexic children (mean age about 12 years) from age-matched good readers. The dyslexic children were as fast on these tasks as a younger group of reading-level-matched good readers (mean age about 8 years), but they remained less accurate. Manis et al. argued that efficient orthographic encoding is critical to accurate word recognition. Carr, Brown, Vavrus, and Evans (1990) found that among elementary and high school students recruited from a university reading clinic, performance in the visual same–different matching task predicted individual differences in both reading comprehension and the ability to decide which of several candidate words best fit into a blank in a text. Because visual same–different matching appears to tap more directly into visual encoding operations uncontaminated by phonological and semantic recoding or post-perceptual guessing than tachistoscopic report or visual search (Carr, Pollatsek, & Posner, 1981; Carr, Posner, Pollatsek, & Snyder, 1979; Smith & Spoehr, 1974), these results are particularly relevant to assessment of orthographic coding.

Evidence for the importance of orthographic encoding can be found in second-language reading as well as first-language reading. Among native speakers of Chinese who are reading English as a second language, the pseudoword advantage over random letter strings in the same–different matching task predicts not only reading comprehension, but also the accuracy of learning new vocabulary words from context. Haynes and Carr (1990) argued from this finding that efficient orthographic encoding plays a primary role in laying down new lexical representations that can be accurately discriminated from other known words and from unknown letter strings when encountered again in the future. This suggestion extends the scope of Manis et al.'s (1990) view on the importance of orthographic encoding to word recognition.

Because the subjects in Haynes and Carr's study were Taiwanese college students with several years of experience reading English, these findings fit well with Gibson's analysis of the experiential basis of orthographic competence. In second-language as well as first-language reading, such development is gradual, sometimes protracted, and it depends on exposure to the language, not simply to developmental maturity. The same properties of orthographic development can be seen in a study of US college students learning to read Spanish as a second language, carried out by Givon, Yang, and Gernsbacher (1990). These investigators used a paradigm developed by Sieroff and Posner (1988; see also Sieroff, Pollatsek, & Posner, 1988), in which a peripheral cue that involuntarily attracts spatial attention is presented either to the left or to the right of each string of letters during a tachistoscopic full report task. Sieroff and Posner showed that among college students receiving random letter strings and familiar English words as stimuli, the spatial cues disrupted report accuracy much more for random letter strings than for familiar English words. Sieroff and Posner argued that spatial attention is required to construct an accurate visual-orthographic representation of the unstructured and unfamiliar random letter strings, but is less necessary for stimuli that can been encoded effectively by the Prestriate VWFS. Thus, according to Sieroff and Posner, the magnitude of attentional disruption effects in tachistoscopic word recognition can serve as an index of the efficiency with which the Prestriate VWFS can produce an integrated orthographic representation of a word. Applying this logic, Givon and colleagues found that beginning students of Spanish treated Spanish like English random letter strings, whereas advanced students treated Spanish words like English words, and concluded that effective orthographic encoding emerges gradually during the first few years of Spanish reading experience.

Many analogous findings, primarily on first-language reading, are described in the reviews cited earlier. Additional arguments like those of Manis et al. (1990) and Haynes and Carr (1990) have been made by Perfetti (1991; Perfetti & McCutcheon, 1987), and, as discussed earlier, current models of word recognition give an imporant place to orthographic analysis. Orthographic encoding skills appear to be related to reading success in ways that are generally consistent with the primary gateway hypothesis.

Phonological and Articulatory Encoding: Structures Near the Sylvan Fissure.

PET evidence on sound-based processes is less analytic than the evidence on orthographic encoding, but it is still instructive. Figure 13.3 shows brain regions that Petersen and colleagues (1989) found to be activated in tasks requiring either overt articulation or explicit phonological analysis. When subjects read visually presented familiar words aloud, requiring overt articulation, frontal regions were active that are known from lesion evidence to be associated with speech production and motor control. Of course, the Prestriate VWFS was also active, as in passive reading, because visual presentation engaged the reading system. However, when presentation of the words was auditory and the task required passive listening without any overt articulation, these frontal regions were not active (and neither was the Prestriate VWFS). Instead, passive listening activated temporoparietal regions apparently involved in phonological but not articulatory coding. Converging evidence on the notion that these temporoparietal structures are involved in phonological analysis came from rhyme judgements about visually presented words, which activated a left temporoparietal region similar to that found to be active in passive listening but did not activate the frontal articulatory structures.

Thus, phonological and articulatory coding appear to dissociate in the PET results that are currently available. Articulation is associated with frontal activation just anterior to the sylvan fissure, whereas phonological analysis is associated with temporoparietal activation just posterior to the sylvan fissure. A temporoparietal locus for phonological analysis is consistent with the earlier discussion of a relatively superior pathway for pronouncing letter strings that involves assembled phonology and extends from occipital cortex through the area labelled PD in Fig. 13.1b. The fact that a task requiring pronunciation of familiar words did not activate temporoparietal cortex, but did activate both occipital cortex and frontal motor regions, is consistent with the existence of a more inferior pathway, passing through the area labelled SD in Fig. 13.1b, which does not involve phonological analysis but deals instead in direct associations between orthographic codes and stored pronunciations. Hence there is a degree of convergence between the available PET findings and the neuropsychological evidence from lesion studies.

The question of whether one or two pathways support the pronunciation of written words is theoretically very important at present (for discussion, see Bernstein & Carr, in press; Besner, Twilley, McCann, & Seergobin, 1991; Carr & Pollatsek, 1985, Coltheart et al., 1993; Manis et al., 1990; Norris, 1994; Olson, Wise, Conners, & Rack, 1990; Patterson & Coltheart, 1987; Seidenberg, 1985; Seidenberg & McClelland, 1989 Seidenberg et al., 1994; Van Orden et al., 1990). Therefore, confirmation of these conjectures about pathway activation via additional PET work would be useful. Because each block of trials requires a new administration of low-level radioactive tracer into the bloodstream, PET studies are usually limited in the number of blocks presented in a session. For this reason, they must be efficiently designed if issues as specific as these are to be addressed.

A straightforward but informative experiment might use a target task that requires subjects to pronounce high- and low-frequency words with regular and exceptional spelling-to-pronunciation correspondences, plus pseudowords, in separate blocks of trials, with an articulatory baseline task that requires pronunciation but not reading, such as repeating a syllable over and over. The baseline task would allow activation associated with the execution of already-planned articulatory programmes to be separated from activation associated with the analysis of phonological organisation and the retrieval or construction

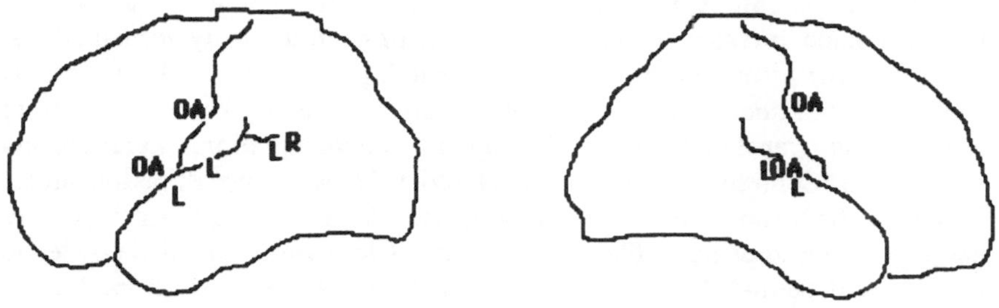

FIG 13.3 Left and right lateral views of the cortex. Regions OA are active during tasks requiring overt articulation of visually presented familiar words. Regions L are active during passive listening to auditorily presented familiar words. Region R, which is in close proximity to the temporoparietal L site, is active when making rhyme judgements about pairs of visually presented familiar words (adapted from Petersen et al., 1989).

of appropriate articulatory plans. Performance on pseudowords and low-frequency words with regular spelling-to-pronunciation correspondences would expose the structures involved when, according to current dual-route or parallel-coding systems theories, phonological analysis is most needed and direct associations to stored pronunciations are least helpful. Performance on high-frequency exception words would expose the structures involved when phonological analysis is least helpful and direct associations most necessary. The remaining two stimulus types represent intermediate cases. High-frequency regular words would expose structures active when both pathways ought to produce an accurate pronunciation and co-operation between them is possible, whereas low-frequency exception words would expose structures active when the two pathways are most likely to produce conflicting pronunciations close enough together in time to interfere with one another. More complex designs employing stimuli of these various kinds could be attempted in studies using FMRI, which allow more blocks of trial and mixing of stimulus types within blocks.

How do the Pathways from Visual Coding to Phonology and Articulation Develop? If it were true that two pathways connect the Prestriate VWFS to the mechanisms of phonological and articulatory encoding, one would need to know how the pathways develop and what factors govern their relative strength and efficacy. Investigations of individual differences have produced a lot of evidence in favour of two contrasting styles or strategies of word recognition. Intuitively, these styles correspond to the two pathways of dual-route theory. One body of evidence comes from neuropsychological studies of the effects of brain damage on the reading of formerly literate adults. This evidence supports the distinction between surface dyslexia and phonological dyslexia we have already discussed. Unsurprisingly, then, one factor that influences the relative strength and efficacy of the two routes is the degree to which they are intact and healthy.

A distinction quite similar in spirit to surface versus phonological dyslexia has been made in respect to the reading styles of neurologically normal adults. Baron and Strawson (1976) argued that some highly literate college students appear to be "Phoenicians", who rely primarily on rule-governed spelling to pronunciation translation processes to support word recognition, whereas others appear to be "Chinese", who rely on direct retrieval of word-specific associations. Baron and Strawson were clear in claiming that these are strategies among highly literate college students—"Phoenicians" can retrieve word-specific knowledge if it is required and "Chinese" do know the general patterns of spelling to pronunciation translation and can deploy them when word-specific knowledge is insufficient. Thus the difference between a group of brain-damaged phonological dyslexics and a group of normal "Chinese" is that the "Chinese" can adopt the other style of word reading if they choose but the phonological dyslexics no longer have that option. The less preferred style may not be as efficacious among "Chinese" or "Phoenicians", if for no other reason than lack of exercise, but it is available. Thus preference, perhaps based on histories of exercise that have magnified initial small differences in skill, is another factor that may influence relative strength and efficacy.

Obviously these distinctions between reading styles call to mind the two major approaches to teaching word recognition, the so-called "phonics" and "sight-word" methods. The explicit goal of the phonics method is to teach general patterns of spelling to pronunciation translation, whereas the explicit goal of the sight-word method is to teach a reading vocabulary consisting of associations between the visual appearances of particular words and their pronunciations. There is some evidence that beginning reading curricula strongly oriented toward one of these methods or the other do instil reading styles consistent with the method (e.g. Carr et al., 1990; Evans & Carr, 1985), and there is considerable evidence that curricula with phonics components produce higher levels of reading achievement than curricula with only sight-word practice (e.g. Adams, 1990; Evans & Carr, 1985; Chall, 1967; 1983; Rieben & Perfetti, 1991). Instruction would appear to be a third factor that influences the relative strength and efficacy of the two pathways.

This last fact, that inclusion of phonics instruction generally results in higher reading achievement, leads us to three points that seem particularly important. First, the strongest relationship between encoding processes and early reading success involve translation from spelling to pronunciation, especially for unfamiliar letter strings, rather than orthographic encoding per se (e.g. Adams, 1990; Carr & Levy, 1990; Perfetti, 1985, 1991; Stanovich, 1982, 1986, 1991; Vellutino, 1991). Secondly, fluent translation from spelling to pronunciation depends on gaining intentional, manipulative command over the phoneme as a unit of linguistic analysis (Alegria & Morais, 1991; Bryant, Chapter 12; de Gelder, Chapter 7; Morais & Kolinsky, Chapter 15; Rozin & Gleitman, 1977; Treiman, 1985). Common measures of this "phonemic awareness" include accuracy in rhyme judgement tasks rather like the one that activated temporoparietal cortex in the experiments of Petersen et al. (1989). Taken at face value, these findings implicate the more superior of the two pathways, passing from the Prestriate VWFS towards temporoparietal cortex, in setting limits on reading success, at least in alphabetic writing systems. This is the pathway that appears to be concerned with phonological analysis and assembled phonological representations.

Finally, according to behavioural-genetic investigations by Olson et al., (1990), the skills associated with this pathway have much higher heritability coefficients than do orthographic encoding or the ability to deploy direct word-specific associations between orthography and pronunciation. Thus it appears that children may differ significantly in their biological preparedness to develop pathways allowing visual input access to the phonological structures of the language system. This conclusion is consistent with the outcome of a training study with dyslexic children and adolescents by Lovett (1991), in which intensive phonics and word recognition instruction improved recognition of trained words but produced little evidence of transfer that would indicate gains in rule-governed phonological assembly. In contrast, heritability coefficients for orthographic encoding and the deployment of word-specific associations are near zero, suggesting that individual differences in the efficacy of the inferior pathway from Prestriate VWFS toward the object recognition structures of temporal cortex are determined primarily by exposure and practice rather than by biological preparedness. This is also consistent with Lovett's (1991) training outcomes, as well as with earlier demonstrations that young dyslexics can learn relatively normally via paired-associate instruction even when their mastery of general orthography-to-pronunciation patterns is near zero (e.g. Rozin, Poritsky, & Sotsky, 1971; see also Levy & Stewart, 1991).

The upshot of the evidence on heritability is that the two pathways transmitting visual codes forward from the Prestriate VWFS for further linguistic processing may differ in the ease with which they can be influenced by instruction. One of these pathways is relatively easy to establish, widely available across members of the human species, and takes advantage of the brain's natural solution to the problem of visual object recognition by treating written words as if they were objects. This is the inferior pathway toward temporal cortex. A more complex pathway, subject to more severe biological constraints on who can master it and who cannot, treats written words as if they were linguistic entities rather than visual objects. This is the superior pathway toward temporoparietal cortex, which gives orthographic encoding processes an immediate connection to phonological analysis and the structures of auditory speech processing. Theorists such as Liberman (Chapter 1) have argued that such a connection ought to make for the most efficient transition from being a speaker–listener to being a reader. Studdert-Kennedy (Chapter 4) puts this view in a particulary intriguing way. Writing, he argues, is an "ethological description of an animal," where the animal is spoken language. Writing is a very powerful and detailed description, because it not only represents important features or properties of the animal's behaviour, but provides instructions for actually reproducing it. If one accepts Studdert-Kennedy's characterisation, it is easy to conclude that the best link between vision and the language system would be the closest link requiring the fewest computational transformations. For an alphabetic writing system this could well be a link between vision and phonological analysis. Although such a view was discredited during the late 1970s and 1980s, it has enjoyed a resurgence with the appearance of new evidence for early, obligatory phonological recoding in word processing tasks (e.g. Lesch & Pollatsek, 1993; Lukatela & Turvey, 1991; Van Orden et al., 1990).

Semantic Encoding and the Frontal Lexical Semantic Area.

What about meaning? Petersen et al. (1989) tried to identify the specific brain regions associated with semantic processing in two different ways. First, they asked subjects to monitor a series of nouns for members of a particular taxonomic category. Blood flow during this category monitoring task was compared to the passive reading task described earlier. Second, they asked subjects to generate an appropriate verb in response to each of a series of concrete nouns and compared this "generate verbs" task to oral reading. In both of these semantic tasks, a site was active in the inferior prefrontal cortex that did not show up in passive reading or in any of the purely phonological and articulatory target tasks they investigated.

Shown in Fig. 13.1a, this inferior prefrontal structure appears to be involved in the operation of semantic memory. We call it the frontal lexical semantic area (FLSA), to distinguish it from the more posterior region commonly called Wernicke's Area, which is also active during many semantic tasks and has long been implicated by lesion data in receptive semantic processing of connected discourse. Our speculation is that Wernicke's Area is devoted more to propositional than to lexical semantics and hence has its closest anatomical associations to the syntactic structures of Broca's Area and the phonological short-term memory processes of temporal cortex rather than to lexical semantic memory. Such a distinction is consistent with a number of reports that semantic priming from a single word has different properties than semantic priming from a sentence frame whose relation to the primed target word depends on propositional integration of the sentence (Merrill, Sperber, & McCauley, 1981; Seidenberg, 1985; Simpson & Krueger, 1991).

It is not yet clear whether all lexical semantic functions are served by the FLSA, but the relatively novel semantic activities required by Petersen and colleagues' category monitoring and generating verbs tasks consistently activate this prefrontal region. The same region showed activation in the PET studies by Chertkow et al. (1990) when subjects were required to make conceptual judgements about the referents of concrete nouns, such as whether each of series of animals was native to Canada. This prefrontal region was not active during imagery-based judgements about the appearance of the referent. As mentioned earlier, these imaginal judgements produced temporal activation in the vicinity of area IT. Thus the FLSA appears to be separate from structures dealing with the more concrete, perceptual knowledge that might be involved in visual object recognition or visual imagery.

Consistent with such a separation, temporal lesions can produce deficits in object recognition. In addition, temporal lesions can produce surface dyslexia if the area identified as SD in Fig. 13.1b is involved. Frontal lesions do not generally interfere with visual object recognition, nor with oral word reading. Frontal lesions do, however, produce deficits both in planning and in novel problem solving that might be consistent with the suggested role for the FLSA in relatively novel semantic-conceptual computations.

Whether the FLSA is involved in the kind of overlearned semantic encoding that is responsible for "automatic" priming from single words remains a matter for investigation. Many cognitive scientists believe that overlearned semantic associations are deployed at subthreshold levels whenever words are read, independently of intention or the direction of attention (for reviews, see Carr, 1992, which brings neural evidence to bear, and Neely, 1991, which provides the most extensive analysis of the cognitive evidence currently available). If so, and if the FLSA were responsible for this sort of semantic encoding, then one might expect some degree of activation (perhaps rather low) in the FLSA even during a nonsemantic task such as passive silent reading. Such activation was not observed by Petersen et al. (1989), but it did occur in the passive reading tasks of both Petersen et al. (1990) and Chertkow et al. (1990). This variability of outcome is consistent with the notion that only rather low levels of semantic activation occur passively. Another aspect of the PET data on passive reading is also relevant. In passive reading, no frontal regions other than the FLSA have been observed to rise above baseline levels of activation. However, in the explicitly meaning-related tasks such as generate verbs and category monitoring, activity in the FLSA has been accompanied by activity in the anterior cingulate gyrus, a medial-frontal structure that appears to be central to the executive control functions of working memory (Carr, 1992; Edelman, 1989; Pardo, Pardo, Janer, & Raichle, 1990; Posner & Petersen, 1990; Posner & Rothbart, 1990). This pattern is consistent with the notion that semantic activity in the FLSA is monitored and modulated by attentional processes when relations with specific properties must be used to guide decisions and actions (Carr, 1992; Neely, 1990; Posner et al., 1989; Posner & Snyder, 1975). Finally, it is not known whether inferior frontal lesions can degrade either attended or automatic semantic priming, but one might expect both to be affected if the FLSA were generally responsible for encoding word meanings and their relations to one another.

Why is the FLSA Located Where it is? Especially given the classic view that semantics are served by Wernicke's Area, the location of the FLSA is a puzzle. Posner and Rothbart (1990) hypothesise that its prefrontal locus arises very early in language acquisition, during late infancy when language production is commonly limited to one word at a time and is closely linked to gestural communication, with gestures and single words often conveying redundant information (see e.g. Bates et al., 1989; Lock 1990). Greenfield (1991) has recently argued that during the period focused on by Posner and Rothbart, language control and control of action are relatively undifferentiated, with Broca's Area exercising planning and control functions for both. As syntactic word combinations emerge in language, and complex, goal-directed movement sequences emerge in action, neural control of these domains differentiates.

Broca's Area develops domain-specific interconnections with other, more anterior prefrontal regions, creating relatively independent circuitry for control of processing in each domain. Greenfield presents evidence that the circuitry for syntax involves interconnections between Broca's Area and medial prefrontal cortex, whereas the circuitry for control of complex manual action involves interconnections between Broca's Area and superior prefrontal cortex. Analysis of electrophysiological data collected by Thatcher (see Thatcher, Walker, & Guidice, 1987) suggests that these two circuits are developing during the third and fourth years of life. Although pure speculation at this point, it is possible that circuitry interconnecting Broca's Area and inferior prefrontal cortex might develop somewhat earlier than the medial and superior circuitry—during or preceding the emergence of the one-word speech that is closely co-ordinated with gesture and prior to the emergence of syntactic word combinations. If early development of such circuitry were observed, it would be consistent with Posner and Rothbart's hypothesis about ontogenesis of the FLSA. Although neural ontogenesis is hard to measure directly, it has proven possible to trace development of pathways involved in visual selective attention in infants through the use of marker tasks that diagnose the involvement of particular neural structures (Johnson, 1990; Johnson, Posner, & Rothbart, 1991). An extension of this logic may allow more explicit tests of some of these speculative ideas.

The stress placed in this argument on early association with gestural communication might lead one to wonder whether the structure we are calling the FLSA might be more heavily involved in tasks that require overt action than in covert tasks. Within the domain of overt taks, one might wonder further whether the FLSA might be more easily accessible to gestural output mechanisms than to oral ones, and perhaps to visual input mechanisms than the auditory ones (given that gestures are perceived visually). If this were true three implications would follow. The first is that the FLSA might be less active when no overt action must be performed on the basis of the semantic computation than when overt action is required. A recent examination of the generate-verbs task by McCarthy et al., (1993), using FMRI rather than PET, found evidence consistent with this speculation. The second is that this structure might be less active during auditory versions of the generate verbs and category monitoring tasks than they are during the visual versions we have already described. It is not clear at present whether or not this is true. Data from Petersen et al. (1989) indicate that left inferior frontal cortex is responsive to auditory inputs among literate adults, but the level of activity may not be as high as when the inputs are visual. McCarthy et al. (1993) presented their stimuli auditorily and found FLSA activity when overt production of the verb was required, just as Petersen et al. (1989) did, but did not compare auditory and visual presentation. More work is needed to decide this question.

The third implication is that the FLSA might develop more rapidly and more extensively, or play a more important role in the language system as a whole, among native signers than among native speaker–listeners. After reviewing the relative timing of early milestones in the acquisition of signed versus spoken language, Meier and Newport (1990) conclude that there is an advantage for sign in the appearance of the first words, but not much of an advantage, if any, in the appearance of the sign combinations indicative of emerging syntax. They suggest that this early advantage for signing single words may arise from earlier maturation of the visual system than the auditory system, allowing concepts to be connected with visual patterns earlier than with auditory patterns, and from earlier maturation of manual motor control than of vocal-tract motor control, allowing connections between concepts and motor patterns to be expressed earlier through the hands than through the throat and mouth.

This suggestion is generally consistent with Posner and Rothbart's arguments concerning close relations between early lexical semantics and gestural communication, and the fact that the developmental precocity of signed language does not extend beyond single words to word combinations is generally consistent with the possibility of two semantic processing systems, one for lexical semantics and another for propositional semantics. At this time it is difficult to evaluate the much stronger hypothesis that a lexical semantic system closely allied with vision and manual motor control might be somehow independent of, as well as developmentally prior to, a semantic system allied with audition and vocal motor control. For the moment, we make the assumption that whatever modality preferences the FLSA may or may not show early in its ontogenesis, it is by the time of its maturity an amodal system—or at least a multimodal one—supplying information about word meanings to a wide range of language-related task performances. The multi-modality or abstraction of the FLSA is certainly achieved by young adulthood, as indicated in the PET studies, and we assume that it may be quite well established by the time reading development ordinarily begins. The truth or falsity of this assumption, of course, carries strong implications for early reading development.

Ultimately, proper tests of the abstractness of FLSA processing during reading development will need to include a systematic array of neural evidence. However, we might gain some preliminary insight from cognitive analysis of repetition effects in reading tasks. Transfer of repetition benefits across changes in the visual surface form of words and text has become a powerful tool for diagnosing the level of abstraction from physical or sensory input at which the encoding mechanisms of reading are operating. A large body of evidence shows excellent transfer across changes in case (wOrD versus WoRd, for example, or WORD versus word) and across changes between typing and handwriting. Recent ERP experiments show discrimination at posterior electrode between repeated and novel words within 200ms following input—the same pattern observed by Compton et al. (1991)—and this effect did not depend on whether the repeated words appeared in the same letter case or changed CASE between occurrences (McClandis, Curran, & Posner, 1994). These transfer effects suggest that the orthographic coding performed by the Prestriate VWFS is relatively abstract

(Brown & Carr, 1993; Carr & Brown, 1990; Carr, Brown, & Charalambous, 1989). A more impressive possibility, consistent with a high level of abstraction for semantic coding as well, is suggested by Potter et al.'s (1986) report that substitution of pictures for concrete nouns leaves text reading almost completely undisrupted under the conditions of the Rapid Serial Visual Presentation task. Alejano and Carr (1991) attempted to discover whether this apparent equivalence between pictures and words extends to the production of repetition benefits in the less esoteric task environment of oral reading. Literate adults, fourth graders, and first graders all showed just as much improvement on the second oral reading of a short paragraph when the first reading was a rebus with pictures substituted for concrete nouns as when the first reading was exactly the same printed text. Alejano and Carr's subjects were first-language speaker–readers of English. Whether this degree of abstraction characterises first-language reading in other languages is not known, nor is it known whether such abstraction is found in second-language reading. Helling and Carr are currently investigating these questions for readers of English as a second language from Chinese, Korean, and Japanese backgrounds. The logographic nature of noun representations in these writing systems has led many investigators to conclude that characters for nouns are processed much more like pictures in Chinese, Korean, and Japanese than they are in English. This hypothesis lends interest to the comparison of transfer between rebus and regular text in English and the logographic writing systems.

EXTENDING FUNCTIONAL–ANATOMICAL ANALYSIS TO DEVELOPMENT

Although we have attempted to examine developmental issues, we have not described very much neural evidence that bears directly on reading performance by developing readers. More often we have resorted to drawing inferences from mental chronometry and other forms of cognitive data, as in the previously discussed speculations about the FLSA's role in transfer of repetition benefits or the earlier discussions of the development of the Prestriate VWFS and its interface with the structures of phonological analysis and articulation.

The reason for the relative absence of neural evidence from developing readers is that there is very little of it available. The use of brain-imaging techniques with children is quite limited. Because PET requires the introduction of low-level radioactive tracers into the bloodstream, its application to children is largely restricted to cases requiring medical diagnosis. ERP techniques do not face such health-related restrictions, but until the relatively recent development of electrode-containing caps, the process of attaching and maintaining electrodes was sufficiently irksome to tax the patience and good will of young subjects. Preliminary ERP results with children in task situations similar to those of Compton et al. (1991) have produced results consistent with the present arguments but much work remains to be done (Posner et al., 1992). Finally, the problems of establishing useful animal models are even greater for the study of development than for investigations of mature function. Assuming a candidate animal model can be found, differences in lifespan and rate of development between animal species and humans make it difficult to extrapolate from maturational processes in animal nervous systems to potentially analogous processes in the human nervous system (Johnson, 1990; Johnson & Karmiloff-Smith, 1991). These various problems leave only a limited data base readily available. Autopsies provide evidence on structural maturation, brain damage provides evidence on functional localisation, and recovery from brain damage provides evidence on plasticity of functional localisation. The evidence on the latter two issues is complex and at present it is hard to see clear patterns that map straightforwardly onto what is known about adult structure-function relations (see e.g. Bates, Thal, & Janowsky, 1991). Therefore, hypotheses about development of the neural substrate of language and reading are quite tentative, often requiring what we have been trying to do—interpretation of cognitive evidence from children in light of neural evidence from adults.

Clearly, the development of neural imaging techniques more amenable to research with children is required to extend functional-anatomical analysis to development in a serious fashion. Although the electrode-containing cap has helped overcome one of the technical obstacles to using ERP, another still remains. This is the problem of identifying the neural structure or structures responsible for generating any given positive- or negative-going component of the ERP profile. The ability to calibrate mathematical computations on ERP data via comparison with PET data (e.g. Besson et al., 1994; Compton et al., 1991), as well as via comparison with lesion evidence (e.g. Knight, 1990), should aid this enterprise. Our own developmental investigations are moving in this direction. Another promising avenue involves magnetic rather than electrical measurements. Both measurement of blood flow by high-resolution FMRI and measurement of the magnetic fields generated by brain electrical activity, called magnetoencephalography, show potential. However, it is too early to draw any conclusions. MRI requires that subjects endure long periods of inactivity inside the confines of the magnetic housing, which may greatly limit its developmental applicability, and debates are currently quite heated concerning the resolving power of magnetoencephalography and whether it does in fact increase the precision with which generators can be localised relative to ERP (e.g. Crease, 1991).

Despite these difficulties, pessimism is unwarranted. A decade or two ago the possibility of imaging cognitive function in the living adult brain with the anatomical precision and computational relevance of current PET work would have seemed an unlikely achievement to most investigators. A decade or two from now, if present trends continue, precise and computationally relevant imaging of cognitive function in the developing brain should be at least as good, and probably quite a bit better, than imaging of the adult brain is now.

SUMMARY

Application of neural imaging techniques is advancing knowledge of the anatomical distribution and functional dynamics of information processing in the human brain. Imaging techniques provide insight into the cognitive computations performed by anatomically localised brain structures and the time course of each structure's involvement in particular cognitive tasks. The best progress to date has occurred in studies of attentional mechanisms and the perceptual encoding operations of word recognition (Posner & Petersen, 1990). Because word recognition is "the foundation of the reading process" (Gough, 1984; Stanovich, 1991), the resulting functional anatomy is relevant to attempts to understand reading development. We attempted to combine this new information on functional anatomy with findings from cognitive studies of lesion patients, normal children, and adults engaged in both first- and second-language reading and language processing.

Using these data, we explored possible changes in the functional organisation of brain structures that might accompany the emergence of literacy and support its exercise. Our major focus was on two anatomically localised structures recently identified by positron emission tomography (PET) in adult readers of English. One, the prestriate visual word form system (Prestriate VWFS), is specialised to support reading. It is an orthographic encoding mechanism that resides in left-medial prestriate visual cortex. This structure appears to develop during the first few years of experience and instruction with an alphabetic writing system—cognitive evidence for such a course of development now exists for children learning to read English as a first language, young adults from nonalphabetic writing-system backgrounds learning to read English as a second language, and young adults from English backgrounds learning to read Spanish as a second language.

What role does this orthographic processing play in reading? We proposed that the Prestriate VWFS acts as a primary gateway interfacing the visual system with the pre-existing structures of the language system that support listening and speaking in the normally developing, sensorily intact language user. At least for alphabetic writing systems such as English, two major pathways appear to transmit orthographic codes forward from the Prestriate VWFS for further linguistic processing. One is an inferior pathway toward temporal cortex that treats written words as visual objects. The other is a more superior pathway toward temporoparietal cortex that gives orthographic codes access to phonological analysis. The two pathways appear to differ in biological preparedness, with substantially greater heritability of individual differences in the temporoparietal phonological analysis pathway than in the temporal object recognition pathway.

The second structure on which we focused, the frontal lexical semantics area (FLSA), is located in left inferior prefrontal cortex and serves semantic functions for listening and perhaps sign as well as reading. The properties of this structure suggest that lexical and propositional semantics may be handled by quite different brain regions with different ontogenies and different evolutionary histories. Lexical semantics may be more closely associated with the referential processes of gesture, at least early in development, whereas propositional semantics appear to be more closely associated with the syntactic and phonological operations of the spoken language system per se. More work is needed to test the merits of these speculative ideas.

ACKNOWLEDGEMENTS

Preparation of this chapter was supported in part by the Rockefeller Foundation via their funding of the Bellagio Conference on Language and Literacy: Comparative Approaches, and in part by the Keck Foundation via a grant to the Institute for Cognitive and Decision Sciences at the University of Oregon. We thank the participants of the Bellagio Conference for much stimulating interaction that helped to shape the chapter.

REFERENCES

Adams, M.J. (1990). *Beginning to read: Learning and thinking about print*. Cambridge, MA: MIT Press.

Alegria, J., & Morais, J. (1991). Segmental analysis and reading acquisition. In L. Rieber & C.A. Perfetti (Eds.), *Learning to read: Basic research and its implications*. Hillsdale, NJ: Lawrence Erlbaum Associates Inc.

Alejano, A.R., & Carr, T.H. (1991, May). *The development of abstract processing operations in reading: Repetition benefit as a diagnostic tool*. Midwestern Psychological Association, Chicago, IL, USA.

Allen, P.A., & Emerson, P.L. (1991). Holism revisited: Evidence for parallel independent word-level and letter-level processors during word recognition. *Journal of Experimental Psychology: Human Perception and Performance, 17*, 489–511.

Aram, D.M., Gillespie, L.L., & Yamashita, T.S. (1990). Reading among children with left and right brain lesions. *Developmental Neuropsychology, 6*, 301–317.

Baron, J. (1979). Orthographic and word specific mechanisms in children's reading of words. *Child Development, 50*, 60–72.

Baron, J., & Strawson, C. (1976). Use of orthographic and word-specific knowledge in reading words aloud. *Journal of Experimental Psychology: Human Perception and Performance, 2*, 386–393.

Baron, J., & Thurston, I. (1973). An analysis of the word superiority effect. *Cognitive Psychology, 4*, 207–228.

Barron, R.W. (1986). Word recognition in early reading: A review of the direct and indirect access hypothesis. *Cognition, 24*, 93–119.

Bates, E., Thal, D., & Janowsky, J.S. (1991). Early language development and its neural correlates. In I. Rapin & S. Segalowitz (Eds.), *Handbook of neuropsychology, Vol. 6, Child neurology*. Amsterdam: Elsevier.

Bates, E., Thal, D., Whitesell, K., Fenson, L., & Oakes, L. (1989). Integrating language and gesture in infancy. *Developmental Psychology, 25*, 1004–1019.

Baynes, K. (1990). Language and reading in the right hemisphere: Highways or byways of the brain. *Journal of Cognitive Neuroscience, 2*, 159–179.

Belliveau, J.W., Rosen, B.R., Kantor, H.L., Rzedzian, R.R., Kennedy, D.N., McKinstry, R.C.,

Vevea, J.M., Cohen, M.S., Pykett, I.L., & Brady, T.J. (1990). Functional cerebral imaging by susceptibility-contrast NMR. *Magnetic Resonance in Medicine, 14*, 538–546.

Besner, D., Twilley, L., McCann, R.S., & Seergobin, K. (1991). On the association between connectionism and data: Are a few words necessary? *Psychological Review, 97*, 432–446.

Besson, M., Jacobs, A.M., Ziegler, J., Rey, A., Montant, M., Nazir, T.A., & Carr, T.H. (1994, November). *Separating component operations of visual word recognition with electrical imaging and computational modelling*. Paper presented at the Annual Meeting of the Psychonomic Society, St. Louis, MO, US.

Bower, G.H., & Clapper, J.P. (1989). Experimental methods in cognitive science. In M.I. Posner (Ed.), *Foundations of cognitive science* (pp. 245–300). Cambridge, MA: MIT Press.

Brooks, L. (1977). Visual pattern in fluent word identification. In A.S. Reber & D.S. Scarborough (Eds.), *Toward a psychology of reading* (pp. 143–181). Hillsdale, NJ: Lawrence Erlbaum Associates Inc.

Brown, J.S., & Carr, T.H. (1993). Limits on perceptual abstraction in reading: Asymmetric transfer between surface forms differing in typicality. *Journal of Experimental Psychology: Learning, Memory, and Cognition.*

Brown, T.L., & Haynes, M. (1985). Literacy background and reading development in a second language. In T.H. Carr (Ed.), *The development of reading skills* (pp. 19–34). San Francisco: Jossey-Bass.

Bryant, P. (this volume). Linguistic skills and learning to read.

Cappa, S.F., Cavalotti, G., Guidotti, M., Papagno, C., & Vignolo, L.A. (1983). Subcortical aphasia: Two clinical-CT scan correlation studies. *Cortex, 19*, 227–241.

Carr, T.H. (1981). Building theories of reading ability: On the relation between individual differences in cognitive skills and reading comprehension. *Cognition, 9*, 73–114.

Carr, T.H. (1986). Perceiving visual language. In K. Boff, K. Kaufman, & J. Thomas (Eds.), *Handbook of perception and human performance* (pp. 1–92). New York: Wiley.

Carr, T.H. (1992). Automaticity and cognitive anatomy: Is word recognition automatic? *American Journal of Psychology* (special issue on automaticity).

Carr, T.H., & Brown, J.S. (1990). Perceptual abstraction and interactivity in repeated oral reading: Where do things stand? *Journal of Experimental Psychology: Learning, Memory, and Cognition, 16*, 731–738.

Carr, T.H., Brown, J.S., & Charalambous, A. (1989). Repetition and reading: Perceptual encoding mechanisms are very abstract but not very interactive. *Journal of Experimental Psychology: Learning, Memory, and Cognition, 15*, 763–778.

Carr, T.H., Brown, T.L., Vavrus, L.G., & Evans, M.A. (1990). Cognitive skill maps and cognitive skill profiles: Componential analysis of individual differences in children's reading efficiency. In T.H. Carr & B.A. Levy (Eds.), *Reading and its development: Component skills approaches* (pp. 1–55). Orlando, FL: Academic Press.

Carr, T.H., Davidson, B.J., & Hawkins, H.L. (1978). Perceptual flexibility in word recognition: Strategies affect orthographic computation but not lexical access. *Journal of Experimental Psychology: Human Perception and Performance, 4*, 678–690.

Carr, T.H., & Levy, B.A. (Eds.) (1990). *Reading and its development: Component skills approaches*. Orlando, FL: Academic Press.

Carr, T.H., & Pollatsek, A. (1985). Recognising printed words: A look at current models. In D. Besner, T.G. Waller, & G.E. MacKinnon (Eds.), *Reading research: Advances in theory and practice* (Vol. 5, pp. 1–82). Orlando, FL: Academic Press.

Carr, T.H., Pollatsek, A., & Posner, M.I. (1981). What does the visual system know about words? *Perception and Psychophysics, 29*, 183–190.

Carr, T.H., Posner, M.I., Pollatsek, A., & Snyder, C.R.R. (1979). Orthography and familiarity effects in word processing. *Journal of Experimental Psychology: General, 108*, 389–414.

Chall, J. (1967). *Learning to read: The great debate*. New York: McGraw-Hill.

Chall, J. (1983). *Stages of reading development.* New York: McGraw-Hill.
Chertkow, H., Bub, D., Evans, A., Meyer, E., & Marrett, S. (1990, October). *Processing of words and pictures in the brain studied with positron emission tomography.* Paper presented at the Montreal Neurological Institute, McGill University.
Cohen, J.D., Dunbar, K., & McClelland, J.L. (1990). On the control of automatic processes: A parallel distributed processing model of the Stroop effect. *Psychological Review, 97,* 332–361.
Coltheart, M. (1985). Cognitive neuropsychology and the study of reading. In O.S.M. Marin & M.I. Posner (Eds.), *Attention and performance,* Vol. X, pp. 1–70). Hillsdale, NJ: Lawrence Erlbaum Associates Inc.
Coltheart, M., Sartori, G., & Job, R. (1990). *The cognitive neuropsychology of language.* Hove, UK: Lawrence Erlbaum Associates Ltd.
Compton, P., Grossenbacher, P., Posner, M.I., & Tucker, D.M. (1990, November). *A cognitive anatomical approach to visual word form activation.* Paper presented at the meeting of the Psychonomic Society, New Orleans, LA.
Compton, P., Grossenbacher, P., Posner, M.I., & Tucker, D.M. (1991). A cognitive anatomical approach to attention in lexical access. *Journal of Cognitive Neuroscience, 3,* 304–312.
Corbetta, M., Miezin, F.M., Dobmeyer, S., Shulman, G.L., & Petersen, S.E. (1990). Attentional modulation of neural processing of shape, color, and velocity in humans. *Science, 248,* 1556–1559.
Corbetta, M., Miezin, F.M., Dobmeyer, S., Shulman, G.L., & Petersen, S.E. (in press). Selective and divided attention during visual discriminations of shape, color, and speed: Functional anatomy by positron emission tomography. *Behavioral Neuroscience.*
Coslett, H.B., & Saffran, E.M. (1989). Evidence for preserved reading in "pure alexia". *Brain, 112,* 327–359.
Courchesne, E., Akshoomoff, N.A., & Ciesielski, K.T. (1990, February). *Shifting attention abnormalities in autism: ERP and performance evidence.* Poster presented at the meeting of the International Neuropsychological Society, Orlando, FL.
Crease, R.P. (1991). Images of conflict: MEG vs EEG. *Science, 253,* 374–375.
Crosson, B. (1985). Subcortical functions in language: A working model. *Brain and Language, 25,* 257–292.
Dale, A.M., & Sereno, M.I. (1993). Improved localization of cortical activity by combining EEG and MEG with MRI cortical surface reconstruction: A linear approach. *Journal of Cognitive Neuroscience, 5,* 162–176.
Damasio, H., & Damasio, A.R. (1989). *Lesion analysis in neuropsychology.* New York: Oxford University Press.
de Gelder, B., & Vroomen, J. (this volume). Speech processing and developmental dyslexia.
Demonet, J.-F., Puel, M., Celsis, P., & Cardebat, D. (1990). "Subcortical aphasia": Some proposed pathphysiological mechanisms and their rCBF correlated revealed by SPECT. *Journal of Neurolinguistics.*
Doehring, D.G. (1976). The acquisition of rapid reading responses. *Monographs of the Society of Research in Child Development, 41*(2), 1–54.
Downing, J., & Leong, C.K. (1982). *The psychology of reading.* New York: Macmillan.
Edelman, G.M. (1989). *The remembered present: A biological theory of consciousness.* New York: Basic Books.
Evans, M.A., & Carr, T.H. (1985). Cognitive abilities, conditions of learning, and the early development of reading skills. *Reading Research Quarterly, 20,* 327–350.
Feustel, T.C., Shiffrin, R.M., & Salasoo, A. (1983). Episodic and lexical contributions to the repetition effect in word identification. *Journal of Psychology: General, 112,* 309–346.
Fox, P.T., Mintun, M.A, Reiman, E.M., & Raichle, M.E. (1988). Enhanced detection of focal brain responses using intersubject averaging and change-distribution analysis of subtracted PET images. *Journal of Cerebral Blood Flow Metabolism, 8,* 642–653.
Frith, U. (1985). Beneath the surface of developmental dyslexia. In K.E. Patterson, J.C. Marshall,

& M. Coltheart (Eds.), *Surface dyslexia*. Hillsdale, NJ: Lawrence Erlbaum Associates Inc.

Galaburda, A. (1990, July). *The cortical substrate of language and reading*. Tutorial presented at the Third McDonnell Summer Institute on Cognitive Neuroscience, Dartmouth College, NH, USA.

Gevins, A.S. (1990). Dynamic patterns in multiple lead data. In J.W. Rohrbaugh, R. Parasuraman, & R. Johnson (Eds.), *Event-related potentials: Basic issues and applications* (pp. 44–56). New York: Oxford University Press.

Gibson, E.J., & Levin, H. (1975). *The psychology of reading*. Cambridge, MA: MIT Press.

Gibson, E.J., Osser, H., & Pick, A. (1963). A study in the development of grapheme-phoneme correspondences. *Journal of Verbal Learning and Verbal Behavior, 2*, 142–146.

Gibson, E.J., Pick, A., Osser, H., & Hammond, M. (1962). The role of grapheme-phoneme correspondence in the perception of words. *American Journal of Psychology, 75*, 554–570.

Givon, T., Yang, L., & Gernsbacher, M.A. (1990). *The processing of second language vocabulary: From attended to automated word recognition*. Technical Report, Institute for Cognitive and Decision Sciences and Center for Cognitive Neuroscience of Attention, University of Oregon, Eugene, OR, USA.

Gough, P.B. (1984). Word recognition. In P.D. Pearson (Ed.), *Handbook of reading research* (pp. 225–253). New York: Longman.

Gough, P.B., Juel, C., & Griffith, P. (1991). Reading, spelling, and the orthographic cipher. In P. Gough, L. Ehri, & R. Treiman (Eds.), *Reading acquisition*. Hillsdale, NJ: Lawrence Erlbaum Associates Inc.

Greenfield, P.M. (1991). Language, tools, and brain: The ontogeny and phylogeny of hierarchically organized sequential behavior. *Behavioral and Brain Sciences*.

Haynes, M., & Carr, T.H. (1990). Writing system background and second language reading: A component skills analysis of English reading by native speaker-readers of Chinese. In T.H. Carr & B.A. Levy (Eds.), *Reading and its development: Component skills analyses* (pp. 375–421). Orlando, FL: Academic Press.

Hillis, A.E., Rapp, B.C., Roman I.C., & Caramazza, A. (1990). Selective impairments of semantics in lexical processing. *Cognitive Neuropsychology, 7*, 191–243.

Humphreys, G.W., Evett, L.J., & Quinlan, P.T. (1990). Orthographic processing in visual word identification. *Cognitive Psychology, 22*, 517–560.

Johnson, J.S., & Newport, E.L. (1989). Critical period effects in second language learning: The influence of maturational state on the acquisition of English as a second language. *Cognitive Psychology, 21*, 60–99.

Johnson, M.H. (1990). Cortical maturation and the development of visual attention in early infancy. *Journal of Cognitive Neuroscience, 2*, 81–95.

Johnson, M.H., & Karmiloff-Smith, A. (1991). *Can neural selectionism be applied to cognitive development and its disorders?* Unpublished manuscript, Department of Psychology, Carnegie–Mellon University.

Johnson, M.H., Posner, M.I., & Rothbart, M.K. (1991). Components of visual orienting in early infancy: Contingency learning, anticipatory looking, and disengaging. *Journal of Cognitive Neuroscience*.

Johnston, J.C., & McClelland, J.L. (1980). Experimental tests of a hierarchical model of word identification. *Journal of Verbal Learning and Verbal Behavior, 7*, 560–572.

Kennedy, M., & Murdoch, B.E. (1989). Speech and language disorders subsequent to subcortical vascular lesions. *Aphasiology, 3*, 221–247.

Knight, R.M. (1990). Neural mechanisms of event-related potentials: Evidence from human lesion studies. In J.W. Rohrbaugh, R. Parasuraman, & R. Johnson (Eds.), *Event-related potentials: Basic issues and applications* (pp. 3–18). New York: Oxford University Press.

LaBerge, D. (1990). Thalamic and cortical mechanisms of attention suggested by recent positron emission tomographic experiments. *Journal of Cognitive Neuroscience, 2*, 358–373.

Lesch, M.F., & Pollatsek, A. (1993). Automatic access of semantic information by phonological codes in visual word recognition. *Journal of Experimental Psychology: Learning, Memory, and Cognition, 19*, 285–294.

Levy, B.A., & Stewart, L. (April, 1991). *Early diagnosis and treatment of reading problems.* Society for Research in Child Development, Seattle, WA, USA.

Livingstone, M.S., & Hubel, D.H. (1988). Segregation of form, color, movement, and depth: Anatomy, physiology, and perception. *Science, 240*, 740–749.

Lock, A. (1990). The development of language and object manipulation: Evolutionary implications. In Wenner-Gren Foundation for Anthropological Research International Symposium No. 110, *Tools, language, and intelligence: Evolutionary implications.* Cascais, Portugal.

Lovett, M. (1991). *Remedial outcome data: Unique perspectives on dyslexic reading acquisition.* Society for Research in Child Development, Seattle, WA, USA.

Lukatela, G., & Turvey, M.T. (1991). Phonological access of the lexicon: Evidence from associative priming with pseudohomophones. *Journal of Experimental Psychology; Human Perception and Performance, 17*, 951–966.

Manelis, L. (1974). The effect of meaningfulness in tachistoscopic word perception. *Perception and Psychophysics, 16*, 182–192.

Manis, F.R., Szeszulski, P.A., Holt, L.K., & Graves, K. (1990). Variation in component word recognition and spelling skills among dyslexic children and normal readers. In T.H. Carr & B.A. Levy (Eds.), *Reading and its development: Component skills approaches* (pp. 207–259). Orlando, FL: Academic Press.

Marsh, G., Friedman, M., Welch, V., & Desberg, P. (1981). A cognitive-developmental theory of reading acquisition. In G.E. MacKinnon & T.G. Waller (Eds.), *Reading research: Advances in theory and practice* (Vol. 3). New York: Academic Press.

McCarthy, G., Blamire, A.M., Rothman, D.L., Gruetter, R., & Shulman, R.G. (1993). Echo-planar magnetic resonance imaging studies of frontal cortex activation during word generation in humans. *Proceedings of the National Academy of Science, 90*, 4952–4956.

McCarthy, R.A., & Warrington, E.K. (1990). *Cognitive neuropsychology: A clinical introduction.* San Diego: Academic Press.

McClandis, B., Curran, T., & Posner, M.I. (1994, November). *Exploring the time course of word recognition for identical and cross-care repetitions.* Paper presented at the Annual Meeting of the Psychonomic Society, St. Louis, MO, US.

McClelland, J.L. (1979). On the time relations of mental processes: An examination of systems of processes in cascade. *Psychological Review, 86*, 287–330.

McClelland, J.L., & Rumelhart, D.E. (1981). An interactive activation model of context effects in letter perception: I. An account of basic findings. *Psychological Review, 88*, 375–407.

Meier, R.P., & Newport, E.L. (1990). Out of the hands of babes: On a possible sign advantage in language acquisition. *Language, 66*, 1–23.

Merrill, E., Sperber, R.D., & McCarthy, C. (1991). Differences in semantic encoding as a function of reading comprehension skills. *Memory & Cognition, 9*, 618–624.

Meyer, D.E., Irwin, D.E., Osman, A., & Kounios, J. (1988). The dynamics of cognition and action: Mental processes inferred from speed-accuracy decomposition. *Psychological Review, 95*, 183–237.

Miller, G.A., Bruner, J.S., & Postman, L. (1954). Familiarity of letter sequences and tachistoscopic identification. *Journal of General Psychology, 50*, 129–139.

Neely, J.H. (1991). Semantic priming effects in visual word recognition: A selective review of current findings and theories. In D. Besner & G. Humphreys (Eds.), *Basic processes in reading: Visual word recognition* (pp. 264–336). Hillsdale, NJ: Lawrence Erlbaum Associates Inc.

Newport, E.L. (1990). Maturational constraints on language learning. *Cognitive Science, 14*, 11–28.

Olson, R., Wise, B., Conners, F., & Rack, J. (1990). Organization, heritability, and remediation of component word recognition and language skills in disabled readers. In T.H. Carr & B.A. Levy (Eds)., *Reading and its development: Component skills approaches* (pp. 261–322). Orlando, FL: Academic Press.

Paap, K.R., Newsome, S.L., McDonald, J.E., & Schvaneveldt, R.W. (1982). An activation-verification model for letter and word recognition: The word superiority effect. *Psychological Review, 89*, 573–594.

Pardo, J.V., Pardo, P.J., Janer, K.W., & Raichle, M.E. (1990). The anterior cingulate cortex mediates processing selection in the Stroop attentional conflict paradigm. *Proceedings of the National Academy of Science, 87*, 256–259.

Patterson, K.E., & Coltheart, V. (1987). Phonological processes in reading: A tutorial review. In M. Coltheart (Ed.), *Attention and performance, Vol. XII: The psychology of reading* (pp. 421–448). Hove: Lawrence Erlbaum Associates Ltd.

Perfetti, C.A. (1985). *Reading ability*. New York: Oxford University Press.

Perfetti, C.A. (1991). The representation problem in reading acquisition. In P. Gough, L. Ehri, & R. Treiman (Eds.), *Reading acquisition*. Hillsdale, NJ: Lawrence Erlbaum Associates Inc.

Perfetti, C.A., & McCutcheon, D. (1987). Schooled language competence: Linguistic abilities in reading and writing. In S. Rosenberg (Ed.), *Advances in applied psycholinguistics* (Vol. 2, pp. 105–141). Cambridge: Cambridge University Press.

Petersen, S.E., & Fox, P.T., Posner, M.I., Mintun, M., & Raichle, M.E. (1989). Positron emission tomographic studies of the processing of single words. *Journal of Cognitive Neuroscience, 1*, 153–170.

Petersen, S.E., Fox, P.T., Snyder, A.Z., & Raichle, M.E. (1990). Activation of extrastriate and frontal cortical areas by visual words and word-like stimuli. *Science, 249*, 1041–1044.

Posner, M.I., (1978). *Chronometric explorations of mind*. Hillsdale, NJ: Lawrence Erlbaum Associates Inc.

Posner, M.I. (1986). *Chronometric explorations of mind* (2nd ed.). New York: Oxford University Press.

Posner, M.I., & Carr, T.H. (1992). Lexical access and the brain: Anatomical constraints on cognitive models of word recognition. *American Journal of Psychology, 105*, 1–26.

Posner, M.I., Kiesner, J., Thomas-Thrapp., L., McClandiss, B., Carr. T.H., & Rothbart, M.K. (1992, November). *Brain changes in the acquisition of literacy*. Paper presented at the Annual Meeting of the Psychonomic Society, St. Louis, MO, US.

Posner, M.I., & McLeod, P. (1982). Information processing models: In search of elementary operations. *Annual Review of Psychology, 33*, 477–514.

Posner, M.I., & Petersen, S.E. (1990). The attention system of the human brain. *Annual Review of Neuroscience, 13*, 25–42.

Posner, M.I., Petersen, S.E., Fox, P.T., & Raichle, M.E. (1988). Localization of cognitive operations in the human brain. *Science, 240*, 1627–1631.

Posner, M.I., & Rothbart, M. (1990, September). *Attentional mechanisms and conscious experience*. Paper presented at the conference on Consciousness and Cognition, St. Andrews, Scotland.

Posner, M.I., & Snyder, C.R.R. (1975). Attention and cognitive control. In R.L. Solso (Ed.), *Information processing and cognition: The Loyola Symposium* (pp. 55–82). Hillsdale, NJ: Lawrence Erlbaum Associates Inc.

Potchen, E.J., & Potchen, M.J. (1991). The imaging of brain function. *Investigative Radiology, 26*, 258–265.

Potter, M.C., Kroll, J., Yachzel, B., Carpenter, E., & Sherman, J. (1986). Pictures in sentences: Understanding without words. *Journal of Experimental Psychology: General, 115*, 281–294.

Raichle, M. (1987). Circulatory and metabolic correlates of brain function in normal humans. In F. Plum (Ed.), *Higher functions of the brain* (Part 2, pp. 643–674). Baltimore, MD: William Wilkins.

Rayner, K., & Pollatsek, A. (1989). *The psychology of reading*. Englewood Cliffs, NJ: Prentice-Hall.

Rieben, L., & Perfetti, C.A. (1991) *Learning to read.* Hillsdale, NJ: Lawrence Erlbaum Associates Inc.
Reicher, G.M. (1969). Perceptual recognition as a function of meaningfulness of stimulus material. *Journal of Experimental Psychology, 81*, 275–280.
Rohrbaugh, J.W., Parasuraman, R., & Johnson, R. (Eds.) (1990). *Event-related potentials: Basic issues and applications.* New York: Oxford University Press.
Rozin, P., & Gleitman, L. (1977). The structure and acquisition of reading: II. The reading process and acquisition of the alphabetic principle. In A.S. Reber & D.L. Scarborough (Eds.), *Toward a psychology of reading.* Hillsdale, NJ: Lawrence Erlbaum Associates Inc.
Rozin, P., Poritsky, S., & Sotsky, R. (1971). American children with reading problems can easily learn English represented by Chinese characters. *Science, 171*, 1264–1267.
Rueckl, J.G., Cave, K.R., & Kosslyn, S.M. (1989). Why are "what" and "where" processed by separate cortical visual systems? A computational investigation. *Journal of Cognitive Neuroscience, 1*, 171–186.
Salasoo, A., Feustel, T.C., & Shiffrin, R.M. (1985). Building permanent memory codes: Codification and repetition effects in word recognition. *Journal of Experimental Psychology: General, 114*, 50–77.
Scherg, M., Vajsar, J., & Picton, T.W. (1989). Source analysis of the human auditory evoked potential. *Journal of Cognitive Neuroscience, 1*, 336–355.
Seidenberg, M.S. (1985). The time course of information activation and utilization in visual word recognition. In D. Besner, T.G. Waller, & G.E. MacKinnon (Eds.), *Reading research: Advances in theory and practice* (Vol. 5, pp. 200–252). Orlando, FL: Academic Press.
Seidenberg, M.S., & McClelland, J.L. (1989). A distributed, developmental model of word recognition and naming. *Psychological Review, 96*, 523–568.
Seymour, P.H.K., & MacGregor, C.J. (1984). Developmental dyslexia: A cognitive experimental analysis of phonological, morphemic, and visual impairments. *Cognitive Neuropsychology, 1*, 43–82.
Shallice, T. (1988). *From neuropsychology to mental structure.* Cambridge, UK: Cambridge University Press.
Sieroff, E., Pollatsek, A., & Posner, M.I. (1988). Recognition of visual letter strings following damage to the posterior visual spatial attention system. *Cognitive Neuropsychology, 5*, 427–449.
Sieroff, E., & Posner, M.I. (1988). Cueing spatial attention during processing of words and letter strings in normals. *Cognitive Neuropsyychology, 5*, 451–472.
Simpson, G.B., & Krueger, M. (1991). Selective access of homograph meanings in sentence context. *Journal of Memory and Language, 30*, 627–643.
Smith, E.E., & Spoehr, K.T. (1974). The perception of printed English: A theoretical perspective. In B.H. Kantowitz (Ed.), *Human information processing: Tutorials in performance and cognition.* Hillsdale, NJ: Lawrence Erlbaum Associates Inc.
Sperling, G., & Dosher, B. (1986). In K. Boff, L. Kaufman, & J. Thomas (Eds.), *Handbook of perception and human performance* (Vol. II). New York: Wiley.
Stanovich, K.E. (1982). Individual differences in cognitive processes of reading. I: Word decoding. *Journal of Learning Disabilities, 15*, 485–493.
Stanovich, K.E. (1986). Matthew effects in reading: Some consequences of individual differences in the acquisition of literacy. *Reading Research Quarterly, 21*, 360–407.
Stanovich, K.E. (1991). Word recognition: Changing perspectives. In P.D. Pearson (Ed.), *Handbook of reading research* (Vol. 2). New York: Longman.
Sternberg, S. (1969). The discovery of processing stages: Extensions of Donders' method. In W.G. Koster (Ed.), *Attention and performance* (Vol. II, pp. 276–315). Amsterdam: North-Holland.
Thatcher, R.W., Walker, R.A., & Guidice, S. (1987). Human cerebral hemispheres develop at

different rates and ages. *Science, 236*, 1110–1113.
Treiman, R. (1985). Phonemic analysis, spelling, and reading. In T.H. Carr (Ed.), *The development of reading skills* (New Directions in Child Development, No. 27). San Francisco: Jossey-Bass.
Van Orden, G.C., Pennington, B.F., & Stone, G.O. (1990). Word identification in reading and the promise of subsymbolic psycholinguistics. *Psychological Review, 97*, 488–522.
Vellutino, F.R. (1991). Has basic research in reading increased our understanding of developmental reading and how to teach reading? *Psychological Science, 2*, 70; 81–83.
Wise, S.P., & Desimone, R. (1988). Behavioural neurophysiology: Insights into seeing and grasping. *Science, 242*, 736–740.

14 Literacy and Linguistic Awareness

Pratibha Karanth, Asha Kudva, and Aparna Vijayan
All India Institute of Speech and Hearing, Manasagangothri, Mysore, India

INTRODUCTION

The assumption that all native speakers of a language have an intuitive knowledge has been the touchstone of linguistic methodology for several decades. Since the 1970s, grammatical judgements, in particular, have been given a central role in linguistic theory and research by the transformational-generative theory of grammar, and the set of sentences that the adult judges upon reflection to be well-formed serves as an important source of data for linguists engaged in formulating linguistic theories.

Developmental psycholinguists, too, have shown interest in grammatical acceptability judgements of children as a means of determining the young child's competence. That the ability of children to make grammatical judgements varies considerably across certain ages has been well established by researchers over the past two decades (see e.g. Bever, 1970; De Villiers & De Villiers, 1972; Fujiki, Briton, & Dunton, 1987; Gleitman & Gleitman, 1970; Hakes, Evan, & Tunmer, 1980; Karanth, 1984; Karanth & Suchitra, 1993; Pratt, Tunmer, & Bowey, 1984; Scholl & Ryan, 1980; Tunmer & Grieve, 1984; Van Kleek, 1982; Vasantha, Sastry, & Murthy, 1989).

What is not so well established or recognised is the observation that not all adults perform equally well on grammaticality judgement tasks. Results from a recently concluded study on brain-damaged and neurologically healthy adults (Karanth, Ahuja, Nagaraj, Pandit, & Shivashankar, 1991) found qualitative differences between the language behaviour of the literate and illiterate, brain-damaged as well as neurologically healthy, adults. Of particular interest was the performance of the literate and illiterate adults on the grammaticality judgement task, wherein the subjects had to judge a given sentence, presented auditorily, on its syntactic accceptability. The literate adults performed significantly better than the illiterate adults on grammaticality judgement. The illiterates generally refused to perform the task, stating that they did not know what was required of them: When they did respond, they did not do so to all of the test items or gave indiscriminate responses. Similar results were obtained in two different adult illiterate populations, speaking two different languages and located more than 2000 miles apart. These observations suggest that literacy per se is a variable affecting grammaticality judgements.

Although it has been known that language as a skill may be handled differently by the literate and illiterate sub-populations and that the effects of literacy are reflected both in one's linguistic skills and one's rational and analytical thinking, these effects have not been clearly understood. Empirical investigations in this area have concerned themselves more with the intellectual consequences (including the emergence of abstract thinking and logical operations) of literacy than with specific linguistic and metalinguistic skills.

Although it is generally agreed that metalinguistic awareness refers to the ability to reflect upon and manipulate the structural features of spoken language, there is considerable debate concerning how and when metalinguistic awareness actually develops (Tunmer, Pratt, & Herriman, 1984). Three main theoretical conceptualisations have been offered. The first claims that metalinguistic awareness is an integral part of the process of language acquisition. Spontaneous speech repairs and language play are cited as evidence in support of this claim. The second view claims that metalinguistic awareness occurs during middle childhood (4–8 years of age) and reflects a new kind of linguistic functioning that is influenced greatly by the cognitive control processes emerging during this period. The third position is that metalinguistic awareness is largely a result of exposure to formal schooling, especially learning to read.

The available literature (Gleitman & Gleitman, 1970; Tunmer, Pratt, & Herriman, 1984) suggests that the ability to reflect on the internal grammatical structure of sentences as measured by tasks involving judgement of acceptability, synonymy, ambiguity, sentence discrimination, sentence correction, and riddle comprehension emerges later than the ability to comprehend sentences. Data from these studies reveal rather striking developmental changes between 4 and 8 years of age, lending some support to the notion that a developmentally distinct kind of functioning emerges during middle childhood. The ability to consciously reflect on the structure of sentences is seen to occur from age 5 onwards, but it is also claimed that before school age children appear to be making judgements on the basis of content (Pratt, Tunmer, & Bowey, 1984; Van Kleek, 1984). This tendency to accept or reject sentences on the basis of their content rather than on the linguistic manner in which they are conveyed is said to decrease to nearly zero by the age of 7, rarely to be seen at later ages (Hakes et al., 1980).

As to cognitive development, it has been suggested that metalinguistic awareness plays an important role in the development of children's thought processes (Donaldson, 1978; Tunmer & Grieve, 1984). The development of metalinguistic awareness is an essential part of the development of metacognitive skills involved in reflecting upon and monitoring one's thought process. Furthermore, these skills are viewed as crucial for the successful completion of many of the abstract tasks that children encounter when they enter formal schooling.

Research into reading and metalinguistic awareness has looked more directly at the role of different language awareness skills in reading acquisition (Ehri, 1979; Tunmer & Bowey, 1980). Tunmer and Bowey argue that different components—phonological, word, and grammatical awareness—all play different roles in the processes involved in learning to read. In respect to grammatical awareness, they point out that once the child has mastered the grapheme–phoneme correspondence rules of the language he or she must consciously begin to organise the text into higher-order syntactic groupings. Because the structures of sentences are crucial to understanding, the child must bring his or her syntactic knowledge of spoken language to bear on the written language, which requires the metalinguistic ability to reflect on the structural features of the spoken language. So, the connection between metalinguistic awareness and education is largely established by extending the conceptual identification of metalinguistic skills with classroom activities together with support from research; this indicates that metalinguistic skills may be necessary for certain educational attainments, especially language-related ones (Karmiloff-Smith, 1979; Herriman & Myhill, 1983; Nesdale & Tunmer, 1983).

Our earlier work on grammaticality judgements in children (Karanth, 1984; Karanth & Suchitra, 1993) indicated that children under the age of 6 years are unable to carry out the metalinguistic task of grammatical judgement. Beginning at age 6–7 years and with a rapid spurt at about 7–8 years, children become increasingly proficient in the grammaticality judgement task, reaching adult-like proficiency by 14 years of age. This is in agreement with much of the earlier investigations in the area and lends support to the theory that metalinguistic awareness occurs during middle childhood, reflecting new kinds of linguistic functioning under the influence of cognitive control processes that emerge during this period. However, our findings on illiterate adults (Karanth et al., 1991) whose performance on grammaticality judgements was significantly different from that of literate adults lend greater support to the position that metalinguistic awareness is largely a result of exposure to formal schooling and learning to read. Taken together, these observations led us to conclude that the emergence of grammaticality judgement in children *around the age at which schooling begins* is not merely coincidental but more directly causal, and that literacy acquisition has a definite role in metalinguistic awareness and skills such as grammaticality judgement. It is also noteworthy that: (1) the general belief that all adult native speakers of a language are capable of making accurate judgements of grammaticality of given sentence structures in their language has not been based on any systematic study and has not in fact stood up to empirical investigation; and (2) the children who showed emergence of metalinguistic skills of the kind required for grammaticality judgement in mid-childhood (including those in our previous studies) were all school-going children. Given this, further investigations would be required to resolve the interrelationships between age, literacy, and metalinguistic skills. Specifically, it would be of interest to see whether: (1) a developmental trend in acquisition of metalinguistic skills, free of the influence of literacy, emerges in children; (2) the extent to which literacy and its acquisition influences the emergence of these skills in children; and (3) the consequences or the implications of the lack of or limited development of metalinguistic abilities for linguistic competence and language use in adults such as the illiterate subjects of our earlier study (Karanth et al., 1991).

It was therefore proposed to investigate the grammaticality judgement skills of two groups of literate and illiterate children and adults, matched for age. Furthermore, as the processes underlying metalinguistic abilities are dependent on familiarity with the language, the subjects' abilities to comprehend and produce the syntactic structures on which they were required to pass grammaticality judgements were also investigated.

METHOD

Two groups of children, one school-going and the other nonschool-going, ranging in age from 6 to 11 years were evaluated on linguistic tasks assessing their comprehension, expression, and grammaticality judgement of specific syntactic structures. Each group consisted of 50 normal, healthy children who were subdivided into five subgroups of one year age interval. All 100 were native speakers of Kannada—the language in which testing was carried out. Whereas all 50 children of one group had continuous noninterrupted schooling up to the time of testing, the 50 in the other group had less than one continuous year of formal schooling and no nonformal exposure to literacy.

In parallel, two groups of adult native speakers of Kannada in the age range of 21 to 40 years were tested on the same materials. One group of 30 were literate adults with an average of 14.67 years of formal education in Kannada, whereas the other group of 30 were illiterate adults who had had no introduction to formal education.

As in our earlier work, the syntactic judgement abilities of all 200 subjects were examined on the Syntax Section of the Linguistic Profile Test (LPT) (for details see Karanth, 1984; Karanth et al., 1991; and Karanth & Suchitra, 1993). Of the 130 test items covering a wide range of syntactic structures 65 were ill-formed sentences violating a particular rule for usage of a particular syntactic marker, and the other 65 were syntactically correct. The randomly arranged correct and incorrect items were presented aurally and the subjects were required to judge the utterances for grammatical acceptability. In parallel, 110 test items of the syntactic section of the RRTC Battery for comprehension and expression of specific syntactic structures were also administered. This test evaluates the subjects' ability to comprehend and express the very same syntactic structures that are investigated in the LPT through picture pointing and picture description tasks.

RESULTS

The mean scores obtained on the LPT by the children in the two subgroups (school-going and nonschool-going) in the five age groups are shown in Table 14.1, along with their standard deviations.

In the school-going subgroup, beginning with a score of around 57, there is a gradual but consistent increase in scores, with a sharp increase at about 8 years of age. In the nonschool-going group the average score was about 48 for the lowest age group tested (6–7 years). A gradual rise in the scores is seen but the rise is less pronounced and the overall scores of the nonschool-going children are much lower than those of the school-going children in the same age group.

The results of an analysis of variance on the significance of literacy and age on grammaticality judgement showed that both main effects were highly significant, as well as the interaction. For school-going children there was an overall developmental trend with a spurt at 8 years of age. Although a similar trend was seen among the nonschool-going children, too, the differences (increase in scores) were far higher for the former compared to the latter.

In addition, the grammaticality sensitivity index A' as given by Linebarger, Schwartz, and Saffran (1983) was computed for each child. The mean scores of the index of grammatical sensitivity A' obtained by the different age groups among the school-going and nonschool-going children (see Table 14.2) once

TABLE 14.1
Mean Scores on the Linguistic Profile Test, Syntax Section, for Both School-going and Nonschool-going Subgroups

	School-going Children	*Nonschool-going Children*
Age Group (yrs)	*Mean Scores (SD)*	*Mean Scores (SD)*
6–7	57.00 (5.20)	48.35 (3.09)
7–8	55.30 (6.90)	50.10 (2.33)
8–9	64.90 (2.70)	53.90 (1.56)
9–10	65.85 (3.65)	53.95 (3.56)
10–11	67.95 (5.75)	55.90 (3.56)

again, although showing an increase in age across both groups, confirmed the poorer performance of nonschool-going children across the entire age range studied. The average grammaticality sensitivity index values across the five age groups of the school-going children is seen to increase from 0.62 to 0.79. However, maximum sensitivity (A' = 1.00) is not achieved even by the age of 11 years, the upper limit of the children studied here. In the nonschool-going children the average values of A' across the five age groups increases from 0.45 to 0.69, the mean A' values for these children being far below the A' values for the age-matched school-going children. The data shows that the average A' values (A' = 0.69) for the oldest nonschool-going group (10–11 years) is comparable to that of the youngest school-going age group (6–7) years, A' = 0.62)

The mean scores obtained by the school-going and nonschool-going children on the syntactic comprehension task were as follows. Of a maximum possible score of 55 the school-going children scored an average of 49.9 in the youngest age group tested, and the maximum score of 55 was reached by age 9. The nonschool-going children on the other hand performed comparatively poorly throughout the age range studied and did not reach the maximum score possible on syntactic comprehension even by the age of 10–11 years. Both literacy and age were found to influence syntactic comprehension significantly.

A comparison of the performance on syntactic comprehension as against grammaticality judgement in the school-going and nonschool-going children shows better performance in comprehension than judgement in both groups across the entire age range (Fig. 14.1). This finding is consistent with earlier studies (Bever, 1970; De Villiers & De Villiers, 1972) that comprehension precedes syntactic judgement ability.

The scores obtained by the two groups of children on syntactic expression are given in Table 14.3. The 6–7-year-olds among the nonschool-going children failed to respond adequately, as a result of which their scores could not be quantified.

TABLE 14.2
Mean Grammaticality Sensitivity Indices (A') for the Literate and Illiterate Subgroups

	Mean Grammaticality Sensitivity Indices A'	
Age Group (yrs)	*Literates*	*Illiterates*
6–7	0.62	0.45
7–8	0.59	0.47
8–9	0.72	0.56
9–10	0.76	0.56
10–11	0.79	0.69

TABLE 14.3
Mean Syntactic Expression Scores for Literates and Illiterates

	Mean Syntactic Expression Scores	
Age Groups (yrs)	*Literates*	*Illiterates*
6–7	39.5	NAR*
7–8	46.0	10.0
8–9	50.5	16.5
9–10	51.5	20.0
10–11	55.0	24.5

*NAR = no adequate responses.

There were important qualitative differences between the syntactic output of the nonschool-going and school-going children. The former tended to respond in single words or phrases that were inadequately marked for syntax. The school-going children, in contrast, used comparatively more complex utterances. These subjects were more explicit in their description of the pictures and used full sentences in their explanations. For example:

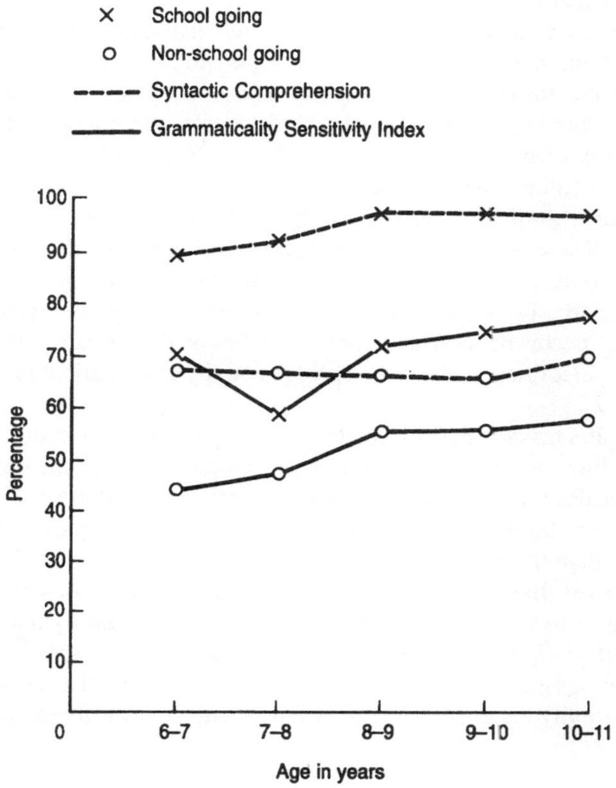

FIG 14.1

Morphophonemic structures:
Question: / *Bombe yellide*?/ (Where is the doll?)
Expected answer: / *Bombe mĕjina mĕle ide.*/ (The doll is on the table.)
School-going subjects' answer: / *Bombe mĕjina mĕle ide.*/ (The doll is on the table.)
Nonschool-going subjects' answer: /*Mĕju*/ (Table); /*Mĕju mĕle* / (on table).

Similar results were obtained with the literate and illiterate adults. On the syntactic judgement task the literate group obtained a mean score of 92.9 against a total possible score of 100, whereas the illiterates obtained a mean score of 72.7. On all subsections of the metalinguistic task the literates consistently performed better than the illiterates. However, even though as a group the illiterates performed poorly, there were instances where certain individuals performed exceptionally well in certain sub-sections, but this did not apply to all subsections.

The mean sensitivity indices for the two groups on the various subsets of the grammaticality judgement tasks are given in Table 14.4. A *t* test was applied to determine the significance of the differences between the grammaticality sensitivity indices of the literates and illiterates and the differences were found to be significant at the 0.01 level across all subtests.

Table 14.5 presents the results for the comprehension task. Despite the fairly simple verbal commands given (e.g. "while playing the boy fell"; distractors: boys playing, boy fallen down on the ground; target: one boy falling down while playing with other boys), the illiterates' performance was not perfect on certain tasks of auditory verbal comprehension involving syntactic markers of participial constructions, conjunctives, quotatives, causatives, tenses, and morphophonemic transformations, all of which are bound morphemes mapped onto the root word in Kannada. There were significant differences between the literates and illiterates in comprehension of participial constructions and predicates. Thus, even in the relatively simple task of auditory verbal comprehension of syntax the illiterates' performance was poorer than that of the literates, although the difference in performance was not as great as on the grammaticality judgement task (Fig. 14.2).

On expression tasks in describing the pictures presented, as in the case of the children, the literate adults tended to use the complete form of the sentence and gave elaborate descriptions using adjectives and modifiers, whereas the illiterates tended to produce incomplete utterances that were syntactically and semantically less complex than those of the literates. For examples, see Table 14.6.

Briefly, the results of the current study confirm our earlier observations that literates and illiterates differ considerably in the metalinguistic task of grammaticality judgement. The data on the school-going versus nonschool-going children suggests that although these skills increase with age in childhood, they are apparently enhanced by acquisition of literacy. Furthermore, the lack

TABLE 14.4
Group Means, Standard Deviations, and *t* Ratios of the Grammaticality Sensitivity Indices for the Various Syntactic Structures in the Syntactic Section of the LPT

Syntactic Structures	*Group*	*Mean*	*SD*	t *Ratio*
Morphophonemic structures	Literate	0.97	(0.222)	5.50
	Illiterate	0.79	(0.178)	
Plural forms	Literate	1.00	(0)	7.20
	Illiterate	0.77	(0.175)	
Tenses	Literate	0.96	(0.064)	7.20
	Illiterate	0.62	(0.252)	
PNG markers	Literate	0.98	(0.022)	5.90
	Illiterate	0.77	(0.193)	
Case markers	Literate	0.93	(0.070)	4.09
	Illiterate	0.75	(0.231)	
Transitives, intransitives,	Literate	0.94	(0.090)	5.20
& causatives	Illiterate	0.82	(0.100)	
Sentence types	Literate	0.98	(0.030)	7.70
	Illiterate	0.77	(0.153)	
Predicates	Literate	0.98	(0.024)	7.00
	Illiterate	0.84	(0.108)	
Conjunctions, comparatives,	Literate	0.93	(0.069)	5.90
& quotatives	Illiterate	0.62	(0.250)	
Conditional clauses	Literate	0.96	(0.036)	7.20
	Illiterate	0.75	(0.155)	
Participial constructions	Literate	0.95	(0.039)	6.09
	Illiterate	0.67	(0.252)	
Raw scores	Literate	92.9	(4.850)	12.60
(Syntax Section of LPT)	Illiterate	72.7	(7.320)	

of comparable syntactic awareness or sensitivity among nonschool-going children and illiterate adults extends to tasks such as auditory verbal comprehension and expression, although not to the same extent as in the metalinguistic task of grammaticality judgement.

Of the three conceptualisations on the development of metalinguistic awareness the first, that metalinguistic awareness is an integral part of language acquisition, is only partially supported by our data, as these skills, although showing some increase with age, are not developed to the same extent among nonschooled illiterates as in schooled literates. The second view, which claims that the metalinguistic awareness developing in middle childhood reflects a new kind of linguistic functioning influenced greatly by cognitive control processes that emerge during this period, also receives only partial support. The significant differences between the schooled and nonschooled suggest that these cognitive control processes are not present to the same extent in the nonschooled illiterates as in the schooled literates. It is likely that

TABLE 14.5
Group Means and Standard Deviations of the Comprehension Scores for the Various Syntactic Structures in the Syntactic Section of the RRTC Battery

Syntactic Structures	*Group*	*Mean*	*SD*
Morphophonemic structures	Literate	5.00	(0)
	Illiterate	4.97	(0.179)
Plural forms	Literate	5.00	(0)
	Illiterate	5.00	(0)
Tenses	Literate	5.00	(0)
	Illiterate	4.98	(0.890)
PNG markers	Literate	5.00	(0)
	Illiterate	5.00	(0)
Case markers	Literate	5.00	(0)
	Illiterate	5.00	(0)
Transitives, intransitives,	Literate	5.00	(0)
& causatives	Illiterate	4.90	(0.300)
Sentence types	Literate	5.00	(0)
	Illiterate	5.00	(0)
Predicates	Literate	5.00	(0)
	Illiterate	4.60	(0.480)
Conjunctions, comparatives,	Literate	5.00	(0)
& quotatives	Illiterate	5.00	(0)
Conditional clauses	Literate	5.00	(0)
	Illiterate	5.00	(0)
Participial constructions	Literate	5.00	(0)
	Illiterate	4.10	(0.860)

schooling itself may contribute to these cognitive processes. Our data lend greater support to the third view that metalinguistic awareness is greatly enhanced by formal schooling, for though some metalinguistic skills were common among the schooled and nonschooled children, and the literate and illiterate adults, those who had exposure to formal schooling performed consistently and significantly better than those who did not receive any formal schooling.

A further observation that the heightened syntactic awareness and sensitivity of the literates is not limited to metalinguistic skills alone, but may also be seen in the relatively easier day-to-day tasks of auditory verbal comprehension and expression, is in line with Luria's (1971) observations on his illiterate subjects as being governed by the "immediate", "concrete", and "practical". These observations lead us to emphasise that the cognitive consequences of literacy and education on language use and metalinguistic skills need to be investigated further.

Theoretical models such as the cognitive-developmental model of metalinguistic development (Tunmer, 1992) propose that reading acquisition is the end-product of a process of cognitive development in which metalinguistic abilities develop as

TABLE 14.6
Picture Description Responses by Literates and Illiterates

		Observed Response	
Description of the Picture	*Expected Response*	*Literate*	*Illiterate*
1. The picture depicts a girl drinking water from a glass	*avalu kudiyutiddăle* (She is drinking)	*avalu kudiyutiddale*	*kudiyutiddăle* (Drinking, she is) by PNG marker only, subject not identified – Gender implied – Incomplete
2. The picture depicts a book on top of a table	*pustaka mejina mele ide* (The book is on the table)	*pustaka mejina mele ide*	*buku stulalli ide* (The book is in the stool) – Morphophonemic locative – marker absent

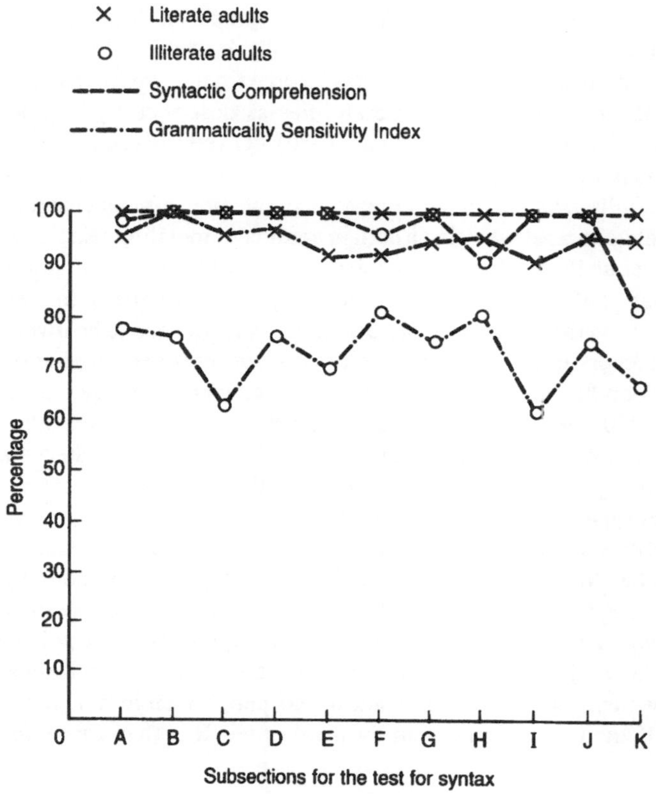

FIG 14.2

a consequence of exposure to language and the process of decentration; this leads to phonological, syntactic and pragmatic awareness, which heighten phonological recoding/decoding and listening comprehension, in turn leading to reading comprehension. Metalinguistic skills are seen as essential for early progress in reading and children who have difficulty in acquiring basic reading are considered to be those who are basically deficient in performing metalinguistic operations. To quote Tunmer (1992, p. 207): "Metalinguistic performances such as separating a word from its referent, dissociating the meaning of a sentence from its form and reflecting on the phonemic constituents of words require the ability to decenter, to shift one's attention from message content to the properties of language used to convey content. An essential feature of both metalinguistic operations and decentration is the ability to control one's thoughts, that is, to invoke control processing." According to the cognitive-developmental model, then, the developmental differences in control processing ability produce differences in the development of metalinguistic abilities necessary for acquiring basic decoding and comprehension-monitoring skills, in turn leading to poor reading.

Our results would suggest a more reciprocal relationship between metalinguistic skills and reading. Although it could be that certain metalinguistic skills are brought about by decentration or control processing with cognitive growth and increasing maturity in children, it appears that the acquisition of reading in itself could lead not only to greater decentration and better metalinguistic skills but also to better listening comprehension. The process of the child learning to map his or her auditory verbal memory onto the newly introduced written forms in reading would necessarily enhance the metalinguistic abilities as described by Tunmer. The "bootstrapping" relationships (Stanovich, 1986) between reading achievement and other aspects of development include, in our opinion, the development of metalinguistic skills, better linguistic competence, and more efficient language use.

Given the interactionist view that a certain amount of metalinguistic awareness may be a prerequisite for literacy acquisition, with literacy acquisition itself further facilitating the development of metalinguistic awareness, the levels of interaction between the two and the factors affecting them need to be investigated further. Researchers in this area have up to now concentrated on phonological awareness, which has been viewed as a bridge between language and literacy (Ehri, 1979, 1980, 1984; Bradley & Bryant, 1983; Tunmer & Nesdale, 1985; Morais, 1991). However, some recent investigations have suggested that it is alphabetic literacy in particular that promotes phonemic awareness as these skills were not seen in illiterate adults exposed to the same languages (Morais, Cary, Alegria, & Bertelson, 1979), nor in those exposed to non-alphabetic scripts (Prakash, Rekha, Nigam, & Karanth, 1993). It is likely that the metalinguistic skills related to syntactic awareness that we have studied here have a special bearing on languages like Kannada, which is a highly inflected polysyllabic agglutinative language. Unlike English, most syntactic markers in Kannada are bound morphemes, some of which result in morphophonemic transformations and are not affected to a great extent by word order. It is therefore likely that literacy acquisition has a greater influence on syntactic awareness in these languages in comparison with those like English, whose syntax is more dependent on free morphemes and word order.

These findings also have important implications for the centrality of syntax and the grammaticality judgement ability in particular in current linguistic theories. Similar differences in performance between English-speaking literate vs. illiterate adults and pre-literate children on metalinguistic tasks such as rhyme detection, phoneme deletion, morphological segmentation, and grammaticality judgement of sentences, led Scholes and Willis (1987a, b) to suggest that illiterates and pre-literates perform at a "level 1 grammar" that is simpler, less abstract and less mature than the "level 2 grammar" of literates. Literacy acquisition is said to bring about the transition from level 1 to level 2 grammar. These divergent facets of metalinguistic awareness, the role of literacy in their development, and their implications both for cognition and language use need to be investigated further and incorporated into models of language and cognition.

REFERENCES

Bever, T.G. (1970). The cognitive basis for linguistic structure. In J.R. Hayes (Ed.), *Cognition and development of language*. New York: Wiley.

Bradley, L., & Bryant, P.E. (1983). Categorizing sounds and learning to read—a causal connection. *Nature, 301*, 419–421.

De Villiers, P.A., & De Villiers, J.G. (1972). Early judgement of semantic and syntactic acceptability by children. *Journal of Psycholinguistic Research, 1*, 294–310.

Donaldson, M. (1978). *Children minds*. Glasgow: Collins.

Ehri, L.C. (1979). Linguistic insight; Threshold of reading acquisitions. In T.G. Waller & G.E. Mackinnon (Eds.), *Reading research: Advances in theory and practice* (pp. 63–111). New York: Harcourt Brace Jovanovich.

Ehri, L.C. (1980). The development of orthographic images. In U. Frith (Ed.), *Cognitive processes in spelling*. London: Academic Press.

Ehri, L.C. (1984). How orthography alters spoken language competencies in children learning to read and spell. In J. Downing & R. Valtin (Eds), *Language awareness and learning to read.* New York: Springer.

Fujiki, M., Briton, B., & Dunton, S. (1987). A grammatical judgement screening test for young elementary school-aged children. *Language, Speech and Hearing Services in Schools, 18*, 131–143.

Gleitman, L.R., & Gleitman, H. (1970). *Phrase and paraphrase: Some innovative uses of language*. New York: Morton.

Hakes, D.T., Evan J.S., & Tunmer, W.E. (1980). *The development of metalinguistic abilities in children*. Berlin: Springer.

Herriman, M.L., & Myhill, M.E. (1983). Metalinguistic awareness and education. In W.E. Tunmer, C. Pratt, & M.L. Herriman (Eds.), *Metalinguistic awareness in children: Theory, research and implications* (pp. 188–205). New York: Springer.

Karanth, P. (1984). *Inter-relationship of linguistic deviance and social deviance*. ICSSR young social scientists fellowship report, Mysore: CIIL.

Karanth, P., Ahuja, G.K., Nagaraj, D., Pandit, R., & Shivasshankar, N. (1991). *Language disorders in Indian neurological patients—A study in neurolinguistics in the Indian context.* A report—an inter-institutional project in collaboration with AIIMS, Delhi, and NIMHANS, Bangalore, funded by the Indian Council of Medical Research (no. 5/8/10–1 (Oto)/84–NCO–I IRIS Cell, ICMR 8403810).

Karanth, P., & Suchitra, M.G. (1993) Literacy acquisition and grammaticality judgements in children. In R. Scholes (Ed.), *Literacy and Language Awareness* (pp.143–156). Hillsdale, NJ: Lawrence Erlbaum Associates Inc.

Karmiloff-Smith, A. (1979). Language development after 5 years. In P. Fletcher & M. Garman (Eds.), *Language acquisition—Studies in first languages acquisition* (pp. 307–323). Cambridge: Cambridge University Press.

Linebarger, M.C., Schwartz, M.F., & Saffran, E.M. (1983). Sensitivity to grammatical structure in so called agrammatic aphasics. *Cognition, 13*, 361–392.

Luria, A.R. (1971). Towards the problem of historical nature of psychological processes. *International Journal of Psychology, 6*, 259–272.

Morais, J. (1991). Phonological awareness: A bridge between language and literacy. In D.J. Sawyer & B.J. Fox (Eds.), *Phonological awareness in reading: The evolution of current perspectives* (pp. 31–71). Berlin: Springer.

Morais, J., Cary, L., Alegria, J., & Bertelson, P. (1979). Does awareness of speech as a consequence of phonemes arise spontaneously? *Cognition, 7*, 323–331.

Nesdale, A.R., & Tunmer, W.E. (1983). The development of metalinguistic awareness: A methodological overview. In W.E. Tunmer, C. Pratt, & M.L. Herriman (Eds.), *Metalinguistic awareness in children: Theory, research and implications* (pp. 36–55). New York: Springer.

Prakash, P., Rekha, D., Nigam, R., & Karanth, P. (1993). Phonological awareness, orthography and literacy. In R. Scholes (Ed.), *Literacy and Language Awareness* (pp. 55–70). Hillsdale, NJ: Lawrence Erlbaum Associates Inc.

Pratt, C., Tunmer, W.E., & Bowey, J. (1984). Children's capacity to correct grammatical violations in syntax. *Journal of Child Language, 11*, 129–141.

Scholes, R.J., & Willis, B.J. (1987a). Language and literacy. *Journal of Literacy Semantics, 16*, 3–11.

Scholes, R.J., & Willis, B.J. (1987b). The illiterate native speaker of English: Oral language and intentionality. In J. Klesins & M. Radeneich (Eds.), *Links to literacy* (pp. 33–42). Miami: Florida Reading Association.

Scholl, D.M., & Ryan, E.B. (1980). Development of metalinguistic performance in early school years. *Language and Speech, 23*, 199–211.

Stanovich, K.E. (1986). (Cited in Tunmer, W.E.) Cognitive and linguistic factors in learning to read. In P.B. Gough, L. Ehri, & R. Treiman (Eds.) (1992). *Reading acquisition*. Hillsdale, NJ: Lawrence Erlbaum Associates Inc.

Tunmer, W.E. (1992). Cognitive and linguistic factors in learning to read. In P.B. Gough, L. Ehri, & R. Treiman (Eds.), *Reading acquisition*. Hillsdale, NJ: Lawrence Erlbaum Associates Inc.

Tunmer, W.E., & Bowey, J.A. (1980). The development of word segmentation skills in children. In A.R. Nesdale, C. Pratt, R. Grieve, J. Field, D. Fillingworth & J. Hogben (Eds.), *Advances in child development: Theory and Research*. Perth, WA: NCCD.

Tunmer, W.E., & Grieve, R. (1984). Syntactic awareness in children. In W.E. Tunmer, C. Pratt, & M.L. Herriman (Eds), *Metalinguistic awareness in children: Theory, research and implications* (pp. 92–104). New York: Springer.

Tunmer, W.E., & Nesdale, A.R. (1985). Phonemic segmentation skills and beginning reading. *Journal of Educational Psychology, 77*, 417–427.

Tunmer, W.E., Pratt, C., & Herriman, M.L. (1984). *Metalinguistic awareness in children: Theory, research and implications*. New York: Springer.

Van Kleek, A. (1982). The emergence of linguistic awareness: A cognitive framework. *Merrill-Palmer Quarterly, 28*, 237.

Van Kleek, A. (1984). Metalinguistic skills—Cutting across spoken and written languages and problem solving abilities. In G.P. Wallach & K.G. Butler (Eds.), *Language and learning disabilities in school age children* (pp. 128–153). Baltimore: Williams & Wilkins.

Vasantha, D., Sastry, J.V., & Maruth, R. (1989). *Grammaticality judgements by Telugu speaking elementary school children*. Interdisciplinary National Seminar on Language Processes and Language Disorders. Hyderabad: Osmania University.

15 The Consequences of Phonemic Awareness

José Morais
Université Libre de Bruxelles, Belgium

Régine Kolinsky
Université Libre de Bruxelles, and Fonds National de la Recherche Scientifique, Belgium

INTRODUCTION

In a recently published paper (Morais & Mousty, 1992), we examined the causes of phonemic awareness. In this chapter, we attempt to deal with its consequences. What is phonemic awareness good for?

The most immediate answer that comes to mind is that phonemic awareness is good for the acquisition of alphabetic literacy. Most of us agree that there is an important and systematic relation between phonemic awareness and literacy acquisition. Peter Bryant and Usha Goswami (1987, p. 439) said that "the discovery of a strong relationship between children's phonological awareness and their progress in learning to read is one of the great successes of modern psychology". This proposal was later emphasised by Isabelle and Alvin Liberman (1990) in a very persuasive paper about conceptions of reading instruction. What seems to raise a problem is the nature of the relation. For some years, there was a polemic about whether phonemic awareness is a correlate, a consequence, or a determinant of literacy acquisition. The polemic has somewhat faded, with most people coming to the conclusion that there must be reciprocal influence between the two.

Although the present text is concerned with the causal roles of phonemic awareness, a few introductory words about the dependence of phonemic awareness on learning to read and write in an alphabetic system may be useful.

Our group contributed to show that phonemic awareness does not emerge spontaneously; rather, it usually emerges during learning to read and write in an alphabetic system. Illiterate normal adults are unable to segment speech into its phoneme constituents in a conscious, intentional way. The fact seemed counterintuitive to many researchers, nevertheless it came out so neatly that sophisticated design and statistics would have just been an ornament. The illiterates scored less than 20% correct in a task involving deletion of a consonant, whereas ex-illiterates, in other words people from the same social and cultural milieu but who learned to read and write at adult age, scored higher than 70% in the same task (Morais, Cary, Alegria, & Bertelson, 1979). This difference was too dramatic to be attributed to chance. The finding was replicated in other countries, and also by comparing alphabetic to nonalphabetic literate people (Read, Zhang, Nie, & Ding, 1986). Thus, that learning to read and write in the alphabetic system promotes phonemic awareness is an unavoidable truth.

In more recent papers we proposed that, if we exclude explicit specific training,[1] phonemic awareness does not develop outside alphabetic instruction (Morais, Alegria, & Content, 1987a; Morais, 1991a, b). Two objections were raised against this idea. One is that the illiterates' lack of phonemic awareness is due to their weak cognitive capacities: Illiterates would be less intelligent than the ex-illiterates. Based on our experience of illiterate people, we never took this objection seriously. However, slightly exasperated by this recurrent objection, we eventually decided to test both illiterates and ex-illiterates with a form of the Raven's Progressive Matrices test (Morais & Cary, unpublished data). We found that illiterates were not poorer than ex-illiterates.[2]

The other objection is that some subjects, among our illiterate subjects, had non-negligible scores. Does this mean that these illiterates are aware of phonemes? We do not think so. A non-negligible score in one particular "phonemic awareness" task does not necessarily indicate the presence of phonemic awareness. Rather, it may reflect the fact that the subjects have found some strategy that is appropriate to deal with the particular task they have to perform. As a matter of fact, we found that, after variable amounts of simple corrective feedback, pre-literate kindergarten children could begin to respond correctly in the deletion task (Content, Kolinsky, Morais, & Bertelson, 1986). We also found that those children remained as poor as untrained children in an oddity task based on the initial consonant (Content, Morais, & Bertelson, 1987). Thus, it seems that the children merely discovered a successful strategy for deletion. This was probably the case, too, of the illiterate adults to whom we gave systematic corrective feedback (Morais et al., 1988): Most of them began, at different times, to respond correctly. In conclusion, it is possible that the few illiterates who obtained non-negligible scores in our earlier study (Morais et al., 1979) were quite efficient in finding a task-dependent appropriate strategy. It should be remarked that, in that study, we provided the subjects with a few

[1]Even this restriction, as we will discuss later, might be useless.

[2]Of course, both groups of subjects were mentally retarded by reference to the norms of educated people! This should not surprise us, as both illiterates and ex-illiterates did not benefit from schooling in childhood, and schooling may influence strongly the ability to perform some visual tasks (see, e.g. Kolinsky, Morais, & Brito Mendes, 1990; Kolinsky, Morais, Content, & Cary, 1987).

examples followed by 15 training trials (i.e. with corrective feedback). This amount of training may be sufficient for the discovery of a specific "trick" by a few subjects.

To obtain more information on this point, we tested more recently 25 illiterate adults in Brazil, giving only a few examples at the beginning, and no training trials at all (Scliar-Cabral, Morais, Nepomuceno, & Kolinsky, submitted). Twenty-four of the subjects did not give a single correct response. But one, a woman, had about 50% of correct responses. Was she aware of phonemes? We think she was not. As a matter of fact, she was also exceptional in a previous task of deletion of an initial vowel that constituted a syllable by itself. Whereas many illiterates are good in this task, she did not give a single correct response. Most of her responses were repetitions. Thus, having a tendency to produce responses beginning with a vowel, she was unable to delete a syllable, but she could often get the right answer in consonant deletion. Further evidence of her lack of phonemic awareness was obtained in an oddity task based on the initial consonant, where she performed at chance level.

Phonemic awareness thus emerges when one has to learn symbols that stand for phonemes. We do not wish to discuss here the question of whether or not phonemic awareness can develop when it is taught in isolation. It is difficult to obtain clear evidence on this issue, because even when the training programme used by the experimenter only includes exercises on intentional phonemic analysis or synthesis, the pre-literate child may be receiving some instruction on the alphabetic code either at home or at school. This extra-experiment training can hardly be controlled, and the conjunction of the two trainings can be entirely responsible for the progress made in phonemic awareness. For the present purpose, it is enough to emphasise that, if we put aside training experiments, there is no unequivocal evidence of phonemic awareness being independent of literacy aquisition.

As regards the other direction of the interaction, namely that phonemic awareness is good for literacy acquisition, most people agree with this proposition, but not everybody does. There are people who, like Goodman (1967) or Smith (1971), reject the usefulness of analytic sequential transcoding for beginning reading. As we will see later, there are also people who recognise the importance of this type of transcoding, but who believe that it may be acquired in an automatic, implicit, associative way (Cossu & Marshall, 1990; Marshall & Cossu, 1990, 1991). Thus, although the idea that phonemic awareness is important for literacy acquisition is not original at all, it certainly deserves careful examination. This will constitute the first part of this chapter.

The role of phonemic awareness may, however, not be limited to its consequences on literacy acquisition. We should not forget that the study of phonemic awareness has been contributing to phonological theorising. The linguistic notion of phoneme was put forward only one century ago, by Baudouin de Courtenay, although in some way and to some extent millions of people had discovered and used it before him.

More importantly for the present purpose, phonemic awareness may have some influence on the processing of spoken language. We have always considered that it is unmotivated to use the illiterates' lack of phonemic awareness as an argument for the idea that phonetic segments cannot be extracted during speech perception and serve in lexical access (Morais et al., 1979). In our opinion, the fact that illiterates do not have conscious representations of phonemes does not tell us anything about the kind of units that are relevant in unconscious processing. Yet, we think that it is important to compare literate and illiterate people in order to check whether or not phonemic awareness affects speech processing. This forms the second part of this chapter.

PHONEMIC AWARENESS IS A CRUCIAL FACTOR OF SUCCESS IN ALPHABETIC LITERACY ACQUISITION

This direction of the interaction is not only more polemic than the other one. It is also more difficult to demonstrate, and the researchers who have attempted to do so needed both much more ingenious experiments and much more sophisticated statistics than were needed in studying the other direction of the interaction. Yet, we think that some of them were successful.

One strong demonstration was provided by Lundberg, Frost, and Petersen (1988). These authors used an 8-month programme to develop different forms of phonological awareness in pre-school children. At the end of the school year, the trained children were no better than the controls in either letter knowledge or higher-order language comprehension. They were, as expected, superior to the controls on metaphonological tests, especially on phonemic segmentation. Later on, in first grade, the children were tested again, but on other abilities. The trained subjects were no better than the controls on either mathematics or the Raven's Progressive Matrices, but they were better on both written-word recognition and spelling. A retest at the second grade showed that the superiority of the trained subjects on these abilities tended to increase.

There are several other indications of the causal influence of phonemic awareness. Ohnmacht (1969), for example, found that first-graders improved in reading to a greater extent if, in conjunction with word learning, they were taught both letter names and sounds than if they were taught only letter names. Williams (1980) observed larger progress in word and pseudoword reading in a group that received training on phonemic analysis and synthesis as well as on letter–sound association during the whole school year than in a group that did not receive such instruction.

Cunningham (1990) taught kindergarden children and first-graders to associate the phonemic constituents of words with wooden chips, to delete a phoneme from an utterance, and to categorise utterances according to common segmental constituents. She found a positive influence of this instruction on reading ability, compared with a control group that was presented with stories and commented on them during the same amount of time. In first-graders, the positive effect was magnified if the programme also included a conceptual training showing both the relevance of phonemic abilities for reading and how these abilities are used in reading.

Ball and Blachman (1988; 1991) observed that training letter–sound knowledge alone has no impact on word reading and spelling, whereas training both letter–sound knowledge and phonemic segmentation has a strong effect. In a similar vein, Helfgott (1976) found that pseudoword reading benefited more from the conjoined training of knowledge of grapheme–phoneme correspondences and phonemic synthesis ability than from training of only one of these abilities. Bradley and Bryant (1983) also reported that children who received instruction on both a phonological task and letter–sound associations became better readers and spellers than controls. Instruction on the phonological task alone did not yield a significant advantage.

To the best of our knowledge, Ball and Blachman's studies and Helfgott's one are the only training studies in which the instruction given to one group did concern only the letter–sound correspondences. These studies, taken together with Bradley and Bryant's (1983) one, where one group received only metaphonological instruction, indicate that either of the two competences, namely knowledge of grapheme–phoneme correspondences and intentional phonemic abilities, is insufficient by itself. It is only when these abilities are trained in conjunction that reading and spelling abilities develop significantly. This is an important notion because it implies that, from the beginning, the acquisition of phonemic awareness and the acquisition of alphabetic literacy are intimately associated. Phonemic awareness is not an external factor that triggers literacy acquistion. It is rather a component of literacy acquisition.

Yet, phonemic awareness is a rather abstract term, which refers to the set of conscious representations of the individual phonemes of a language (Morais, 1993; Morais et al., 1987a). Our group called attention to the necessary distinction between phonemic awareness and phonemic abilities, which are the abilities to use the conscious representations of phonemes in particular situations (Morais et al., 1987). Different phonemic abilities, as for example analysis of utterances into phonemes and synthesis of phonemes into larger phonological units, may require different types of operations as well as different memory capacities. We explicitly mention these two abilities because phonemic training studies suggest that spelling may benefit mostly from phonemic analysis (Helfgott, 1976), and reading mostly from phonemic synthesis (Ball & Blachman, 1991; Lundberg et al., 1988). A different type of study, in which partial correlations were calculated at different times of the school year, also suggests that phonemic synthesis, but not phonemic analysis, significantly contributes to reading (Perfetti, Beck, Bell, & Hughes, 1987).

Recently, Bryant, MacLean, Bradley, and Crossland (1990) outlined three models of the relations between phonological abilities and reading acquisition. In one of the models, which is attributed to our group, learning reading and spelling leads to phoneme detection. We do not recognise ourselves in this model for two reasons. First, it does not incorporate the reverse influence; and second, it does not consider the possibility of a common factor to rhyming and phonemic skills (see discussion of this point in Morais, 1991a). The other two models postulate only an unidirectional influence from phonological abilities to reading and spelling. We think that all these models are too simple and do not capture the "special magic", as Adams (1990) calls it, that lies in the linking of these two types of skills.

This special magic has a name: It is the alphabetic principle, which is based on the association between graphemes and phonemes. Not surprisingly, its understanding requires the knowledge of both. Moreover, the importance of integrating knowledge both of the graphemes and of the linguistic units onto which they map is probably not limited to the alphabetic principle. As a matter of fact, Amano (1989), a Japanese researcher, found that reading and spelling in Hiragana improved to a greater extent when a programme of teaching reading and spelling in this system was preceded by a programme of syllabic analysis than when it was carried out alone.

Our view implies the usefulness of analytic sequential transcoding for beginning reading. It also implies that this phonological transcoding is acquired through *explicit* knowledge of both phonemes, graphemes, and of their correspondences. So, it is very important for this view, which is the dominant one in the domain, to investigate to what extent this knowledge has to be conscious in order to support phonological transcoding in reading and writing.

Cossu and Marshall (1990) and Marshall and Cossu (1990; 1991) took a position that is at odds with this view. These authors presented the case of a child, T.A., who displays excellent phonological transcoding abilities, but who would have not developed phonemic awareness. They concluded from this apparent dissociation that *implicit* operations on graphemic and phonological strings may be sufficient to establish phonological transcoding. They (Cossu & Marshall, 1990, p. 38) suggested that: "the only cognitive prerequisites for the development of T.A.'s transcoding skill lie in his (limited) abilities in the domain of *spoken* language". Under this proposition, phonemic awareness would be optional with no causal effect on literacy acquisition.

The theoretical motivation for this proposition is the notion that many of the components of the cognitive system involved in reading and spelling have a biological origin and are modular. We share this belief with Cossu and Marshall. For example, in a recent paper (Morais & Mousty, 1992), we present phonemic awareness as a metalinguistic capacity with both linguistic and metalinguistic precursors, and we relate difficulties in acquiring phonemic awareness to anomalies in phonological development. However, we diverge from Cossu and Marshall when they consider that a marked insistence on the causal role of phonemic awareness is more consistent with the notion that the alphabetic system is a pure cultural invention than with the notion that literacy has biological roots. Indeed, the orthogaphic systems derive from and represent language (see Studdert-Kennedy & Goodell, Chapter 4), which is biologically determined. Still, not everything that is allowed by biology develops spontaneously. No orthographic system develops spontaneously as a consequence of cognitive and linguistic maturation. In the history of mankind, literate men and women constitute a minority, yet we never heard that they could be considered mutants. In the particular case of the alphabet, phonemic awareness is an essential part of its mastery. There is no reason why a view that relates written to spoken language cannot insist on the importance of phonemic awareness to the acquisition of alphabetic literacy.

Moreover, we disagree with Cossu and Marshall's conclusions, because we think that the lack of phonemic awareness is not demonstrated in the cases they studied. Regarding the case of T.A. (Cossu & Marshall, 1990), which we mention because it was presented by the authors as good support for their position, one should remark that the subject has a full-scale IQ of 47 and a digit span of 2 items. Thus, it is very likely that he is cognitively too impaired to understand the instructions provided in most metalinguistic tests. In particular, he was competely unable to understand what the examiner asked him to do in rhyming and blending tests. Secondly, it is important to note that at school he received explicit "analytic" training in grapheme–phoneme correspondences. Thirdly, in a test requiring the deletion of the first two phonemes from words with 4–5 and 8–9 phonemes, he obtained 43% correct responses. This is, we think, an excellent performance for a child who is mentally impaired and has a digit span of 2 items. Clearly, he has understood this task. It is at least premature to state that this child has no phonemic awareness. Yet, even if we consider that 43% is a non-negligible score, it does not necessary reflect phonemic awareness. Indeed, since we have no information about the items on which T.A. succeeded nor about the nature of his errors, it is possible that he succeeded sometimes by writing mentally the spoken word, then deleting the first two letters, and finally, reading mentally the remaining part. This implies conscious segmentation of the alphabetic material, which he is highly familiar with. Perhaps T.A. has assimilated the link between graphemes and phonemes without separating these two entites as we do. A further possibility is that he succeeded on items in which the first two phonemes correspond to the initial syllable.

For those who prefer to look at the empty half of the glass rather than at the full one and who are thus convinced that 43% is a poor score, remember that deleting two phonemes from a relatively long utterance is one of the most difficult tasks used so far to tap phonemic awareness. After the identification of the two first phonemes of the utterance, T.A. has probably no more memory capacity available to complete the task. Phoneme detection and classification may provide much easier tasks, but the research strategy used by Cossu and Marshall was oriented towards the confirmation of their position rather than to the testing of it.

Another possible interpretation of T.A.'s "poor" performance is that he has acquired a primitive form of phonemic awareness that is sufficient to understand grapheme–phoneme correspondences,[3] but insufficient to perform correctly in phonemic awareness tasks. The notion underlying this interpretation is that a child may learn to attend to the phonemic constituents of speech without developing a concept of phoneme that could be used in any kind of mental manipulation. This distinction was suggested to us, for instance, by the results of the Brazilian illiterate study mentioned earlier (Scliar-Cabral et al., submitted), in which we gave no training trials. In this study, we tested, in addition to illiterate people, a group of people who had normal schooling for 4 years and who can read and write to some extent. Unexpectedly, the 4-year schooling group was as poor as the illiterate group in the consonant deletion task (3% and 2%, respectively). As they were provided with a few examples, but not with training trials, this suggests that those subjects had no easy access to the concept of phoneme. On the other hand, they were probably able to attend to the phonemic constituents of speech, as suggested by the fact that they performed above chance, and far better than illiterates, in an oddity task based on the initial consonant.

Whatever the right interpretation of T.A.'s results, and whether or not we should distinguish several levels of phonemic awareness, it would be foolish to cast doubt on the association between phonemic awareness and alphabetic literacy on the basis of the kind of data presented by Cossu and Marshall. In normal children, the association between phonemic tasks scores and literacy measures is high because the phonemic tasks reflect phonemic awareness fairly well. This latter association is not obscured by other components of the phonemic tasks, which we refer to as general cognitive demands. However, in hyperlexic children, these general cognitive demands of the tasks may be a source of difficulty, and may thus hide the relation between phonemic awareness and alphabetic literacy. If we are right, T.A. should have shown as much difficulty in deleting the two initial syllables of a multisyllabic utterance as in deleting the two initial phonemes. We know that normal pre-literate children and illiterate adults are usually able to segment utterances into syllables. Assessing whether or not T.A. was *specifically* unable to manipulate phonemes intentionally is a further test of their interpretation, which Cossu and Marshall should have carried out, but which they have not.

More recently, Cossu, Rossini, and Marshall (1993) reaffirmed their view on the basis of a similar argument: They found several children with Down's syndrome to be able to read to some extent but to be unable both to count phonemes and to delete the first two phonemes of an utterance. Their paper received several criticisms. Bertelson (1993) and Byrne (1993) formulated methodological remarks close to those we presented earlier. With Philippe Mousty we are currently investigating whether children of low IQ (around 50) who can read and write are

[3]Unfortunately, the authors did not indicate whether or not they tested T.A. for his knowledge of letter–sound correspondences.

able or unable to perform phoneme deletion and segmentation on short items. Our results are clearly positive, thus suggesting that the subjects' failure reported by Cossu et al. (1993) is related to the difficulty of the tests used.

We cannot but disagree with Cossu and Marshall's proposal that the mapping between phonemes and graphemes occurs "automatically" in normal learning to read and write. There is strong evidence, we repeat, of the causal role of the awareness of phonemes in the acquisition of alphabetic literacy. We have seen that phonemic awareness training contributes, in conjunction with training on grapheme–phoneme correspondences, to rapid improvements in reading and spelling. This could not be the case if the mapping between graphemes and phonemes was merely an implicit learning phenomenon. Furthermore, the results of the training studies are inconsistent with any model (such as the one recently proposed by Morton & Frith, 1993) that would not accept a direct, interactive influence between phonemic awareness and knowledge of grapheme–phoneme correspondences.

Cossu and Marshall's proposal is also unable to afford a reasonable interpretation of why instructional reading methods should matter for reading success. Indeed, in their view, any method allowing exposure to grapheme–phoneme correspondences should work equally well. Our own experience in the comparison of the effects of instructional methods is that the *phonic* methods lead to much faster acquisition of word and pseudoword reading than the whole-word methods. Moreover, we did not find one single child who could read a substantial number of novel words, or of pseudowords, without having received beforehand some instruction on the alphabetic code. In one study (Alegria, Morais, d'Alimonte, & Seyl, submitted), we found that more than half of the first-graders who were learning to read according to a whole-word method read fewer words than the worst reader among the children who were learning to read according to a phonic method. Moreover, about one-third of the "phonic" children read more words than the best reader among the "whole-word" children.

The great majority of the "whole-word" children were unable both to read pseudowords and to segment into phonemes. However, we found in this group a few subjects who were able both to read pseudowords and to score high in the consonant deletion task. For all of the subjects except one, we could inquire among their relatives. The inquiry showed that the children had received explicit instruction on the alphabetic principle at home.

We also found a few subjects who were able to read pseudowords but were unable to perform the consonant deletion task. Interestingly, all of these exceptional subjects were from a highly literate milieu. At first sight, then, it would seem that it is possible to develop phonological decoding without phonemic awareness. However, we were puzzled by the fact that all these exceptional subjects were surprisingly poor in syllable deletion, so perhaps they failed the consonant deletion test for reasons other than the lack of phonemic awareness. One possible reason, related to the fact that we used pseudowords, is that they might have some reluctance to operate on these stimuli. Another possible reason, contributing to artefactual good performance in pseudoword reading, is that the pseudoword reading test was created by changing only one consonant in words that were highly familiar to the subjects. Therefore, the following year we examined 37 first-graders from the same setting, using words in the deletion task, and pseudowords differing in every consonant from familiar words in the reading test. This time we found no exceptional subject. All children who manifested phonological decoding also displayed phonemic awareness.

The question of whether or not a child can discover the alphabetic principle while receiving no explicit instruction of it at all has now been clearly answered in a very systematic and elegant set of experiments carried out by Brian Byrne (see Byrne, 1992). The general technique Byrne devised may be illustrated as follows. A pre-literate child with no knowledge of grapheme–phoneme correspondences is taught to read the words *mat* and *sat*. The child is then presented with the written word *mow* and required to choose between *mow* and *sow* as pronunciations.

Performance in this forced-choice transfer task was at chance level for all children. However, the transfer performance was high if the symbols stood for words or even nonsense syllables rather than phonemes. Thus, failure to transfer in the phonemic-based test was not due to general difficulty. A similar transfer failure was also observed for another intra-syllabic constituent, namely the rime. Learning first a word-based correspondence did not put the child in a position more advantageous to discover a phoneme-based correspondence. Moreover, providing the child with more than one item sharing the same initial phoneme and the same initial letter did not contribute to elicit above-chance transfer performance, thus suggesting that using phonemic-based word families without making the correspondence explicit is of no help.

A further set of experiments (Byrne & Fielding-Barnsley, 1990) highlights the conditions of success. When the children received training on phonemic segmentation before given the paired associate learning and transfer tests, it came out that none of the children who succeeded in phonemic segmentation (two-thirds of the group) was able to accomplish the transfer test correctly. Phonemic segmentation without knowledge of the correspondences is inefficient. In contrast, when the children received phonemic training (both on segmentation and on segment identity) as well as instruction on letter–sound correspondences, all the children who succeeded both to segment syllables into phonemes and to associate sounds to letters reached the criterion on the transfer test. It is important to remark that those children who learned to associate sounds to letters but who remained unable to segment into phonemes failed the transfer test. Thus, learning letter–sound correspondences alone is also insufficient to acquire the alphabetic principle and to be able to use it in reading new words.

One may conclude from these results that reading new words can only be achieved if the children receive *explicit* instruction both on the phonemes and on their graphemic correspondents. Of course, as mentioned by the authors themselves, one cannot discard the possibility that exposure to larger families of phonemically related words than the ones they used would lead to spontaneous discovery of the alphabetic principle. However, we have no empirical demonstration of this.

We have seen that, contrary to Cossu and Marshall's view, learning to read an alphabet-based orthography requires or, at least, receives a strong impulse from the conjunction of phonemic awareness and knowledge of grapheme–phoneme correspondences. At this point, one can ask whether these two competences, which seem to be necessary to alphabetic literacy acquisition, are also sufficient. Indeed, all the children who succeeded in the transfer test had also learned to segment syllables and to associate sounds to letters. However, about 10% of the children who acquired these two abilities were unable to achieve the transfer test (Byrne & Fielding-Barnsley, 1991). It seems that, for a minority of children, something more is needed. The additional ability may be the understanding of how to use phonemic awareness and knowledge of grapheme–phoneme correspondences when reading. One should remember Cunningham's (1990) suggestion about the usefulness of conceptual instruction in addition to procedural training.

To state that the child needs to develop phonemic awareness and knowledge of phoneme–grapheme correspondence in order to develop reading in an alphabetic system does not imply, however, that the child is merely passively learning the (explicitly thought) alphabetic principle.

In Byrne and Fielding-Barnsley's (1990) study, most, though not all, of the children who were successful in the training test could generalise the newly acquired knowledge of one particular grapheme–phoneme correspondence to another, and could also generalise from one word position to another. For example, training on the identification of /s/–/m/, followed by training on reading *sat–mat*, then by training on the phonemic correspondences for "f" and "b", and finally by learning to read *fin–bin*, was sufficient to allow successful transfer to *fun–bun*. In other words, there was no need of a phonemic training on /f/–/b/. Knowledge of the alphabetic principle may be displayed for untrained phonemes, which means that there is no need to master the whole alphabet in order to possess the alphabetic principle. Likewise, learning the identification of one phoneme at the beginning of the word allowed the application of the alphabetic principle at the initial as well as at the final position, and vice-versa.

These findings are important, because they suggest that the child *both learns and discovers* the alphabetic principle. The child does not seem to be able to apply the alphabetic principle if he or she does not receive explicit instruction on the phonemic representation of language and on the alphabetic code. On the other hand, it is also correct to say that the child discovers the alphabetic principle, for the explicit instruction received concerns a set of examples, not the principle itself. The child extracts a general rule from the examples. Being provided with explicit information about phonemes and about grapheme–phoneme correspondences, the child discovers the alphabetic principle.

THE EFFECTS OF PHONEMIC AWARENESS ON SPEECH RECOGNITION ABILITIES

In this section of the chapter, we examine` the possible influences of phonemic awareness on the processes used in spoken word recognition. Although the ability to recognise spoken words is well developed before the acquisition of literacy, and therefore of phonemic awareness, the acquisition of phonemic awareness might elicit additional and perhaps more efficient procedures to cope with spoken words.

In the past years, in collaboration with S.L. Castro, from the University of Porto (see Morais, Castro, & Kolinsky, 1991), we have compared literate and illiterate people on some phenomena that are observed in speech recognition tasks and that seem to involve phonetic or phonemic processing. In order to study speech recognition, i.e. in order to tap unconscious processing, simple perceptual or recognition tasks are more appropriate than metaphonological tasks like segment monitoring (see, for discussion, Dupoux, & Mehler, 1992; Morais, 1985). Yet, the speech recognition system itself involves several stages of processing. Distinguishing those phenomena that are affected by alphabetisation from those that are not may contribute to a better understanding of the architecture of the speech recognition system. It is our working assumption that those phenomena affected by alphabetisation have their origin at relatively late stages of processing.

The demonstration of alphabetisation effects on spoken word recognition may also be relevant for the theoretical confrontation of modular and interactionist approaches of lexical access. Let us consider an interactionist model that postulates the interactive activation between layers of speech units, from say phonetic features to words, and from words back to features. If so, any factor that influences one layer, even at a high structural level, should influence the lower levels. In other words, an entirely interactionist model predicts that the effects of alphabetisation, if any, should occur everywhere in the structure of the speech system, and should not be circumscribed to only one or some of the levels. This is of course not the case of a modularist model. Indeed, one might attempt to accommodate the finding of a circumscribed effect of alphabetisation, suggesting that this finding is the spurious consequence of a very different pattern of connection weights between the levels affected by alphabetisation and those not affected. However, this kind of objection, besides making the empirical confrontation of modular and interactionist models very hard, would lead to attributing to the interactionist structure a modular functioning, which means anyway at least partial rejection of the interactionist principle.

There is a further motivation for the study of alphabetisation effects on speech recognition. This study may contribute to distinguish abilities that would be at the origin of reading impairments from those that would be mere consequence of reading backwardness. In Morais and Mousty (1992), we reviewed several demonstrations of correlations between phonological anomalies and reading difficulties. However, even when the correlation may be supposed to result from a direct cause–effect link between two variables, one needs additional evidence in order to specify the direction of causality. This additional evidence may be provided, in the present case, by testing illiterates. If illiterates show no indication of the phonological anomalies displayed by the backward readers, then these anomalies cannot be the consequence of a low level of literacy. They might, instead, be a cause of dyslexia, or be associated to one of its causes.

The observation of alphabetisation effects on speech recognition does not mean necessarily that these effects are due to the fact that alphabetic literates, contrary to illiterates, possess phonemic awareness. Those effects might be due to other competences possessed by literates, but not by illiterates. It is the analysis of the requirements of the tasks used that may allow or not the consideration, in each case, of phonemic awareness as a possible causal factor.

Generally speaking, the results of our studies have shown that there is no literacy effect on the phonetic processing of the sensory input. For instance, the rate of occurrence of phonetic feature blendings (Cutting, 1976; Day, 1968), which seem to occur when the acoustic information is evaluated by reference to speech categories, as well as the slopes of the phonetic categorisation curves (Liberman, Cooper, Shankweiler, & Studdert-Kennedy, 1967), are not affected by whether the subject is literate or illiterate (Castro & Morais, in preparation, a; Morais, Castro, Scliar-Cabral, Kolinsky, & Content, 1987b).

Phonetic feature blendings were observed in a dichotic listening situation in which two different Portuguese CVCV words were presented simultaneously, one to each ear (Morais et al., 1987b). Two facts are worth noting. First, blendings of the phonetic features of the dichotic initial consonants (which were always double-contrast stops) were obtained even when the consonant reported was unvoiced, which precludes an interpretation of the effect in terms of acoustic combination of the pre-voicing present in the voiced consonant with the stimulus delivered in the opposite ear. Moreover, the vowel following the initial consonant was different in the two ears, which means that the place of articulation value involved in the dichotic blending was abstract (phonetic) information, rather than physical (acoustic) (see also Studdert-Kennedy, Shankweiler, & Pisoni, 1972). Secondly, there was no correlation between the number of dichotic feature blendings and the total number of errors made. This finding suggests that the automatic, pre-attentive processes of phonetic processing do not contribute in any significant way to individual differences in performance. Indeed, one would expect a modular (biologically constrained) system to contribute much less than attentional, i.e. optional (learned), procedures to performance variability. It is also worth noting, in the context of the latter remark, that when differences in overall performance are controlled for, illiterates and literates show similar rates of right-ear advantage in the recognition of the same material (Castro & Morais,

1987). It seems that the cerebral organisation of the processes used to deal with spoken words is not affected by literacy (see Carr & Posner, Chapter 13, for some suggestions about changes in the cerebral organisation of the processes used to deal with written words during literacy acquisition).

In Castro and Morais (in preparation, a), phonetic categorisation curves were obtained for pairs of Portuguese words differing in voicing ("bala"–"pala" and "gola"–"cola"). Different durations of pre-voicing were either added to an unvoiced stimulus or deleted from a voiced stimulus, yielding prevoicing durations of 0, 20, 40, 60, 80, and 100msec. As already indicated, no consistent differences in the slope of the identification curves were observed as a function of alphabetisation. Alphabetic literacy does not seem to affect categorical perception. Identification curves were also obtained in a further study (Morais, de Gelder, & Verhaeghe, in preparation) for the /ba–da/ continuum. Their slopes were similar in literates and illiterates. This situation was also used in conjunction with optical information about the speaker's lip movements, for comparison of the susceptibility of the two populations to the McGurk effect (cf. McGurk & McDonald, 1976). The shift of the identification curve when a visual "da" rather than a visual "ba" was used was similar in the literates and illiterates. The lack of an alphabetisation effect on this phenomenon reinforces the proposition put forward by Liberman and Mattingly (1985), according to which the integration of acoustical and optical information about speech is achieved by a modular, biologically programmed system.

The findings reported so far indicate no difference in speech perception between literates and illiterates. If one assumes that speech processes insensitive to alphabetisation are likely to take place rather early, before the intervention of attention, than in later stages, then the present findings suggest that feature blendings, categorical perception and auditory-visual integration of speech information are all preattentive phenomena.

This argument holds if one observes significant differences between literates and illiterates as regards other, hence presumably later, processes of spoken word recognition. As a matter of fact, we found differences between literates and illiterates with respect to listening strategies that bear on the phonemic level.

In Morais et al. (1987b), all the segments of the two CVCV dichotic stimuli presented on each trial were different (with the exception of the last V, in some trials). The subject's task was to report the stimulus presented in one ear, which was previously indicated to the subject. We calculated the proportion of errors that differed from the actual stimulus in only one segment (*segmental errors*, such as giving "pano" for "cano"), and the proportion of errors in which at least one syllable was completely misrecognised (*global errors*, such as "dono" for "cano"). Among segmental errors, those on the initial consonant were by far the most frequent. On the assumption that phonemic awareness (which has certainly been acquired by the literate subjects but not by the illiterate ones) elicits the development of an attentional procedure focusing on the phonemic constituents of speech, we predicted that the proportion of segmental errors would be greater in the literate than in the illiterate subjects. As a matter of fact, we did observe that difference: The proportion of errors limited to the initial consonant increased with literacy (0.24, 0.29, 0.39, in illiterates, semiliterates, and literates, respectively), whereas the proportion of global errors decreased (0.23, 0.19, and 0.13, respectively).

However, the errors made by subjects who present a high rate of correct responses may approximate the stimulus to a greater extent than those made by the poorest subjects, so that the difference observed between literate and illiterate subjects could be a trivial consequence of the higher performance obtained by the literates. In order to take this into account, we compared subgroups consisting of the poorest literates and the best illiterates in terms of correct responses, so that the mean performance of the two subgroups was exactly the same. Despite similarity in overall performance, a higher proportion of segmental errors was still found in the literate subgroup compared to the illiterate subgroup. It thus seems that literate and illiterate people use to some extent different procedures, and this difference seems to concern the segmental structure of speech in some way.

There are in the literature some indications that literate people can use a strategy of focusing attention on phonemes in order to improve speech recognition. For example, Nusbaum, Walley, Carrell, and Ressler (1982) showed that the listener may avoid the illusion of phonemic restoration by attempting to focus attention on the processing of the phonetic structure of the stimulus. Moreover, Samuel and Ressler (1986) found that selective processing of the critical phoneme in the phonemic restoration situation was possible when both the lexical identity of the stimulus and the identity and position of the critical phoneme were known in advance. In our situation, nothing pushed the subjects to focus attention on the phonemic constituents of the stimulus. It may be, however, that literate people tend to use such a procedure in difficult listening conditions. Actually, in a situation in which the CVCV word was presented in one ear with noise in the other ear, we again obtained the difference between literates and illiterates in the proportion of segmental errors (Castro & Morais, in preparation, b). This effect is thus not specifically tied to the dichotic listening situation.

It remained to show that the procedure of attentional focusing on the phonemic constituents of speech, which would be at the origin of a significant part of the segmental errors, is really a strategy, under subject's control. In order to obtain evidence on this point, we attempted to manipulate attention in literate subjects (university students). We asked explicitly the subjects of the experimental group to attempt to recognise the word presented under noise masking by focusing attention on the constituent phonemes. More precisely, these subjects received the following instruction: "All the words you are going to hear are sequences of CVCV, and the first consonant is always taken from among /b, d, g, p, t, k/. Try to pay attention to these constituents, to the elementary sounds, not to the global word, and tell me which word you hear". The subjects of the other, control, group were simply asked to recognise the same words. The results showed the same level of accuracy in the two groups, but in the experimental group the proportion of segmental errors was higher (0.32) and the proportion of global errors was lower (0.15) than in the control group (0.26 and 0.22, respectively), the interaction between groups and error types being significant (Castro & Morais, in preparation, b). It thus seems that literate subjects can attend to phonemic constituents in recognition tasks, and that this process is, at least partially, under voluntary control.

The segmental vs. global type of errors distinction is, as we have just seen, influenced in all likelihood by phonemic awareness. Not all effects of alphabetisation are, of course, mediated by phonemic awareness. The phenomenon called "phonological fusion" (cf. Cutting, 1975) is, as we shall see, influenced by alphabetisation, but in this case it is orthographic knowledge that is the critical factor.

The phonological fusion phenomenon is observed in the dichotic listening situation, like the dichotic feature blending. It consists in the combination of the initial consonants of the two dichotic stimuli so that the listener perceives illusorily a consonantic cluster. For example, the presentation of "lack" and "back" yields the incorrect perception of "black". This illusion, contrary to the feature blending, may have its origin relatively late in the perceptual process: It is little influenced by acoustic factors, respects the phonotactic constraints of the language ("lback" is never heard), and occurs more frequently when the output of the eventual consonantic clustering yields a word than when it yields a nonword (Cutting, 1975).

In one of our experiments (Castro & Morais, unpublished data), we used pairs of words in such a way that the phonological fusion would be either consistent or not with the spelling of the corresponding word. Thus, in the case of "cara"–"lara", and "pena"–"lena", the phonological fusion of the two initial consonants ([kl] and [pl], respectively) is consistent with the spelling of the words ("clara" and "plena"). In these cases, we observed a high percentage of phonological fusions (on the average about 60%), and this percentage was roughly the same in the illiterate and the literate subjects.

However, in the case of the pairs "fiz"–"liz" and "par"–"lar", the phonological fusion is not consistent with the spelling of the resulting words, since the words [fliʃ] and [plar][4] are spelled "feliz" and "pelar", respectively, i.e. with a silent "e" between the two consonants. For these pairs of words, the illiterates showed 55% of phonological fusions, thus a percentage similar to the one observed for resulting words which are not spelled with a silent "e". Interestingly, the

[4]These pronunciations correspond to European Portuguese, not to Brazilian Portuguese, but this is irrelevant here, as the experiment was run in Portugal.

phonological fusions for these pairs of words were observed much less frequently in the literate subjects (17%). It thus seems that knowledge of the orthography can inhibit the occurrence of the phonological fusion. For people who know how [fliʃ] and [plar] are spelled, the phonological fusion can hardly be accepted, although the corresponding written words were not presented to them, nor were they asked to write what they heard.

It is not the first time that a phonological decision is shown to depend on orthographic knowledge. For instance, such an influence was observed by Seidenberg and Tanenhaus (1979) in a task requiring the subjects to judge whether or not two words rhyme, and by Taft and Hambly (1985) in a task of detection of a sequence of phonemes. However, the effects shown in those two studies should be distinguished from ours; they were a kind of Stroop effect, in the sense that the orthographic representation, after being activated from its connections with the corresponding phonological representations, interferes with the latter at the decision stage and provokes a response delay. There is, however, no substantial effect, if any, at the level of response accuracy. In the case of the alphabetisation effect on phonological fusions, the mechanism must be different, because it is the conscious perceptual output that is affected, not only the response time. Two different decision stages are involved in the two cases. In the rhyme judgement and phoneme detection situations the spelling effect occurs at the *response* decision stage, whereas in our situation it takes place at the stage of *recognition* decision. Thus, the effect of orthographic knowledge of phonological fusions is the more precocious effect of this type of knowledge on phonological processing obtained so far. This implies that the upper level of the system responsible for the recognition of spoken words cannot be only lexical or morphophonemic, but must include (or must be connected with) the representations of orthographic forms.

The effect of phonological fusion gives evidence of intrasyllabic analysis. The [b] of "back" can only precede "lack" in the conscious perceptual representation if it is previously (unconsciously) separated from the remainder of the syllable (the rime). Thus, it seems that, in both English and Portuguese, an unconscious analysis into phonemes is carried out during the perceptual processing of spoken words. The fact that illiterates display the phonological fusion effect, too, and at roughly the same frequency of occurrence as literates, implies that the unconscious segmentation of utterances into phonemes is not a consequence of alphabetisation. We knew already (see first section of this chapter) that illiterates do not possess conscious representations of phonemes. We now discover that illiterates do possess unconscious representations of phonemes. This dissociation is consistent with the notion of an emergence of (unconscious) phonemes in preliterate children (see Studdert-Kennedy & Goddell, Chapter 4).

Concluding from the work reviewed in this section, one can tentatively locate phonetic processing (as evidenced by phonetic feature blendings, categorical perception, and auditory-visual integration, all of which are unaffected by alphabetisation) in the first stages of the perception of speech.

The activation of phonemic representations might occur at three different stages. Given that illiterates show as many phonological fusions as literates when the resulting word is consistent with the corresponding orthographic form, there must be an activation of phonemes at a relatively early stage. A later stage of phonemic processing can be hypothesised from the observation of an alphabetisation effect on the rate of segmental vs. global errors in word recognition. The third stage of phonemic analysis is the conscious identification of these units in metaphonological tasks. Alternatively, one may consider that stages 2 and 3 of phonemic processing are only one: It would involve the same type of conscious representations of phonemes, but these would be used for different purposes, in one case for word recognition, and in the other case for metaphonemic analysis.

The dissociations that occur within the speech recognition process as a function of the literacy status of the listeners suggest that the speech recognition process is better viewed as a partially modular system than as completely interactive.

For a long time illiterates have been ignored in the inquiries into speech recognition. This is not only because it is difficult to find and test illiterates in the countries where cognitive psycholinguistics (and science in general) is highly developed, but also because, until very recently, there has been an underestimation of the importance of the interactions between spoken and written language. Illiterates are a key population for the study of these two topics—speech and reading—which this volume is contributing to link, and above all for the study of this link.

ACKNOWLEDGEMENTS

Preparation of this chapter benefited from the Belgian Fonds National de la Recherche Scientifique (FNRS)—Loterie Nationale (Convention no. 8.4505.92), as well as from the Belgian Ministère de l'Education de la Communauté française ("Action de Recherche concertée": *Language processing in different modalities: comparative approaches*, Convention no. 91–96/148). The second author is Research Associate of the Belgian FNRS.

REFERENCES

Adams, M.J. (1990). *Beginning to read: Thinking and learning about print.* Cambridge, MA: MIT Press.

Alegria, J., Morais, J., d'Alimonte, G., & Seyll, S. (submitted). *The development of speech segmentation abilities and reading acquisition in a whole word setting.*

Amano, K. (1989). Phonological analysis and acquisition of reading and writing in children. *Psychologia, 32*, 16–32.

Ball, E.W., & Blachman, B.A. (1988). Phoneme segmentation training: Effects on reading readiness. *Annals of Dyslexia, 38*, 208–225.

Ball, E.W., & Blachman, B.A. (1991). Does phoneme awareness training in kindergarten make a difference in early word recognition and developmental spelling? *Reading Research Quarterly, 26*, 49–66.

Bertelson, P. (1993). Reading acquisition and phonemic awareness testing: how conclusive are data from Down's syndrome? (Remarks on Cossu, Rossini, & Marshall, 1993). *Cognition, 48,* 281–283.

Bradley, L., & Bryant, P.E. (1983). Categorizing sounds and learning to read: a causal connection. *Nature, 301,* 419–421.

Bryant, P.E., & Goswami, U. (1987). Beyond grapheme-phoneme correspondence. *Cahiers de Psychologie Cognitive, 7,* 439–443.

Bryant, P.E., MacLean, M., Bradley, L., & Crossland, J. (1990). Rhyme and alliteration, phoneme detection, and learning to read. *Developmental Psychology, 26,* 429–438.

Byrne, B. (1992). Studies in the acquisition procedure for reading: Rationale, hypotheses, and data. In P.B. Gough, L.C. Ehri, & R. Treiman (Eds.), *Reading acquisition* (pp. 1–34). Hillsdale, NJ: Lawrence Erlbaum Associates Inc.

Byrne, B. (1993). Learning to read in the absence of phonemic awareness? (A comment on Cossu, Rossini, & Marshall, 1993). *Cognition, 48,* 285–288.

Byrne, B., & Fielding-Barnsley, R. (1990). Phonemic awareness and letter knowledge in the child's acquisition of the alphabetic principle. *Journal of Educational Psychology, 81,* 313–321.

Byrne, B., & Fielding-Barnsley, R. (1991). Evaluation of a program to teach phonemic awareness to young children. *Journal of Educational Psychology, 83,* 451–455.

Castro, S.L., & Morais, J. (1987). Ear differences in illiterates. *Neuropsychologia, 25,* 409–417.

Castro, S.L., & Morais, J. (in preparation, a). *Categorical perception in illiterate adults.*

Castro, S.L., & Morais, J. (in preparation, b). *Listening to phonemes as a way to recognize words.*

Content, A., Kolinsky, R., Morais, J., & Bertelson, P. (1986). Phonetic segmentation in prereaders: effect of corrective information. *Journal of Experimental Child Psychology, 42,* 49–72.

Content, A. Morais, J., & Bertelson, P. (1987). *Phonetic segmentation in prereaders: A transfer of learning approach.* Paper presented at the Second Meeting of the European Society for Cognitive Psychology, Madrid.

Cossu, G., & Marshall, J.C. (1990). Are cognitive skills a prerequisite for learning to read and write? *Cognitive Neuropsychology, 7,* 21–40.

Cossu, G., Rossini, F., & Marshall, J.C. (1993). When reading is acquired but phonemic awareness is not: A study of literacy in Down's syndrome. *Cognition, 46,* 129–138.

Cunningham, A.E. (1990). Explicit versus implicit instruction in phonological awareness. *Journal of Experimental Psychology, 50,* 429–444.

Cutting, J.E. (1975). Aspects of phonological fusion. *Journal of Experimental Psychology: Human Perception and Performance, 1,* 105–120.

Cutting, J.E. (1976). Auditory and linguistic processes in speech perception: Inferences from six fusions in dichotic listening. *Psychological Review, 83,* 114–140.

Day, R.S. (1968). Fusion in dichotic listening (Doctoral dissertation, Stanford University). *Dissertation Abstracts International, 29,* 2649B (University Microfilms No. 69–211).

Dupoux, E., & Mehler, J. (1992). Unifying awareness and on-line studies of speech: A tentative framework. In J. Alegria, D. Holender, J. Junça de Morais, & M. Radeau (Eds.), *Analytic approaches to human cognition* (pp. 59–75). Amsterdam: Elsevier.

Goodman, K.S. (1967). Reading: A psycholinguistic guessing game. *Journal of the Reading Specialist, 6,* 126–135.

Helfgott, J. (1976). Phoneme segmentation and blending skills of kindergarten children: Implications for beginning reading acquisition. *Contemporary Educational Psychology, 1,* 157–169.

Kolinsky, R., Morais, J., & Brito Mendes, C. (1990) Embeddedness effects on part verification in children and unschooled adults. *Psychologica Belgica, 30,* 49–64.

Kolinsky, R., Morais, J., Content, A. & Cary, L. (1987). Finding parts within figures: a developmental study. *Perception, 16,* 399–407.

Liberman, A.M., Cooper F.S., Shankweiler D., & Studdert-Kennedy, M. (1967). Perception of the speech code. *Psychological Review, 74*, 431–461.

Liberman, I.Y., & Liberman, A.M. (1990). Whole language versus code emphasis: Underlying assumptions and their implications for reading instruction. *Annals of Dyslexia, 40*, 51–76.

Liberman, A.M., & Mattingly, I.G. (1985). The motor theory of speech perception revised. *Cognition, 21*, 1–36.

Lundberg, I., Frost, J., & Petersen, O.-P. (1988). Effects of an extensive program for stimulating phonological awareness in preschool children. *Reading Research Quarterly, 23*, 263–284.

Marshall, J.C., & Cossu, G. (1990). Is pathological development part of normal cognitive neuropsychology?—A rejoinder to Marcel. *Cognitive Neuropsychology, 7*, 49–55.

Marshall, J.C., & Cossu, G. (1991). Poor readers and black swans. *Mind and Language, 6*, 135–139.

McGurk, H., & McDonald, J. (1976). Hearing lips and seeing voices. *Nature, 264*, 746–748.

Morais, J. (1985). Literacy and awareness of the units of speech: implications for research on the units of perception. *Linguistics, 23*, 707–721.

Morais, J. (1991a). Constraints on the development of phonemic awareness. In S.A. Brady & D.P. Shankweiler (Eds.), *Phonological processes in literacy. A tribute to Isabelle Y. Liberman* (pp. 5–27). Hillsdale, NJ: Lawrence Erlbaum Associates Inc.

Morais, J. (1991b). Phonological awareness: A bridge between language and literacy. In D.J. Sawyer & B.J. Fox (Eds.), *Phonological awareness in reading. The evolution of current perspectives* (pp. 31–71). New York: Springer.

Morais, J. (1993). Phonemic awareness, language and literacy. In R.M. Joshi & C.K. Leong (Eds.), *Reading disabilities: Diagnosis and component processes*. Dordrecht: Kluwer.

Morais, J., Alegria, J., & Content, A. (1987a). The relationships between segmental analysis and alphabetic literacy: An interactive view. *Cahiers de Psychologie Cognitive* [*European Bulletin of Cognitive Psychology*], *5*, 415–438.

Morais, J., Cary, L., Alegria, J., & Bertelson, P. (1979). Does awareness of speech as a sequence of phones arise spontaneously? *Cognition, 7*, 323–331.

Morais, J., Castro, S.L., & Kolinsky, R. (1991). La reconnaissance des mots chez les adultes illettrés. In R. Kolinsky, J. Morais, & J. Segui (Eds.), *La reconnaissance des mots dans les différentes modalités sensorielles. Etudes de psycholinguistique cognitive* (pp. 59–80). Paris: Presses Universitaires de France.

Morais, J., Castro, S.L., Scliar-Cabral, L., Kolinsky, R., & Content, A. (1987b). The effects of literacy on the recognition of dichotic words. *Quarterly Journal of Experimental Psychology, 39A*, 451–465.

Morais, J., Content, A., Bertelson, P., Cary, L., & Kolinsky, R. (1988). Is there a critical period for the acquisition of segmental analysis? *Cognitive Neuropsychology, 5*, 347–352.

Morais, J., de Gelder, B., & Verhaeghe, A. (in preparation). *Auditory-visual integration of speech in illiterate adults*.

Morais, J., & Mousty, P. (1992). The causes of phonemic awareness. In J. Alegria, D. Holender, J. Junça de Morais, & M. Radeau (Eds.), *Analytic approaches to human cognition* (pp. 193–212). Amsterdam: Elsevier.

Morton, J., & Frith, U. (1993). What lesson for dyslexia from Down's syndrome? (Comments on Cossu, Rossini, & Marshall 1993). *Cognition, 48*, 289–296.

Nusbaum, H.C., Walley, A.C., Carrell, T.D., & Ressler, W.H. (1982). Controlled perceptual strategies in phonemic restauration. *Research on Speech Perception Progress Reports, 8*, 83–103. Bloomington, IN: Department of Psychology, Indiana University.

Ohnmacht, D.C. (1969). *The effects of letter knowledge on achievement on reading in first grade*. Paper presented at the American Educational Research Association, Los Angeles (cited in Adams, M.J., 1990, see above).

Perfetti, C.A., Beck, I., Bell, L., & Hughes, C. (1987). Phonemic knowledge and learning to read are reciprocal: A longitudinal study of first grade children. *Merrill-Palmer Quarterly, 33*, 283–319.

Read, C., Zhang, Y., Nie, H., & Ding, B. (1986). The ability to manipulate speech sounds depends on knowing alphabetic writing. *Cognition, 24*, 31–44.

Samuel, A.G., & Ressler, W.H. (1986). Attention within auditory word perception: Insights from the phonemic restauration illusion. *Journal of Experimental Psychology: Human Perception and Performance, 12*, 70–79.

Scliar-Cabral, L., Morais, J., Nepomuceno, L., & Kolinsky, R. (submitted). *Phonemic awareness versus phonemic sensitivity: A study of Brazilian adults of different literacy levels.*

Seidenberg, M.S., & Tanenhaus, M.K. (1979). Orthographic effects on rhyme monitoring. *Journal of Experimental Psychology: Human Learning and Memory, 5*, 546–554.

Smith, F. (1971). *Understanding reading: A psycholinguistic analysis of reading and learning to read.* New York: Holt, Rhinehart & Winston.

Studdert-Kennedy, M., Shankweiler, D., & Pisoni, D. (1972). Auditory and phonetic processes in speech perception: Evidence from a dichotic study. *Cognitive Psychology, 3*, 455–466.

Taft, M., & Hambly, G. (1985). The influence of orthography on phonological representations in the lexicon. *Journal of Memory and Language, 24*, 320–335.

Williams, J.P. (1980). Teaching decoding with an emphasis on phoneme analysis and phoneme blending. *Journal of Educational Psychology, 72*, 1–15.

16 Mechanisms of Word-retrieval: Neuropsychological Investigations of Patients with Parkinson's Disease

J.M. Gurd and J.C. Marshall
University of Oxford, and The Radcliffe Infirmary, Oxford, UK

INTRODUCTION

Word-retrieval deficits are common in patients with Parkinson's disease (PD). The impairment seems to be linked to deficits in word search, rather than to problems with task-switching, or other functions of the supervisory attentional system (Baddeley, 1986; Norman & Shallice, 1986). Verbal fluency tasks have often been employed to assess the word-finding difficulties that many patients with PD complain of. These tasks require the subject to produce as many words as possible within a limited time; it is usual to require retrieval from a single predefined category, such as animals or words beginning with the letter s. Preliminary results on such tasks are described and discussed. Word-search deficits linked to fluency impairments are then reported, followed by presentation of task-switching experiments in which subjects must, for example, produce words alternately from the two (or more) categories.

WORD-RETRIEVAL DEFICITS IN PARKINSON'S DISEASE PATIENTS

Introduction

The verbal fluency task is widely employed in cognitive psychology (Bousfield & Sedgewick, 1944; Graesser & Mandler, 1978; Gruenewald & Lockhead, 1980; Hampton & Gardiner, 1983; Mandler, 1975; Osgood, 1958); and neuropsychology (Allen & Frith, 1983; Benton, 1968; Dunn, Russell, & Drummond, 1989; Goodglass

& Kaplan, 1972; Grossman, 1980; Isaacs & Kennie, 1973; Milner, 1964; Newcombe, 1969; Perret, 1974; Ramier & Hecaen, 1970; Schechter et al., 1985; Ulatowska, Hayashi, Cannito, & Fleming, 1986). The task is particularly sensitive to the word-retrieval deficits characteristic of patients with Parkinson's disease (PD) (Gurd & Ward, 1989; Girotti et al., 1986; Huber, Shuttleworth & Paulson, 1986; Lees & Smith, 1983; Levin et al., 1989; Megna et al., 1985).

Methods and Results

Gurd and Ward (1989) tested 27 nondemented patients with idiopathic PD (mean age: 62.15; mean onset: 8.07, SD 4.56 years; mean Webster [1968] severity: 11.67, SD 6.40), of whom over 50% produced response scores falling more than two standard deviations below the control mean ($N = 27$, mean age: 63.11). The tasks involved letter-initial and semantic categories: animals, furniture, animals and furniture, S-words, A-words, S- and A-words, foods and occupations, foods, occupations. Subjects were requested to produce as many category exemplars as possible within 60 seconds per category. Only subjects who were able to complete all 12 fluency tasks within one session were included in the study. All patients were well-medicated, and tested while on their levodopa/carbidopa medication.

The tasks were administered in both single (one category at a time), and alternating (items from two different categories) conditions. The alternating condition yielded *no* additional deficit for the PDs. In contrast, a patient with frontal lobe atrophy due to Pick's disease (Gurd, Ward, & Hodges, 1990) showed impaired fluency performance overall, compounded by an *additional* deficit on the alternating fluency conditions.

Control measures were taken to pinpoint the cognitive locus of the PD fluency deficit. Rapid speaking rate was measured for over-learned sequences (i.e. days of the week), that is, so-called "automatic speech". There were no significant correlations between these values and fluency scores for either the PD or the control group. It would seem then that the PD fluency deficit was not caused (solely) by motor-speech slowing per se. Having concluded that the fluency deficit was not simply an artifact of motor factors, a link with more cognitive word-finding functions was sought. The first approach was to measure word-finding in a picture naming task. Error scores on the Boston Naming Test (Goodglass & Kaplan, 1983) correlated significantly with verbal fluency values for PDs. This evidence points to a lexical-semantic locus for the PD fluency deficit.

Discussion

Counter-evidence? These experimental findings were subsequently addressed by others; Hanley et al. (1990) suggested that the results described above (Gurd & Ward, 1989) were invalid. Although Hanley et al. reported verbal fluency deficits in Parkinson's disease patients (using the tasks F-words, A-words, S-words, animals, clothing, vegetables), they suggested that the deficit was due to age and current verbal ability, rather than to more specific word-finding difficulties.

Therefore, it became necessary to investigate these factors further in our study. We were able to construct an excellent pair-wise match between PDs and controls (N total = 40), whose age and education levels were strictly comparable. Nonetheless, a fluency deficit was again found in the PD group, and Hanley et al.'s criticisms did not invalidate our results.

On closer examination, several flaws in the Hanley et al. study were noticed. Their groups were not well matched for length of education (and hence were probably not well matched for verbal IQ), and their controls were overall more highly educated than their PDs. Secondly, Hanley et al. violated the prerequisites for using analysis of variance, by having standard deviations that were significantly different between groups (for the letter-initial fluency tasks). (Our between-group standard deviations did not differ significantly.) Thirdly, it appears Hanley et al., violated the assumptions for performing an analysis of covariance (ANCOVA), with age as covariate. On ANCOVA, their age variable was only just marginally significant for the semantic condition ($P = 0.049$), and failed to reach significance for the letter-initial condition ($P = 0.065$). Overall, it appears that age may not have been a significant variable in their study. The validity of entering age as a covariate on the ANCOVA is thus doubtful. Each additional factor added as a covariate reduces the degrees of freedom in calculating the significance level (P) of the F-value, and hence reduces the likelihood of obtaining a significant difference between the main dependent variables (Armitage, 1971). Furthermore, Hanley et al. did not state whether their data conformed to the prerequisites of (a) linearity of association between the dependent variable (fluency) and independent variables (age or Mill Hill); and (b) equivalence of slopes (i.e. no significant difference between slopes) of the regression equations (on the listed variables) for the two groups.

Gurd and Ward (1989) were justified in *not* performing an ANCOVA with age as a covariate on our original data ($N = 54$), because our data violated prerequisite (a) above. In our control group, there was no significant linear relation between age and fluency, ($r = -0.09$, n.s.) although our PD group did show linearity ($r = -0.43$, df = 25, $P < 0.02$, 2-tailed). Prerequisite (b) was *not* violated in our data. There was no significant difference between the slopes of the regression lines for the two groups ($t = 0.0003$, n.s.), but as the regression line for the controls was not a meaningful representation of the data, the slope difference calculation is irrelevant.

The Theoretical Notion of "Dementia". How the theoretical notion of "dementia" relates to specific cognitive impairments found in PD is rather more complicated. Hanley et al. (1990, p. 737) state: "It is therefore possible that in a study like Gurd and Ward's, which does not employ a general mental status examination, that differences in verbal fluency performance might reflect a general intellectual impairment rather than a selective word-finding deficit."

According to a modular view of cognitive deficits, the suggestion that verbal fluency deficits reflect general intellectual impairment is akin to suggesting that a patient was experiencing heart trouble due to feeling unwell. It is important to note that "dementia" or "general intellectual impairment" is a clinical classification, typically based on the presence of: ". . . acquired persistent deterioration in mental function involving at least three of the following areas of neuropsychologic activity: language, memory, visuo-spatial skills, personality or emotion, and cognition (abstraction, calculation)". (Cummings, 1982, p. 93)

Clearly, it is possible in point of logic for a patient to fall under the diagnostic label "demented" without having a verbal fluency deficit. Our view is that the clinical diagnosis of presence or absence of "dementia" is *theoretically* irrelevant (see Marshall, 1987, for discussion) to the hypothesis that verbal fluency deficits in PD may reflect cognitive word-finding problems. According to the clinical definition, a patient with language problems (e.g. a fluency deficit) *and* visuo-spatial problems *and* calculation problems is "demented". However, analysis of the precise nature of the language problems is not advanced by observing that the patient also has other, nonlanguage, impairments. This "modular" approach to the "dementias" is well-argued in Schwartz (1990).

Empirical issues such as the relationship between Fluency and Mill Hill Synonyms vocabulary, or Mini-Mental score dementia measures, were not addressed in Gurd and Ward (1989). These tasks were not included in our original protocol. Nonetheless, NART–IQ (Nelson & O'Connell, 1978) estimates are available for a subset of the original sample (N = 13 each, matched for age and education between groups, and equivalent in age, education, fluency, PD onset, and severity to the larger group). The Nelson Adult Reading Test (NART) is frequently used in clinical practice, and in experimental research, to derive estimates of pre-morbid verbal IQ. The decision to employ NART rather than MH synonyms is based on the assumption that NART does indeed reflect *pre-morbid* verbal IQ. If verbal fluency impairments in PD are due to cognitive disorder of the lexicon, one might expect the disease process to perturb performance on the synonyms test, too. Appropriate matching of controls and patients accordingly ought to be based upon a pre-morbid estimate of lexical knowledge.

PDs did not differ significantly from controls on NART (t = 1.56, df = 24, n.s.). The correlation between NART and fluency was significant for PDs (r = +0.78, df = 11, $P < 0.01$, 2-tailed). The correlation between NART and fluency was not significant for controls (r = +0.46, df = 11, n.s.), although there is a trend in the same direction. In this sample of patients and controls, the between-group difference on verbal fluency remained significant (df 1,24; F = 11.16, P = 0.003). On analysis of covariance, the between-group difference on fluency held up with NART–IQ partialled out (df = 1,23; F = 8.34, P = 0.008).

Although there was no between-group difference on regression slopes for fluency by NART, the failure to find a significiant regression between NART and fluency in the control group renders this analysis statistically insecure. Furthermore, Raskin, Sliwinski, and Borod (in press) have carefully documented verbal fluency impairments in a group of PDs ($N = 25$) who are demonstrably "nondemented" on the Dementia Rating Scale.

We suggest that if Hanley et al. had matched their two groups for length of education, their between-group verbal fluency differences would have reached significance. Their groups were not matched for verbal IQ, and the controls were, overall, more highly educated than the patients. Education would be expected to correlate with Mill Hill Synonyms (MH) scores, and hence could account for the between-group difference on MH. We also note that the two studies did not employ identical versions of the fluency task, and that Hanley et al. did not measure picture-naming accuracy, or rapid speaking rates.

Incidence of Verbal Fluency Deficits in Parkinson's Disease. It is important to stress that small patient groups may not be statistically representative of larger patient populations. Studies of the type described here are not large enough to discover the range of inter-individual variability; we did not aim at the scale of epidemiological research. That a verbal fluency deficit was observed in the study of Gurd and Ward (1989) does not imply that others, using different groups of PD patients, will invariably observe the same phenomenon. Nonetheless, many studies have found verbal fluency deficits in patients with PD (Lees & Smith, 1983; Megna et al., 1985; Girotti et al., 1986; Levin, Llabre, & Weiner, 1989; Raskin et al., in press). Oyobode et al. (1986) reported that verbal fluency was the best cognitive indicator of PD severity; of the PDs studied by them, 78% fell below the 25th percentile of the control sample on verbal fluency, and 33% had scores below the control range. It would seem, then, that such deficits are a frequent, but not inevitable concomitant of Parkinson's disease.

Information Processing Approaches to Verbal Fluency. The finding of a verbal fluency by picture-naming correlation in PD is the first step toward fractionation of the fluency task in the service of PD deficit analysis. With reference to a model such as that of Patterson (1972), there are several possible "loci" of word-finding dysfunction that could underly the reduced PD output (of words per unit time). We know from the literature that PDs typically have other, "nonword-finding", problems, such as "starting" motor tasks in general; these have accordingly been filtered out of our studies from the start—time measurement began with the first word produced, rather than with the initial cue to begin.

Two fundamental loci of possible dysfunction are: (1) "pick a word, or subcategory"; and (2) "test the word, or subcategory". Deficient performance on the verbal fluency task could result from erroneous, or from slowed, functioning in either or both of these two mechanisms. *Erroneous functioning* could be characterised as picking the wrong word or subcategory, i.e. not the one intended, or not the one which belongs to an appropriate semantic category. It could also be characterised as failure to test the word or category due to mnemonic failure, i.e. forgetting those words or subcategories that have already been produced. *Slowed functioning* could be manifested in correct choice of words or subcategories, but with long inter-item/inter-subcategory times, caused by slowed picking, and/or slowed testing of the words or subcategories. Slowed picking could be re-expressed as a function of slowed retrieval from long-term memory, and slowed testing as slowed retrieval from short-term memory stores.

VERBAL FLUENCY AND WORD SEARCH IN PARKINSON'S DISEASE PATIENTS

The verbal fluency task has largely remained unfractionated in its employment within cognitive neuropsychology. Using a case-series methodology, we discovered highly significant correlations between PD verbal fluency scores and performance on a measure of word-search time, which we designed using a modified Neisser memory-search paradigm. As the PDs were also significantly slowed on their cognitive word-search component (once the motor factors were subtracted out), the evidence was interpreted as supporting a wordsearch deficit underlying the PD verbal fluency impairments (Gurd, 1993). Our results were consistent with the original findings of Neisser (1963), in that it took longer to search for items from larger-sized semantic sets than it did to search for items from the smaller ones. However, there was no interaction on the between-group and between-condition analysis of variance for the PDs, as compared to matched controls. The PDs were slowed overall on the cognitive component of this task. By contrast, our frontal Pick's patient (F.M.) was differentially impaired on the larger-sized semantic set search times.

Overall, the data were interpreted as supporting the role, as measured here, of word-search time as a possible rate-limiting step in the performance of verbal fluency tasks. This type of conclusion could not have been reached without the results from neuropsychological patient studies. However, it was possible, as might be suggested by Baddeley (1986), that the link between fluency and search was simply an artifact of working memory dysfunction (underlying slowing on both the tasks). Further experiments were therefore designed to address this issue.

VERBAL TASK ALTERNATION IN PARKINSON'S DISEASE PATIENTS: 1

Introduction

In the experiments described so far, the focus has been on difficulties of word-finding underlying PD verbal fluency impairments. It remains possible, however, that the locus of cognitive dysfunction lies outside the language module per se. For example, it is important to determine whether deficits on tasks such as verbal fluency may be due to short-term memory problems of a central executive (e.g.

SAS, Norman and Shallice, 1986). The supervisory attentional system (SAS) may also be responsible for task-switching functions: the focus of this next experiment, in which the modality of output and the types of cues provided, are similar to those used in the fluency–automatic speech paradigm described earlier.

We designed a verbal category alternation task (referred to as "continuous series") that was as similar to fluency as possible. There was also a titrated switching between number of categories from which words were produced in an ongoing task. All categories from which the words were drawn were "overlearned", such as days of the week, months of the year, and letters of the alphabet. Thus, the modality of output and types of cues provided were similar to those used in the fluency and automatic speech tasks.

Methods

Forty matched elderly subjects were tested, of whom 20 had PD (onset 3–15 years; mean onset 8.00 years, SD 3.75) (see Gurd, 1993, for further details). The continuous series task requires subjects to produce words orally in alternating series, as rapidly and accurately as possible. The tasks are divided into two parts, A and B, each comprising three tasks administered in fixed order. In part A, for example, the task A–2 requires a subject to alternate between saying the days of the week and the letters of the alphabet, beginning with the day "Monday", and the letter "A". This is followed by a three-category alternation, and then a four-category one. The same pattern holds for part B. Subsequent tasks in part A add the category *numbers*, followed by *months* of the year. All categories commence at the "natural" start of the series (i.e. "Monday, A, One, January"). In section B, the same categories are used, but the beginning points are varied. For example, task B–2 begins with "Wednesday" and the letter "C", task B–3 with "Wednesday" and the letter "C" and the number 9, and task B–4 adds the month "April" to make a four-category task. Parts A and B are administered within the same session. A maximum of 21 iterations were recorded for each task (for example, each subject was stopped once they had gone through 21 "days of the week").

The tasks thus varied in: (1) the number of categories between which the subject was required to alternate (ranging from 2 to 4); and (2) the starting point within the given categories. In this way, the generation of items becomes progressively less "automatic", and it becomes less likely that an item in one category can serve as a direct cue for the item in a subsequent one. The tasks were administered in a fixed order of hypothesised difficulty. The tasks were:

A2: Days and alphabet: beginning with "Monday", "A".
A3: Days, alphabet, and numbers: beginning with "Monday", "A", "1".
A4: Days, alphabet, numbers, and months: beginning with "Monday", "A", "1", "January".

B2: Days and alphabet: beginning with "Wednesday", "C".
B3: Days, alphabet, and numbers: beginning with "Wednesday", "C", "9".
B4: Days, alphabet, numbers, and months: beginning with "Wednesday", "C", "9", "April".

Within a given part, the subjects proceeded to subsequent sets of alternations only if previous ones had been completed with less than 20% errors. Subjects were permitted to quit within part A once the task became too difficult. However, they were then asked to proceed to part B. All responses were timed, tape-recorded and transcribed.

Results

Overall, the PDs completed significantly fewer tasks to criterion than did controls. On average, over the total of six tasks, the PDs reached criterion on half the tasks. Controls, in contrast, reached criterion on over 80% of tasks, which reflects the compound difference in rate and accuracy between the two groups. Significant between-group differences were found on both parts A and B.

There were no significant interactions (group × number of category shifts) on the analysis of variance, and the PDs did not make more errors than controls. PDs tended to quit, rather than make errors. The errors were broadly categorised as errors of: sequencing, repetition, category-switch, or other (e.g. memory), and there was no significant difference between groups on the first three types of error. PDs did, however, produce more errors within the "other" category, and these tended to be memory-retrieval problems. Also, one PD subject produced items from a "wild" category that was not part of the task. The PDs tended to produce their first error significantly sooner in the series than did controls, and they produced significantly more deletions (in which the target was omitted) than did controls.

Furthermore, when the PD mean times per number of category switches were correlated with their difference values on (single–alternating) fluency, no significant relationships were observed.

Discussion

Between PDs and controls, there were significant differences on number of tasks performed to criterion, response time, efficiency, and error rate (and type). On all these measures, the PDs as a group performed more poorly than controls. However, for the purposes of discussion here, the most interesting result is the *lack* of correlation in the PD sample between measures of task-switching titration (changes in score with increasing numbers of task-switches) and verbal fluency (single vs alternating score differences per subject).

These data do *not* suggest that PD verbal fluency deficits are related to task-switching problems. We note that for controls there was a significant correlation between the slope of a task-switch regression line and the fluency (single vs. alternating) difference score. This suggests that the task *is* suitable for testing the relationship between task-switching functions and verbal fluency performance.

That PDs did not show significant correlations between fluency and continuous series indicated that the psychological locus of PD fluency dysfunction lies elsewhere than in task-switching functions per se. In this task, all items were by definition, pre-specified and overlearned. There was therefore no real need to "search" for a suitable word to produce. However, there was a considerable short-term memory component to the task.

Several modifications to the continuous series task were recommended:

1. The distinction between A and B task types (with differences in initial starting points) did not prove to be helpful. The effects in controls may have been overshadowed by stronger practice effects, and the effects in PDs may have been confounded by fatigue effects. Thus, in subsequent experiments, it is desirable to forego the use of A-type tasks. B-type tasks (with non-initial starting points) are preferable, and each titration should commence at a different starting point to avoid the confounding effects of within-task practice.
2. Some subjects found the category of letters of the alphabet quite difficult. Subsequent usage of this set should be preceded by a suitably controlled rehearsal phase.
3. Measures of switch cost could be more accurately calculated; before a subject begins a continuous series, the time it takes to say all the category items (as rapidly and accurately as possible) should be measured. This would provide rehearsal as well as subject-specific normative data from which to calculate the switch cost.

Several other qualitative observations of interest can be derived from the results. From those PDs who reached an arbitrary criterion of task completion with greater than 80% accuracy, there was no time difference between their mean and the control mean. Thus, the PDs who reached criterion were truly "normal" in that they did not need to sacrifice speed to meet the accuracy criterion. However, from the total-time values (criterion plus noncriterion tasks), it can be seen that PDs were significantly slower than controls. The PDs who were slow also tended to make more errors; their performance was poor overall. Furthermore, the fact that PDs found the task more arduous than controls (although both groups commented on its difficulty) is reflected in the large percentage of PDs who declined to attempt the four-category switch task conditions (A4 and B4).

For the PDs, there was an increase in response time, between two and 3 switches, of approximately 10% for part A, and 33% for part B. This compares with the control values of 38% and 28% respectively. Practice and fatigue effects may be responsible for these differences. For the three and four switches, the PD and control differences in rate were virtually identical at between 5% and 6%. That is, the PDs who attempted the four-way switch (50% of the original sample) showed a switch-cost differential identical to that of controls. Nonetheless, the PDs' task performance was overall less "efficient" than the controls'.

VERBAL TASK ALTERNATION IN PARKINSON'S DISEASE PATIENTS: 2

The continuous series experiment was subsequently redesigned and administered to a new set of matched subjects. All beginnings were at noninitial starting points and the tasks used were: two categories (alternating between saying numbers and days of the week); three categories (alternating between numbers, days of the week, and months); and four categories (alternating between numbers, days of the week, months, and letters of the alphabet). The task administration was preceded by baseline practice tasks for each category. The PDs were overall significantly slower than controls, and there was a significant difference, for both groups, between conditions; responses were slower on the four- vs. three-switch conditions. There were no significant between-group differences on number of errors produced.

DOUBLE DISSOCIATIONS

The processes involved in performing the different tasks described so far are to a large extent distinct. We observed double dissociations between PD word-search and their continuous series scores. For example, one PD patient (Caa), scored intact on search, but was impaired on continuous series (his score was 1.88 standard deviations below the control mean on continuous series). In contrast, one PD subject (Rgo) was impaired on search (3.75 standard deviations below the control mean), but was intact on continuous series (0.94 standard deviations below the control mean). There were *no* double dissociations between fluency and search.

Thus, although PDs may have had impairments on both fluency and continuous series, it is unlikely that there was any necessary relation between the deficit processes common to the two tasks. On the other hand, the relationship between fluency and search is further strengthened by the *lack* of dissociations, and the strongly significant correlations for PDs, between fluency and word search.

CONCLUSION

Some PDs have switching problems, but these are dissociable from their fluency impairments. Both types of deficit may be found in PD, but reflect dysfunction in different underlying mechanisms. The two impairments are unlikely to be due to some shared underlying dysfunction of a "central cognitive processor"—"executive" or "control" function, such as Norman and Shallice's SAS (1986). This is not to say that central executive functions are not involved in the performance of the two tasks of fluency and continuous series. Rather, the relevance of "central executive" functions differs between the two tasks.

Fodor (1983) claims that the functions of any central cognitive processor can not be fractionated. Allport (1992) has suggested that several distinctions be made between different central executive functions associated with Baddeley's (1986) working memory and Norman and Shalice's SAS (1986) models. The precise functions, mechanisms, and capacities of a "central processor" remain to be specified (see Allport, 1992). Also, Allport (1992) notes the difficulty in separating out the effects of task-switching vs. interference effects (e.g. proactive inhibition) in continuous tasks of task-switching such as ours.

With the improved experimental design of continuous series, double dissociations between continuous series and search were obtained. This finding augments the PD double dissociation between fluency and automatic speech. For automatic speech, the stimulus is the instructions to produce words in a fixed sequence from a category that contains items of fixed identity (e.g. days of the week). In response to the instruction, internal accessing of semantic memory must take place. The abstract target word form, or "lemma" (Levelt, 1989), is retrieved from storage, and specifies the phonological/articulatory form for output.

In verbal fluency, by contrast, the stimulus instructions specify a semantic category only (e.g. animals). The identity and sequence of the items produced from the set is under the control of the subject. Thus, the mechanism of access to lexical-semantic memory is now nonroutinised. A further difference is that once the words have been retrieved, they must be stored or tagged in some form; a buffer specifically set up for this task may be involved. Before subsequent items are produced, there is some form of checking to ensure that the item has not already been produced in the current series. (If a buffer comes into play in automatic speech, then it would be required to hold only a single item at a time, and this would be continually updated.)

The double dissociation between automatic speech and verbal fluency shows that there is a difference between the rate-limiting steps for the two tasks. The differences are in respect to routinised vs. nonroutinised lexical-semantic retrieval, and the number of items held in the (task-specific) buffer. Fluency and automatic speech are similar in that both involve access to, and production from, a lexical semantic store. The manner of accessing, however, is indicated by the task instruction, and probably differs between fluency and automatic speech. It is highly unlikely, for example, that any semantic effects of competitive inhibition operate in the automatic speech task.

REFERENCES

Allen, H.A., & Frith, C. (1983). Selective retrieval and free emission of category exemplars in schizophrenia. *British Journal of Psychology, 74*, 481–490.

Allport, A. (1992). Attention and control. Have we been asking the wrong questions? A critical review of 25 years. In D.E. Meyer & S. Kornblum (Eds.), *Attention and performance, XIV: A silver jubilee*. Cambridge: MA: MIT Press.

Armitage, P. (1971). *Statistical methods in medical research*. Oxford: Blackwell.

Baddeley, A.D. (1986). *Working memory*. Oxford University Press.

Benton, A.L. (1968). Differential behavioral effects in frontal lobe disease. *Neuropsychologia, 6*, 53–60.

Bousfield, W.A., & Sedgewick, C.H.W. (1994). An analysis of sequences of restricted associative responses. *Journal of General Psychology, 30*, 149–165.

Cummings, J.L. (1982). Cortical dementias. In D.F. Benson & D. Blumer (Eds.), *Psychiatric aspects of neurologic disease*, Vol. III (pp. 93–121). New York: Grune & Stratton.

Dunn, N.D., Russell, S.S., & Drummond, S.S. (1989). Effect of stimulus context and response coding variables on word retrieval performances in dysphasia. *Journal of Communication Disorders, 22*, 209–223.

Fodor, J.A. (1983) *The modularity of mind*. Cambridge, MA: MIT Press.

Girotti, F., Grassi, M.P., Carella, F., Soliveri, P., Mussico, M., Lamperti, E., & Caraceni, T. (1986). Possible involvement of attention processes in Parkinson's disease. In M.D. Yahr & K.J. Bergmann (Eds.), *Advances in neurology* (Vol. 45, pp. 425–429). New York: Raven Press.

Goodglass, H., & Kaplan, E. (1972). *The assessment of aphasia and related disorders*. Philadelphia, PA: Lea & Febiger.

Goodglass, H., & Kaplan, E. (1983). *The Boston Naming Test*. Philadelphia, PA: Lea & Febiger.

Graesser, A., & Mandler, G. (1978). Limited processing capacity constrains the storage of unrelated sets of words and retrieval from natural categories. *Journal of Experimental Psychology: Human Learning and Memory, 4*, 86–100.

Grossman, M. (1980). The aphasics' identification of a superordinate's referents with basic object level and subordinate level terms. *Cortex, 16*, 459–469.

Gruenewald, P.J., & Lockhead, G.R. (1980). The free recall of category examples. *Journal of Experimental Psychology: Human Learning and Memory, 6* , 225–240.

Gurd, J.M. (1993). *Studies of verbal fluency deficits in patients with Parkinson's disease (Vols I and II)*. D. Phil thesis, Oxford University.

Gurd, J.M., & Ward, C.D. (1989). Retrieval from semantic and letter-initial categories in patients with Parkinson's disease. *Neuropsychologia, 28*, 737–741.

Gurd, J.M., Ward, C.D., & Hodges, J. (1990). Parkinson's disease and the frontal hypothesis: Task alternation in verbal fluency. In M.B. Streifler, A.D. Korczyn, E. Melamed, & M.B.H. Youdim (Eds.), *Advances in Neurology, Vol. 53, Parkinson's disease anatomy, pathology, and therapy*. New York: Raven Press.

Hampton, J.A., & Gardiner, M.M. (1983). Measures of internal category structure: A correlational analysis of normative data. *British Journal of Psychology, 74*, 491–516.

Hanley, J.R., Dewick, H.C., Davies, A.D.M., Playfer, J., & Turnbull, C. (1990). Verbal fluency in Parkinson's disease. *Neuropsychologia, 27*, 743–746.

Huber, S.J., Shuttleworth, E.C., & Paulson, G.W. (1986). Dementia in Parkinson's disease. *Archives of Neurology, 43*, 987–990.

Isaacs, B., & Kennie, A.T. (1973). The Set Test as an aid to the detection of dementia in old people. *British Journal of Psychiatry, 123*, 467–470.

Lees, A.J., & Smith, E. (1983). Cognitive deficits in the early stages of Parkinson's disease. *Brain, 106*, 257–270.

Levelt, W.J.M. (1989). *Speaking. From intention to articulation*. Cambridge, MA: MIT Press.

Levin, B.E., Llabre, M.M., & Weiner, W.J. (1989). Cognitive impairments associated with early Parkinson's disease. *Neurology, 39*, 557–561.

Mandler, G. (1975). Memory storage and retrieval: Some limits on the reach of attention and consciousness. In P.M.A. Rabbitt & S. Dornic (Eds.), *Attention and performance, V* (pp. 499–516). Hove, UK: Lawrence Erlbaum Associates Ltd.

Marshall, J.C. (1987). Behavioural fractionation in the dementias. In R.A. Griffiths & S.T. McCarthy (Eds.), *Degenerative neurological disease in the elderly* (pp. 150–156). Bristol: Wright.

Megna, G.F., Craca, A., Fiore, P., Del Prete, M., Calabrese, S., & Nardulli, R. (1985). *Neuropsychological evaluation in Parkinson's disease.* Paper given at the VIIIth International Symposium on Parkinson's Disease. New York, June 9–12.

Milner, B. (1964). Some effects of frontal lobectomy in man. In J.M. Warren & K. Akert (Eds.), *The frontal granular cortex and behavior* (pp. 313–331). New York: McGraw-Hill.

Neisser, U. (1963). Decision-time without reaction-time: Experiments in visual scanning. *American Journal of Psychology, 76*, 376–385.

Nelson, H.E., & O'Connell, A. (1978). Dementia: The estimation of premorbid intelligence levels using the new adult reading test. *Cortex, 14*, 234–244.

Newcombe, F. (1969). *Missile wounds of the brain. A study of psychological deficits.* Oxford: Oxford University Press.

Norman, D.A., & Shallice, T. (1986). Attention to action: willed and automatic control of behaviour. In R.J. Davidson, G.E. Schwartz, & D. Shapiro (Eds.), *Consciousness and self-regulation*, Vol. 4 (pp. 1–18). New York: Plenum Press.

Osgood, C.E. (1958). *Method and theory in experimental psychology* (2nd ed.) New York: Oxford University Press.

Oyebode, J.R., Barker, W.A., Blessed, G., Dick, D.J., & Britton, P.G. (1986). Cognitive functioning in Parkinson's disease: In relation to prevalence of dementia and psychiatric diagnosis. *British Journal of Psychiatry, 149*, 720–725.

Patterson, K.E. (1972). Some characteristics of retrieval limitation in long-term memory. *Journal of Verbal Learning and Verbal Behavior, 11*, 685–691.

Perret, E. (1974). The left frontal lobe of man and the suppression of habitual responses in verbal categorical behavior. *Neuropsychologia, 12*, 323–330.

Ramier, A.M., & Hecaen, H. (1970). Role respectif des atteintes frontales et de la latéralisation léssionnelle dans les déficits de la "fluence verbale". *Revue Neurologique, 123*, 17–22.

Raskin, S.A., Sliwinski, M., & Borod, J.C. (in press). Clustering strategies on tasks of verbal fluency in Parkinson's disease. *Neuropsychologia.*

Schechter, I., Korn, C., Yungreis, A., Koren, R., Sternfeld, R., Motlis, H., & Bergman, M. (1985). The word retrieval fluency test: What does it assess? *Scandinavian Journal of Rehabilitation Medicine (Suppl.)*, 12, 76–79.

Schwartz, M.F. (Ed.) (1990). *Modular deficits in Alzheimer-type dementia.* Cambridge, MA: MIT Press.

Ulatowska, H.K., Hayashi, M.M., Cannito, M.P., & Fleming, S.G. (1986). Disruption of reference aging. *Brain and Language, 28*, 24–41.

Webster, D.D. (1968). Critical analysis of the disability in Parkinson's disease. *Modern Treatment, 5*, 257–282.

Wheeldon, L. (1989). *Competition between semantically related words in speech production.* Paper presented to the Experimental Psychology Society, London, 6 January.

Author Index

Subject Index